AMERICA'S BLACK CAPITAL

AMERICA'S BLACK CAPITAL

HOW AFRICAN AMERICANS REMADE ATLANTA IN THE SHADOW OF THE CONFEDERACY

JEFFREY O. G. OGBAR

BASIC BOOKS

NEW YORK

Basic Books
Hachette Book Group
1290 Avenue of the Americas, New York, NY 10104
www.basicbooks.com

Printed in the United States of America

First Edition: November 2023

Published by Basic Books, an imprint of Hachette Book Group, Inc. The Basic Books name and logo is a trademark of the Hachette Book Group.

The Hachette Speakers Bureau provides a wide range of authors for speaking events. To find out more, go to hachettespeakersbureau.com or email HachetteSpeakers@hbgusa.com.

Basic Books copies may be purchased in bulk for business, educational, or promotional use. For more information, please contact your local bookseller or the Hachette Book Group Special Markets Department at special.markets@hbgusa.com.

The publisher is not responsible for websites (or their content) that are not owned by the publisher.

Library of Congress Cataloging-in-Publication Data
Names: Ogbar, Jeffrey O. G., author.
Title: America's Black capital : how African Americans remade Atlanta in the shadow of the Confederacy / Jeffrey O. G. Ogbar.
Description: First edition. | New York : Basic Books, 2023. | Includes bibliographical references and index.
Identifiers: LCCN 2022059138 | ISBN 9781541601994 (hardcover) | ISBN 9781541602007 (ebook)
Subjects: LCSH: African Americans—Georgia—Atlanta—History. | Atlanta (Ga.)—History. | Atlanta (Ga.)—Race relations.
Classification: LCC F294.A89 B53 2023 | DDC 975.8/23100496073—dc23/eng/20221228
LC record available at https://lccn.loc.gov/2022059138

ISBNs: 9781541601994 (hardcover), 9781541602007 (ebook)

LSC-C

Printing 1, 2023

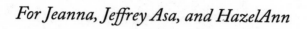

For Jeanna, Jeffrey Asa, and HazelAnn

CONTENTS

INTRODUCTION

Atlanta's Dixie Heritage
From the Heart of the Confederacy to the Black Mecca

On January 4, 2021, one day before a critical runoff for both of Georgia's seats in the US Senate, the president-elect, Democrat Joseph Biden, told crowds in Atlanta that the fate of the country lay in their hands: "One state can chart the course [of our country], not just for the next four years, but for the next generation." On that same day, outgoing president Donald Trump, who refused to concede his loss to Biden and promoted baseless claims of widespread voter fraud, spoke to crowds in Georgia, some of whom waved Confederate flags. Trump insisted that "our country is depending on you. The whole world is watching the people of Georgia tomorrow." Sharing the stage with Trump, conservative Republican incumbent Kelly Loeffler evoked the words of her predecessors: "We've got to hold the line." Fear-stoking terms of the past such as abolition and integration were supplanted by a new one: socialism. According to Loeffler, the progressive Democratic candidates, Raphael Warnock and Jon Ossoff, were aiming to lead the country astray with far-left agendas: "We're the firewall to stopping socialism in America."[1]

On January 5, 2021, in a stunning upset, both Democratic candidates defeated the Republican incumbents, effectively granting control of the legislative branch to the Democratic Party. Warnock, the first black senator in the state's history, is the senior pastor of Ebenezer Baptist Church, the church in which Martin Luther King Jr. was raised and served as pastor. Like the many historical figures who animate this book, Warnock arrived in Atlanta to attend one of its black colleges. He stayed to contribute to his new hometown in remarkable and indelible ways.

Political analysts repeatedly drew attention to the unprecedented voting power of Democratic-leaning African Americans, especially in the Atlanta metropolitan area.[2] Although many grassroots organizations and people are responsible for this electoral transformation, no single figure has been more celebrated than Stacey Abrams, who first appeared in the press in 1992 as an eighteen-year-old activist demanding that the image of the Confederate battle flag be removed from the state flag.

In 2022 Abrams and Warnock both entered electoral races drawing national attention. Abrams ran for governor against Republican incumbent Brian Kemp but ultimately lost. However, Warnock ran against Herschel Walker, a former football star who is also black. Although Walker has been called a "token" candidate put forth by the Republican Party, he had the support of Trump and other GOP leaders, including most white Georgians. The circumstances forced white Georgia voters to choose between two black senatorial candidates for the first time. Although Walker garnered an estimated 70 percent of white voters, the groundswell of support among African American voters (about 90 percent cast Democratic ballots) gave Senator Warnock a victory for a full six-year term. Warnock represents the political transformations wrought by generations of African American voters, activists, and institution builders, especially in the Atlanta metropolitan area.

This book examines the remarkable story of Atlanta, starting when the municipality barely existed and continuing on to the present day, in which the Gate City has gained a place among the world's leading metropoles.

Atlanta has been called a variety of famous (and infamous) nicknames over the last 175 years. No two names capture the contrast of the city's history as much as "Imperial City," for the Ku Klux Klan, and the "Black Mecca." The former name emerged in the 1920s, when the nation's largest and oldest terror group peaked with an estimated four million members. Its international headquarters was based in Atlanta, where the mayor, most police officers, and many local and statewide politicians were open members of the Klan. Neo-Confederate white nationalism had a firm grip on all corners of Atlanta's landscape, from politics to education to popular culture. At the start of the decade, although there were public high schools available for black students in cities and towns across the South, they were barred from all of Atlanta's public high schools. From the country's most popular movie, *Gone with the Wind* (as well as the Margaret Mitchell novel on which it was based), to the 1946 movie *Song of the South* and other filmic and novelistic presentations, the Gate City was firmly associated with Old South tropes.

A half-century after it was known as the "citadel of the Klan," Atlanta was dubbed the "Black Mecca" and would be the first major southern city to elect a black mayor. Another half-century later, the former bastion of hardened white nationalism would boast inordinate black achievement. Over the decades, multiple magazines have heralded the city as the "best city" for African Americans. By 2020, the city had the highest concentration of black-owned businesses and black millionaires, and an exceptional imprint on the national political economy. More black people migrated to Atlanta than to any other metropolitan area in the United States between 1990 and 2020, giving it the largest number of black people in any metro area after New York City. The world's busiest airport, based in the city, had been under unbroken black executive administration for more than thirty years while achieving nearly twenty years of awards for efficiency and innovation by leading airline industry associations. Today, the airport has more than 80 percent of all minority-owned airport business contracts in the United States. In terms of population, African Americans are overrepresented in the administration of the city: schoolteachers, administrators, police officers, and firefighters. They are overrepresented in upper administration as well as lower-skilled occupations in the municipal and county governments. In terms of political activity, on Election Day 2020, African Americans cast more votes in the Atlanta metro area than in any other state's metro area. Atlanta has the largest concentration of black colleges and universities in the country, and it has an imprint on African American culture that exceeds that of all other cities. Scores of films, production companies, reality shows, and record labels centered on black creative expression have positioned Atlanta as a near "Wakanda," or black utopian landscape.[3] This book explores how a city that once outlawed black ownership of property, black voting, black assemblage, and black education—and even criminalized black people wearing clothing "above their station"—evolved into the veritable capital of black America.

This is a history of Atlanta from the uncertain moments before the conflagration of war subsumed the city to the present. Although dozens of books have explored various components, themes, and periods of the city's history, this one uniquely centers its attention on the resilience of two ideals: neo-Confederate politics and Afro-self-determinism. This book explores the historical arc of the Confederacy's rise, reprise, and demise in the Gate City while simultaneously drawing attention to the exceptional achievements of the city's black community, which occurred in spite of neo-Confederate antipathy. The meaning of the term *neo-Confederate* is self-evident, but I define *Afro-self-determinism* as the belief that the interests of African Americans are best advanced by establishing collective control of institutions in their community, such as churches, businesses, schools, and social and political groups. This concept critically differs from black nationalism in that Afro-self-determinism does not disavow US citizenship or seek territorial separatism, as did classic black nationalists, such as the Universal Negro Improvement Association and the Nation of Islam. Although it lacks the conspicuous cultural centering of black aesthetics found in the late 1960s, it ideologically presages the black power movement by sharing two similar core principles: (1) privileging black institution building while not centering integration with whites as a central goal for black people's advancement, and (2) affirming the right in practice and theory for (armed) self-defense by black people.

In telling the history of how black people made extraordinary achievements in Atlanta in spite of the constraints consistently imposed on them by neo-Confederate white nationalism, I follow the stories of several individuals who illuminate the contested definitions of freedom, democracy, and citizenship. Among them are the nineteenth-century Georgia senator and wartime mayor of Madison, Joshua Hill, and a child whom he enslaved, William Edward Evans. The lives of both, tied together through intersecting fates on a plantation sixty miles from Atlanta, illuminate the contested definitions of freedom, democracy, and citizenship.

At age nine, Evans found his freedom from slavery in November 1864, at the moment Union troops marched through Madison. After the fall of Reconstruction, he settled in the state capital, drawn by the prospect of new opportunities, especially those emanating from the concentration of black colleges and universities, and found early work as a plasterer. These schools were foundational to the unique development of black advancement in Atlanta. They were early local expressions of the Afro-self-determinism that Evans personifies. Still in his twenties, the formerly enslaved Evans was hired to help build an iconic building at Atlanta University, Stone Hall, which would house the office of an eminent Harvard-educated scholar, also named William

Edward. Evans was active in Friendship Baptist Church, the early Atlanta home for both Morehouse College and Spelman College. He lived through disenfranchisement, survived the 1906 Racial Massacre, and witnessed the New Negro movement in Atlanta. He helped build academic halls at local black colleges, including a Morehouse College dorm, Robert Hall, where a young Martin Luther King Jr. eventually lived. After working with leading black construction firms, he started his own, which was one of several black-owned construction companies in the city. When he died, in 1944, Evans owned a home larger than that of his former enslaver, Senator Hill. He and his wife, Sarah, a schoolteacher, had raised several children, some of whom were graduates of the local black colleges and taught generations of the city's black children. Atlanta's history is full of people like Evans, who through their commitment to Afro-self-determinism transformed the city into a place where black people could make substantial advancement. Atlanta's history includes colorful, complex, and often inspirational figures, such as Tunis Campbell, Henry Grady, John and Lugenia Burns Hope, Ivan Allen Jr., Grace Towns Hamilton, Maynard Jackson, Shirley Franklin, and Rodney Strong.

In contrast to many histories that highlight how progressive the city has been, I shift the gaze to focus on African American leaders as critical actors who forged remarkable achievements despite the powerful forces opposing them at nearly every front. This theme runs throughout the history of the city, from the earliest black landowners in the nineteenth century through the multimillionaire tycoons of the 1970s. Black success in the city is too often explained by how "progressive" Atlanta is rather than by the ingenuity and persistence of black people who managed to achieve success in spite of the relentless waves of neo-Confederate white nationalism. For example, the sprawling and bucolic black colleges and universities (and, importantly, their alumni) are used as proof of how racially progressive Atlanta is without putting the very existence and need of these colleges in context. They were not forged because the neo-Confederate leadership valued black education. The success of these schools is not because "Atlanta" had elevated and poured resources into black education. These black achievements are nothing short of remarkable when measured against the obstinate forces that, in every way, stood against them. This book tells that story.

The narrative begins before the Civil War, with the emergence of the white southern nationalism that would shape much of the city's core character for generations. The story advances through the 1864 siege of Atlanta, which was a consequence of the city's fierce commitment to white southern nationalism. However, its fantastic rebirth evinced a resilience that was greater than the city itself. Atlanta emerged in the late nineteenth century as the veritable capital of the New South. And with a Janus-faced affection for its Confederate past, it also looked to the future from the vantage point of a progressive, modern city that was simultaneously prepared for industrial capitalism and a full integration into the fabric of American identity. It transcended the stultifying occupations of sectional discord and embraced its Americanness even as it built conspicuous altars and monuments to the Confederacy. In fact, Atlanta's identity after the Civil War cannot be extricated from its Confederate roots. Although Atlanta was not totally unlike other southern cities, its Confederate culture was especially pervasive. From the naming of schools, streets, statuary, and holidays to the cultural depictions in literature, film, and music to the civic groups and law, Atlanta's essential character was forged in the fire of its *bellum ultimum*. The seal for the city of Atlanta was a testament to how fundamental the war was to the city. Adopted in 1900, it has two dates: 1847, the year the city was chartered, and 1865, the year the Civil War ended and the city emerged from the ashes of Union bombardment and destruction. The seal prominently features the mythical phoenix rising from flames with the word *Resurgence*. The city's official history explains the design of the Atlanta seal:

Just as the phoenix, fabled bird of myth and story, rose from its
ashes to begin a new life, the people of Atlanta returned to the
ashes of their city without bitterness or self-pity, and began the
gigantic task which lay before them. Their seal is an enduring
symbol of the courage, vision and selflessness they brought to that
task . . . reminders of a gallant past, of the civic spirit which will
make tomorrow the full realization of today's hopes and plans.[4]

Atlanta emerged after the war as a mélange of competing forces:
a locus of federal power—militarily and politically—but also a site of
Confederate Redeemer power. It embraced an ambitious business community that heralded industrial capitalism, but its economy remained
strongly tethered to a preindustrial feudal system of agrarian debt
peonage. The city became home to the state's largest black population
and its largest concentration of black colleges, yet it had an obstinately
racist local and state government that grossly mistreated and oppressed
its black citizens. Amid this complicated landscape, there remained
a fierce loyalty to the principles of the failed Confederate experiment
among the most powerful sectors of the city. The fundamental ideological thrust of the Confederacy—white nationalism—shaped every
aspect of the city's landscape: politically, socially, culturally, and
beyond. Black people were liminal citizens who were required to pay
taxes that supported public high schools, public parks, public roads,
public utilities, and public health services that were designated for the
exclusive use of whites. Black citizens were denied municipal jobs and
even modern conveniences such as sidewalks and streetlights. In fact,
hundreds, if not thousands, of southern cities and towns—including
Birmingham, Alabama, and Jackson, Mississippi—would establish
black public high schools before Atlanta.

Atlanta forged an identity as a principal municipal heir to the Confederacy itself. Those who saw themselves as loyalists to the Confederacy
established homages to the rebel cause throughout the city and region.

Only Virginia, where the actual capital of the Confederate States of America (CSA) existed, had more Confederate statues. Public-school textbooks celebrated the treasonous war against the United States as "patriotic" and expunged the defense of slavery as its raison d'être.

Over the century and a half after the Civil War, Atlanta grappled with its relationship with the Confederacy and that failed project's notions of freedom, democracy, and citizenship. As a neo-Confederate enterprise, the state and local governments enacted a series of laws in the Gate City to extend and fortify principles of white nationalism. The notion that whites alone should have full and unfettered participation in the civic and political life of the state—as citizens—is foundational to white nationalism. It is based upon the principles of a government in the exclusive control of white people. This belief was essential to the Confederacy. Given that nomenclature often shifts over time, I have chosen to use white supremacy and white nationalism interchangeably; however, when appropriate, I prefer the latter to draw emphasis to the strictly political dimension, not the social pseudoscience of nineteenth-century biology. In the nineteenth and most of the twentieth century, racists who argued for complete and absolute white control of the political apparatus generally identified as "white supremacists." They fought for white supremacy, as expressed in their own speeches and writings. They advocated for the political, economic, social, and cultural supremacy of white people and for their domination of people of color. This was, as Chapter 1 details, supported by pseudoscientific and theological justifications. By the late twentieth century, some white nationalists began abandoning unscientific and biblical arguments that claimed a biological, innate superiority of whites over all others. Instead, they argued for an exclusive and sovereign white racial state: white nationalism. They have sometimes identified as white separatists or racial separatists. Many of them also, of course, believe in an innate superiority of whites over all other people. Therefore, I generally employ "nationalism" as a broad category: it captures white supremacy but is not centered on it as the fundamental driver. Absolute control of the state by white people is the dominant expression. Although its adherents may believe in racial hierarchies, white nationalism is not synonymous with white supremacy as it is currently defined.[5]

Chapters 1–3 focus on the significance of the Civil War in shaping Atlanta. The shadow of the war covered every facet of the city, from education to health care. A separate and grossly unequal city arose from the ashes of war, but African Americans, with the power of local colleges and universities, forged remarkable opportunities for black brilliance, creativity, and enterprise to thrive. While much of the book explores the interconnected histories of black and white Atlanta, Chapter 4 gives special attention to the incredible resilience of the neo-Confederate cause and ideological conflict among whites who see themselves as honoring that cause. This and Chapter 5 detail how the intersections of electoral politics and race are rarely static.

As much as the city centers its identity in its rebirth from the ashes of the Civil War, the 1906 Atlanta Racial Massacre, as Chapter 6 details, destroyed and traumatized much of black Atlanta. Similar to the resurgence after Sherman's 1864 destruction of Atlanta, the black community rebounded with an acute focus on institution building. The efforts transformed the city and drew newcomers from across the country. Chapter 7 illuminates the exceptional social, economic, and cultural world of black Atlanta during the New Negro era of the 1920s–1930s. The city had a higher percentage of black people than almost any other city in the country. And despite the attention focused on Harlem in this era, Atlanta alone boasted new black suburbs, multiple black college and university presidents, black corporate executives, a black-owned amusement park, black hotels, and the country's only daily black newspaper. This all occurred while the city was headquarters to the KKK, which viewed Atlanta as a practically sacred city. By the time of the modern civil rights movement, a generation later, Atlanta, despite popular belief, was perhaps the least progressive major southern city. Although there were moderate members of the white leadership class, they remained marginal in the wider white community. Neo-Confederate control of the city prevented integration of schools, public transportation, policing, public housing, and public accommodations until later than nearly every other city in the country. Local black civil rights groups, for their part, tepidly pushed for integration, much to the chagrin of their national leadership. Black Atlanta leaders, as discussed in chapters 8 and 9, were more concerned with controlling institutions and resources critical to black people than with demanding integration into largely white-controlled spaces. This approach culminated in the election of Maynard Jackson, the South's first black mayor of a major city.

The successful models of Mayor Jackson's "Atlanta Plan" became a gold standard for cities seeking to effectively expand municipal contracts to minority firms, as shown in Chapter 10. The significance of Jackson's success is in conspicuous display in the actual physical landscape of Atlanta. In addition to academic buildings, offices, skyscrapers, and the airport, the city's three largest professional sports stadiums were fully or partially built by black firms. Chapter 11 explores how the Black Mecca became firmly placed as a veritable black capital for America after Jackson's tenure. No longer synonymous with *Gone with the Wind* and Confederate celebrations, Atlanta has a cultural imprint on African American culture larger than that of any other US city.

Few people would have imagined that the former Confederate stronghold, the bastion of hardened neo-Confederate white nationalism—Atlanta—would emerge as a locus of such black political power, influence, and affluence. In the shadows of Confederate monuments, along streets named after rebels, one is always reminded of the city's local history. The through-lines connecting the city's past to its present are palpable. But as Scarlett O'Hara concluded, "Tomorrow is another day."

1 | Capturing the Heart of the Confederacy
Secession, War, and the Making of Atlanta

> I need not call your attention to the fact that [Atlanta] is to the Confederacy
> almost as important as the heart is to the human body. We must hold it.
> —Georgia governor Joseph Brown to CSA president Jefferson Davis, July 1864

In the generation before the Civil War, as sectional disputes became increasingly acrimonious, no industry was more transformative to the country than the railroads. They were swiftly making commerce and travel easier and bringing people together in some ways. Yet in other ways the industry had widened sectional chasms. As easterners gained easier access to new territories in the West, disputes arose over whether to use enslaved or wage labor in the newly acquired lands. But another, tangentially related consequence of the expansion of railroads was the creation of entirely new communities, often called "rail towns." A railroad agent wrote in *Harper's Magazine* that "every temporary terminus of track laying became a city; wicked, wonderful and short-lived." Urban cosmopolitans from the Northeast dismissed these towns as bland, characterless constructs. They were "dropped at random upon the flat and featureless prairies along our western railroads." They were never expected to thrive or amount to any cultural, economic, or political importance. A critic in the *American Architect and Building News* observed that "in the ordinary course of civilization, such characterless sites are not the ones to which populations cleave."[1] Despite a veritable consensus that these rail towns were boom-and-bust locales of little significance, the formidable South Carolina statesman, political philosopher, slaveholder, and vitriolic proponent of southern nationalism John C. Calhoun saw something promising in one such small rail town: Atlanta.

Calhoun, a former US vice president, secretary of war, senator, and wealthy planter, had been at the center of sectional crises for decades. He believed that states had a right to nullify federal laws with which they disagreed; more significantly, he believed that the Constitution did not prevent any state from seceding from the Union. Although he would die more than a decade before the start of the Civil War, he provided much of the intellectual and political foundations upon which secessionists would justify disunion. In 1846, four years before his death, Calhoun met F. M. Haygood, a prominent religious leader from Georgia. When the aging statesman learned that Haygood lived in DeKalb County, he was intrigued: "You may be proud of your country, for Atlanta is in DeKalb. Before you are as old as I am, it is probable that a southern confederacy will be formed; it will doubtless locate its capitol in Atlanta."[2] Calhoun didn't live to witness the establishment of the Confederate States of America, the expansion of Atlanta into a major hub of its war machinations, or the Confederacy's collapse, but his prediction was prescient.

Atlanta had been formed around the "zero milepost" marker (at present-day Five Points) for the Western and Atlantic Railroad line after the Georgia General Assembly authorized the establishment of a railroad link to connect lines between Savannah and midwestern states in 1836. Originally known as "Terminus," the village included six buildings and thirty residents in 1842, when it was renamed "Marthasville" after Georgia governor Wilson Lumpkin's daughter. The development of the railroad at Marthasville made the town an important node for transportation, a strategic point of trade that would indelibly shape the region for the next 150 years and beyond.

By 1845, the town broke the first of many transportation-related records when the new 173-mile Augusta to Marthasville line became the longest railroad track in the world.[3] As the town grew around the intersection of the railroad lines, J. Edgar Thomson, the chief engineer of the Georgia Railroad, recommended that the town be renamed in honor of its importance to continental railroad travel. Thomson's proposed name, "Atlantica-Pacifica," gained currency, but it was shortened to "Atlanta" by locals and others in Georgia. Finally, four days after Christmas 1847, the town was formally incorporated as Atlanta.[4] In late 1860, it was still a relatively small city, ranked fourth in size in Georgia after Savannah, Augusta, and Columbus (and one hundredth among the country's hundred largest cities). By 1864, however, it had become one of the most important and strategic cities for a rebel government and its enterprise in maintaining its slavery empire. When Union general William T. Sherman led the siege of Atlanta in the summer of 1864, the event captured the attention of the entire country: the fate of the war and the national elections would be shaped by its outcome.

Through the close of the Civil War, Atlanta was an intrinsic part of the Confederacy and consequently exemplified ideas about race, democracy, and power that were foundational to the rebel state. The southern nationalist project was explicitly devoted to white supremacy and the right to enslave and otherwise subjugate black people. These Confederate principles were the cornerstone for Atlanta as it fashioned its own identity as a new city during and after the Civil War. Moreover, Atlanta was critical to the rebel government's survival.

Across the South, lawmakers passionately debated the merits of secession in the wake of Abraham Lincoln's election on November 6, 1860. The prospect of the country following many other nations—Mexico, Colombia, and the empires of France and Britain—in outlawing slavery was so repulsive to so many southerners that rebellion and forging a new country seemed the only alternative.

Despite the swiftness with which secessionist sentiment spread across the region, the South did not come upon the decision to dissolve the Union easily. There were fierce debates from Virginia to Texas. These debates were significantly shaped by the degree to which state populations were entangled with slavery. In fact, the first six states to join the Confederacy (South Carolina, Mississippi, Florida, Alabama, Georgia, and Louisiana) also had the highest ratios of slaveholding families and of people enslaved in their borders. Among the fifteen states that legally allowed slavery, the four states with the lowest proportions of enslaved people or slave owners (Delaware, Maryland, Missouri, and Kentucky) refused to secede.[5] Although slavery was the primary driver for secession, many slave owners also vigorously fought secession. And most white southerners did not enslave anyone.

In 1860, as it had been since its inception, the United States was a white-nationalist project that had established citizenship based on *universal whiteness*: it welcomed any indigenous person from Europe as a possible citizen. Its first naturalization law of 1790 affirmed that only "free white persons" could become naturalized citizens. Because of that standard, people from every corner of Europe had become American citizens by the start of the Civil War. Whether from Ireland, Russia, Greece, or Italy, immigrants arrived and secured citizenship. The first census, also in 1790, had a racial category for whites that made no distinction between those whites born in the United States of various faiths or ancestries. These ethnic groups of German, Irish, English, Polish, French, Protestant, Jewish, or Catholic extraction were not barred from public schools, state militias, voting, jury service, or marriage with other whites, whereas East Asians or Africans could not be naturalized citizens at all. According to the Supreme Court's 1857 *Dred Scott v. Sandford* decision, even black people born free in the United States were not citizens. According to Chief Justice Roger Taney, they "are not included, and were not intended to be included, under the word 'citizens' in the Constitution, and can therefore claim none of the rights and privileges which that instrument provides for and secures to citizens of the United States."

White nationalism did not originate with the Confederacy; it was inherited from its mother country, along with the ideology of universal whiteness. When the Civil War began, both sides of the conflict explicitly declared that only white men could serve in the militaries as soldiers. However, the emphasis on whiteness for the Confederacy articulated a more virulent expression of white nationalism than what was typical in the United States. Given its commitment to slavery, the Confederacy was much more vociferously antiblack. Finally, southern white nationalism was undergirded by the belief that God endorsed slavery, white supremacy, and the subjugation of black people. Whites were, the architects of the Confederacy argued, a "superior race." This was a biological and spiritual superiority, fixed by nature, not a malleable and mutable condition that could be ameliorated by social, cultural, and political intervention. Therefore, African slavery was ordained and natural.

The Confederate beliefs in white nationalism were so inveterate that adherents chose to rebel against their own country rather than to relinquish their right to enslave black people. Several weeks after Lincoln's election, South Carolina was the first state to secede, on December 20, 1860. The "cause for secession" of the first state did not confuse the fundamental cause for rebellion:

> A geographical line has been drawn across the Union, and all the States north of that line have united in the election of a man to the high office of President of the United States, whose opinions

and purposes are hostile to slavery. He is to be entrusted with the administration of the common Government, because he has declared that that "Government cannot endure permanently half slave, half free," and that the public mind must rest in the belief that slavery is in the course of ultimate extinction. This sectional combination for the submersion of the Constitution, has been aided in some of the States by elevating to citizenship, persons who, by the supreme law of the land, are incapable of becoming citizens; and their votes have been used to inaugurate a new policy, hostile to the South, and destructive of its beliefs and safety.[6]

Subsequent articles of secession from other states similarly evoked slavery as the driver for rebellion against the United States.

In Georgia the debate over secession was dramatically played out in the state assembly and in newspapers across the state. In Atlanta hostile crowds milled about in the streets denouncing Lincoln as an abolitionist who would bring doom upon the South. They cheered calls for secession and burned Lincoln in effigy at the appropriately named Planters' Hotel in downtown.[7] Governor Joseph E. Brown, a lawyer and enslaver, firmly believed that the state should join South Carolina and other slave-holding states to protect the right to practice slavery against Lincoln's ambition: "I do not doubt that submission to the administration of Mr. Lincoln will result in the final abolition of slavery. If we fail to resist now, we will never again have the strength to resist."[8]

Despite the governor's warnings, other Georgia lawmakers who were similarly invested in protecting slavery found secession extreme. Herschel V. Johnson, who was a former Georgia governor and the vice-presidential nominee of the Douglas wing of the Democratic Party in the 1860 US presidential election, opposed secession, as did former US representative Alexander Stephens. These two men, who together enslaved 149 people in 1860, insisted that the political landscape did not favor the antislavery politics of Lincoln.[9] The Republicans were a minority in both houses, and the Supreme Court had recently ruled in favor of slavery in the Dred Scott case. Moreover, the debates in the press had clearly demonstrated the North's aversion to secession and war. Johnson and Stephens even proposed to the Georgia Secession Convention that Atlanta host a February 16 conference of all slaveholding states to discuss ways to protect slavery without seceding. Only after all negotiations failed would secession result. Their proposal was soundly rejected.[10] One of the most outspoken advocates for remaining in the Union was Benjamin H. Hill, a state senator who was celebrated as "the peerless orator" of the state assembly. As the only non-Democratic member of the Georgia Secession Convention, he passionately denounced secession, reasoning that resistance to the "abolitionist" efforts of Lincoln would be best fought through the constitutional process. Hill and others at the convention did not equivocate on the profitability of slavery and their natural right to enslave people at birth. But that right, Hill insisted, was guaranteed in the Constitution itself. One member of the Georgia delegation to the US Senate, Joshua Hill (no relation to Benjamin), also advised against secession. A member of the American Party, he was a slaveholder from Madison who saw the "fire-eaters" (rabid defenders of slavery and secession) who dominated his state's affairs as unreasonable. Both Hills believed that the best defense of slavery would be waged while remaining a part of the United States and through extant legal tools. But many more people in the state argued forcefully for secession.

Thomas R. R. Cobb, a lawyer, politician, and delegate at the secession convention, agreed with Benjamin Hill that slavery was morally, economically, and socially justified. Cobb, a founder of the University of Georgia School of Law, had written that the "negro race seems . . . peculiarly fitted for a laborious class" and that "their mental capacity renders them incapable of successful self-development, and yet adapts them for the direction of the wiser race." Finally, whites need not feel any moral or ethical conflict over enslaving babies or the elderly because black people's "moral character renders them happy, peaceful, contented and cheerful in a status that would break the spirit and destroy the energies of the Caucasian."[11] In fact, there was little disagreement at the convention about the merits of racial oppression and the rightness of slavery. Of course, the fundamental crux of the debates centered on the response to Lincoln's election and any threat that it posed to slavery. For Cobb, and most at the convention, Lincoln was such a danger that Georgia had to leave the Union. Benjamin Hill's passionate argument was in vain.

When South Carolina seceded, on December 20, 1860, many in Atlanta fired cannons, released balloons, and mobilized a torchlight procession through the streets in their support for the embryonic stages of southern independence. When Florida seceded, on January 10, 1861, citizens in Augusta organized an honorific firing of a hundred guns.[12] The secessionist sentiment was strongest in the parts of Georgia with the highest concentration of enslaved people. In order to draw non-slaveholding whites into the cause, especially those in the mountainous areas of North Georgia, Governor Brown made a special appeal. He argued that if Lincoln had his way, slavery would end, but not without compensation to the enslavers, who would be paid for their property losses—much as had been done with the slaveholders in Great Britain. The necessary two-billion-dollar cost to pay for this emancipation would be collected in taxes. The slaveholding elites would then buy "all the land and make tenants of the [white] small farmers."[13]

On January 29, 1861, the Georgia Secession Convention issued its "declaration of its causes of secession," which read, in part, that the party of president-elect Lincoln is "admitted to be an anti-slavery party." Given that the Republican Party sought ideals that were anathema to Georgia, such as "the prohibition of slavery in the territories, hostility to it everywhere, [and] the equality of the black and white races," secession was required to maintain the integrity of the values of the state of Georgia. It further argued that "if we submit to [Lincoln's ideals], it will be our fault and not theirs."[14] Benjamin Hill, Stephens, and Johnson, though disheartened by the vote, became ardent support- ers of the Confederacy. Hill and Johnson joined the Confederate Pro- visional Congress when Georgia joined the CSA. Hill was soon elected by the Georgia State Assembly to the Confederate States Senate, where he served throughout the war. Johnson was elected to the Second Con- federate Congress. Congressman Joshua Hill resigned from the US Senate in January, even though he was ambivalent about his delega- tion's fervent move toward disunion. He remained opposed to disunion and war. In fact, Henry Winter Davis, the eloquent and scholarly Republican congressman from Maryland, argued that Hill was among the "only three devoted Union men in the South."[15] Hill's devotion to American nationalism caused him to be disparaged in newspapers and by public speakers, and he was burned in effigy across Georgia.[16] He returned to his plantation in Madison and saw his son, Hugh Legare, depart from his own politics and join the Georgia state militia, part of the Confederate Army. Despite his early opposition to secession, Hill returned to office and served as mayor of Madison during the war. Ste- phens became vice president of the Confederate States of America.[17]

Although most Georgians who were not inclined to secede resigned themselves to their fates, there were pockets of Unionist sentiment and considerable anxiety about the dramatic effort to sever ties with the United States. Antisecessionist Georgia House representative Garnett Andrews, witnessing the cheers, cannons, balloons, and general jubila- tion, sought refuge at home, "darkened the windows, and paced up and down the room in the greatest agitation. Every now and then, when the noise of the shouting and the ringing of bells would penetrate the closed doors and windows, he would pause and exclaim: 'Poor fools! They may ring their bells now, but they will wring their hands—yes, and their hearts, too—before they are done with it.'"[18]

However, Andrews was in the minority among Georgians: others energetically sought to widen the number of seceding states by using some Confederate proselytizing. In crafting the fundamental ideals of the new nation, architects of the Confederacy affirmed the earliest sentiment from South Carolina and Mississippi. CSA vice president Stephens offered a cogent, succinct declaration in his famous "Cornerstone Speech." The Confederacy's "cornerstone rests . . . upon the great truth that the negro is not equal to the white man." He continued to note that "slavery subordination to the superior race is [the] natural and normal condition" of black people.[19] Other states similarly affirmed their defense of both the right to enslave people and to maintain white supremacy as an immutable natural law. They made clear their objections to any intimations of or open support for equality, justice, or freedom for all people.[20]

With a new government, military, currency, and collection of laws in place, the Confederacy moved swiftly to adopt a new flag in March 1861: its first national flag, known as the "Stars and Bars." Because of its red and white stripes, a blue canton, and white stars, some Confederates criticized it for being too similar to the US Stars and Stripes. Not only was it confusing on the field of battle, but some Confederates also thought it a "servile imitation" and a "detested parody" of the US flag.[21] William T. Thompson, publisher of the *Savannah Morning News*, argued that the flag of the Confederacy was more than a practical matter on the battlefield. It was also a near-sacred representation of the cause of the Confederacy, its beliefs, and core principles. It would remind soldiers and civilians alike of their cause: "As a people, we are fighting to maintain the Heaven-ordained supremacy of the white man over the inferior or colored race; a white flag would thus be emblematical of our cause. . . . As a national emblem, it is significant of our higher cause, the cause of a superior race, and a higher civilization contending against ignorance, infidelity, and barbarism. Another merit in the new flag is, that it bears no resemblance to the now infamous banner of the Yankee vandals."[22]

As essential as pro-slavery ideology and white supremacy were to the Confederacy, most whites in the South did not own slaves. In fact,

75 percent of whites in the South were not slaveholders, yet they had also been ideologically invested in protecting the interests of the region's ruling class, even if they received few material returns. And they mostly supported secession and were eager to serve the Confederacy. The Confederacy granted all white people a certain level of privilege, regardless of their class. This white civic equality was a critical expression of the efficacy and significance of white nationalism. It gave white nationalism meaning. It offered something to whites that—at the level of participation in civic affairs—offered a semblance of democracy, equality, and justice. In the face of enormous chasms of wealth between the slaveholding elite ruling class and the semiliterate, poor, barefoot mass of white southerners, white nationalism meant little without a group for whom civic access was otherwise denied. As Cobb, the Georgia secessionist and eventual Confederate Army officer, wrote in *An Historical Sketch of Slavery*, "Every citizen feels he belongs to an elevated class. It matters not that he is no slaveholder; he is not the inferior race; he is freeborn; he engages in no menial occupation." In truth, most whites in Georgia (and throughout the South) did engage in menial occupations—subsistence farming—and were poor, often going without shoes. And although Cobb may have conveniently overlooked the vast divide between rich and poor whites, he did draw attention to the civic equality enjoyed by whites. The poorest white man shares a "republican equality" with the richest white man and "meets him in every public assembly."[23]

As noted earlier, white nationalism was national in scope, but in the Union it was forced to evolve in the travails of war. At the start of the Civil War, most states across the United States denied black citizens the right to vote. Cities across the North denied black children access to public schools. In Philadelphia, New York, and Boston, black people founded their own schools because local governments denied them access to the all-white public ones, which also welcomed immigrant children from Europe.[24] The federal government itself banned black troops yet welcomed people from every corner of Europe into all-white units, with equal pay relative to service duties. Once black soldiers could join, they were denied equal pay, were not eligible to be commissioned as officers, and were segregated from white troops. Whites, regardless of their ethnicity, fought in whites-only units with higher pay. Despite ahistorical notions of European immigrants being legally or socially designated as "non-white," the concept of *universal whiteness*—the legal definition of whiteness that extended to any people indigenous to Europe—had been forged during the earliest legal regulation of race in the United States. Even Confederates openly recognized that they shared with their northern counterparts a commitment to universal white supremacy and the natural subjugation of black people.[25]

The Confederacy allowed whites who were Irish, such as General Patrick Cleburne, or Jewish, such as Secretary of State Judah Benjamin, access to the same universal whiteness as the poor and illiterate white Anglo-Saxon Protestant turnip farmer. In fact, there were more Irish-born generals in the Civil War (twelve Union and six Confederate) than in any other country.[26] In the Union, however, all black regiments were led by white officers. Some officers, as high up as the rank of general, were loath to have any black regiments even after these were legally mandated. The pervasive belief in white supremacy across the country shaped virulent antiblack sentiment among Yankees. Union rank-and-file soldiers routinely expressed contempt for black people—free or enslaved. They were referred to as "niggers," "darkies," "childlike," and other hateful epithets by white soldiers on both sides of the conflict. In Ship Island, Mississippi, white Union troops refused to provide support for the soldiers of a black unit and fired guns at them instead. A Massachusetts soldier, in a letter home, referred to black troops as "regular Congoes with noses as broad as a plantation and lips like raw beefsteaks. . . ."[27] If the impetus behind southern secession was to *protect slavery*, the mission behind Union mobilization was not to put an end to slavery but to *protect the United States*. Union mobilization was a direct response to secession, not an effort to promote racial equality.

Whereas Jefferson Davis, president of the Confederacy, insisted that black people were an inferior race, his counterpart, Lincoln, argued that in regard to the war, black people had "nothing to do with it," and as late as 1862 he entertained the possibility of expunging free blacks from the United States.[28] However, the circumstances of war forced into existence new phenomena. In addition to new technologies and tools of war, from the Gatling gun to the ironclads, there were new ethical, moral, and legal notions that slowly undermined the white nationalism of the United States. But southern nationalism was a much more resilient force, spawned from circumstances that did not permit the same sorts of challenges to its expression of white nationalism as had faced the Union.

The secessionist appeal transcended the wealthy planter elites. Confederate officials understood that secession would not be successful without widespread support from the white poor—the majority of whites in the region. Similarly, Georgia governor Brown rejected any speculation that equality or freedom should be enjoyed by all in his country. Though affirming his commitment to white supremacy, he simultaneously proclaimed that equality could and must exist only among whites, even the poorest among them: "Among us the poor white laborer is respected as an equal. His family is treated with kindness, consideration and respect. He does not belong to the menial class. The negro is in no sense of the term his equal."[29] CSA vice president Stephens explained that "with us, all of the white race, however high or low, rich or poor, are equal in the eye of the law. Nor so with the negro. Subordination is his place."[30] White nationalism maintained that all people of European descent were granted access to the enclaves of power and privilege regardless of nationality or religion.

Secretary of State Benjamin and the many generals and officers of Irish, Polish, and Italian extraction are cases in point. The trope of universal whiteness had circulated for decades and was most acute in the rhetoric of southern elites who extolled the utility of slavery. A generation before the Civil War, Calhoun explained that there was only one division of any consequence in the United States, a racial one between whites and blacks: "With us the two great divisions of society are not the rich and the poor, but white and black, and all the former, the poor as well as the rich, belong to the upper class, and are respected and treated as equals."[31] This notion of universal whiteness was a foundational expression of white nationalism. Of course, gendered and class-based forms of discrimination still attenuated its application, but whiteness itself—through a social contract—was the sole and immutable criterion for one's eligibility for citizenship and investment in the project of "democracy."

Although most whites in the South were rural, unlettered yeomanry or poor, they were universally invested in two institutions: the church and the government. Their citizenship—especially for white males who could vote—had special value. Even in poverty, they enjoyed the civil rights of suffrage, jury duty, securing public-sector jobs, and serving in the militia and slave patrols. Of course, the very existence of the slave patrol fueled fears that slave insurrection could at any point be a threat to all white people—slaveholders or not. It was with the grand and pervasive machinations of southern institutions that secessionist sentiment was galvanized, undergirded by the sensibilities of white supremacy, which was something that had been enjoyed by all whites in the region. Not only had an "abolitionist" president-elect put white supremacy under threat; the very existence of white people, they insisted, was in peril.

Southern elites pandered to the fears and racial paranoia pervasive among the region's white population. The yeomanry who could not afford to enslave people were as committed to the protection of slavery as slaveholders were. They were essential in vigilance campaigns to ensure that the enslaved never found freedom. Slave patrols across the South employed poor whites who were able to exercise a degree of governmental-sanctioned authority over the mobility and assemblage of black people. They were hired as overseers and security on plantations across the region. And, of course, being a slaveholder was an aspiration for many. But the institution of slavery was also a reminder of the freedom and power that whiteness itself conveyed.[32]

The meaning of whiteness was dependent on the contrasting meaning of blackness. And no institution made the power of freedom, whiteness, and justice more acute than slavery. Blackness was as synonymous with weakness, degradation, slavery, and barbarism as whiteness was with power, prestige, freedom, and civilization. Confederates argued that any threat to slavery would not only undermine the sovereignty of the region and its right to enslave people; it would also foster a dystopia of racial equality at best. At worst, Lincoln's efforts would foment a massive, bloody slave insurrection, engulfing the region and enveloping all whites, regardless of slaveholding status.

Henry Louis Benning, a Georgia judge, explained that if slavery were abolished, poor and rich whites alike would suffer unimaginable horrors as newly freed people would run amok in genocidal campaigns against them: "We will be completely exterminated, and the land will be left in the possession of the blacks, and then it will go back to a wilderness and become another Africa. . . . Suppose they elevated Fred Douglass, your escaped slave, to the presidency? What would be your position in such an event? I say give me pestilence and famine sooner than that."[33]

The call for secession conveniently protected the interests of elite slaveholding whites by galvanizing the mass of whites who were not slaveholders. Ironically, the South was so notoriously parsimonious with its wealth that public schools, public parks, and other public institutions were rare in comparison to the North.[34]

Politicians, whose elected positions required that they appeal to people outside of the planter class, were not alone in arguing that secession was in the best interest of all white people. Southern newspaper publishers and journalists were essential to cultivating secessionist support as well. In fact, the press, which was a massive industry in the second half of the nineteenth century, was the chief vehicle by which politicians' sentiments were spread among the people. Virginia had 120 newspapers in 1861, including four daily newspapers in Richmond: the *Dispatch*, the *Enquirer*, the *Examiner*, and the *Whig*. Although the Confederate capital consisted of only 37,910 people (in a county of 61,616, where 20,041 were enslaved), these four newspapers were circulated across the South and were critical to CSA propaganda and the general dissemination of news about the war.[35] Newspapers and their editors, from the *Charleston Mercury* to the *Memphis Daily Appeal*, published hundreds of articles and editorials denouncing Lincoln both as a tyrant and an abolitionist. They also regarded him as an advocate of racial equality, a wild-eyed radical who would destroy southern society.[36] On December 6, a month after Lincoln's election, South Carolina's *Carolina Spartan* argued that the US Constitution had "proved impotent to protect us against the fanaticism of the North. The institution of slavery [therefore] must be under the exclusive control of those interested in its preservation, and not left to the mercy of those that believe it their duty to destroy it." After naming members of Lincoln's cabinet as threats to slavery, the paper insisted that with "treasonous advice," these men and the newly elected "Black Republican President" were then able to "carry out their long cherished designs against the peace and prosperity of the South." Finally, the paper noted, secession and the establishment of a "Southern Confederacy" were the only means by which the institution of slavery could be guaranteed and protected from devious abolitionists.[37]

Given slavery's importance to Georgia, it is not surprising that Atlanta saw an early call for action against threats to slavery emanating from the North. Slavery was the foundation of wealth in Georgia, even as most whites—63 percent—were not slaveholders and were mostly poor subsistence farmers. In 1860 property directly related to slavery in the state was worth more than $400 million, accounting for at least half the state's total wealth. The elite planters were so rich that their wealth had a staggering effect on the state average. At the dawn of the Civil War, the per-capita wealth of the white Georgia household was almost double that of white families in New York and Pennsylvania, despite most whites being yeomanry with little or no wealth.

It comes as no surprise that a newspaper in a Georgia rail town would emerge as a vocal advocate for protecting slavery—the state's uncontested source of great wealth.[38] On February 15, 1859, nearly two years before Lincoln took office, James P. Hambleton, a zealous advocate of slavery and vigilance against federal efforts to end it, launched his newspaper, presciently named the *Southern Confederacy*. Hambleton, a fire-eater, understood the importance of newspapers and their roles as influential forces in society. His efforts were part of a body of hundreds of papers across the South that pushed for secession and supported the Confederacy, acting as polemic news outlets for the southern public. By shaping public opinion, the press was especially important in shoring up support for public policy, both influencing lawmakers and operating as a tool for politicians to influence the public. In a town with fewer than ten thousand inhabitants and a relatively small percentage of enslaved people (20 percent), Atlanta may have seemed like an odd location for Hambleton to establish a newspaper so devoted to the cause of slavery.[39]

However, Atlanta was important to the transportation of staple crops such as cotton—the nation's number-one export. Slave labor not only fueled the national economy; Atlanta's development was also dependent on it, even if the city did not have a large population of enslaved people. The city was not disengaged from the direct commerce in slavery, of course. In what became the Five Points section of downtown, there were auctions to buy and sell children, women, and men. The city was a growing hub of goods produced from slave labor across the region. Financial institutions in the North provided loans, insurance, and finished products (clothing, tools, home goods, for example) to the slaveholders and others. Businessmen met in Atlanta to negotiate deals, and northern-based railroad industrialists and engineers planned and built new rail networks through the city and the region. However, despite whatever financial ties the city had with northerners, the local press reflected and influenced popular sentiment toward several national connections.

When Lincoln was elected, Hambleton was livid. Lincoln's elevation portended nothing short of irrevocable harm to the region. After weeks of lamenting the impending inauguration of the "greatest threat to the American republic," Hambleton's paper devoted special coverage to the transition of power from the notoriously feckless James Buchanan to Lincoln. On March 4, the *Southern Confederacy* reported on the oath of office of the country's sixteenth president: "If one single man, to-day, in Washington, can be glad, he is either insensible to havoc and ruin, or must be a Bedlamite." Like most southern newspapers, the Atlanta paper viewed Lincoln as an abolitionist who schemed through deceit, lies, and corruption to end slavery. Lincoln's proclamations to limit slavery only where it currently existed were dismissed as mendacious efforts to bamboozle the southern people. The *Southern Confederacy* condemned Lincoln as "a Black Republican" who "should of all men, be the most wretched, for he had the will to commit a treason against Liberty, heinous enough to damn a world." Lincoln was little more than a "stupid rail splitter" whose election would result in "the overthrow of the best Government that ever existed."[40]

Perhaps hinting at and encouraging the irreconcilable sectional tensions in the weeks before the first shots of the Civil War, Hambleton's newspaper reported on the desperate attempts to avert war with hastily proposed laws to mollify the South by protecting slavery. The infamous Corwin amendment, introduced by Ohio representative Thomas Corwin, to "forever prohibit an interference by constitutional amendment or by Congressional action against slavery," was introduced shortly before Lincoln took the oath of office. Despite outcry from abolitionists, so many Americans wanted to avoid war that the amendment to guarantee protection of slavery—beyond even the reach of the US Constitution—passed both houses of Congress. It was endorsed by outgoing president Buchanan, and on March 4, Lincoln, eager to avoid war, expressed "no objection" to the amendment. The only obstacle to the would-be Thirteenth Amendment was the secession of the seven states of the newly formed Confederate States of America: they refused to ratify the law. The hard-line *Southern Confederacy* endorsed these seven states, reporting that "anti-seceders and Northern apologists" were "besotted in their ignorance and bigotry" to fall for a plan endorsed by Lincoln himself.[41] The arrogance of the secessionists not only undermined added protection of their right to enslave people; it also guaranteed war.

When the Civil War started in April with the Confederate attack on Fort Sumter in South Carolina, Hambleton eagerly joined the Georgia militia, part of the Confederate Army, and sold his newspaper to C. R. Hanleiter and G. W. Adair, the co-owners of the Atlanta newspaper *Gate-City Guardian*. Hanleiter and Adair, in the spirit of their moment in history, continued with the name *Southern Confederacy* for their new paper.[42]

As the war progressed, Atlanta's role in the Confederacy only expanded. The city continued as a critical hub of war matériel and agriculture for the region, and it was also an important locus for Confederate propaganda when New Orleans, Mobile, Jackson, and Memphis were captured by Union forces. Scores of Confederate-sympathizing newspapers were shut down in the border states and the Upper South early in the war. After Memphis was captured by Union forces in June 6, 1862, the region's biggest paper, the *Daily Appeal*, fled to various cities before settling in Atlanta, where it was published, under its original name, until Atlanta was also captured by federal troops.[43]

The press was not the only institution that fervently endorsed slavery. As Gordon Rhea explains, "The South was defined by slavery." It shaped the theological, political, economic, and racial identity of the region and its people. In a region with high rates of illiteracy and virtually no public school systems beyond isolated and limited primary schools, churches were extremely powerful and influential. Southern churches, connected through larger regional denominations, invested in both slavery and the subjugation of black people. When former South Carolina governor James Henry Hammond advocated for secession and slavery, he was careful to exploit religious sensibilities. Slavery and white supremacy were morally sound and congruent with the will of Jesus. Slavery was "especially commanded by God through Moses and approved by Christ through His Apostles."

Hammond's proclamations were used to affirm that the Christian gospel endorsed the efforts to protect slavery through secession, but a religious secession had occurred a generation before the establishment of the Confederacy. Across the South, major congregations seceded from their national bodies over the issue of slavery when Presbyterians, Methodists, and Baptists broke away and established southern denominations between 1837 and 1845. In 1850, a decade before secession, a southerner wrote to *DeBow's Review*, a southern business periodical, to affirm the biblical justification for slavery. Citing several figures of the Bible who enslaved people, including Abraham, the writer insisted that white Americans were kinder and more just than slaveholders of antiquity: "Now, we all know, that the condition of the servant of the Roman empire, was much less free than that of the southern negro." After asserting the biblical support for slavery, the author noted that "if that book is of divine origin, the holding of slaves is right: as that which God has permitted, recognized and commanded, cannot be inconsistent with his will."[44] Many others—ministers, politicians, and laypeople—wrote articles in the popular press and in journals similarly justifying slavery as a Christian practice.

To southern Christians, those who sought slavery's destruction were a threat not only to the South and to white people but also to the faith itself. Abolitionists were anti-Christian and therefore immoral. A Presbyterian minister, Benjamin Morgan Palmer, delivered a sermon titled "The South, Her Peril and Her Duty" soon after Lincoln's election. Incensed at the prospect that the president-elect was an abolitionist, Palmer argued that white southerners had a "providential trust to conserve and to perpetuate the institution of slavery." Palmer described how slavery "has fashioned our modes of life, and determined all of our habits of thought and feeling, and molded the very type of our civilization." Without any other option but to submit to the "undeniably atheistic" governance of an abolitionist president, nothing "is now left but secession."[45]

One Confederate official, William Harris, addressed a Georgia audience and warned that the Confederacy would "rather see the last of her race, men, women, and children, immolated in one common funeral pyre than see them subjugated to the degradation of civil, political and social equality with the negro race." Moved by the visceral denunciation of Lincoln and the abolitionist North, the Georgia State Legislature printed a thousand copies of his speech for public consumption.[46]

The planters dominated the entirety of the South's political, economic, cultural, religious, and social spheres. They had been inexorably moving toward a new nationalism that was framed as an heir to the American Revolution. The enthusiasm for nation building and southern nationalism was ubiquitous across the slaveholding states, so a new country with new ideals and a new protection for slavery was born. In various ways, the small rail town of Atlanta would be central to that new country's short existence.

By the end of May 1861, the Confederate States of America had eleven states, an army, a national government, a constitution, and a president in place at its provisional capital of Montgomery, Alabama. In its search for a permanent capital, the CSA asked lawmakers to propose a centrally located city with a hundred square miles available to form a district for the federal government. Of the literally thousands of options, the debates centered on three bids: Atlanta, Opelika (Alabama), and Richmond. And although discussions and debates highlighted the many benefits of Atlanta, including its central location, well-developed rail connections, industrial base, and deep interior position, the bid went to Richmond. Stephens, the new vice president, pushed hard for Virginia to join the CSA. Virginia had the largest southern white male military-age population as well as substantial industrial capacity and natural resources. Stephens thus supported Richmond over his own state's Atlanta. Although Atlanta lost its bid, it would remain an important city for the rebel cause, and the Confederacy would remain an indelible component of the city's identity more than a century after the collapse of this short-lived government.[47]

The war waged on through early 1861, with victories and defeats exchanged between both sides. The small communities of African Americans in the North clamored to enlist when Lincoln requested on April 15 that all governors (including those in southern states) provide 75,000 soldiers to put down the rebellion in the South. However, the Department of War rejected black men and issued a statement that it had "no intention to call into service of the Government any coloured soldiers." In fact, both the Union and the Confederacy barred blacks from their militaries.[48] But the question of black soldiers would remain intensely debated in Lincoln's cabinet and among generals in the field.

On August 30, 1861, Major General John C. Frémont, an ardent abolitionist, declared a "Proclamation of Emancipation." As commander of the Union Army in St. Louis, he declared that those "who shall be directly proven to have taken an active part with their enemies in the field" (Confederates and their agents) would have their property confiscated by Union forces. This property included people who were enslaved. Frémont's order actually ruled that slaves "are hereby declared freedmen." Lincoln removed Frémont from his post, rescinded the order, and replaced him with General David Hunter.[49] But given the centrality of race and slavery, even Hunter struggled to "keep 'the Negro' out of the war." The administration was famously anxious about giving border states reasons to secede. Arming black men, Lincoln and many others rationed, would affirm fears that the president (1) endorsed racial equality, (2) would ultimately abolish slavery, and (3) would inspire slave insurrections across the country. Yet in the early stages of the war, some Union commanders found it prudent to destabilize the enemy by freeing the enslaved and attaching them to the Union Army.

General Hunter was later made commander of the Department of the South, where he was based on the South Carolina coast and also oversaw operations in Florida and Georgia. Hunter issued his own emancipation proclamation on April 13, 1862, freeing all people throughout his area of command who were theretofore enslaved:

> The three States of Georgia, Florida and South Carolina, comprising the military department of the south, having deliberately declared themselves no longer under the protection of the United States of America, and having taken up arms against the said United States, it becomes a military necessity to declare them under martial law. This was accordingly done on the 25th day of April, 1862. Slavery and martial law in a free country are altogether incompatible; the persons in these three States—Georgia, Florida, and South Carolina—heretofore held as slaves, are therefore declared forever free.[50]

In May, Hunter even organized the first "African" troops to serve in the Union Army. When congressmen from border states demanded an explanation for the reports of black troops, General Hunter offered a sharp-witted, sarcastic reply that subtly and adroitly addressed the politics of language and his task at hand as military commander. In a letter dated June 23, 1862, he explained that "no regiment of 'Fugitive Slaves' has been . . . organized by this Department. There is, however, a fine regiment of persons whose late masters are 'Fugitive Rebels,'— men who everywhere fly before the appearance of the National Flag, leaving their servants behind. . . ." Hunter mocked the rebels for fleeing their plantations and the people whom they enslaved, and for "dodging behind trees." Instead of questioning the organization of loyal men, Congress would be better served with a "Fugitive Masters Law" to apprehend treasonous rascals, he quipped. "The loyal persons composing this regiment," Hunter detailed, were "working with remarkable industry to place themselves in a position to go in full and effective pursuit of their fugacious and traitorous proprietors." He answered the critics who argued that he had no authority to enlist black soldiers. Hunter had, in fact, been given instructions to "employ all loyal persons offering their services in defence of the Union and for the suppression of this Rebellion in any manner I might see fit. There is no restriction as to the character or color of the persons to be employed, or the nature of the employment." In describing the nature of the men who filled his ranks, Hunter reported that "the experiment of arming the Blacks, as far as I have made it, has been a complete and even marveilous [*sic*] success. They are sober, docile, attentive, and enthusiastic, displaying great natural capacities for acquiring the duties of the soldier." He hoped to raise up to fifty thousand of these "hearty and devoted soldiers" by the next fall.[51]

Lincoln rescinded Hunter's edict soon thereafter. His black troops were also disbanded. Radical Republicans grew weary of Lincoln, arguing that he was too conciliatory to the border states, to the point that these states exercised political influence in far excess to any capacity deserved or realized before the war. All evidence suggested that abolition would prove destructive to efforts to forge national unity in the war effort.[52]

However, the organization of black soldiers was even more outrageous to Confederates. The state of Georgia had been in Hunter's military district, and rebels personally witnessed his edict and understood the act as a firm reification of their argument and greatest fears. To them, the Union was driven by the unfathomable ambition to secure total destruction of slavery. These Confederates were not entirely wrong. Several months after Hunter's edict, Lincoln called his cabinet together for his unveiling of new war plans. On August 25, 1862, General Rufus Saxton of the Department of the South was officially given the authority to recruit "volunteers of African descent" into the ranks of the United States military as full-fledged soldiers.[53] Hunter's original regiments had been reorganized by November, much to the chagrin of South Carolina and Georgia Confederates who "resented with burning bitterness" the use of black soldiers and considered fighting them on the battlefield a "crowning indignity."[54] In a society that trafficked in the rhetoric of slave loyalty, contentment, happiness, and (perhaps most important) passivity, the effort to militarize a class of people believed to be inherently weak and cowardly was an affront to white southerners in the most fundamental way. This was the first of a bold series of measures that struck powerful blows at the Confederacy and the US institutions that had heretofore relegated black people to the margins of citizenship.

On September 22, 1862, a little more than a year after Frémont's renegade military orders in Missouri, the president shared his plans to issue a proclamation of emancipation as a wartime order. His cabinet, which included abolitionists and others who wished only to contain slavery rather than destroy it, endorsed his plans. The spread of abolitionist measures frightened white southerners and Confederate leadership. Rumors spread of slave conspiracies. Alleged conspirators were beaten, tortured, and killed. Georgia's governor Brown argued that there was a massive Christmas conspiracy in 1862, perhaps in anticipation of the impending Emancipation Proclamation, which went into law on January 1, 1863.[55] That famous edict freed all people enslaved in Confederate-controlled areas. However, it did not outlaw slavery in all other places, including the border states, partly because of Lincoln's fear of losing them to the Confederacy. Additionally, Lincoln did not have the constitutional authority to outlaw slavery in those states by executive order. Lincoln knew quite well that slavery was sacrosanct for far too many Americans for him to unilaterally outlaw it—even in war.[56]

Confederate president Jefferson Davis renounced the proclamation to free nearly four million people from slavery as final proof of Lincoln's abolitionist ambitions: "The most execrable measure recorded in the history of guilty man is tempered by a profound contempt for the impotent rage which it discloses." Moreover, the liberation of black people from bondage would lead to their ultimate destruction. African people, Davis insisted, were inferior to whites and, if not enslaved, would go extinct. The proclamation was "a measure by which several millions of human beings of an inferior race, peaceful and contented laborers in their sphere, are doomed to extermination."[57] The infamous Confederate Georgia senator Benjamin Hill argued that the Emancipation Proclamation was, in effect, an "Insurrection Proclamation" and that US soldiers must be understood as its enforcers. Given that insurrection against slavery in the Confederacy was a treasonous offense, northern troops had the "intent to incite insurrection and abet murder" and should therefore "suffer death" rather than be offered any opportunity to surrender. Hill's suggestion to treat all Union soldiers as it had treated black ones did not become law.[58] Again, the rhetoric of black servile docility was employed as a moral intervention to charges of slavery's cruelty. This trope of black docility simultaneously implied that physically and mentally inferior black men would never be viable soldiers in any white man's war. This would also prove to be untrue.

As enlistments into the Union military decreased among northerners, the federal government rescinded a 1792 law that prohibited the arming of black citizens in the country's military. On May 22,

1863, the War Department issued General Order 143, establishing the United States Colored Troops. Black men, seeking to hasten the end of slavery, poured into recruitment offices across the country by the thousands.[59] African American leadership, across the ideological spectrum of the clergy, abolitionists, emigrationists, and black nationalists, found a special promise in black military service. This would not only be a war to end slavery; it would also simultaneously affirm black humanity and serve to prove, if not codify, full citizenship for black people.

Black privates were paid $10 per month, compared to their white counterparts, who were paid $13 per month. Additionally, black soldiers were assigned menial tasks and given secondhand amenities, arms, and other resources. White officials actually argued that black troops were best used for noncombatant duties; many thought that black men were too cowardly to be competent soldiers. When forced to explain why black soldiers were paid less than their white counterparts, President Lincoln insisted that it was "a necessary concession" to even allowing the presence of black troops.[60]

The father of black nationalism, Martin R. Delany, who had no faith in the ability of the United States to live up to its ideals of freedom, justice, and equality, abandoned his efforts to establish a black nation-state in Africa. With great alacrity, he began recruiting black soldiers across the Northeast. It was a chance to deliver a "death blow" to the "tyrants" in the South who held millions in chains. Similarly, black leadership across every region including Henry Highland Garnett, Mary Ann Shadd, and Tunis Campbell joined the efforts of the most famous African American of his time, Frederick Douglass, in rallying black communities for service.[61] Douglass, who also published and edited the *North Star* newspaper, famously issued his "Men of Color! To Arms!" broadside and spoke across the country, recruiting thousands. In no uncertain terms, the brilliant orator anchored black service into a long tradition of resistance to slavery: "Remember Denmark Vesey of Charleston; remember Nathaniel Turner of Southampton; remember

Shields Green and Copeland, who followed the noble John Brown, and fell as glorious martyrs."[62] Douglass, who was likely a product of a white man's rape of his mother, had been enslaved at birth and beaten as a youth. Around the age of twenty-two, he escaped slavery to become its most visible black antagonist. With profound and characteristic charisma, he evoked both sacred and secular themes in his speeches. This was a moral and Christian struggle of freedom against the forces of evil and slavery.

General Hunter, who had been targeted with "execution" along with black troops, made his own direct reply to Jefferson Davis in spring 1863. Circumventing military channels of communication, Hunter wrote to Davis, warning him that "I now give you notice, that unless this order is immediately revoked, I will at once cause the execution of every rebel officer, and every rebel slaveholder in my possession." Hunter poignantly argued that black people are "fighting for liberty in its truest sense." A master of semantic engagement, Hunter pointed out that while "you say you are fighting for liberty," it was a hollow and morally void corruption of its meaning. Confederates were "fighting for liberty . . . to keep four millions of your fellow-beings in ignorance and degradation—liberty to separate parents and children, husband and wife, brother and sister . . . liberty to seduce their wives and daughters, and to sell your own children into bondage;—liberty to kill these children with impunity." Addressing the pervasive practice of rape, destruction of families, cruelty, and beatings, Hunter, like Frederick Douglass, framed the war in salient moralistic and religious terms. This was unequivocally a war between good and unmitigated evil: "[Yours] is the kind of liberty—the liberty to do wrong—which Satan, Chief of the fallen Angels, was contending for when he was cast into Hell."[63]

The threats of retribution for cruelty against US prisoners of war appeared to temper Confederate action against black soldiers after the Union Army forced Confederate POWs into the line of fire as prison laborers in retaliation for the same act that the Confederate Army committed against black POWs.[64] But the spring of 1864 witnessed more brazen and violent acts by troops in both the Union blue and the Confederate gray. These included the raiding and sacking of homes, assaults on civilians, rape, and murder. However, few war crimes were as infamous as the Fort Pillow Massacre.[65]

An enslaver and slave trader, Major General Nathan Bedford Forrest commanded around two thousand Confederate soldiers during their raid of Fort Pillow on April 12, 1864. The fort was occupied by about six hundred troops, many from Tennessee and about evenly composed of black and white soldiers. Many of the black men at the fort had escaped slavery to serve in the Union Army. They were members of the 6th US Regiment Colored Heavy Artillery and a section of the 2nd Colored Light Artillery, and they served under the command of Major Lionel F. Booth, who, like all commanders of black regiments, was white.

The Confederates significantly outnumbered the Union forces and held sniping advantages from elevated positions nearby. The battle lasted hours before the fort was breached. When the defenses were broken, Union soldiers retreated toward a Union ship in a nearby river, but some surrendered to the enemy. Ordered to disarm, Union troops raised their hands when the Confederates charged. What followed was a wholesale slaughter of hundreds of men. The black troops were especially hated by Confederates and, as noted above, often fell victim to outright murder at the hands of rebels rather than being given quarter. White southerners who fought for the Union as well as white officers of black troops were likewise killed.[66]

Reports from witnesses, including some Confederates disgusted at the horror, described the massacre of civilians, including women and children. Achilles V. Clark, a Confederate soldier at the battle, wrote to his sister two days after the fight:

> The slaughter was awful. Words cannot describe the scene. The poor deluded negros would run up to our men fall on their knees

and with uplifted hands scream for mercy but they were ordered to their feet and then shot down. The whitte [*sic*] men fared but little better. The fort turned out to be a great slaughter pen. Blood, human blood stood about in pools and brains could have been gathered up in any quantity. I with several others tried to stop the butchery and at one time had partially succeeded but Gen. Forrest ordered them shot down like dogs and the carnage continued. Finally our men became sick of blood and the firing ceased.[67]

Northern newspapers were livid. The *Chicago Tribune* demanded justice for the "blood of four hundred United States soldiers, shot down after they had surrendered as prisoners of war, and their bodies hacked and slashed to pieces." The editors were clear that the war criminals needed a "retributive lesson of humanity." They wrote that "we must fight these rebels with their own weapons. If they shoot and starve our prisoners, treat theirs to the same dose. We must take off our gloves and go into this business as if we meant something."[68] William Tecumseh Sherman, major general and commander of the Military Division of the Mississippi, commanded forces in Tennessee and was one of the many Union military outraged at the massacre. Sherman wrote that there was "no doubt Forrest's men acted like a set of barbarians, shooting down the helpless negro garrison after the fort was in their possession."[69]

President Lincoln and the War Department considered in-kind punishment of Confederate POWs. Some argued that roughly four hundred rebels should be executed in a strong response to the massacre. However, this idea struck some as particularly savage. Others reasoned that any retributive barbarism was to prevent further war crimes from being committed by the Confederates. Ultimately, Lincoln and his generals decided to hold responsible the specific perpetrators at Fort Pillow, including, of course, Forrest. In the meantime, the story spread throughout the ranks of the Union Army, enraging and motivating soldiers with greater determination against a foe that was, to many, as vivid a manifestation of evil as ever witnessed in war.[70]

After many notable campaigns, various white newspapers, military commanders, and politicians celebrated black soldiers. Their performance cut short the lives of many Confederate soldiers, prompting one white soldier to note that "many a proud master found in death that freedom had made his slave his superior."[71] By the end of the Civil War, 10 percent of the entire US Army was black (roughly 179,000 soldiers). Black people constituted roughly 15 percent of the country in 1860, but about 90 percent of US blacks were enslaved and were concentrated in the states that formed the Confederacy. Therefore, it is remarkable that such a high ratio of black men served in the Union military. The proportion was higher than that of white men serving from the South but also higher than that of non-southern white men serving for the Union. Another 19,000 black servicemen were in the Union Navy.[72]

More than any other single event, the service of black men in the United States military undermined the white-nationalist project that had been woven into the fabric of the country since its inception. Even while forced to be in segregated units and denied pay equal to even that of foreign-born whites who had just arrived from Ireland, Germany, and other countries, these black troops, against incredible obstacles, proved their mettle on the battlefield and beyond. The status of free black people who had never lived anywhere but the United States had long been a liminal state of being neither citizen nor alien. As Martha Jones explains, in the course of the decades leading to the Civil War "lawmakers and jurists fumbled, punted, confused and otherwise failed to settle the question" of black citizenship.[73] Notions of "rights" being fixed to "citizenship" were muddled. Plenty of citizens—including, most visibly, white women—were not granted certain rights afforded their male counterparts. However, their status as citizens was never in question, even if they did not have rights equal to those granted to white men. One thing was certain: white men universally enjoyed access to nearly all levels of the federal, state, and local governments—even those white men who were newly arrived and naturalized. At the start of the Civil War, the United States was a white-nationalist project like its enemy, the Confederacy. For the US, however, the demands of war forged expanded notions of democracy and freedom.

The Civil War and black service in the Union Army forced a substantive reevaluation of what freedom, democracy, and citizenship meant. In the face of a brutal history of legalized oppression in every region of the country, black men and women campaigned, organized, and recruited black men to serve the Union. Even black nationalists were quick to heed the call to serve. Although most may have been motivated by the desire to destroy slavery more than to serve the United States, their participation in the US military set a path for an expanded notion of democracy and citizenship in the country. Still, these new, more capacious applications of democracy would remain in abeyance until after the war against the Confederacy was won. And the Atlanta Campaign would be a defining event in the summer of 1864.

2 | "No Capes for Negroes"
Quasi-free Blacks and Civil War Atlanta

"Very few white people were in sight, but lots of Negroes watched us as we marched along. . . . [Black people] hailed our men as their deliverers of God."
—UNION SOLDIERS ON MARCHING ON ATLANTA, 1864

"[Sherman was] the Nero of the nineteenth century . . . [overseeing] the most ruthless, Godless hand ever organized in the name of patriotism."
—MARY A. H. GAY, WHITE GEORGIAN, 1864

When *Williams' Atlanta Directory, City Guide and Business Mirror*, the city's first documented listing of its inhabitants, was published in 1859, few imagined how the names listed therein would be soon transformed by the sweeping forces of war. Solomon Luckie and his barbershop and bathing saloon were among the many people and businesses highlighted. His establishment was located in the Atlanta Hotel, built by the Georgia Railroad in 1845 and run by Dr. Joseph Thompson. At two stories, it was initially the largest among the hotels in the city and was regarded as the best hotel in town. Reflecting the centrality and power of the railroad industry in the city, this hotel was positioned in the prime central business district, literally next to a railroad. On the northwest side of the city's central State Square, the hotel sat on Pryor Street between what was then Marietta Street and the railroad.

The city's first mayor, Moses Formwalt, lived there, and Associate Justice Francis H. Cone of the Georgia Supreme Court savagely stabbed Alexander Stephens, future vice president of the Confederacy, there in 1848. Cone had accused Stephens, who was a Whig congressman, of being a "traitor to the South" for tabling the Clayton Compromise, which was meant to ease sectional tensions over the Oregon Territory. Hospitalized for weeks, Stephens refused to press charges against his assailant. Many other privileged and powerful locals and visitors patronized the barbershop and bathing saloon, making Luckie a comfortable man.[1]

By his thirties when the war began, Luckie was married to Nancy Cunningham, with whom he had three children, Camilla, Loduska, and Odie. When most Georgians were either subsistence farmers, in poverty, or enslaved, the Luckies, a very attractive couple, were photographed in fine clothes. In a striking photo, Solomon wears a suit, a large bow tie, and a pleasantly confident stare while balancing his left arm on a table in a classic pose that subtly draws attention to his pinky ring, itself a quiet mark of his status. Despite his relative wealth, Luckie's security and that of his family were always precarious. The Luckie family's five members accounted for more than 20 percent of all free black people in Atlanta in 1860. The tiny number of free blacks—23 in total—stood in contrast to the 1,917 who were enslaved, yet there they were: free, wealthy, well-dressed, and well-connected enough to secure a business and protect it against petitions from white barbers who protested his existence.

He was the first wealthy black Atlantan, but his wealth could not fully protect him in the travails of war or peace in the city of his day.[2]

By the eve of the Civil War, Georgia was one of the most inhospitable places to black people anywhere. Forty-four percent of all people in the state were enslaved, a higher rate than most southern states. More than 99 percent of black people in Georgia were enslaved, again a rate higher than that of most southern states. For the fraction of 1 percent of black people who were free, life included a range of extremely hostile laws that outlawed or constricted their ability to travel, associate with others, receive an education, or own firearms. In 1818 the state ruled that free black people had to annually register with authorities and that they could not purchase land unless they had a white guardian. It was also illegal for them to purchase anyone in slavery (partially a measure to prevent people from buying someone to surreptitiously manumit them) unless they had a white guardian. They could not "beat drums [or] blow horns," be taught to read and write, or be employed as scribes. It was illegal to free anyone from slavery—even through a last will and testament—except with a special ruling by the Georgia State Assembly. Between 1835 and the defeat of the Confederacy, the state approved manumission of only one person. Black people were not citizens by any measure.

However, there were challenges to this notion, and in these cases the courts were unequivocal. In 1853, Chief Justice of the State Supreme Court Joseph Henry Lumpkin ruled that black people had no citizenship rights, regardless of status as "free": "We maintain that the status of the African in Georgia, whether bond or free, is such that he has no civil, social, or political rights whatever, except those bestowed on him by statute." A free black person, the court argued, "can act only by and through his guardian; that he is in a condition of perpetual pupilage, or wardship."[3] Even in this daunting landscape, Atlanta managed to make even greater constrictions through its municipal racial laws.

The Gate City was a deeply hostile space for black people, even in comparison to other cities in the South. Washington, Charleston, and New Orleans all had sizable free-black populations. The extraordinary wealth of some free blacks in these cities has been well documented. Some owned opulent hotels, restaurants, and barbershops; enslaved people; and lived in mansions. Even if they could not vote, they managed to protect their wealth and create a black elite social world onto themselves.[4] In contrast, free and enslaved black people in antebellum and Civil War–era Atlanta were severely limited in their ability to move about the city and lived under a hypervigilant structure of laws and regulations. The city was explicitly hostile to black institution building: black churches, black schools, and black social organizations were illegal. The municipal government was determined to prevent free black people from entering Atlanta.

An enslaved black person could be brought as property to Atlanta, but free black people had to petition to settle there. If they were approved, they then paid a fee to live in the city. If they had not registered within five days of arrival, they could be arrested and leased out to white people for labor—in effect, enslaved. They had to secure a special license to operate a business. They could not sell certain products, including alcohol. When one black businessman applied for a permit to sell ice cream, the city rejected his request. They lived under curfews and had to secure a white guardian to traverse the city in ways that were mundane for whites. In addition to being unable to have firearms, they were barred from having canes or wearing capes—should their sartorial expressions appear too grand for their "proper status." Local laws mandated that they seek city council approval to entertain friends or family from out of town. The city council rejected multiple petitions of black people who attempted to move into the city, even under these conditions.[5] For the nearly two dozen free black people, a range of laws attempted to prevent them from achieving success. Yet, as this chapter details, through a consequence of incredible fortitude, cunning, and determination, African Americans brought about extraordinary successes that would prove foundational for generations of black institution builders in the city. This was especially so in the fog of war, which eroded much of the legal (and social) structures built to contain human aspiration and ability.

Despite Atlanta's relatively low percentage of enslaved people, the city was deeply tied to the institution of slavery. The city had nine businesses in particular that profited from human trafficking.[6] One business even offered groceries *and people* for sale. The largest slave trader was Crawford, Frazer & Company, where prospective slavers could survey children, women, and men in chains, in pens, in cages, and tethered to tables. One could purchase an eight-year-old girl, a twenty-year-old woman, or a person of any other age or gender variation. In these venues, people were treated as chattel and were physically inspected, prodded, and handled in the most dehumanizing ways. One such venue was the building at 8 Whitehall Street, which was centrally located, had plenty of foot traffic, and was proudly exposed to the public gaze. Wails from children being pried from their mothers could easily emanate out to the passing pedestrians.[7]

Two years after the Civil War started, Atlanta emerged as a central depot for buying and selling people. In April 1863, three months after the passage of the Emancipation Proclamation, the city's largest slave trader made extraordinary profits, evincing the Confederates' faith that their cause was destined to be a victorious one. Crawford, Frazer & Company sold entire families to traffickers or parceled off mothers from children and husbands from wives. A nine-year-old child was sold for $2,150 ($50,561 today). The *Atlanta Intelligencer*, a perennial booster for the city, lauded the city for its regional dominance in slave trading. The Gate City was "almost up to Richmond as a negro mart."[8]

Under these conditions, it is truly remarkable that some African Americans managed to achieve any semblance of success. Yet despite these circumstances, some—even those legally enslaved—were able to do just that. Along with the unique circumstances of the well-connected

Solomon Luckie in antebellum Atlanta, one of the most fascinating stories of early black efforts of self-determination is that of Laura Lavinia Kelley, a woman who was never enslaved and who managed to purchase land in 1854, becoming the first black landowner in the city of Atlanta.

Kelley was born in 1825 in Augusta to free parents who had relocated to Georgia from South Carolina in the early nineteenth century. Her parents had purchased at least two parcels of Augusta land by 1816—two years before the state outlawed any black person from buying land without a white guardian. She moved to Atlanta around 1849 as an employee of Dr. James F. Alexander, who left Augusta to start a medical practice. She was listed as a washer and ironer in the city's registration of free people of color. Alexander emerged as the city's leading physician in the treatment of smallpox.

Shortly after her arrival in Atlanta, Laura met John Combs, who was held in bondage there. The two married by 1854. Of course, few free black people lived in the city, making marriage options with a free African American limited. Across the South, some free black people married those held in slavery. Many ultimately purchased the freedom of their spouses. However, this was illegal in Georgia. Yet Laura found a loophole.

As a domestic worker confronted with the virulent forces of racism and patriarchy, Laura Combs managed to cobble enough resources to purchase land, becoming Fulton County's only person of color listed as a landowner and taxpayer in the 1854–1858 period. Around 1856, she negotiated a complex exchange with a third party that included a "land swap" of her plot in "city lot 10, land lot 78" for her husband, owned by Mary and Jane Combs. These women, who were sisters, had inherited John when he was a child and, most likely, willingly circumvented state law to negotiate with Laura. Doing so gave John freedom to be with his wife and granted the Combs sisters new real estate. Although he was technically still their property, John managed to live a life in de facto freedom from the white Combs family. Around 1857, the Laura and John Combs family settled in Augusta.[9]

Alexander was the person who, as Laura's guardian, made possible her initial land purchase. He was also one of the founders of the Atlanta Medical College in 1854. Alexander emerged as a full-throated secessionist in the following decade, serving in the Confederate Army's Eighth Georgia Infantry as a surgeon. Simultaneously, Laura's oldest son, Thomas, served in the Union Army, rising to the rank of sergeant and military band leader.

Beyond the remarkable story of Laura and John Combs, there were other African Americans who lived in a liminal space as professionally and socially privileged yet technically enslaved. A particularly fascinating account is that of Roderick Badger, the city's first black dentist, who, surprisingly, grew successful by attracting a white clientele. He was born on Independence Day 1834 in DeKalb County to Martha, a woman enslaved by Joshua Badger, a wealthy plantation owner and dentist. Joshua had several children from his wife and at least two, Roderick and Robert, from women he enslaved. He taught his two black sons and a white one, Ralph, the trade of dentistry.

In 1855 Roderick married Mary Murphey, who was the daughter of an enslaver, Charles Murphey, and who was still held in bondage. Although Roderick was legally enslaved, in 1856 Joshua granted his son resources and support—as his owner—to settle in Atlanta and establish a practice. Similarly, Mary was given permission to live with her husband in Atlanta, where they eventually had eight children.

Despite the incredibly hostile environment, Roderick's dental practice thrived. He attracted a sizable clientele of whites who proved loyal to his business. Although it was not unusual for whites to patronize black barbers, dentistry was a highly specialized profession that conferred prestige even among whites. This fact was not lost on white competitors, who seethed at Badger's success.

In line with the city's general hostility to black development of any kind, a body of whites (believed to be bitterly jealous dentists) petitioned the Atlanta City Council to prevent a capitalist market with any measure of fair competition. In 1859 they argued that it was unfair to compete with black businesses: "We feel aggrieved as Southern citizens that your honorable body tolerates a negro dentist (Roderick Badger) in our midst; and in justice to ourselves and the community it ought to be abated. We, the residents of Atlanta, appeal to you for justice."[10] In their moral and ethical universe, where equal opportunity was considered unjust, they appealed to the state to prevent black professionals from existing.

Despite the petition, Badger was able to maintain his practice. He had close ties with powerful whites. Roderick was the son and, more importantly, legal property of a wealthy white planter who was his guardian. His wife, Mary, was the daughter and legal property of a sitting state senator, former member of the US House of Representatives, and wealthy lawyer in nearby Decatur. These relations, as well as

Solomon Luckie was the first documented wealthy black Atlantan. He owned a barbershop and bathing saloon in the Atlanta Hotel, catering to the city's elites and those who visited the city. In a city that had some of the most repressive antiblack laws anywhere in the country, where black people could not form organizations (including churches or schools) or even wear certain clothing, Luckie was a profound outlier. Luckie and wife, Nancy, pictured here, along with their three children, represented over 20 percent of the city's miniscule free-black population. CREDIT: PART OF THE KENAN RESEARCH CENTER AT THE ATLANTA HISTORY CENTER REPOSITORY some of his clientele, likely gave Badger some insulation from punitive action from the city council, which did, however, pass a series of laws that constricted business opportunities for free black people. They were assessed a $5 tax (about $175 today) to live in Atlanta and were required to submit $200 (about $7,000 today) to be allowed to relocate to the city.

The Luckies and the Badgers must have measured their privilege against that of the mass of black people while simultaneously recognizing the chasms of privilege, power, and basic rights that separated them from whites across class lines. They enjoyed many things that poor whites did not; however, their full citizenship and basic ability to travel freely, gather with friends and family, conduct business, and live a peaceful life with equal protection under the law were starkly curtailed by the most basic principles of white nationalism. Their talent, grit, industriousness, and integrity were never enough to realize civil rights for all in a system that inherently found meritocracy anathema—even among those designated as free.

After Abraham Lincoln's election, in homes, private parlors, streets, and hotels, people engaged in debates and curious conversations about the future of the country and the region. Would the federal government attempt to destroy slavery? Would war ensue? What would become of the South? Of black people? The Luckies and the Badgers were aware that as war neared, life for them and their children would be fundamentally changed. Of course, the degree to which it would be changed remained unknown to all.

Charles Murphey, the father of Mary Badger, served as one of two delegates from DeKalb County during the debates over secession. He intended to vote for the Union but died on the first day of the convention. Ultimately, 208 voted for secession and 89 against it. By the time Lincoln was inaugurated, in March 1861, the breakaway republic organized militias in every state, and men in and around Atlanta swiftly assembled their own brigades or joined others. The Gate City

Guards, the Atlanta Cadets, the Fulton Blues, the Atlanta Grays, the Fulton Dragoons, the Georgia Volunteers, and the Davis Infantry had all formed by the time Lincoln was sworn in. The southern nationalist cause appealed to various European immigrants as well. The all-German Steuden Yagers and the Atlanta Irish Volunteers organized among the city's respective immigrant communities.

The local newspapers were excited about what the war would portend for their city and region. "Upon one point he is perfectly plain," the *Atlanta Intelligencer* wrote about Lincoln. "He decides for war. We are prepared to meet it. We are a united and homogenous people. . . . Every man in the South is a soldier." The paper wrote in classic form, disregarding the 44 percent of its state's population that was black and almost entirely held in chains or the 35 percent of the people in the South in similar conditions. With remarkable confidence, the paper concluded that the Confederacy was a formidable military force and that the citizens of Atlanta would rise to serve with alacrity. As the article concluded, "We say then, to Lincoln and his myrmidons, come on!"[11] A month later, the Gate City Guard left for service in Florida, where the Confederates planned to surround, if not capture, US military installations, including Fort Pickens in Pensacola. The Atlanta Hotel and the Trout House (another of the main hotels) were brimming with excitement as thousands of Atlantans gathered to send off the rebels. The city was ready to support white southern nationalism with force.

Confederate president Jefferson Davis, who visited the city in April, was met with throngs of cheering locals. Children curiously and dutifully followed directions to "scatter flowers in Mr. Davis's pathway" as he waved at the excited citizens lining his route. More than sending eager troops off to war, Atlanta was an early critical source of war matériel as well. The Confederate government designated the city as an industrial producer of weaponry. Gunsmiths worked overtime to produce an arsenal. The state militia was headquartered there, and the whirl of machinery, commerce, and excitement animated the city as war neared.[12] Even with this level of preparedness and excitement, few would anticipate the scope of the conflagration before them or the degree to which Atlanta would be central to its unfolding.

In 1861 scores of cities, from Haverhill, Maine, to Quincy, Illinois, including more than a dozen southern ones, were more populous than Atlanta. Despite its small population, Atlanta was an important cog in the Confederate war machine by 1863. The *New York Times* reported that the city, as part of a transportation network, "furnished forth half its war material to the entire Confederacy from the Rappahannock to the Rio Grande."[13] That the war was in its third year surprised most. People on both sides had assumed that it would end after its first several months. Although the industrial output of the North far exceeded the South, it was at a distinct disadvantage by being forced to have its soldiers march sometimes hundreds of miles into enemy territory. Defeating rebels required capturing the several cities that were essential to feeding the Confederate war machine with manufacture and transportation of munitions, as well as illegally traded crops, including cotton. That trade relied on rail networks through the Black Belt cotton-rich regions of the South, and no city was as strategically important as Atlanta to that trade. The US War Department identified Atlanta's capture as critical to victory.

In spring 1864, the famed General Sherman, with the horror of Fort Pillow still fresh, led the Military Division of the Mississippi in a major campaign into Georgia to capture Atlanta. The Union forces comprised three divisions: the Army of the Tennessee, under General James B. McPherson; the Army of the Ohio, under General John M. Schofield, and the Army of the Cumberland, under General George Henry Thomas. The massive group of 98,000 Union soldiers terrified Confederates and their sympathizers.

Confederate general Joseph E. Johnston, who commanded a much smaller group of troops (53,000), futilely resisted the push of Sherman's soldiers but continued to fall back toward the prized city. A pall of fear fell across much of Atlanta as its residents awaited the Yankee advance. To temper the growing anxiety, on June 6 the Atlanta City Council passed a resolution requesting Mayor James M. Calhoun to issue a special proclamation. Calhoun steadfastly urged calm, faith, and patience, and he established June 10, 1864, as "a day of Fasting, Humiliation and Prayer . . . to Almighty God . . . to bless and crown our arms with success, and to cause our enemies to return discomforted to their homes."[14] There is little doubt that black Atlantans also prayed, but for a distinctly different outcome than did Calhoun and his white compatriots. For them, the federals were harbingers of freedom, not the demons described by Confederates.

On June 27, after several weeks of pushing into Georgia, Sherman led an ill-fated assault on Kennesaw Mountain, more than twenty miles north of Atlanta. The rebels, under Johnston, held their positions and pushed back the federal army, which had charged from all sides. As typical of battles through history, the carnage, which had started in the morning, concluded just hours later, by midday. Union casualties were estimated at 2,500, whereas Johnston calculated around 800 Confederate dead. The battlefield was littered with corpses, which began to rot in the summer heat. The two sides agreed on a truce to gather their dead comrades for burials.[15] Despite the failed charge, white locals remained rightfully terrified at the prospect of Sherman's push. The Union general had already established a reputation for strong repression of local Confederate vigilantism and resistance. Among other things, he exiled pro-Confederate civilians and commandeered their crops, cattle, businesses, and homes. There was little recourse when Sherman's troops, a veritable juggernaut, moved across the southern landscape.

The day after the assault on Kennesaw Mountain, Georgia governor Joseph Brown wrote to CSA president Jefferson Davis begging for more troops. Brown was particularly alarmed about Atlanta. Brown explained that "I need not call your attention to the fact that this place is to the Confederacy . . . almost as important as the heart is to the human body. We must hold it." Brown, desperate for the most savage of generals, suggested that Nathan Bedford Forrest be summoned to cut off Sherman's supply line from the rear. When Richmond refused to send Forrest or any more soldiers, Brown was livid. The governor complained that upward of fifty Georgia regiments were in Richmond defending the Confederate capital when they could be protecting Atlanta instead. Brown was an outspoken critic of Davis, and his hostility to conscription only intensified with Sherman's march. Brown undermined the wider Confederate war effort when he refused to send further militia to CSA federal authority in order to avoid "surrendering the last vestige of sovereignty of the state."[16] In a twist of irony, the Confederate federal government witnessed its own weakening in the face of vituperative protests against violations of "states' rights" from within its own constituent states.

The situation for the rebels seemed dire, but the Yankees' charge had, for the moment, stopped. Perhaps cautious about rushing into another major assault on Johnston's positions, the two armies remained at Kennesaw Mountain until Johnston and his weary troops fled to Smyrna on the night of July 2. Sherman, emboldened, pushed forward with his soldiers, making his way closer to Atlanta.[17]

Throughout the Georgia Campaign, Confederate leaders scrambled to raise militia and even guerrilla groups to attack Sherman. Benjamin Hill, the politician and ardent white supremacist, enjoined the civilian population of his state to rise up against Union soldiers. In outright desperation, he even implored slaveholders to direct their enslaved men to attack Union troops, as long as the enslaved did not have firearms. Making a calculated distinction, Hill called for "every citizen with his gun and every Negro with his spade and axe" to attack federal troops. Other Georgia politicians directed the people to "burn all bridges and block up the road in [Sherman's] route. Assail the invader by day and night—let him have no rest."[18] The fear across Confederate leadership—political and civil—was palpable. The highly regarded rebel General P. G. T. Beauregard, whose troops had first fired on Fort Sumter, demanded that the people of Georgia "arise for the defense of [your] native soil" and "rally around your patriotic Governor and gallant soldiers! Obstruct and destroy all roads in Sherman's front, flank, and rear and his army will soon starve in your midst."[19] To the Confederate leaders' dismay, the people refused to confront Sherman on any notable scale.

Many white Georgians fled Sherman's approach, hiding in fields, forests, basements, and attics. They did not charge the Union troops, and, as the *Richmond Dispatch* reported, "nor did they destroy any property or drive away their cattle."[20] Atlanta's *Southern Confederacy* newspaper, which had become a powerful mouthpiece for Confederate leadership, had just a few weeks earlier graphically admonished rebel soldiers to repulse Sherman's troops: "Rise to the field of battle! Sink down in your own blood and hail it as a joyful deliverance, in preference to submission to the heartless abolition Yankees."[21] The reference to abolition was a clear reminder to rebel soldiers of slavery's significance to their fight. According to millions across the South, abolition was an infernal evil itself. In a moral universe that celebrated the right to enslave as "freedom" and the abnegation of that right as "tyranny," the appeal to Confederate resistance seemed only strengthened by the Emancipation Proclamation and the reports of newly freed black men joining the ranks of the US military. Perhaps the only thing worse than Sherman's advance on Atlanta would have been regiments of black soldiers under his command.

The editors of the *Intelligencer* shared the anxiety and alarm that pervaded the city. The paper insisted that Jefferson Davis provide more troops to repulse the approaching federals. The *Intelligencer*, like people across the North and South, understood the critical importance of the city's fate. There was "no greater prize in the Confederacy" outside of Richmond, as Robert O'Connell notes. "If the South had a workshop

for war, it was Atlanta."[22] Johnston could not withstand the advancement, and the industrial hub was too important to be lost: "Should
Atlanta fall, fearful indeed will be the responsibility. . . . The Richmond
in Virginia is the political Richmond, but the Richmond in Georgia is
Atlanta, which to the Confederacy is a more important point."[23] Significant national attention focused on the Gate City and the massive
forces assembling to determine its fate. Lincoln, who was running for
reelection, faced challenges from Democrats who had grown weary of
the war, as well as members of his own party who felt that he was too
conciliatory to the Confederates and too short on battlefield victories.
During the siege, given the casualties and the war fatigue from northern families and soldiers alike, the president confided in a colleague
that "I am going to be beaten and, unless some great change takes
place, badly beaten."[24]

By mid-July, the Union forces were on the outskirts of Atlanta, the
would-be capital of the Confederacy. The War Department in Richmond,
desperate to repulse Sherman, relieved Johnston of his duties and replaced
him with Lieutenant General John Bell Hood on July 17. Hood, known
as bold and audacious, eagerly embraced the charge. Even some other
Confederates considered the young officer brash and reckless. Robert E.
Lee warned that Hood was "all lion, none of the fox."[25] Though smaller in
number, Hood's troops attacked the Union line at various points, hoping
to disrupt the forces and isolate the much larger regiment. Confederates
attacked from Peachtree Creek, Decatur, and Ezra Church. However,
these assaults were futile against the might and military maneuvers of
Sherman and his commanders. Hood lost fourteen thousand troops to
casualties, and his aggressive tactics proved for naught.[26]

The numbers, strength, and military command of the Yankees
overwhelmed the rebels. Hood retreated to Atlanta, which was fortified with troops and parapets positioned across the city in homes and
buildings. He prepared for the Union assault and appealed for reinforcements, but these were never authorized. The situation appeared

increasingly desperate for the Confederates across the state. In fact, by
1864 there had emerged a peace movement tacitly supported by Alexander Stephens, the stern CSA vice president. A Georgia native, Stephens was known as a "master at managing relations with journalists,"
and he exploited his relations with state newspapers, including Atlanta's famed *Southern Confederacy*, to promote the notion that a negotiated
peace with the North was viable.[27] In essence, Stephens endorsed the
platform of the Democratic Party, which argued the same in the 1864
presidential election cycle. While the local movement for "unbowed"
peace spread, General Hood anxiously calculated his options.

In the oppressive heat of the Georgia summer, Sherman patiently
established encampments along a stretch of the city and began a brutal
siege. The shelling went on for weeks and destabilized the city in every
way. Daily reports on the front kept others throughout the Confederacy abreast of the siege of Atlanta. On July 9 the *Southern Confederacy*
reported that "the echo of a few heavy guns has been heard in the city
in the morning." In an attempt to provide some degree of comfort, the
paper noted that "our readers may rest assured we shall keep them duly
posted of further developments of the enemy, and as such the disposi-
tion of our own troops as may not betray the movements and designs of
our commander in chief." However, the iconic newspaper made no further reports on the siege. That report was in the last published issue of
the *Southern Confederacy*, which ceased operations in Atlanta as Union
forces bombarded the city.[28] The collapse of the newspaper was an omi-
nous sign for the rebellion across the South.

The wartime population had doubled to more than twenty thousand:
war production drew both wage labor and enslaved workers to the city.
With huge shortages of wage labor, enslavers across the region profited
by leasing enslaved men and women to work for the Confederate war
machine. Many of these people were forced to work in hospitals, in factories, on the railroads, or in any other space deemed necessary by the
rebel government. Forced-labor camps with thousands of people from

throughout Georgia were used to produce war matériel as well as dig massive ditches around the city to fortify against Union attack. The final result of months of backbreaking labor was several miles of fortifications, thousands of skirmish holes for armed soldiers, and "a man-made wall as impregnable as any titanic storm-tossed ocean waves broke upon."[29]

However, the chaos and mayhem caused by war and the siege enabled waves of escapes to freedom. First dozens, then scores, and finally hundreds of enslaved people fled to freedom after reaching Atlanta. The rapidly growing population of black people brought more opportunity for escape and melting into crowds of urban anonymity. Newspapers reported large rewards to reenslave people who had escaped bondage. The proximity of the Union Army only exacerbated fears that people would escape slavery. A resident of Marietta, outside of Atlanta, advertised a reward of a thousand dollars to capture a husband and wife, Jesse and Delia, who were likely "making their way for the enemy."[30] The uncertainty and the fog of war provided a perfect arena for emancipation. By the July bombardment campaign, most Atlantans had fled the city. Thousands of people fled slavery from plantations, factories, and other leased positions as management, overseers, and authority itself eroded.

But even as Atlanta was threatened by Union forces, some people were still moving into the city for various reasons. The city was a depot for people fleeing conflict in the countryside and for soldiers either en route to battle or returning from it as casualties. Local hospitals tended to the wounded from the front, as well as civilian needs. At one point, the city had twenty-six hospitals. As the Yankee forces moved closer to the city, health-care workers fled with other civilians. The strain on and demand for the handful of physicians who remained were extraordinary. The most famous of the wartime health-care workers was Dr. Noel D'Alvigny, a French-born surgeon who joined the Ninth Georgia Battalion of the Confederate Army and tended to all manner of trauma. Like many other foreign-born people in Georgia,

he committed himself to the cause of southern nationalism. His son
Charles served in Company G of the cavalry battalion of the Georgia
Legion, which had been organized by the wealthy slave owner Thomas
Reade Rootes Cobb, and he eventually served with Robert E. Lee in
Virginia.[31] By July, the Atlanta Medical College was the only hospital
still in operation in the city and Noel D'Alvigny its only physician. The
horrifying specter of a siege was being realized, with very few resources
to attend to its carnage.

Those who remained spent weeks preparing for bombardment.
Civilians prepared "bombproofs" in their yards and around their homes
as defenses against shelling. Confederates created parapets stretching
across the city as well. For weeks the salvos continued with an occasional lull, but no breaks lasting much more than a day. National newspapers covered the siege, and Americans eagerly anticipated updates
on the Atlanta Campaign. Richmond was in regular communication
with General Hood, who clamored for more resources and troops. In
an effort to reassure its shaken readers, the *Intelligencer* reported that
the Confederacy need not fear capture of the prized city. The fortifications and the spirits of the people were strong. The fate of the Gate City
was in the capable hands of Hood and his soldiers. In fact, the rebels
were winning against the "abolitionist" invaders: "The Yankee forces
will disappear before Atlanta before the end of August."[32] Of course,
the Yanks had other plans.

As Sherman's forces penetrated farther into Georgia, Confederate troops met them on July 21 at the Battle of Atlanta, southeast
of the city. Early on, Confederate skirmishers shot and killed General McPherson. Rated first in his 1853 West Point graduating class,
McPherson was the second-highest-ranking Union officer killed in the
war. Coincidentally, Confederate general Hood was a classmate and
friend of McPherson's, and he wrote that the death of his "classmate
and boyhood friend" caused him "sincere sorrow." Although they were
on opposite sides of the conflict, Hood claimed that the war had not

lessened his friendship with McPherson.[33] Sherman swiftly promoted General Oliver Otis Howard to replace McPherson as the commander of the Army of the Tennessee. Howard, who had also attended West Point with Hood, advised Sherman that "I knew [Hood] well at West Point. He won't give up."[34] Howard's words resonated with the indefatigable Sherman, who then calculated a strategy to crush the rebels. Sherman knew that a broken supply line, coupled with constant shelling, would break the most obstinate resistance. A full bombardment of the city would follow. In early August, as Sherman wrote to Howard, "Let us destroy Atlanta and make it a desolation."[35]

The shells raining into the city horrified its inhabitants, prompting a steady flow of excited civilians to move south out of the city for safety. Many of the people, accurately fearing pillaging soldiers, fled with as much as they could carry. People frantically loaded trunks with clothes and valuables, and many even tried to move furniture from their homes onto crowded trains. "Everyone seems to be hurrying off," reported one newspaper. "Wagons loaded with household furniture and everything else that can be packed upon them crowd every street, and women old and young, and children innumerable are hurrying to and fro. Every train of cars is loaded to its utmost capacity. The excitement beats anything I ever saw."[36] Confederate lieutenant Andrew Neal, a native of Atlanta, witnessed the shelling while in Hood's command. He wrote to his sister that although their hometown had not been captured, "they have ruined its value to us in great measure."[37]

The shelling caused fires throughout the city, which was ablaze day and night. The Union forces targeted militarily important positions, but scores of homes and other private properties of no military importance were hit with shells, shrapnel, and bullets or were destroyed by fire. The *New York Times* reported on one powerfully symbolic casualty of Union shelling: a downtown business that sold babies, the elderly, and all manner of people in between. The sign across the facade of the bombarded building read "Auction Sale of Negroes." The shelling "was but uttering the condemnation of God and the civilized world, against the diabolical traffic." The Yankee projectiles were compared to "thunderbolt[s] from Heaven . . . speaking for humanity, and carrying the destruction to the accursed tenement wherein the dearest rights of man have been violated."[38] On August 7, Sherman wrote to Major General H. W. Halleck in Washington, informing him that the military operation against the fortified Confederate stronghold was moving favorably: "One thing is certain, whether we get inside Atlanta or not, it will be a used-up community by the time we are done with it."[39] The bombardment proved to be a powerful display of modern warfare, laying waste to both military and civilian structures, and demoralizing the population.

On August 9, two days after Sherman's letter to Halleck, Luckie, the black businessman who operated out of the Atlanta Hotel, was on his way to work as he had for years. Although most residents had evacuated, he was one of the civilians who had not fled the city. Why he chose to stay is unclear. Perhaps he considered travel with his family in the chaos of war to be too risky. The city and region were infiltrated with thieves, looters, violent opportunists, and others who could with impunity commit almost any manner of offense against black women, children, and men. In his years in Atlanta, Luckie was able to forge favorable relationships with enough powerful whites that he enjoyed a modicum of a protective bubble. Outside of this, his and his family's safety was uncertain. Luckie was aware that any random, unlettered, barefoot, poor white man with no resources, or perhaps a covetous soldier, could steal everything of worth and even take their lives.

That morning, as Luckie ventured toward his shop, he and others quickly became aware that the Union onslaught had escalated. Shells were more numerous than before, and the sounds of their screams across the sky were more intense. "Shot and shell rained in every direction," wrote journalist Walter P. Reed. "Great volumes of sulphurous smoke rolled over the town, trailing down to the ground, and through this stifling gloom the sun glared down like a great red eye peering through a bronze colored sky."[40] One of the day's estimated five thousand Union shells fired into the city landed near the corners of Whitehall and Alabama Streets, just as Luckie neared the intersection. The shell ricocheted off a lamppost and sent fragments tearing through his leg, ripping it open. Luckie was lying helplessly on the ground when passersby came to his aid. Captain E. C. Murphy, commanding the 1st Volunteer Fire Department; Johnny Magee, also from the fire unit; and Tom Crusselle wrapped Luckie in a blanket and transported him to Atlanta Medical College, where Dr. D'Alvigny amputated his leg. Like most Civil War soldiers who suffered similar injuries, Luckie never recovered; he died within hours.[41]

Just as Luckie was on the precipice of witnessing the great abolition that so many Confederates feared, he was felled by a Union shell and attended to by a physician who was committed to saving rebel lives. Luckie did not live to see the full scope of black freedom and the defeat of the southern nationalist cause. However, his wife, Nancy, and their three children survived the horrors of that hot August day to grapple with a life without Solomon, witnessing the slow collapse of the Confederate experiment around them. In the meantime the city remained enveloped with fear, anxiety, and instability. Smoke billowed in the air as terrified civilians sheltered in place, hoping to be spared direct hits or the resulting fires. One journalist referred to the bombardment as "the red day of August, when all the fires of hell, and all the thunders of the universe seemed to be blazing and roaring over Atlanta."[42]

During the weeks leading up to the siege, many people from the countryside poured into Atlanta, and many others moved out. People escaping slavery drifted to the city, as well as yeomanry and the poor, who constituted most whites in Georgia. These subsistence farmers and the formerly enslaved often sought refuge from the encroaching troops, the skirmishes, the bombs, and the stench of death that followed. All these groups found refuge in the Gate City, adding to the sense of frenzy and instability.

In the unprecedented upheaval of the social, political, and cultural institutions and sensibilities of the region, black people positioned themselves to take advantage of the disorder. Few were as colorful as Robert Webster. Like Solomon Luckie, he was a successful barber, but like Roderick Badger, he was regarded as "half-slave and half-free." Webster was legally enslaved, although in many respects he lived much better than the average white man—anywhere.

Webster was born in Washington, DC, in 1820 to a woman enslaved by John Gadsby, owner of the largest hotel in the city. Records are unclear on Webster's paternity, but he chose his surname based on the belief that his father was Daniel Webster, the powerful Massachusetts senator and former secretary of state. Like women held in slavery across the country, Robert Webster's mother was vulnerable to sexual abuse, even from white men other than her owner. Regardless of Robert's parentage, Gadsby, following law and custom, enslaved him at birth and raised him in the National Hotel among thirty-eight other enslaved workers.[43] Considered the most luxurious of the capital city's hotels, the impressive five-story structure offered shops, ballrooms, and spacious accommodations to the country's elite. Congressmen rented rooms there, presidents and dignitaries hosted balls there, and others met at the opulent bar. In the hotel, Robert navigated a world of power, pedigree, and urbane cosmopolitanism. Gadsby later gave Robert to his son, who lost him in a poker game soon thereafter. His new owner sold him, and he was eventually sent to a plantation in South Carolina. An incredibly wealthy lawyer and planter, Benjamin Yancey, worked with the owners of the plantation and eventually bought Robert after he convinced the politically connected Yancey to purchase him and his wife. Yancey transported his new property to his plantation in Alabama and found Webster to be particularly valuable, even worthy of management roles. Yancey called him "truthful, sober, affectionate, honest. . . . He was a faithful servant, much attached to me, my wife and children."[44] In 1856 Yancey, eager to take advantage of the exploding growth in Atlanta, relocated to the city with his family, Webster, and other captives. Circumstances shifted for both men when President Buchanan tapped Yancey, who had served in the Alabama senate, to serve as a diplomat to Argentina in 1858.

During his absence in South America, Yancey granted Webster the opportunity to settle in Atlanta, establish a barbershop, and pay a part of his profit to Yancey. Yancey later claimed that "I gave him practical freedom and the means of making and using money." Webster, despite the countervailing forces against him, managed to succeed extraordinarily. Like Luckie and Badger, his clientele included whites with resources and power. Perhaps his familiarity with the mannerisms, sensibilities, and interests of elites positioned him to appeal to the local Atlanta crowd. He thrived and then opened multiple business enterprises, employed people, and bought a new home by the time that Yancey was serving as a colonel in the Confederate Army. Because the law would not allow a slave to purchase a home in Atlanta, Webster had to register the purchase in Yancey's name. However, this did not fundamentally change the fact that he was growing wealthy in the Gate City even as the tumult of war and the collapsing Confederate economy meant that the richest members of the planter class were losing wealth as the war continued.

By the summer of 1864, when most people had fled Atlanta, Webster had established himself as a trader in the underground economy of gold, tobacco, and currency, acquiring more prestige, power, and influence even as he was still enslaved. A confluence of expected deprivations and disruptions from the chaos of war made food increasingly scarce in the city, especially for the poor, who had experienced food insecurity even before the siege. Many Atlantans complained of the influx of "rabble": the dirty "ruffians" and random strangers in their midst. Many were becoming increasingly desperate.

A brigade of Confederate soldiers, struck by the deprivations of the city's refugees, donated rations to the starving in early August.

Perhaps the circumstances of such social, political, economic, and cultural upheaval disabused people of the need to enforce what may have appeared as trite and petty laws of racial etiquette and policing. Hunger, fear, and widespread instability meant that Webster's ability to secure goods granted him access and resources in ways that were otherwise unavailable. Moreover, he was technically the property of a well-established and powerful white man. This would, of course, deter threats against him from envious parties. However, his visibility did not go without challenge or suspicion.

Throughout the war, there were pervasive concerns about spies in the city. As the population of the city surged in 1862, the *Intelligencer* told its readers that "spies of the enemy have been and are still in Atlanta." In an almost direct reference to Webster, the paper complained of "suspicious characters" and lamented that the city had become "Head Quarters for itinerant speculators, in gold, bank notes, Confederate Currency, meat and bread." The paper even called for martial law to be imposed to constrict movement of the "secret enemies" roaming about the Gate City. The fear of Union sympathizers in Atlanta remained throughout the war effort. To root out suspected spies, locals pressed Mayor John Calhoun, himself a Unionist before the war, to enact more punitive or vigilant measures against the increased numbers of black people who populated the city. As noted earlier, many were enslaved and leased to work in factories, whereas others drifted among a bourgeoning influx of migrants in the earliest years of the war. Some, it was argued, had escaped from slavery and posed a fundamental threat to the institution itself. Any of them could subvert the war effort as possible spies for the Union. Another prominent black barber, William Dougherty Hutchins, lost his business in the destruction of Atlanta. And although Hutchins may have provided his family some semblance of comfort through his profession, his son, Styles, left Atlanta and joined the Union Army in 1864.[45] Many local whites, despite rhetoric about "loyal Negroes," were clear-minded enough to suspect that most, if not nearly all, local black people harbored Union sympathies.

To some degree, Webster was the embodiment of these fears and was not protected from being molested by agents of the rebel state. In July 1864, Confederate soldiers invaded Webster's home under the pretense of seeking people who had escaped slavery. They eventually stole jewelry from Robert and his wife, Bess. Although he had little recourse against the weight of the Confederate Army, the de facto free Robert used his connections and privileges to travel to and collaborate with Union soldiers in various ways. He gave them food, traded with them, and even provided the means for at least one soldier to escape. He had "done all in his power to help break the Confederacy's back."[46]

When Yankee prisoners of war passed through the city, Webster took advantage of his position—neither a Confederate nor a Yankee—to surreptitiously contact and conduct business with northerners held captive. Webster traded US currency for Confederate money with Atlanta civilians and Union POWs so that the captives could purchase food or other goods. It was an underground market that he dominated, earning as much as three hundred Confederate dollars for one US dollar. Though dangerous, his commerce in currency was a boon for the living and breathing oxymoron called Webster. According to court testimony from white Atlantans after the war, as well as from Webster himself, the quasi-free barber and boss of the unregulated, untaxed, underground market had profited handsomely during the war. He eventually purchased a warehouse and traded in produce among other commodities. He insisted that "I never made less than $100 a day" (about $4,000 in today's dollars). Regardless of whatever false, socially imposed limitations and assumptions about the innate and immutable superiority of whites and the fecklessness of blacks that premised the Confederate (and American) project, Webster rose to unprecedented heights. "No man in the place," he argued later, "stood higher than I did." He was, according to a white Atlantan, "one of the biggest traders we had here." Although enslaved, he amassed more than $16,000 during the war (more than half a million in today's dollars): "Even as the war crushed the fortunes of many white neighbors, Webster got richer."[47]

A white Unionist would later argue that Webster was not simply capitalizing on the instability of war for his own pecuniary interests; he was also dedicated to the defeat of the Confederacy: "Mr. Robert Webster was one of the 35 or 36 loyal men of the city during the war." Assisting the Union Army was central to his efforts, despite the incredible risks, which included execution if found guilty of "insurrection" or "treason," as the Confederates ironically constructed their legal language regarding those who aided the military of the United States. Webster and his wife were not isolated in their activities. The liminally free Websters were close associates of white Union loyalist Cyrena Stone, so much so that as part of an underground Unionist network they mutually assisted each other during the war.[48]

Webster, who was black and was enslaved in a white-nationalist, pro-slavery society, thrived during the instability of war, but many whites, whether enslavers or not, saw their circumstances worsen terribly. The *Columbus Sun* insisted that "the poor in Atlanta are said to be suffering for something to eat." Nearly two weeks later, the *Intelligencer* reported that there is "but very little in the city, and, since the 22d July last, there has been scarcely any provisions for sale here." Intermittently, trains from Macon provided watermelons, apples, and beef. The situation was becoming even more untenable as foragers stole from private gardens and looted the homes of families who had fled.[49] General Hood, under great duress and anger, reached out to his Union counterpart, protesting the shelling of civilians and other nonmilitary targets. But Sherman did not waver from his determination to lay waste to the city that had been a critical cog in the Confederate war machine. His charge and mission, as a commander of US military forces, Sherman said, was to vanquish its enemies and incapacitate their ability to fight.

Furthermore, he insisted that women and children should not have been put at risk by being in the city during the weeks of shelling.[50]

As Sherman and the scores of thousands of federals under his command settled into a siege, the general focused his energy on one artery of trade. Uncle Billy, as his troops affectionately called him, knew how essential it was to capture the Macon road, which controlled the traffic of goods to and from Atlanta. As Sherman explained, "Its possession, by us would, in my judgement, result in the capture of Atlanta." Moreover, "Atlanta was known as the 'Gate-City of the South,' . . . full of founderies [sic], arsenals, and machine-shops, and I knew that its capture would be the death-knell of the Southern Confederacy."[51] The Union strategy crippled resistance.

Hood's former West Point classmate Howard commanded formidable forces that were slowly sealing the fate of Hood's southern troops. The Confederates were fatigued, were without sufficient reinforcements, and were outmanned. After the Union forces shelled the city for weeks, severing supply lines and routing rebels, Hood and his soldiers fled on September 1. Hood, with his tenacity, grit, and what some would call arrogance, finally capitulated to the might of the military juggernaut before him. The retreating troops destroyed anything that could be of military use to the Union forces. They burned railroad cars and other tools of war that could not be transported with the retreating soldiers. Rebel ammunition trains, which included eighty-one loaded cars and seven locomotives, were set ablaze. Sherman, who was miles away, assumed that Union bombing had caused the explosions and night glare. Businesses, homes, and human bodies rocked at the reverberations.[52] However, Union major general Henry Warner Slocum accurately suspected that retreating Confederates were destroying munitions.

The fleeing rebels never officially surrendered the city to the federals. That duty was left to civil administrators. On September 2, Mayor Calhoun surrendered the city. He solemnly and soberly reached out to some of the most prominent men in the city, eight in total: Alfred Austell, Thomas Crusselle (who was among the men who immediately attended to the mortally injured Solomon Luckie), Julius Hayden, Thomas Kile, William Markham, E. E. Rawson, J. E. Williams, and, quite conspicuously, Robert Webster. Calhoun led the delegation to the Union troops with a white flag in hand. After finding the ranking officer, Colonel John Coburn, the mayor addressed him: "The fortune of war has placed Atlanta in your hands. As Mayor of the City I come to ask your protection for noncombatants and for private property." Colonel Coburn responded that unless lurking rebel forces attacked, citizens and their property were safe. Otherwise, "neither person nor property would be safe."[53] The victory was significant.

On September 3, General Sherman, who was outside of Atlanta and unable to personally accept Calhoun's surrender, was pleased to telegraph Washington to report the victory: "So Atlanta is ours, and fairly won."[54] Uncle Billy was adored and celebrated across the North. General Halleck called the Atlanta Campaign "the most brilliant of the war," and newspapers fawned over Sherman. Some went as far as to call him "the greatest general since Napoleon."[55] As previously mentioned, Lincoln, after surveying the political landscape before his election and the stalled conditions of war, had complained on August 31 that "I am a beaten man, unless we have some great victory."[56] He finally had that victory.

Many did not know what to expect from Sherman, whom Confederates widely viewed as a marauding monster. One thing was clear: when Yankees marched into Atlanta on September 2, 1864, that day would mark the last time that any black person would be legally held in slavery in the city. For that reason, Sherman, despite his fierce and brutally effective siege, was celebrated by black people. Black people were not alone in welcoming federals. The city of Atlanta also had a subtle diversity among its white population. Those remaining after the civilian and military exodus were a mix of pro-Unionist and pro-Confederate civilians. There were northern transplants who worked in the city and maintained Unionist sentiments. Some white southerners were also pro-Union, perhaps from a convenient change of heart or a genuine evolution under the fatigue of war. Some had never endorsed secession.[57] It is notable, Stephen Davis writes, that the eight men chosen by Mayor Calhoun to surrender to the Union forces were "to a man, Union loyalists."[58] Webster, the lone black, had "won quiet acclaim among Atlanta's 'secret Yankees,' tending to wounded Union prisoners." More than that, however, Webster offered money and a means of escape for them. When Yankee POWs were left starving and thirsty in City Park after the Confederates fled, Webster attended to them with his own goods, even paying local black people—some experiencing their first moments of freedom—to help him dress the soldiers' wounds and give the wounded men food. Many of the POWs screamed in agony as they were moved to a local hospital. Maggots had infested bandages that were wrapped around inflamed limbs, and howls circulated the air as men languished in the scorching summer heat amid the dead and the nearly dead. White onlookers later testified at the sight of black Atlantans helping the wounded, suffering Union prisoners of war. One insisted that "many of the wounded would certainly have died if it had not been for the attention of these men."[59]

The logic of black people welcoming Sherman's forces is clear. The Yankees were harbingers of liberation, a freedom from the horrifying thralls of intergenerational slavery. In a region that openly trafficked in the rhetoric of freedom, the Union victory brought the realization of liberty closer than ever. For those who by accident of birth were enslaved, no amount of hard work, intelligence, virtue, faith in Jesus, or patriotism could prevent their children and grandchildren from a fate of bondage, beatings, torture, or even rape. At least this was the driving philosophy of the Confederates. Federal forces violently overturned these principles when they swept Atlanta. Black people joyfully and openly celebrated the victors. One Union soldier reported on the racial landscape of the city upon his arrival: "Very few white people were in sight, but lots of Negroes watched us as we marched along." Many cheered and celebrated the presence of the triumphant yet war-worn Yanks. Another soldier, from Massachusetts, proclaimed that black people "hailed our men as their deliverers of God."[60] Black people, aware of the Emancipation Proclamation—which applied only to people in Confederate areas under Union control—cheered, praised God, and warmly greeted Sherman's soldiers. Some of their previous enslavers were shocked at the abrupt change in relationships between them. Instead of immutable loyalty to their captors, men, women, and children escaped when given the opportunity for safe passage.

The city's first black dentist, Roderick Badger, legally the property of his father, had become an assistant for Confederate officer Milton Candler. Candler, in addition to being the brother of Coca-Cola founder Asa G. Candler, was the man who was the practical owner of Roderick's wife, Mary. After Sherman captured Atlanta, however, Roderick and Mary could finally enjoy actual freedom. They relocated to free territory and settled their family in Chicago, where they lived for nearly two years.[61] Across Atlanta, other people escaped to freedom. On August 10, Lucie Harvie Hull, who lived on Peachtree, wrote in her diary that "our servants all ran away, except 'Uncle Dick,' and 'Mammy.'" One white Atlantan, perhaps capturing widespread sentiment among his cohort, called Sherman "the most unwelcome guest in the city's history."[62]

The advancement of Union soldiers evoked great excitement for both blacks and whites—the enslaved and the free—for different reasons, of course. Mary A. H. Gay, a white woman from a wealthy family, documented the moment that Sherman's troops advanced toward her home in Decatur: "'Yank! Yank!' exclaimed our deaf negro girl, Telitha, as she stroked her face as if stroking beard, and ran to get a blue garment to indicate the color of their apparel, and this was our first intimation of their appearance in Decatur. If all the evil spirits had been loosed from Hades, and Satan himself had been turned loose upon us, a more terrific, revolting scene could not have been enacted."[63] Despite Colonel Coburn's promise that the property of nonhostile civilians would be safe, many Atlantans—black and white—witnessed Union troops stealing and destroying. Gay describes a coarse, obstreperous horde of Yankees forcing themselves into her property:

> Advance guards, composed of every species of criminals ever incarcerated in the prisons of the Northern States of America, swooped down upon us, and every species of deviltry followed in their footsteps. My poor mother, frightened and trembling, and myself, having locked the doors of the house, took our stand with the servants in the yard, and witnessed the grand *entre* of the menagerie. One of the beasts got down upon his all-fours and pawed up the dust and bellowed like an infuriated bull. And another asked me if I did not expect to see them with hoofs and horns. I told him, "No, I had expected to see some gentlemen among them, and was sorry I should be disappointed."[64]

Many enslaved people did not even bother with warning their captors of the encroaching Yankees. They simply vanished into freedom. The racial landscape of the city had been indelibly transformed, leaving their former owners bewildered, fearful, and angry. Their hold on power and their sense of order were being torn asunder in the most dramatic ways. The unmitigated and sudden realization of freedom to black people proved as traumatic to their former captors as it was liberating to the newly freed. A week following the capture of Atlanta, Sam Richards wrote in his diary of the trauma to his city and its social world: "One unpleasant feature of present circumstances is the impudent airs the negroes put on, and their indifference to the wants of their former masters. Of course they are all free and the Yankee soldiers don't fail to assure them of that fact. . . . So our negro property has all vanished into air."[65]

Anger, contempt, and fear for Union soldiers became more acute after they settled into the city. A week after the surrender, Sherman issued Special Field Order 67 on September 8: "The city of Atlanta being exclusively required for warlike purposes, will be evacuated at once by all except the armies of the United States, and such civilians as may be retained."[66] A truce was implemented to aid the evacuation. The mayor and city council appealed to Sherman to abandon the scheme: "We most earnestly and solemnly petition you to reconsider your order, or modify it, and suffer those unfortunate people to remain at home."[67] Their appeal was unsuccessful. The evacuation accelerated the separation of the newly freed from their former owners. The belief of an immutable black obeisance to their white masters further evaporated with evacuation. Contrary to popular legend and rhetoric about the loyal slaves who would give their lives for their masters, people widely and swiftly embraced freedom rather than remain with their captors.

Mayor Calhoun's family enslaved about thirty people, but after the evacuation the mayor's son, Patrick, complained that all thirty of the newly freed people chose to go north to Union-controlled areas rather than to Rough and Ready, the area under control of Hood's Confederate forces.[68] One family, the Perkersons, documented the moment when Dan, a man they held in bondage, faced them in the aftermath of the evacuation order. Turning to the family, Dan reportedly "bowed politely" and informed them that "I now bid *adieu* to you and slavery." And with those final words, "off he went," disappearing from their gaze and their control into his new life as a free man.[69] Although precise numbers do not exist on the ratio or proportion of black people who went north, it is clear that most chose to break ties with their enslavers. Some negotiated employment with either the Union forces or other whites.[70]

The evacuation was jarring for most white Atlantans. Gay fumed that the evacuation was especially cruel. Calling Sherman the "Nero of the nineteenth century," Gay referred to his soldiers as "the most ruthless, Godless band ever organized in the name of patriotism."

Had it not been for "a few noble spirits" among these soldiers, Yankees "would not have left a Southerner to tell the tale of their fiendishness."[71] Even Hood denounced Sherman's "cruelty." In a heated exchange of letters between him and Sherman, Hood vociferously attacked his counterpart:

> You came into our country with your army avowedly for the purpose of subjugating free white men, women, and children, and not only intend to rule over them, but you make negroes your allies and desire to place over us an inferior race, which we have raised from barbarism to its present position. . . . You say, "let us fight it out like men." To this my reply is, for myself, and, I believe, for all the true men, aye, and women and children, in my country, we will fight you to the death. Better die a thousand deaths than submit to live under you or your Government and your negro allies. . . .[72]

Sherman tersely responded to Hood, "we have no 'negro allies' in this army; not a single negro soldier left Chattanooga with this army or is with it now."[73]

Sherman was confident that both the Atlanta Campaign and Special Field Order 67 were squarely within rightful standards of warfare. He had earlier told Halleck that those who would accuse him of barbarity must recognize that "war is war and not popularity seeking." Following his exchange with Hood, Sherman forwarded his correspondence to Halleck and justified his evacuation order:

> The residence here of a poor population would compel us sooner or later to feed them or see them starve under our eyes. The residence here of the families of our enemies would be a temptation and a means to keep up a correspondence dangerous and hurtful to our cause, and a civil population calls for provost guards, and

absorbs the attention of officers in listening to everlasting complaints and special grievances that are not military. These are
my reasons, and if satisfactory to the Government of the United
States it makes no difference whether it pleases General Hood
and his people or not.[74]

About half of the population went north, according to the
Intelligencer. The newspaper accused many of the whites of being
northern-born "secret Yankees." Many other whites were immigrants
who had little fealty to southern nationalism. A member of the 5th
Connecticut wrote that "many of the Irish and German, and colored
people gladly availed themselves of the opportunity to get away north,
but most of the native born preferred to go south."[75] Of course, "native
born" meant white native born, in this instance and in virtually every
other instance when race is not specified in both northern and southern correspondence. This is most notable in the conspicuous references
to the influx of poor people from the countryside into Atlanta in this
tumultuous time.

As noted above, most whites in Georgia and in Atlanta enslaved
no one and were in poverty, as were most white southerners. As the
war endured, desertion and outright rejection of the Confederate
cause spread among the white yeomanry and the poor. Many whites,
displaced by war, like others, found refuge in Atlanta. What unfolded
in the looting of Atlanta's shops, mansions, and upscale homes was,
in part, a class rebellion, an inexorable rejection of the reach, power,
and authority of the ruling class of the region. Class tensions intensified among whites who had been tethered by a racial confraternity,
premised on the principles of white nationalism and racial superiority. Whiteness, which found its greatest utility as the teleological
racial unifier, was being strained and threatened during the end of the
Confederacy.

The capture of Atlanta mortally weakened the strength and vitality of southern nationalism. After a succession of defeats, food shortages, and the utter devastation of the southern landscape, its major cities, and the economy, morale was low. Across the region, poor southern whites, in particular, had grown critical of the machinations of the war and its leadership of wealthy planters who granted exemptions to the draft to their own military-age sons. General scarcity and the commandeering of animals, food, and other resources from civilians had caused riots in southern cities. One observer argues that "it became clear to many poor southern whites that the war was being waged by the rich planters and the poor were fighting it."[76] Unlike the wealthy, poor whites had no hotel rooms or boardinghouses to serve them in the city under siege. Unsure about what was to follow, many of the rural poor milled about the town. Their presence only added to the anxiety that swept Atlanta. As Franklin Garrett writes,

> For the people of Atlanta, [there] came the awful hours of waiting—waiting for the unknown. Men with wives and daughters stayed home, weapons at hand, ready for any emergency. The center of the city began to fill with the flotsam and jetsam of war—riffraff, stragglers and deserters; with Negroes delirious and confused over their strange sense of freedom, and with lean and haggard [white] men and women of the lowest class plundering stores and vacant dwellings. They picked up buckets, tinware, canteens, pieces of furniture, old tents; anything lying around loose.[77]

Universal whiteness and its ability to blunt class divisions were being tested as they never had been before. Class conflict between whites had long been a threat to white-nationalist dogma in the region, and in the waning days of the Civil War these tensions grew more acute.

Securing the city was not limited to municipal surrender. In addition to the wide-reaching ramifications of the battle on the national

General William T. Sherman, leaning on gun breech, and staff at Federal Fort No. 7. The Battle of Atlanta was one of the most consequential ones in the Civil War. The Union victory resulted in a cascading effect of more Confederate retreats and losses, and a reelection victory for President Lincoln, who, before Atlanta was captured, was widely expected to lose. On September 3, one day after the mayor of Atlanta surrendered, Sherman sent a telegraph to Lincoln: "So Atlanta is ours and fairly won." CREDIT: PUBLIC DOMAIN

stage, Sherman's troops were inclined to do what conquerors had always done: they conspicuously and ceremoniously celebrated their victory over the defeated. Thousands of Union soldiers formed a dynamic river of blue as they marched down Marietta Street in the heart of the city. Some locals, perhaps too exhausted by war and willing to celebrate its inevitable end—even as a Union victory—were lined up side by side with native southern Unionists. Other, more obstinate locals with strong Confederate loyalties remained distressed, angry, and seething with resentment at the sight of victorious Yankees parading through the "heart of the Confederacy." Overwhelmed, outnumbered, and subdued, in a feeble and symbolic act of resistance "the small boys of staunch Confederate families whistled 'Dixie' and 'The Bonnie Blue Flag,' for the benefit of, but not to the amusement of Sherman's boys, who retorted, via brass bands, with loud renditions of 'Yankee Doodle' and 'The Battle Hymn of the Republic.'"[78] The Confederates were devastated.

Across the country, both sides of the war emotionally received the news of the Union capture of Atlanta. Despair fell across the Confederacy. Thomas Cooper De Leon, who lived in various southern cities during the war, remarked that Atlanta's capture was particularly traumatizing for the South: "A sullen and increasing gloom . . . seemed to settle over the majority of the people."[79] In the Confederate capital the *Richmond Examiner* lamented "the disaster at Atlanta," which would likely "save the party of Lincoln from irretrievable ruin. . . . [It] obscures the prospect of peace, late so bright. It will diffuse gloom over the South."[80] Similarly, Mary Boykin Chesnut, the famed Civil War diarist from South Carolina, wrote in September 1864 that "since Atlanta fell, I have felt as if all were dead within me forever."[81] For the North, however, the Battle of Atlanta was an extraordinary moment of joy and celebration. It reinvigorated a doubtful and fallen spirit among Unionists in profound ways.

Cheers erupted in cities across the North upon the news of Atlanta's capture. The *New York Times* extolled the bravery and military prowess of Union soldiers who chased the rebels from the fortified city. Quoting Sherman, the newspaper blasted "Atlanta is Ours."[82] Similarly, newspapers in Washington, Philadelphia, Chicago, and Boston made General Sherman a war hero whose fierce and formidable leadership personified the vitality, strength, and power of the US military in the face of treasonous insurrection. The victory also had massive implications for the political landscape.

Horace Greeley, the famed antislavery editor of the *New York Tribune*, had only a tepid endorsement of Lincoln for reelection. Like many others who thought the president a poor commander in chief and too conciliatory with the slave powers, Greeley sought alternatives to the incumbent. Earlier in August, fearing a Democratic victory and "peace with slavery protected," he even conspired to secure a new Republican nominee to replace the weak-kneed Lincoln. Following the victory in Atlanta, however, the *New York Tribune* celebrated the military success and threw its full weight behind Lincoln's reelection.[83] The Battle of Atlanta turned the tide in Lincoln's favor in concrete ways.

John C. Frémont, the famed abolitionist general whom Lincoln relieved of duty when he refused to rescind an emancipation edict in Missouri in 1861, had been an outspoken critic of the president. Similarly, Salmon Chase, the secretary of the treasury and a Radical Republican, had pushed Lincoln to be more aggressive with the Confederacy while simultaneously intimating his own interest in the presidency or in supporting another Republican candidate. But as Doris Kearns Goodwin explains, "The fall of Atlanta produced a remarkable transformation in the mood of Republicans."[84] The historical significance of this victory cannot be overstated. In fact, as fate would have it, Union troops occupied Atlanta on the very day that the Democratic National Convention officially nominated George McClellan as its presidential nominee. It was widely believed that McClellan would win not only the military vote but the general election as well. That confidence evaporated even as the Copperheads ("Peace Democrats") argued that the war was a stalemate and scampered to try to make peace with the Confederates.

In the midst of incredible fatigue, vexing doubts, and struggles within his own party and administration, Lincoln was elated at the news of Atlanta. He quickly celebrated the victory as one for the integrity of the United States and its very survival. On the same day that Sherman telegraphed Washington, Lincoln congratulated him "and the gallant officers and soldiers of his command before Atlanta, for the distinguished ability and perseverance displayed in the campaign in Georgia, which under Divine favor, has resulted in the capture of Atlanta." The letter insisted that the "military operations . . . must render it famous in the annals of war."[85]

Lincoln's reelection campaign and the viability of the Union war effort had been so invigorating that it not only benefited the president; reverberations of the victory were felt across the political landscape, affecting both state and local elections. John George Nicolay, private secretary to Lincoln, wrote this about the Atlanta effect: "Three weeks ago, our friends everywhere were despondent, almost to the point of giving up the contest in despair. Now they are helpful, jubilant, hard at work and confident of success."[86] Sherman's triumph over the Confederates in Atlanta stalled the presidential campaign of the very popular McClellan. The former Union general was more popular than Lincoln in many sections of the country, and his victory would have brought a negotiated peace with the Confederacy. That Democratic victory would have likely included preserving slavery.[87] Lawyer and diarist George Templeton Strong chronicled this excitement, writing that in the midst of the contentious national election process, the capture of Atlanta was "the greatest event of the war" and "glorious news" for the country.[88]

Lincoln was quick to capitalize on the victory and to affirm his wartime leadership, ordering one-hundred-gun salutes in the nation's capital and a dozen other cities. Secretary of State Seward was greeted with a large jubilant crowd at his home, including several hundred men who eagerly volunteered to serve.[89] The squabbles within the Republican Party and surreptitious efforts from Chase and others to challenge Lincoln in the 1864 election quickly dissolved. Political adviser and journalist Thurlow Weed explained to Seward that "the conspiracy against Mr. Lincoln collapsed" after Sherman's triumph. The political climate improved for Lincoln in almost every arena. Following the Atlanta victory, Frémont, who enjoyed support from Radical Republicans, pulled out of the race as a candidate for the Radical Democratic Party and endorsed Lincoln.[90] Major abolitionists such as Frederick Douglass were finally inspired to follow and endorse Lincoln. "When there was any shadow of a hope that a man of more decided antislavery conviction . . . could be elected, I was not for Lincoln," Douglass explained. "All dates changed with the nomination of Mr. McClellan."[91] Of course, no such candidate withdrawal was expected from the Democratic Party, even after the momentous victory in Atlanta.

The Democrats had endorsed an immediate truce with the Confederacy; restoration of the Union would include slavery, fully protected. Draft riots a year earlier, the loss of hundreds of thousands of lives, and the carnage of maimed young men returning to towns across the country all taxed the support for the war. But the capture of Atlanta emboldened the North, increased morale, and provided important momentum for Lincoln's campaign, which he won against McClellan, taking all but three states. And despite McClellan's popularity with the Union soldiers, the military overwhelmingly supported Lincoln by a margin of nearly three to one.[92]

Lincoln's agenda was affirmed with a landslide victory in the Electoral College, 212–21. The Confederate Army was in retreat, losing battles and suffering accelerated rates of desertion.[93] The victory in Atlanta was a turning point that inexorably stressed Confederate politicians. To make matters worse, in the fall of 1864 Georgia lawmakers and slaveholding planters such as Benjamin Hill fumed at the cascading effects of the victory. A significant Confederate stronghold with important military value was lost, and Lincoln was reelected, eliminating the possibility of the Democratic Party's offer of peace with slavery. It also opened Sherman's subsequent March to the Sea, which was not only devastating to Hill's political sensibilities and worldview; it also significantly diminished his wealth: Union soldiers freed the many people enslaved on his plantation. Joshua Hill faced a similar fate when Sherman's soldiers marched through Madison. As with other wealthy planters, the two Hills' wealth almost totally evaporated as Yankee soldiers enforced the Emancipation Proclamation in regions under their control. Garnett Andrews, who, like the Hills, had opposed secession, was left "financially prostrated" when the many people he held in bondage were liberated.[94]

The region was in shambles as Union troops swept through a war-fatigued Georgia, weakened by the loss of an important hub of industrial production and trade. Sherman was well aware of the significance of his victory to the outcome of the war. As for the obstinance among Confederate sympathizers, Sherman quipped that his victory at Atlanta would demonstrate two things: "we were in earnest," and "if they were sincere in their common popular clamor 'to die in the last ditch,' that the opportunity would soon come."[95]

By the spring of 1865 and after the deaths of more than seven hundred thousand Americans, the gruesome war was near an end. Out of desperation, the nearly fanatical white-nationalist government debated the possibility of allowing black men—free or enslaved—to fight for the Confederacy. In early 1864, Irish-born Confederate general Patrick Cleburne proposed reinvigorating the rebel military by using black men as soldiers, not as camp slaves or unarmed manservants. For serving, enslaved men would secure their freedom. The use of free or enslaved black men would "dry up two of [the Union's] sources of recruiting; it will take from his negro army the only motive it could have to fight against the South. . . ." Given that a third of southerners were enslaved, the use of this pool would "enable us to have armies numerically superior to those of the North."[96] Cleburne's proposal was rejected. Two weeks after Sherman captured Atlanta, a panicked Georgian Confederate appealed directly to Jefferson Davis to allow black soldiers into the military. The rebel military should "force them into the army . . . upon the condition, if necessary, of freedom after the war."[97] It was against the principles upon which the Confederacy was based, and Jefferson Davis initially rejected the idea.

In November 1864, following the successive Confederate losses after Atlanta, Lincoln's reelection, and the South in retreat, Davis, in deep desperation, also came around to the possibility of black Confederate troops. However, the Confederate Congress denounced the idea. Howell Cobb, a fervent secessionist from Georgia, argued that the use of black soldiers was "the most pernicious idea that has been suggested since the war began." Cobb reminded his colleagues of the cornerstone of the rebel government, as articulated by fellow Georgian and Confederate vice president Alexander Stephens: white supremacy and its dependent principle, black inferiority, guided their mission. Cobb argued that "the day you make soldiers of them is the beginning of the end of the revolution. If slaves will make good soldiers our whole theory of slavery is wrong."[98] However, the performance of black Union soldiers could not be ignored. Black men could serve with bravery and distinction. In fact, Congress was so impressed with their service that it sought to provide resources for them by chartering an entire bank, Freedman's Saving and Trust Company. Lincoln signed the charter into law on March 3, 1865, providing the first bank designated for black soldiers, their families, and their communities.[99]

Robert E. Lee, with tattered and desperate troops, relented. The slaveholder and white nationalist argued that enslaved people should be recruited "without delay" and be granted freedom for serving. The venerated general's appeal was moving. After considerable debate and hand-wringing, only five days after Lincoln signed the Freedman's Bank into law, the Confederate Congress voted for the "Barksdale Bill" (named for Mississippi CSA congressman Ethelbert Barksdale) by the thinnest possible margin: one vote.[100] It allowed the CSA president to raise levies "from such classes, irrespective of color . . . as the . . . authorities . . . may determine." Davis signed the bill on March 13, and it went into effect on March 20. However, no black soldiers, free or enslaved, ever formally fought for the Confederacy in battle because Lee surrendered to Grant at Appomattox Court House on April 9, less than three weeks later.[101]

The treasonous southern effort failed after four years of unprecedented national bloodshed. There was no question about the Confederacy's foundational principle being the protection of white people's right—as humanity's superior race—to enslave and subjugate black people. Therefore, it was particularly disruptive—even apocalyptic—for wealthy enslavers to lose their greatest wealth. An even greater offense was the expansion of citizenship rights, making the formerly enslaved full-fledged Americans during the years that followed under Reconstruction.

The city of Atlanta had quickly developed from a rail town into an important component of the machination and efficacy of the Confederate States of America. The fundamental driver of southern white nationalism had led to the city's development; however, it was also the reason for which Atlanta was all but destroyed. The city, so vital to the Confederacy's war industry, was an important symbol for both sides. It was a highly visible conquest for one and a miserable, disheartening defeat for the other. For many, the Union victory brought a well-received increase in morale, a political boost for an incumbent president Lincoln, and a signal pointing to peace and abolition. For others, particularly those devoted to the principles and philosophies upon which the Confederacy was based, the fall of Atlanta was an omen of horrifying possibilities, including abolition and racial equality. When the Yankee victors marched down Marietta Street, some recalcitrant Confederates refused to fully capitulate but could offer only the hollow resistive act of "whistling 'Dixie.'" That subtle protest was born in Atlanta's Confederate defeat, but over the course of the next century, Dixie's Confederate spirit would remain unusually resilient and formidable in ways that few imagined in 1864.

Atlanta was, as Sherman promised, made a desolation. "The burnt district of Richmond was hardly more thoroughly destroyed than the central part of Atlanta," wrote one observer.[102] A huge number of the city's businesses, government buildings, railroad buildings, and private homes were destroyed. All hotels except the Planters' Hotel were burned down. In the immediate years to come, the citizens of Atlanta made ambitious strides at rebuilding their city. Blacks and whites poured into the Gate City. Notably, the nucleus of the black community was built near the Union camp and was appropriately known as Shermantown—by all Atlantans. Each new building, public square, school, or church was a testimony to the resilience of the Atlanta spirit. However, this resilience was more than just grit and determination to transcend the dispiriting destruction of the city in the war.

After the war, the gas lamppost that was damaged by Union shelling, resulting in Solomon Luckie's mortal shrapnel injury, was dismantled and stored for posterity's sake. Unlike the other forty-nine gas lampposts installed in 1855, this one was special. City leaders were willing to rebuild, but Atlanta's leaders had no intention of forgetting. Artifacts, diaries, songs, poems, novels, and more would keep alive the memory of the failed southern nationalist effort in the Gate City. Indeed, Atlanta cultivated a civic identity that was intimately dependent on the Civil War experience. With former Confederate leadership reestablishing firm controls in the state and local spheres of power, it appeared that the Civil War was less a loss for the South than it was a compromise. A critical and essential element of local identity included fealty to the city's Confederate heritage, which, as Chapter 3 details, found black "freedom" a necessary nuisance that had to be heavily regulated and constricted in order to maintain the proper racial order, one that naturally fit the New South.

The Atlanta Medical School, which James Alexander had helped found, adhered to its white-nationalist principles in the century following the war. It excluded black students, physicians, and nurses, eventually evolving into the Emory University School of Medicine, which continued to exclude people of color until successful lawsuits in the 1960s. The white Combs family benefited financially by their exchange with Laura Combs. Instead of losing wealth when John was liberated by war, they were able to ultimately pass the land through inheritance and sell it to the YMCA a generation later, in 1886.[103]

After the war, Laura Combs returned to Atlanta from Augusta because she believed that postwar Atlanta offered more opportunities for black people. It had originally been a thoroughly antiblack city that, in its resurgence, offered moral, ethical, and physical renewal. It was not that most of Atlanta's white population had suddenly embraced racial equality, democracy, and basic notions of a meritocratic society with justice for all. To the contrary, most would reject those ideas for the next century and instead continue to honor the white-nationalist project of the Confederacy. In this effort—which was not unlike what unfolded in other southern cities—African Americans were legally excluded from the social, political, economic, and civic centers of power. But unlike most other cities in the South or elsewhere, there was a high concentration of new institutions for black advancement. Atlanta emerged as an exceptional space for black institution building. Black organizations that had been illegal—churches, schools, and social clubs—were now available in ways that few cities offered. They met the spiritual, intellectual, and financial needs of the people. Combs deposited her money in the Freedman's Savings and Trust Company. At its height, it had deposits from more than a hundred thousand black people and black institutions across the country, with a collective worth of over $57 million: $115 billion in today's dollars. Coincidentally, Dr. Roderick Badger was appointed secretary of the Atlanta branch.[104]

Laura Combs's children took advantage of and contributed to African American institution building in a multitude of ways. Although she died in 1872, two years after returning to Atlanta, seven of her ten children lived into adulthood. Her oldest son, Thomas, who was a Union Army veteran, moved to New Orleans, where he continued with his military band work and became a celebrated musician, essentially being part of a number of black veterans who formed a new genre of music: jazz. At least two of her children, Jacob and Oswell, attended Atlanta University. Her namesake daughter, Laura (known as "Annie"), became a teacher, taught black children at Gray Street School, and became a landowner like her mother. Oswell, who was born in 1861, graduated from Atlanta University and eventually became a professor of classics and music at Morris Brown College, a school founded by the African Methodist Episcopal Church. Dr. Badger served on its board of trustees.[105]

In a fascinating twist of historical fate, Laura's son James enrolled in Shaw University (now Rust College) in Holly Springs, Mississippi, where he dated a talented younger student, Ida B. Wells. Wells recalled that James was her "first love." He was also her first heartbreak: he ended the relationship and married Anna Johnson. He then started a career in education, remaining in the Holly Springs area for several years. There, Wells was constantly reminded of the "impermanence of love," which, according to her biographer, made her trepidatious about committing to one person.[106] By the time Wells eventually married, in her early thirties, she had become an internationally renowned leader as an investigative journalist, suffragist, civil rights activist, and cofounder of the NAACP. A brilliant woman, she poured her talents into work of enormous consequence. She was a personal friend of Frederick Douglass, W. E. B. Du Bois, Jane Addams, Mary Church Terrell, and many other notables. The tract of land that Laura Combs owned eventually became the intersection of Peachtree (the most prominent street in the city) and "Sweet Auburn," which was eventually dubbed the "richest Negro street in the world."[107]

Dr. Badger returned to Atlanta with his family and several children in 1866, and he opened a practice at 39 Peachtree Street. He was a delegate to the 1870 convention to create a new state constitution. He advocated for civil rights for all people and supported black uplift with self-determination. He eventually acquired multiple properties throughout the city, and when the *Constitution* ran a story on the city's black wealthy class, the paper listed Badger as being the largest black landowner in Atlanta. He was firmly in place as part of the city's black elite, sitting on the boards of various organizations and helping to shape black Atlanta. When he died, in 1890, the *Constitution*, which had been a mouthpiece of unfiltered racism for years, extolled Badger's "untiring industry," whereby "he earned the respect and esteem of the best citizens of Atlanta to the day of his death."[108]

Except for Solomon, all members of the Luckie family survived the war. Nancy died in 1912 and was buried in South-View Cemetery. Their daughter Camilla, who became a seamstress, named her only son Solomon Walter Luckie, after her notable father. Born one year after the Civil War, Solomon was a tailor and became the first black postal carrier in Atlanta. He and his wife, Ellen Euphrasia Beale, had three children, Ambrosia Luckie, Solomon Walter Luckie Jr., and Charles Edgar Luckie. Solomon, the grandson of the famed barber, took advantage of the educational institutions that black people built in the city. He graduated from Clark University in Atlanta before earning a master's degree from Fordham University in New York. He served in World War I and taught junior high school in New York City for nearly forty years, dying at age eighty-three in 1976.[109]

In all, the city of Atlanta's resurgence from the flames of war offered something new to a wide variety of demographics. White Atlantans were a diverse group. Some were northern industrialists with no interest in neo-Confederate politics. They sought large profits in a city eager to rebuild. Others were ambitious northern missionaries driven with a moral and religious calling to uplift the newly freed. Most white southerners schemed to approximate the white-nationalist politics of the Confederacy, as much as allowable by new laws that granted freedom and citizenship to all people. Poor white migrants aligned with white southern industrialists, or "Bourbons," to forge a white-nationalist project that provided civic equality to whites but concentrated economic power in the hands of Bourbons. When neo-Confederates barred black people from schools, black people formed their own, most often with the help of white missionaries from the North. African Americans (whether formerly enslaved or not) found the city ripe for building new institutions. New churches were immediately created and emerged as nuclei for educational, political, social, and economic life. By the time the YMCA purchased land once owned by Laura Combs, there were multiple black colleges and universities in the city and dozens of black-owned businesses, black physicians, black dentists, and black academics. However, most black people suffered incredible poverty, squalor, and deprivation. The Gate City was emerging as a veritable city on the hill for people from across the country, but these people often had deeply polarized interests, as Chapter 3 will show.

3 | Sherman's Shadow

Reconstruction-Era Georgia and Atlanta's Renewal

> The freedom, as I understand it, promised by the proclamation, is taking us from under the yoke of bondage, and placing us where we could reap the fruit of our own labor, take care of ourselves and assist the Government in maintaining our freedom.
>
> —GARRISON FRAZIER, FORMERLY ENSLAVED BAPTIST MINISTER,
> TO GENERAL WILLIAM T. SHERMAN, 1865

Atlanta was "left a desolation" after the siege and bombardment. Confederates were in retreat, and General Sherman had become a war hero. The Union military, under Sherman's "hard-war" policy, led a devastating campaign across a swath of Georgia in the fall, capturing Savannah by the winter. In this campaign Sherman freed thousands of people from slavery and, in the process, eviscerated the wealth and power of the Confederate ruling class across the state. By the time that his soldiers reached the Atlantic, tens of thousands of freed people had followed Sherman's troops, many of them volunteering to work for food and protection while in an uncertain and tenuous freedom. They served as cooks, spies, and washers, and they tended to a wide range of other needs for the federal soldiers. Despite having abolitionists in his family, Sherman, who witnessed slavery up close while working in Baton Rouge before the war, did not oppose it when the war began. He also agreed with most white Americans of the time that whites were a superior race. However, his hard war meant that the brutal campaign against the Confederacy would remove the enemy's source of labor and wealth. Given its strategic importance, Sherman welcomed the liberation of thousands of people from bondage. It helped cripple the Confederate war machine by stripping it of a labor supply while simultaneously demoralizing rebels by the very act of freeing the people who had literally been the foundation for the Confederacy's wealth and its raison d'être. In fact, an estimated half a million people in Georgia were liberated after the Union victory, resulting in a staggering loss of $272 million ($9 billion in today's dollars) for enslavers.[1] Moreover, the extension of freedom undermined long-held beliefs of the proper racial order, believed by many to be sanctioned by God.

The March to the Sea culminated with the capture of Savannah on December 21, 1864. Two weeks after Uncle Billy offered the city as a Christmas present to President Lincoln, Sherman, who had been promoted to major general, received a visit from Edwin Stanton, the secretary of war. Stanton had heard reports of Sherman's commanders, especially General Jefferson C. Davis, head of the 14th Corps, mistreating black people during the Georgia Campaign. Hundreds of newly freed people followed the coincidentally named Davis, as they had other Union forces across the state. At Ebenezer Creek, Davis directed his troops to construct a bridge for their use but dismantled the pontoons once his soldiers had crossed, forbidding hundreds of black men, women, and children from crossing, leaving them to fend for themselves on the opposite riverbank. With Confederate troops in pursuit, many fled toward the water. Frightened children held by protective but powerless parents faced the armed rebel soldiers, who drew weapons. Scores, if not hundreds, frantically waded into the freezing river, and others were beaten, shot, and enslaved by the rebels.

The national press, including the *New York Tribune* and other newspapers, reported the criminal actions. In a Senate military commission, Major James Connolly called the action "inhumane [and] barbarous."[2] Despite the Ebenezer Creek action, Sherman did not condemn or penalize Davis. This raised concerns among some that the celebrated military hero did not limit his viciousness to Confederate combatants and their supporters. Despite his victorious efforts in the Georgia Campaign, many had come to think that Sherman, who refused to have black soldiers in his ranks, was especially hateful toward black people. There was no doubt that black freedom was incidental to his victories, but it was not the goal of his campaign. Secretary Stanton wanted to know more.

Stanton requested a meeting with black leaders to investigate charges of abuse and rumors that Sherman had "almost a criminal dislike of the negro." Sherman, who had met with many local whites and blacks, offered up a group of men whom he considered "the most intelligent of the negroes."[3] The meeting with Sherman was held on January 12, 1865, and included Stanton and Brigadier General Rufus Saxton. Both Stanton and Saxton supported abolition and had aided the enlistment of black men into the military. There is no doubt that the sentiment for creating some meaningful policy in the interest of men, women, and children just freed from the horrors of enslavement was strong in this meeting.

These twenty black men represented the nascent leadership class among African Americans. They were mostly ministers, and five of them had never been enslaved, although they lived in slaveholding states, preaching to free and enslaved black people. Nine of the twenty had gained freedom as federal troops entered their communities and enforced the Emancipation Proclamation. Six men had been freed before the war, three of them manumitted by their owners and the three others purchasing their freedom. All but three lived or were born in Georgia. Among those three who purchased their freedom was sixty-seven-year-old Garrison Frazier, who in 1857 bought himself and his wife for $1,000 (about $30,000 in today's value) after saving for years as a Baptist minister.[4]

Sherman and Stanton asked twelve questions of the group. Frazier, who was their designated spokesman, answered them. In addition to investigating allegations made against Sherman, the government delegation was concerned with measuring the general sentiment of freed people, assuming that these men, who represented thousands across their churches and many in various camps, would have a grasp of collective black sentiments. What was their understanding of the war? How did they view the federal government? Would black people fight for the Confederacy if it were an option? And, importantly, how could black people take care of themselves and assist the government in protecting their freedom? Frazier directly and cogently answered this last question: "The way we can best take care of ourselves is to have land, and turn it and till it by our own labor—that is, by the labor of the women and children and old men; and we can soon maintain ourselves and have something to spare." Intrigued, Sherman and Stanton asked a follow-up question that speculated how the postwar racial landscape might look: "State in what manner you would rather live—whether scattered among the whites or in colonies by yourselves." Frazier, perhaps considering that his answer would be received as slightly off-putting by the white men present, cautioned that he could speak only for himself and not the group: "I would prefer to live by ourselves, for there is a prejudice against us in the South that will take years to get over; but I do not know that I can answer for my brethren." When the question was subsequently put to the nineteen others in the room, only Jason Lynch disagreed with Frazier. Lynch, twenty-six years old, born in Baltimore and never enslaved, was optimistic about the prospect of living together with southern whites. He alone thought that former Confederates, former enslavers, and their sympathizers would be magnanimous in defeat. They would be sufficiently fair-minded, just, and humane to help establish a thriving democratic region for blacks and whites alike, the ironically named Lynch argued. The other eighteen men were less optimistic and felt that black people would be better off with self-reliant, independent communities under black control, but fully incorporated into the United States. The desire to be fully recognized as US citizens was clear. The fealty to the United States was so strong, Frazier explained, that black people were "willing to make any sacrifice to assist the Government of the United States." In fact, "I do not suppose there are a dozen [black people] that are opposed to the Government."[5] However, they did not believe that most whites would morally advance enough from their commitment to white supremacy. And even if white southerners would not concede that they actually hated black people, they would not equivocate on their belief that black people should not enjoy equality, democracy, or any of the rights of citizenship.[6] There was little faith that most white southerners would, in the near future, be moral, ethical, or Christian-like in their relations with black people.

The collective sentiment—with one dissent—is a foundational belief of organic African American political thought, what I call *Afro-self-determinism*. This is the belief that black people would be best served by creating institutions for, by, and in the best interests of black people, including social, educational, cultural, economic, and political ones. It is simultaneously pessimistic regarding the notion that whites would, collectively, be fair, just, or ethical in their relations with black people, hence self-determination's need.[7] Moreover, although this term certainly shares much with the concept of black nationalism, it fundamentally differs in its assertion of US citizenship. Unlike conventional black nationalism, Afro-self-determinism does not forfeit or deny the United States as the country that belongs to African Americans, regardless of whatever racism or corruption that may be endemic to it. In contrast, black nationalism stresses the need for the establishment of an independent black nation-state free of and autonomous from the United States, in North America, Africa, or elsewhere. Conversely, integrationists have advocated for the optimism of Jason Lynch: in the near term, most whites can be morally and ethically reformed to be fair, just, and democratic in their relations with black people, who, in turn, can live peacefully and enjoy full citizenship and rights in an integrated country.[8] The prefix *Afro* distinguishes this brand of self-determination from any general form. It draws attention to the specific racial element of this sense of collective work and implies a particular set of circumstances and historical context around how and why it functions as a response to wider racialized forces of marginalization and oppression.

By the last year of the Civil War, it became increasingly clear to many black and white Americans that slavery would not outlive the Confederacy, which, itself, was in its death throes. The expansion of civil rights, the liberation of hundreds of thousands of people from slavery, and the valiant performance of black troops all converged to bolster notions that black people were becoming full-fledged citizens of the United States, no longer relegated to a liminal status as neither citizen nor foreigner. Robert Purvis, a black leader of the abolitionist movement and a conductor on the Underground Railroad in Philadelphia, summed up the predominant sentiment among African Americans: "The children of the black man have enriched the soil by their tears, and sweat, and blood. Sir, we were born here, and here we choose to remain."[9] Remaining in the country of their birth also meant carving out a space for their sustenance, general welfare, and posterity. This process required the development of institutions for, by, and about the black community. In many cases the spirit of social, cultural, and religious autonomy dominated the earliest activities of freed people.

As this chapter demonstrates, African Americans advanced the concept of Afro-self-determinism. Though not given a name, the concept developed in various ways across the state of Georgia and in Atlanta, in particular, during Reconstruction. Indeed, inasmuch as white supremacy was national in scope, Afro-self-determinism had organically developed across America in various ways, manifesting according to local circumstances. Naturally, it helped shape black communities by forging collective notions of self-determination, intraracial benevolence, self-reliance, community, and black politics. In many respects the development of this belief was a logical response to the forces of white supremacy and Confederate retrenchment. Black people, it would appear, would have little option other than to follow such self-determinative practices when they were systematically shunned, oppressed, terrorized, and marginalized by racists.

Although this perception is true, what occurred in Atlanta was an especially virulent expression of neo-Confederate politics. The legacy of the Civil War was profound in shaping virtually every aspect of the city's character. In doing so, there emerged a particularly acute notion of racial subjugation. African Americans responded with ambitious efforts at black self-determination that did not advocate for racial integration of social space. Instead, black leadership, across generations, demanded more in the way of resources for black people than shared resources with whites. Like the ministers who met with Sherman on that January night, black people generally felt that they were prepared and equipped to govern themselves, and would be better for it, than to be left to the devices of an intractably hostile white majority in schools, parks, neighborhoods, or elsewhere.

One of the boldest early examples of Afro-self-determinism in Georgia was a northern transplant, Tunis Campbell. In 1812 Campbell was born in Middlebrook, New Jersey, in the waning years of the revolutionary era, the eighth of ten children of a blacksmith, John, and his wife (whose name is lost to history). In this young country, Tunis was shaped by the provincial sensibilities of the time. In the Northeast he had access to education, became a passionate reader, and was influenced by the abolitionist movement. Though of humble origins, Campbell exceeded the education of most Americans by graduating from a private Episcopal school in Babylon, New York. He came of age during the Great Awakening, was spiritually influenced by it, and planned to do missionary work in Africa, but grew skeptical of the intentions of the project. After spending some time working in hotels in New York City and Boston, Campbell published *Hotel Keepers, Head Waiters, and Housekeepers' Guide* in 1848. This was regarded as the first book to outline a scientific management approach to the hotel business in the country, and Campbell's future in hotel management seemed quite likely. But he turned toward abolitionist work instead. Earlier, after he had rejected the mission of the American Colonization Society (ACS), he formed an abolitionist group that was openly critical of the ACS and that committed to abolition until all enslaved people were freed.[10]

As sectional crises over slavery intensified, Campbell became more deeply involved in resisting the slaveholding elite, which increasingly pushed for nullification and secession. When the Civil War began, Campbell, forty-nine years old and married with three children, volunteered to serve in the army, but as were all black citizens in the earliest months of the war, he was rejected. Black people, of course, had been barred from militia service following the American Revolution. Virtually all states—north and south—also allowed voting only for white men. Despite provincial expressions of environmentalism, fairness, and rhetoric regarding democracy and equality, Campbell was well aware of antidemocratic laws that made such notions theoretical at best. He knew that he lived a life of exception as a relatively privileged black man in an antiblack society. However, the war disrupted much of the conventional notions of citizenship, freedom, and access to rights and justice. He was positioned to help expand that disruptive process.[11]

Campbell joined the Union Army as a chaplain to black soldiers when the ban on black troops was lifted in 1862. By 1863, the Emancipation Proclamation had been issued, there were thousands of black soldiers serving in the Union military, and northern states were slowly passing legislation granting civil rights to all people. Campbell, who had become a minister in the African Methodist Episcopal (AME) church, shared a friendship and the lecture circuit with acclaimed abolitionist Frederick Douglass, and he had risen to prominence with the Colored Convention movement a decade earlier. He joined Douglass in recruiting black troops and speaking at AME congregations throughout the Northeast.[12] Through this process, he witnessed the intrinsic value of black institution building, something that Douglass had practiced and valued.

Only four years before the war, in one of his most famous speeches Douglass argued that black people should demand, struggle, and sacrifice for freedom: "Power concedes nothing without a demand. It never did and it never will." Yet many white people wished to lead black people rather than see them practice agency over their fate. Some demanded that blacks be allowed to fight but insisted that they "must fight like the Sepoys of India, under white officers. This class of Abolitionists don't like colored celebrations, they don't like colored conventions, they don't like colored antislavery fairs for the support of colored newspapers. They don't like any demonstrations whatever in which colored men take a leading part." In essence, they don't like black independent action, or self-determination. Douglass admitted that some critics called him "an ingrate" for not assuming a subordinate position to a white leader. Instead, he chose "to stand up on [my] own and to plead our common cause as a colored man, rather than as a Garrisonian."[13] It is in this ideological vein of community work that Campbell matured as a leader.

Campbell's commitment to and zeal for the cause of freedom accelerated his renown. By 1863, his visibility reached the White House, and Secretary of War Stanton commissioned him to work with the US Army organizing freed people and black refugees in Port Royal, South Carolina. General Sherman's March to the Sea exponentially increased the need for services for freed people and simultaneously expanded Campbell's professional portfolio. He was appointed to oversee the resettlement of black people, primarily in Georgia, through the Bureau of Refugees, Freedmen, and Abandoned Lands (Freedmen's Bureau), which the federal government had formed in March 1865 to aid newly freed people as well as poor and displaced whites.[14] Campbell's path now crossed with Sherman's literally and figuratively. And it was Sherman's meeting with black leadership in January 1865 that helped set the stage for Campbell's ascendance and that of black politics in Georgia.

It is difficult to overstate how significant Sherman's Georgia Campaign had been. Much like the desolation of Atlanta, this campaign had shaped the destiny of black political power in the state and, of course, the trajectory of Campbell's career, as well as the careers of many other black (and white) politicians. Freeing people during the March to the Sea may have been militarily expedient, but it also generated great affection for Sherman from those he helped free, as Secretary Stanton learned. Garrison Frazier, the black Baptist minister, explained to Stanton that black people in Savannah "looked upon General Sherman, prior to his arrival, as a man, in the providence of God, specially set apart to accomplish this work, and we unanimously felt inexpressible gratitude to him, looking upon him as a man that should be honored for the faithful performance of his duty." And whatever racial attitudes Sherman exhibited and embraced before the war, he had grown increasingly sympathetic to black people. Frazier stated that Sherman's "conduct and deportment toward us characterized him as a friend and a gentleman."[15]

After considerable discussion about the most pressing needs of the newly freed people, the clergy at the meeting with Sherman and Stanton explained that, more than anything else, the people needed land. They needed space to forge communities for their survival, health, and posterity. Additionally, there was a keen sense that those communities would be more likely to thrive if they were not under the constant threat of Confederates, white supremacists, or other agents of the old racial order. Their vulnerability was clear. The meeting of black leaders was significant and was beneficial to Sherman, who appreciated their praise. After some reflection, Secretary Stanton asked Sherman to devise an action that would be "positive and concrete" for the freed people.[16] Four days later, on January 16, Sherman issued Special Field Order 15, which provided for the confiscation of four hundred thousand acres of land from Confederate planters for the exclusive use of black people.[17] This provided the space and climate for the cultivation of black political mobilization, especially under the auspices of Campbell, who parlayed his work as an administrator of the Freedmen's Bureau into grassroots political engagement and elected office.

Despite the intransigence of so many in Georgia, and the forces hostile to Campbell and other black officials, elections sent several black officials to the state assembly and even one to the US House of Representatives. In all cases the shadow of the Civil War loomed large: it had inflections in the educational, cultural, social, and political arenas of Atlanta for decades to come. Redeemers—Confederate sympathizers who sought white domination of the South after the war—fought tirelessly to slow, if not halt altogether, the incremental progress made in the new spaces of freedom enjoyed by the people of the state.

Full citizenship, as demanded by black leaders such as Douglass, meant equal access to education, employment, accommodations, the vote, and military service. It was, Douglass argued, "personal freedom; the right to testify in courts of law; the right to own, buy and sell real estate."[18] Freedom was not simply being free of chains. It was unfettered citizenship and, of course, a repudiation of white nationalism. Perhaps the most essential and immediate need for newly freed people was land ownership, as Douglass envisioned. It was in response to this demand that Sherman again made critical contributions to the destiny of Georgia's black citizens in the waning months of the war. His Special Field Order 15 declared the boundaries of the land to be provided to freed black people: "The islands from Charleston south, the abandoned rice-fields along the rivers for thirty miles back from the sea, and the country bordering the Saint Johns River, Fla. [near Jacksonville], are reserved and set apart for the settlement of the BLACKS now made free by the acts of war and the proclamation of the President of the United States." Additionally, the order explained that these areas were to be for the cultivation of black communities, free from the threat of racist reprisals or other racial hostility. Sherman ordered that "no white person whatever, unless military officers and soldiers detailed for duty, will be permitted to reside; and the sole and exclusive management of affairs will be left to the freed people themselves, subject only to the United States military authority and the acts of Congress. By the laws of war and orders of the President of the United States the negro is free, and must be dealt with as such."[19]

The order, which was approved by President Lincoln, redistributed the land to newly freed families in forty-acre segments. The order was practical in several ways. It provided resources to the refugees from slavery who had been following Sherman's troops for months. It granted them the ability to settle and to establish communities but freed the Union soldiers from the potential challenges of a civilian population in their midst during battle. It also deprived the enemy of land use for any military purpose. Simultaneously, it was demoralizing to the Confederates, who lost land to the very people whom they fought to keep enslaved. It was a foundational disruption of their world. Although there was no mention of mules in the order, Sherman later ordered that they also be provided to these new homesteads.[20]

The order was immediately controversial. Confederates had long regarded Sherman as a vicious general bent on destroying the world of white southerners. He was referred to as a "rude barbarian" and a "fiend whose soul is stamped with the devil's own hideous image."[21] Confiscating their lands and parceling them out to former slaves was a profound indignity and a gross injustice, they believed. Of course, the notion of reparations for intergenerational enslavement, rape, brutality, and gross exploitation made this field order a promising recompense.

Several weeks after Sherman's order, President Lincoln established the Freedmen's Bureau, which had the authority to oversee the process of securing legal title to the land transfer of the four hundred thousand acres of land to freed people. The scope of the land redistribution even included areas beyond those affected by Sherman's order. Southern whites loyal to the United States were also positioned to receive land confiscated from Confederates. Through the process of seeking administrators, Campbell was offered the job of being the administrative official responsible for overseeing this land transfer as well as the general organization of freed people on the Georgia coast. He eagerly accepted the task and moved his family from South Carolina to Georgia, settling on St. Catherine's Island, where he organized local people. When the war ended, in April, the newly freed faced an uncertain future. Some were positioned to till their own lands, but the vast majority were homeless, unemployed, and illiterate, with few means to ensure safety or procure resources. However, the will to move forward was clear and constant. Voting was essential to that process, and Redeemers, fully aware of the power of the vote, struggled to regain suffrage and to repress the vote of freedmen. The fate of the New South rested in the integrity of its democratic process, and the forces at work to undermine its integrity were national in scope.

The day after the establishment of the Freedmen's Bureau, Lincoln was sworn in for his second term in office. For those very few African Americans who could vote in 1860, Lincoln had been a deeply flawed presidential candidate, but almost alone he offered some open challenge to the expansion of slavery, even while he affirmed protection of it where it existed. During the first half of his first term, he remained committed to the principles of white nationalism; however, Lincoln ideologically evolved as the political landscape of the country dramatically convulsed under the conditions of war. The Confederacy, through its own recalcitrance and obstinate rejections of any compromise, precipitated the destruction of the institution of slavery that it was founded to defend. Furthermore, the rebel enterprise inadvertently sowed the seeds of the demise of white nationalism. In the four years of war, President Lincoln and many other lawmakers, from Congress to state and local governments, eventually committed to abolition, the use of black soldiers, some black officers, and even black citizenship. Lincoln's reelection evinced an expanding national interest in advancing the cause of democracy and freedom in ways that few imagined four years earlier.

Lincoln's second inauguration on March 4, 1865, drew an estimated fifty thousand people, including thousands of African Americans who had previously been excluded from presidential inaugurations.[22] He delivered his speech against a backdrop of more than half a million dead Americans and mourning families from every corner of the country. The president implied that divine punishment had befallen the country for its immoral and cruel investment in slavery. Since the nation's formation, millions of souls had emerged from their mothers' wombs, only to be enslaved at first breath. These guiltless babies were raised to be abused in every barbaric manner in an inhumane system that was thoroughly protected by US laws. The catastrophic loss of life over the last four years seemed biblical to the ill-fated leader: "Fondly do we hope—fervently do we pray—that this mighty scourge of war may speedily pass away. Yet, if God wills that it continue, until all the wealth piled by the bond-man's two hundred and fifty years of unrequited toil shall be sunk . . . so still it must be said 'the judgements of the Lord, are true and righteous altogether.'"[23] This deeply moral and religious castigation of slavery inspired millions and offered a sense of vision for a nation nearing peace and the freedom of millions from bondage. If the enslavement of a people was unjust, one perspective might suggest that the denial of basic rights for the newly freed would also be against the will of a loving God. Thousands cheered these words, including Douglass, who later joined the president at the White House as the first black guest to an inaugural reception there.[24]

Five weeks later, General Lee surrendered to General Grant, effectively ending the war. Celebrations erupted across the country. Crowds assembled in cities and towns as newspapers spread the news. The country seemed positioned to emerge anew, with a revitalized and expanded meaning of freedom and democracy. Five days after the South's surrender, however, a Confederate sympathizer assassinated Lincoln in Washington, DC. The news was horrifying to most Americans, who had only just begun to consider the scope and vast transformation that the war had rendered. For African Americans, the death was particularly distressing. Douglass argued that "no people or class of people in this country, have a better reason for lamenting the death of Abraham Lincoln, and for desiring to honor and perpetuate his memory, than have the colored people." In fact, as the great orator explained to a largely black audience at Cooper Union in New York, no president had ever before come close to affirming the humanity and rights of black people: "Abraham Lincoln, while unsurpassed in his devotion to the welfare of the white race, was also in a sense hitherto without example, emphatically the black man's President: the first to show any respect for their rights as men."[25] But many Confederates rejoiced at the assassination of the President. South Carolinian diarist Mary Boykin Chesnut did not hide her contempt for the slain leader: "The death of Lincoln—I call that a warning to tyrants. He will not be the last president put to death in the capital, though he is the first." In Atlanta there was Confederate revelry, but also dismay and anger among local whites. The *Atlanta Constitution* announced the murder an "OUTRAGE" on its front page, and the *Atlanta Daily Intelligencer* called it a "fearful tragedy."[26] The killing of Lincoln was disruptive to early Reconstruction plans in so many ways. Most immediately, it elevated Andrew Johnson to the presidency, profoundly undermining the initial steps toward citizenship for freed people.

Johnson was the only southern senator who refused to resign from office when his state, Tennessee, seceded in 1861. He crafted his own presidential reconstruction, which was overtly conciliatory to Confederates, offering them a swift return to power and opportunities for them to pass a series of racist laws constricting black rights. Known as "black codes," they swept former Confederate states with legislation that prevented black people from voting, serving on juries, and owning weapons, along with vagrancy laws that arrested blacks and forced them into involuntary servitude. These former Confederates sought, without guile, to reaffirm an unmitigated southern white nationalism. In order to hold office, secure confiscated properties (including land), and regain other rights, ex-Confederates swiftly applied for amnesty at the clerk of pardons. Johnson, conspicuously sympathetic to rebels, had established the office and appointed a former Confederate colonel, M. F. Pleasants, as its head. More than one hundred pardons were granted each day by September 1865.[27] Amnesty enabled the immediate and systematic resistance to black advancement.

The optimism about the promise of reparations was tempered when President Johnson nullified Special Field Order 15 in the fall of 1865. Although Sherman would later claim that he had not intended to make the distribution of land permanent, the people who had come to settle on the lands, as well as the Confederates who lost the land, believed otherwise. Campbell and other black leaders protested against Johnson's order to strip freed people of land. One group of freedmen appealed to Freedmen's Bureau Commissioner, Oliver O. Howard, insisting that they were desperate and without options:

> We are at the mercy of those who are combined to prevent us from getting land enough to lay our Fathers bones upon. We Have property In Horses, cattle, carriages, & articles of furniture, but we are landless and Homeless, from the Homes we Have lived In In the past we can only do one of three things Step Into the public

road or the sea or remain on them working as In former time and subject to thire will as then. We can not resist It In any way without being driven out Homeless upon the road.[28]

Coastal freedmen offered strong support for Campbell, who emerged as the most visible leader among African Americans living near the Atlantic. He insisted, with allies in Congress, that Sherman's order was legally binding and final. Campbell argued that in the course of war the insurgents who had taken up arms against the United States had forfeited their rights inasmuch as they renounced their citizenship and were criminals. Therefore, their treasonous war had required the federal government to usurp their property as contraband, which included, in addition to cattle, agriculture, and war supplies, land that may or may not have been abandoned. Although Campbell was unsuccessful in his effort to retain these lands, he managed to purchase 1,250 acres of land in McIntosh County, along the coast. He then parceled out the land to black families.[29]

An indefatigable agent for freed people, Campbell was widely appreciated by the locals, who elected him to the state senate in 1868. As a significant agent of the spirit of Afro-self-determinism, Campbell was at the forefront of cultivating new black political methods in the state. He was, as Eric Foner explains, the creator of "the only real enclave of political power" for black people in Georgia.[30] For African Americans who were recently freed and made birthright citizens, this era marked an entirely new moment in history. The main expression of black people's politics was no longer abolition. They were no longer occupants of a legally liminal class of neither citizen nor foreigner, constricted by nebulous legal mandates, historical precedent, and provincial proclivities. The Fourteenth Amendment did not equivocate on their status, and leaders such as Campbell and AME minister Henry McNeal Turner made essential demands for full realization of these rights. And given the hundreds of years of cruel and inhumane intergenerational slavery, some recompense in the form of land seemed an appropriate start at granting these new citizens resources to start their lives as free people.

However, resistance to any form of reparations was immediate and formidable. Many still denied that slavery was wrong. Those former Confederate sympathizers who retained their lands, such as Mary Jones of Liberty County, protested that black people would be unfit to govern themselves in freedom. Jones, whose family had enslaved people on their large plantation, wrote extensively about her experience with Sherman's troops and their raids on her land. Some of the newly freed people also faced brutality from Yankee troops who stole from, beat, and even sexually assaulted them. These acts affirmed Jones's argument that white northerners were no more kind or just than their southern counterparts. Free black people would, she explained, face "extermination" in freedom. A staunch supporter of the Confederacy, she argued that an alternative to black extermination would be a postwar "benevolent" form of slavery.[31] Black people in this scenario would not be granted full citizenship rights or access to justice equal to whites. They would, instead, work as laborers for whites—many of them former masters—in a mutually agreeable contract. This veritable compromise between freedom and slavery was, in fact, realized in a wave of hostile legislation that circumscribed the freedom of black people.[32]

It was clear to most that if left to their own devices, former Confederates would, by whatever means possible, render black people a marginalized and exploited class open to every form of vitiation of rights and human dignity. In 1866 the state passed legislation to arrest people for violating a range of new laws, including "vagrancy." Once convicted, these people, most of whom were black men, were hired out to private companies as quasi-slaves. Former plantations, as well as railroad companies, notably the Georgia and Alabama Railroad, used people in this system.[33] All the former Confederate states except Arkansas adopted convict-lease programs and expanded their inmate populations. By 1880, in every southern state black people were arrested at higher rates than whites. (In Texas, white inmates were higher in raw numbers—1,585 to 1,578.) Georgia led every state in the numbers of black people incarcerated.[34] Only seven formerly enslaved black people were imprisoned in Georgia when Sherman invaded the state in 1864. By the time Campbell was elected to the state senate, in 1868, the number had increased to 147. Although this is a relatively small number in a state with several hundred thousand African Americans, it was the start of an especially insidious form of social control.[35] However, the most effective method of this social control would be extralegal intimidation in the form of physical harassment, beatings, arson, lynching, and other forms of terrorism, as well as quotidian acts such as landlord demands of sharecropping families. The diversity of methods quickly manifested in the earliest months of freedom. Hundreds, if not thousands, were beaten each year across the state for various violations of unwritten racial etiquette or resistance to discriminatory or cruel acts. Georgia swiftly emerged as an epicenter of lynching. Although some whites were also the victims of lynch mobs, 95 percent of those who were killed were black.[36]

The fierce devotion to racial subjugation was so virulent in Georgia and across the former Confederacy that in March 1867, Congress passed the First Reconstruction Act. Under this law, Georgia, together with Alabama and Florida, became part of the Third Military District, supervised by General John Pope. In Georgia, Campbell cast himself as a loyal agent of the Freedmen's Bureau and closely followed the direction of General Pope. In the process, Campbell would help shape the earliest expressions of black political leadership in the state. Simultaneously, under Pope's leadership, Atlanta's importance and visibility in the state and therefore the country would be indelibly strengthened in no small part to Confederate recalcitrance.

Pope, under congressional authority, registered 95,214 white and 93,457 black voters, a major historical advancement of the democratic

process in the state. Although former Confederates had formed terrorist organizations and militias of various sorts, including the Ku
Klux Klan, military supervision helped repress violence and aided
voter turnout from October 29 through November 2, 1867, when delegates for another constitutional convention were selected. Campbell
was elected as a delegate to this convention, along with other African
Americans who joined whites from December 1867 to March 1868 in
order to craft a new state constitution.

The presence of black lawmakers was outrageous to most white
Georgians. Death threats and general threats of violence and terrorism circulated. Violence against white and black Republicans had
continued at such a pace that the expansion of democracy in the state
seemed uncertain. The level of racist threat may have altered the fate of
Atlanta, which had been the headquarters for General Pope. Reports
that innkeepers in Milledgeville, the state capital, would bar black delegates from accommodations prompted Pope to move the convention
to Atlanta, where delegates met at city hall.[37]

Redeemers met in Macon for their own two-day "Conservative
Convention" and passed resolutions denouncing military command
and Pope's leadership. Despite full-throated objections—vitriolic rhetoric against the official convention in Atlanta—Redeemers appeared
impotent relative to the forces at hand. The authority and power of a
much larger community of Republicans and Democrats, backed by
the full weight of the federal government, forced the most recalcitrant
Confederates to relent to the new political landscape, or so it appeared.

The official convention in Atlanta hosted hundreds of black and
white men in bustling new hotels and inns. It was a city swept with
an enthusiastic anticipation for the promise of future opportunity.
Black delegates such as Campbell, Philip Joiner, and Turner arrived
in Atlanta, which, though destroyed by war, seemed eager to rebuild
and take new shape as something better and more dynamic than ever.
There was even a greater promise for black advancement, compared

to the more hostile rural towns in other parts of Georgia. Although the city had no public schools, there were efforts to educate African Americans, including the formation of colleges that served as primary and secondary schools as well. Various black enterprises—barbershops, tailors, churches, and craftsmen—opened in the aftermath of the war. For Campbell, Joiner, and Turner, the city provided a glimpse of the possibilities of freedom as they navigated new political terrain. They established relationships with the small but expanding class of black business and religious leadership in Atlanta. The general contentment that delegates experienced in Atlanta was not lost on the city council.[38]

Atlanta's officials, never willing to pass up an opportunity to boost their beloved city, made a proposal to the convention in February 1868 to make Atlanta the new state capital. Unionists and former Confederates alike found common ground in promoting the city in this way. The Atlanta City Council offered to provide buildings for the governor, supreme court, legislature, and other state offices free of charge for ten years. Joseph E. Brown, former Confederate governor of Georgia and justice of the state supreme court, welcomed the move: "The State can build a splendid granite Capitol . . . with convict labor, at a very light cost."[39] The promise of a growing city with outstanding transportation networks appealed to the convention, and in April 1868 it formally voted: "The seat of government of this State, from and after the date of the ratification of this constitution, shall be in the city of Atlanta, and the general assembly shall provide for the erection of a new capitol, and such other buildings as the public welfare may require." Atlanta became Georgia's fifth and last capital.[40]

Three months later, the state assembly ratified the Fourteenth Amendment, and Georgia was readmitted to the Union. Later that month, however, the state Democrats met in Atlanta to host "the largest political mass meeting ever held in Georgia," where the party argued that even if black men could vote, they had no right to hold public office. With a groundswell of support from Georgia's white majority, conservatives in the state assembly cobbled together an alliance of Democrats and enough conservative white Republicans to purge twenty-eight black officeholders. In September 1868 all black legislators were removed from office, and flashes of violence unfolded as Redeemers waged terrorist campaigns to return to a codified form of racial subjugation. In protest, Philip Joiner, a black elected state assemblyman, organized a march to a Republican rally in Camilla, where the local sheriff and other local whites opened fire, killing about a dozen men and wounding around thirty. Known as the Camilla Massacre, the killings made national news, and it was further proof to Congress that Georgia had not been sufficiently reformed and that military supervision was still required.[41]

The massacre caused outrage, demands for justice, and a stronger federal military presence. Additionally, as Georgia's former Confederates were reelected to office—from county sheriff through governor—the practice of being "reformed" appeared hollow at best. Shortly after the war, in a letter to Radical Republican senator Charles Sumner, Frederick Douglass argued that former enslavers could not be trusted to govern and protect the freedom of people whom they stopped enslaving only after losing a protracted and bloody war. That these people had fought and died to protect their right to hold children, women, and men in bondage evinced their incapacity to govern justly. In the end, "the freedmen cannot be safely left to the care of their former masters."[42]

In alignment with the neo-Confederate ascension, protests against suffrage for black men spread across the South. In Georgia, as in other states, conservatives proffered religious, cultural, biological, and political reasons why black men should be denied the right to vote. The vote made formerly enslaved men "vain." Redeemers pined for the old social order, one that demanded black obsequiousness, timidity, and pliant behavior. That black people would express any political agency and self-assurance was anathema. Political independence, when blacks exercised it, was a haughty and arrogant act rather than civic engagement. Classically paternalistic ideas that white southerners knew best for black people manifested themselves in the argument that black political organization was but a mere appendage to white radicals, who "enslaved the Negro to [their] own schemes no less than the South had done before to its interests." To be sure, many continued to traffic in language that fanned flames of sectional discord, where Radical Republicans were the party of "foreigners" from "abroad," citizens of a veritable alien country. These carpetbaggers encouraged "Negro rule" and with it the subjugation of native white southerners under an unfair, despotic, and corrupt government. Benjamin H. Hill, the former Confederate senator from Georgia, rejected black suffrage "whether with or without the aid of the mischief-making adventurers from abroad, or selfish apostates from their own blood at home."[43] More than anything else, suffrage affirmed black citizenship and legal equality in a way that simple emancipation had not.

Voting granted access to the levers of political power that had previously been available only to white men. One Georgian conservative decried the expansion of suffrage and excoriated whites who supported it. Black men, he complained, had been "elevated into a seat of power, so lavishly granted such possibilities for mischief, so grovelingly worshipped for a formidable factor of the master-race."[44] Neo-Confederates and their sympathizers argued that abolitionists thrust black people into a more desperate state of existence through their "spurious humanitarianism," which made carefree slaves into a clueless, inept mass of helpless citizens who were unfit and unworthy of the responsibility of said citizenship. Unfit for survival in, or the responsibilities of, a civilized society, black people would, they insisted, devolve into barbarism. They would likely decline toward extinction, as had Native Americans. The most civilized among the Redeemers denied that they harbored any hatred for black people. Instead, they fumed that white northerners were the nefarious ones who had "ravished the [black] race in their own interests . . . [and] left the Negro worse off than when they picked him up. He was now left on the doorstep of the [white] Southerners, who were to bear the responsibilities of his presence but were not permitted freedom in solving the riddle."[45] However, the most barbarous defenders of the old order proved exceedingly malevolent. Various terrorist groups operated as enforcers of the old order, zealously and violently repressing black political activity. A former member of the White Brotherhood, John W. Long, explained that "the chief purpose of [klanism] was as I understood it to keep the negroes from elevating themselves to white people and keep them from going to the polls and voting and to over throw the republican party."[46] To that end, black men, women, and even children were publicly tied to trees or posts, whipped, tortured, and murdered before jeering packs of onlookers across the state.

Thousands fell victim to unimaginable cruelty because of their efforts to vote, politically organize, or advocate for other rights. White federal agents, some of whom may have been hardened by the carnage of war, were shocked at the barbarity directed at freed people. Mobs of whites milled about frothing at the mouth, screaming and reveling in the ritualistic torture and beatings of men, women, and children. In language that could only offend Native Americans, one white observer remarked that an Indian "is not more delighted at the writhings and shrieks of his victims at the stake, than many Georgians are at the agonizing cries of the African negro at the whipping post."[47] Months after the war, a black newspaper in Savannah reported on the rape of a black woman. The rapists had declared to punish those whose families served in the Union Army, but white newspapers were reticent about reporting on such violence, arguing that the racist terrorism was not reflective of most whites. The editor of the black paper explained that this reasoning was a "miserable plea . . . for shielding criminals and thwarting the demands of justice." The social, political, and cultural landscape of white "high society," as Leon Litwack explains, may have "deplore[d] the excesses" of terror, but "many of them assumed an indifference that came close to approval or sympathy."[48]

Many others had been accused of sexual assault or "disrespecting" whites, but the mob violence that followed was a process of deracinating legal rights and enforcing political subjugation by denying due process. In many cases mob violence was directed against entire households. Some of these actions included sexual violence against black women and girls, including rape in front of the victims' families.[49] Yet the allegations of black male sexual violence against white females emerged as an essential trope of the wider politics of racial subjugation during Reconstruction. Threats to white sexuality operated as an easy rhetorical tool when arguing for the oppression of black people. At times, simple rhetoric about "Negro rule" fell short of evoking the passion that Redeemers demanded. And, of course, allegations of black political corruption did not strike the same degree of visceral rage and fear that sexual violations of white women had. One Redeemer even admitted that "the rapist is a product of the reconstruction period." He explained that the black rapist's "chrysalis was a uniform. . . . He came into life in the abnormal atmosphere of a time rife with discussions of social equality theories, contentions for coeducation and intermarriage."[50]

Racist terrorism shook the black community and its nascent political leadership. However, Tunis Campbell did not easily capitulate to the rise of Redeemers. He and other black officials, including Henry McNeal Turner, successfully appealed to the federal government for intervention. With the presence of federal troops and other oversight, conservatives eventually relented to the federal government, but without a hint of magnanimity. Once seated, the editor of the Georgia legislative manual in Atlanta refused to provide the traditional biographic profiles for black lawmakers. In absolute bitterness about the presence of black publicly elected officials, he fumed that "though Congress could compel him to associate with negroes in a deliberative body . . .

neither Congress, Military Government, a triple Reconstruction nor even another amendment to the . . . United States Constitution, could compel him to publish their biographies in this book."[51] The absence of their biographies notwithstanding, black lawmakers impressed their marks in the annals of Georgia law.

Political office was an essential component of the development, funding, and protection of black institutions across the state. From health care to rations, Campbell used the resources of the federal government to establish and strengthen the communities of freed people along the coast. Few institutions were as valued and proved more important to the community than schools. In his capacity as the Freedmen's Bureau agent in the region, Campbell established two schools and, with the assistance of the bureau, the AME Church, and various black and white missionaries, taught hundreds how to read and write. The bureau simultaneously organized voters and taught new landowners about property management. Various black and northern white missionaries supported the religious, educational, and health-related institutions, but the local people were the critical foundation of these efforts.[52] Black people poured into schools as they did throughout the South. In 1868 one observer noted that they "were to be seen at every corner, and between the hours of labor poring over the elementary pages."

The alacrity with which black people sought education alarmed many local whites, who were doubly fearful of the type of education that freed people received from their (primarily) white northern teachers. Stephen Elliott, who was the former presiding bishop of the Protestant Episcopal Church of the Confederate States of America, was forced to free the people whom he enslaved, and he remained embittered by his loss. In the aftermath of the war, he witnessed white people educating former slaves and teaching on a range of topics, including civil rights. Wildly upset at the intimation of racial equality and the presence of white northerners in black schools, Elliott's southern nationalism was stoked: "Every person imported from abroad to teach these people is an influence . . . widening the breach between the races." African Americans were being taught to regard their citizenship and freedom as natural and inalienable. Simultaneously, they were being instructed to read, write, manage household affairs, and do things that had been long thought impossible for them. They were, in no uncertain terms, being taught to be subversive to the old order and—importantly—hold it in deep contempt. And although northern teachers were not required to foment contempt for slavery and the Confederacy, some transplants were explicit in their disdain for the rebel cause. One who taught in Savannah wrote, "I am just at this time feeling as if it would be pleasant, had I the power, and an *iron heel* strong enough, to grind every one of the Secessionists deep into the earth."[53]

These teachers knew that Redeemers remained a constant threat to their work, and the newly freed fully understood the scorn that their educational advancement invited. Some freed people gained literacy, voted, and emerged as local leaders through the beneficence of these educational institutions. Many, in turn, faced extraordinary resistance from Redeemers. Washington Eager harnessed the power of education and eventually became "too big a man" to local Klansmen, who murdered him and destroyed a library that Eager and other black people used: "They would just dare any other nigger to have a book in his house."[54]

There is no doubt that hostility to black education was pervasive in Georgia, but sympathy for the educational advancement of black people was present among some white Georgians. In McIntosh County, under the jurisdiction of Campbell, Harriet Atwood Newell Hart was one such local white who proved sympathetic to the cause of black advancement. Although born abroad and raised outside of the South, Hart had lived in Georgia for many years, marrying a local planter who died in 1866, leaving her in debilitating debt. Desperate to secure financial stability, Hart converted part of her home into a schoolroom for black people in the area. She gained financial support from the Presbyterian Committee on Missions for the Freedmen, and grew passionate about her work teaching people who had only recently been enslaved. Hart reported that "if they have one leaf to a spelling book, they will bring it and go over it until they do better. They have set their heart to learn, and they will learn in spite of everything, and it won't be long before the whites see it, and acknowledge it, but it will be a bitter pill for them to swallow."[55] Being foreign-born likely mitigated any racist inclinations that Hart might have had, but native-born white Georgians were also counted among teachers at black schools. About a third of the white teachers in Georgia Freedmen's Bureau schools were native whites, and male teachers far outnumbered female teachers in these schools. Some grew enthusiastic about black students, humanizing them and investing in their successes, but others viewed the students with contempt and the job as a socially unacceptable but reliable source of income.[56]

Through the early development of public schooling in the South, those at the forefront of its creation had largely been Radical Republicans—black and white. And despite their enmity for these radicals, poor whites significantly benefited from black political empowerment in Georgia when Campbell, Joiner, Turner, and others pushed for the expansion of public schools for all children. The investment from the Freedmen's Bureau, black and white northern missionaries, and local black officials, as well as the demand from black pupils, precipitated a rapid expansion of black schools across Georgia. In some sections of the state, more black students were enrolled than white ones: black people, who had been legally prevented from reading, enrolled at every age level, whereas adult whites were less likely to need or desire basic literacy, although they suffered much higher rates of illiteracy than their northern counterparts. The Old South antipathy toward public education gave way as Redeemer interests in public white schools swiftly developed as a rejoinder of sorts to black education.[57]

The education of black people, it appeared to Redeemers, had become a necessary burden, but one that could be used to control freed people if it was effectively administered. In an effort to control the information and quality of education that black people received, one apologist for the Old South argued that "if the Negro were to be correctly educated, it must be done by [white] Southerners." Local communities sought former Confederates, their wives, and widows as teachers in black schools across the state.[58] As Jacqueline Jones explains, "These were the community leaders who would later give their support to a statewide system of public education and speak in favor of segregated black schools taught by native whites."[59] This education of black and white students in public schools expanded under the aegis of white paternalist polemics that forged historical narratives of the noble struggle for southern independence, a chivalrous Old South of honor, pride, and dignity—and, of course, happy slaves.

However, Campbell and other black leaders rigorously fought to maintain black control over the newly created black institutions. Aware of the power of black control and the danger of Redeemers in the classroom, Campbell employed his family members, including his wife and son, as teachers in the local schools, and he maintained supervision over the operations of said schools. He oversaw schools on St. Catherine's Island and Sapelo Island with eighty and sixty students, respectively.[60] Even with the daunting work that enveloped his new life in Georgia, Campbell's local organizing did not deter his statewide political efforts. He was elected vice president of the state's Republican Party and, in that capacity, promoted a range of voter-registration efforts.

Campbell was eventually elected as a justice of the peace, becoming one of the earliest black people in that capacity in the country. As a state senator, he represented the Second Senatorial District, which included Liberty County, the home of Mary Jones, who abhorred the possibility that the people whom she once enslaved would have the capacity to determine her political fate as elected officials.[61] As a woman, of course, she was denied the vote, yet as a wealthy white woman, she enjoyed the material and social benefits afforded to her class (benefits that had been denied to most white men or women). In this moment, however, the hardened notions of patriarchy trumped the barriers to suffrage that had once denied black men the right to vote.

Campbell was one of the earliest members of the black political establishment in Reconstruction Georgia. While serving as a state senator from the Second Senatorial District, Campbell advocated for a range of laws expanding civil rights and social justice for all of Georgia's citizens, including integrated jury boxes, equal access to education, homestead exemptions, open access to public facilities, voting rights, and abolition of the quasi-slavery convict-lease system. Despite great opposition, death threats, and backlash from protectors of the old racial order, he introduced a total of fifteen bills before losing his seat in the infamous 1872 election, which was marred by terrorism and fraud. In the wake of racist violence directed at Republicans and freed people who sought the vote, Campbell pushed for stronger public safety and security in McIntosh County. Fully aware that the state disregarded the protection of black citizens, he insisted that self-defense was critically necessary for the community. To that end, after failed appeals to the federal authorities, he organized a militia that was estimated to include as many as three hundred African Americans armed to protect Campbell's home and family. Local terror organizations and random violent thugs relented and regrouped. They were not entirely pacified but reasoned that a pause in violence was better than a conflict that the racists would likely win but would also cost many white lives.[62] Campbell's application of the principles of Afro-self-determination proved useful to an array of actions, including establishing schools, forming political organizations, and even advocating self-defense. His actions helped fill voids when the scourge of racism meant that public institutions failed to meet the needs of their black citizens. Generations of African Americans would similarly find efficacy in the principles of self-determination in innovative ways.

Immediately following the war, the Radical Republicans in control of Congress had passed laws that expanded democracy beyond the bounds of whiteness. These new freedoms were not limited to states below the Mason-Dixon Line. The expansion of the right to vote unfolded across the country. Reconstruction transformed and expanded American democracy.[63] Governments in states across the former Confederacy worked with the Freedmen's Bureau to create schools, hospitals, infrastructure, and various public works, and even provided rations and distributed land to whites and blacks alike. Although white southerners—most of whom were poor—also benefited from these resources, there was hostility about their availability to the newly freed people.

In Benjamin H. Hill's Georgia, Reconstruction found black citizens positioned to enjoy freedom and rights never imagined before a few years earlier. Leaders such as Turner and Campbell and scores of local religious leaders organized black institutions across the state: churches, schools, and chapters of the Union League. There was a conspicuous excitement about black elected officials on the municipal, county, and state levels. However, the conservative majority of the white population, as noted above, resisted any expansion of rights to black Georgians. In fact, Georgia had perhaps the most dismal record of black political power among all southern states. The life span of Reconstruction was cut short through a systematic and far-reaching violent lawlessness from various terrorist organizations and vigilantes across the state. As Foner writes, Georgia made "the most comprehensive effort to undo Reconstruction."[64]

The sentiment against racial equality was so deeply entrenched that several terrorist groups organically emerged to resist it. The Pale Faces, Knights of the White Camelia, Native Sons of the South, the Society of the White Rose, the Red Jackets, the Knights of the Black Cross, the '76 Association, and White Brotherhood joined the Klan as terrorist organizations that targeted those (white or black) who attempted to realize civil rights for all citizens. Black lawmakers were targeted and were often viewed as existential threats to white southerners. The outrage at general black advancement fueled violent resistance in various forms.

Joshua Hill, the mayor of Madison in 1866, reported on the rise of sectional vitriol and violence against black people and radicals. The hatred was "almost as great as it was in the days of the rebellion," wrote the former slaveholder. In Georgia, it was reported that "parties of rebels [are] now going through the state murdering loyal citizens in their houses at night and shooting them from the bushes during the day. Thirty-seven good citizens were murdered in this way in about 3 days." The murderers were said to be "composed chiefly of slaveholders' sons who are mad at the loss of their slaves."[65]

Chief among the ambitions of these terror groups was the nullification of black civil rights—if not de jure nullification, de facto would suffice. The political goal—to prevent black voting and attract white voters to an antidemocratic cause—explicitly appealed to ignorance and fear. Everything—black "insolence," lawlessness, "radical" corruption, "Republican rule," and miscegenation—had been used to try to attract Democratic voters. Fear of racial amalgamation or miscegenation was a dominant theme. As one white southerner complained, "If we have social equality . . . we shall have intermarriage . . . we shall become a race of mulattoes. . . . [I]t is a matter of life and death with the Southern people to keep their blood pure." On the issue of race mixing, black people were perhaps most flummoxed. For hundreds of years, white sexual predators had violated black women and girls with impunity. Throughout the South, on plantations large and small, biracial children were born from the wombs of black women, not white ones. In 1861 the famed white diarist Mary Chesnut privately wrote that "our men live all in one house with their wives and their concubines; and the mulattoes one sees in every family partly resemble the white children. Any lady is ready to tell you who is the father of all of the mulatto children in everybody's household but her own. Those, she seems to think, drop from the clouds."[66]

Republicans, white and black, directly addressed the rhetorical device that underscored the threat of miscegenation. Sexual predation, racial intermarriage, and miscegenation were not the goals of black people. Turner offered a rejoinder to these fanatical and baseless fears: "What do we want with their daughters and sisters? We have as much beauty as they. Look at our ladies, do you want more beauty than they? The difficulty heretofore has been, our ladies were not always at our own disposal. All we ask of the white men is to let our ladies alone, and they need not fear us."[67] On more than one occasion, black people made references to the irony of white fears of race mixing, given their history and its nearly sole initiators. In Augusta a black newspaper noted that the white man "seems to be afraid that some of his daughters may do what a good many of his sons and himself has done time and again, and therefore he wants laws made to prevent *them* doing so."[68] It was not a fear of interracial intimacy as much as a fear of white men no longer exclusively controlling the sexual practices of everyone else, especially white women, the newspaper suggested. But even as the fear of interracial marriage spread, other existential threats to white supremacy were cast in a national debate about the nature of American governance. As many argued, the machinations of American democracy would function well only if they were wedded to exclusive white citizenship.

Across the country, various forces resisted the spread of democracy to all citizens. In fact, the 1868 Democratic Party's campaign slogan for the Horatio Seymour–Frank Blair Jr. ticket was "Our Ticket, Our Motto, This Is a White Man's Country; Let White Men Rule."[69] Seymour, the presidential candidate, was a former governor of New York, not a southerner. Still, the promise of a nation that universally endorsed civil rights for all citizens remained appealing enough. The Republican ticket of Civil War general and hero Ulysses S. Grant won the election. As the nation moved toward expanding freedoms, however, the provincial forces of retrenchment proved formidable.

The only black member of Congress from Georgia during the nineteenth century, Jefferson Franklin Long, was one of more than twenty black members of Congress in the first three decades after the Civil War. South Carolina and Mississippi, both with mostly black populations, elected eighteen and seven African Americans to Congress, respectively. North Carolina, which had a smaller percentage of black people than Georgia, sent seven black men to Congress.[70] On February 1, 1871, Long became the first black representative to speak before the House when he denounced a bill that would allow former Confederate politicians to return to Congress without swearing allegiance to the US Constitution. Because of election disputes and Georgia's refusal to ratify the Fourteenth Amendment, Long was forced to serve a shortened term. Georgia's only black representative served just three months in office, the shortest term of any black member of the history of the House. Undaunted by the Redeemers in his home state, Long pushed for voting rights for blacks and loyal whites, and against voting rights for unrepentant ex-Confederates. Intimately aware of the violence that swept the South as former Confederates waged terror campaigns against black suffrage, he supported legal measures against unreformed Confederates: "Do we, then, really propose here to–day . . . when loyal men dare not carry the 'stars and stripes' through our streets . . . to relieve from political disability the very men who have committed these Kuklux [sic] outrages? I think that I am doing my duty to my constituents and my duty to my country when I vote against such a proposition."[71] Presciently, Congressman Long appealed to his fellow lawmakers, arguing that, if enfranchised, unrepentant rebels would systematically and categorically oppress black citizens. Viewing black advancement as an affront to the proper racial order, Georgia newspapers accused him of a "malicious attempt to disfranchise whites." Long's arguments were not enough to prevent the seating of unrepentant Confederates. The House's final vote was 118 to 90 to grant Confederates amnesty.[72]

Long's protests against amnesty were far from isolated. The indefatigable Douglass warned vigorously against the pliant ways in which

Congress treated recalcitrant rebels. Just two months after Long's
speech, in his column "Shall We Surrender to the Ku Klux?," Douglass denounced the "Ku Kluxism [that] now moves over the South like
the pestilence that walketh in darkness and wasteth at noon-day."[73]
The Klan had been, as Douglass warned, one of the greatest threats to
peace in the aftermath of war. Through various terrorist organizations,
former rebels defended Redeemer politics, namely the subjugation of
black people, and no terror group was as visible and widespread as the
KKK. As David Blight wrote, the famed abolitionist, newspaper publisher, and advocate for human rights "believed slavery itself still lurked
everywhere in the South, and like an incipient disease, it would infest
all aspects of life if not once and for all killed."[74] Douglass insisted that
the notion of freedom was so distasteful among the "ex-rebel Klan"
that they would murder and maim people and destroy institutions that
served the cause of freedom. They were, he noted, one of the greatest
threats to American democracy and the stability of the country itself.

Though an advocate of black people being fully woven into the fabric of the United States and not segregated or sequestered into isolated
communities, Douglass actually agreed with some fundamental positions of Afro-self-determinism and agreed with the sentiment of Frazier and the others who met with Sherman in the last days of the war.
The war had ensured a "purification" and moral renewal for the United
States, which had destroyed a cruel system of unimaginable wicked-
ness. But unless assiduous efforts were made to protect those newly
freed, the former rebels would "by unfriendly legislation . . . make our
liberty . . . a delusion, a mockery."[75] As previously noted, in a letter to
Congressman Charles Sumner, Douglass explained that "the freedmen
cannot be safely left to the care of their former masters." They showed
no inclinations toward justice, fairness, and appreciation for peace, so
they could not be "trusted to legislate."[76]

The warnings made by Douglass, black and white journalists, and
government observers helped shore up resources for congressional

reconstruction, including the presence of federal troops. Of course, the troops could not be at all places at once. Across the region, men, women, and children were beaten, raped, murdered, and intimidated by Redeemers. Black schools, homes, and churches were burned and vandalized. Long's home state emerged as a bastion of an especially powerful expression of white supremacy. Its citizens swiftly reelected Confederates into government, ensuring that laws, policies, appointments, and allocation of resources would be firmly in the authority of the same people who had led the rebellion only a few years earlier.[77]

A century before Atlanta received the sobriquet "Black Mecca," it was a small but rapidly growing center of the new economy of the Reconstruction South. In some respects it was suited to take advantage of the new economic landscape of the post-slavery era in a way that other, less industrialized cities were not. As noted earlier, Atlanta had the lowest percentage of enslaved people among Georgia's five largest cities. Transportation, agricultural commerce, and financial enterprises were growing sectors. Paper and textile mills were also established, creating a greater need for cheap labor as millworkers toiled to serve the expanding middle classes and the wealthy. And because it was the home base of the Union forces from Sherman's army, it became an important site of governmental work. As well, the Freedmen's Bureau established regional headquarters in the Gate City. There was a growing professional class, and black and white poor people migrated into Atlanta seeking a better life.

At first prevented from entering a military camp, hundreds eventually found their way in, seeking refuge from the instability, uncertainty, and insecurity of life in rural Georgia during the war. That insecurity was particularly acute for black people, most of whom had escaped slavery and were seeking to secure employment, housing, or simple safety from whites who sought to reenslave or otherwise threaten them. The city's population ballooned with refugees fleeing the agrarian crisis in the rural areas, as well as the many freed people who were escaping terror as well as economic collapse. Union soldiers, many believed, would provide some safety. Dozens and then hundreds of people and families established shanties around the Union camp. When most of Sherman's troops departed for the March to the Sea, freed people continued to pour into Atlanta and settle in the camp, known as Shermantown. It did not always offer the security that its inhabitants had desired. Just two years after the war, nine soldiers from the McPherson Barracks (later Fort McPherson) rampaged through the area, beating people and destroying property. However, greater violence in the city only expanded Shermantown as African Americans gathered there for safety.[78]

Although there was not a sizable population of black people—free or enslaved—in Atlanta in the antebellum era, there were already separate black settlements in different wards across the small city. By 1867, there were 10,940 whites and 9,288 blacks in Atlanta. The city limits were expanding outward to accommodate the growing numbers of migrants. Jenningstown, which was formed near Diamond Hill, was one of the earliest black settlements. Others included Mechanicsville, Summerhill, and Shermantown. Black people in the city formed contiguous residential spaces in three major areas. On the west side, African Americans established themselves with small businesses, churches, and homes near Atlanta University. Others settled on Wheat Street and also established churches and small shops. Atlanta University—as well as all the other black educational institutions—was critical to the development of the city's black population. Atlanta University's North Hall (Gaines Hall today), built in 1869, was one of the city's first iconic landmarks.[79]

The way in which black communities developed mirrored formations across the state and region, including these separate all-black residential spaces, was not uniformly a southern phenomenon. In many instances, whites and blacks, though rigidly segregated in terms of public accommodations, education, and beyond, found themselves in relatively close proximity in residential areas. However, Atlanta formed a more rigid spatial separation to complement the segregation that was institutionalized in legal form.[80]

Migration into the city was not exclusive to black people, yet many local whites were particularly hostile to black newcomers. Many used alarmist language to describe a "flocking" to Atlanta. White observers complained that their cities were "overrun" and "crowded, crammed, packed with multitudes of lazy worthless negroes."[81] In addition to the sheer numbers of black people in cities, the notion that these people were untethered to the absolute control of white enslavers was especially troubling. The presence of black people was not unusual for most white southerners, but the sight of *free* black people evoked discomfort, if not outright anger and fear. Nearly half of the city was black in 1870, and few events were as bold a display of black freedom as Atlanta's Independence Day celebrations immediately after the war.[82]

Across the South, the significance of July 4 diminished as the Confederacy formed its own nationalist identity as a new republic. Following the war, July 4 reemerged in Atlanta as a vibrant affirmation of American nationalism and freedom. However, it was dominated by the city's black citizens. The *Atlanta Daily Intelligencer* described the festive events of July 4, 1867: "The celebration of this day in Atlanta was surrendered almost entirely—if not wholly so—by our citizens to the negro population, who appeared upon our streets in the high state of enthusiasm in immense throngs from the early morn to a late hour in the evening."[83] The paper reported how Atlanta's "citizens" had been marginalized by members of "the negro population," who organized in conspicuous odes to "freedom," "democracy," and their own American citizenship. In some ways, these gatherings were subversive and bold. Black Atlantans, in a grand public spectacle, subverted southern white nationalism by "pedestalizing" symbols that had been maligned and hated by Confederates. For example, a group of African Americans from the city's Third Ward organized the "Lincoln Union Republican Club." One banner from the Fifth Ward read, "The Death of Slavery, July 4th '67."[84] For the city's white and black citizens, civil and national pride was deeply marked by the legacy of the Confederate cause. For

black people, the size and character of the city—including its federal troops—afforded new expressions of a freedom that were civic
in nature. These citizens were a part of the social civic body as never
before, and their allegiance to the United States was clear.

Black people celebrated Independence Day, but thousands of
white Atlantans gathered annually on April 26 to celebrate Confederate Memorial Day. Like groups of neo-Confederates and Confederate sympathizers across the South, locals adorned the city cemetery's
graves of fallen rebels and held parades, heard speeches, and otherwise
exalted the Lost Cause. For their part, black Atlantans, in addition
to July 4, celebrated January 1 as Emancipation Day. The anniversary
of the Emancipation Proclamation was an opportunity to celebrate
and honor the legacy of Abraham Lincoln's wartime attempt to lib-
erate many people from slavery. African Americans marched through
the streets with American flags and joyfully brought in the new year
while affirming their own deliverance from hundreds of years of bondage. The connections to the Civil War and the Union's victory were
unequivocal. These public displays of black civic identity not only centered black people and their own cultural agency; they simultaneously
connected this identity with a larger national narrative of patriotism
and Americanness. Independence Day and Emancipation Day parades
in Atlanta had become especially black events that were keen on using
public space and American nationalistic symbols and rhetoric, while
also extolling black freedom and black citizenship and patriotism.
These had become a foil to the Confederate culture that was becoming institutionalized across the South. In a city, state, and region that
viewed being a black American as an oxymoron, these events were subversive. In fact, in the antebellum era black citizens in various northern
and southern cities were barred from participating in public gatherings or patriotic parades. Atlanta's black citizens had carved out a clear
space for their own civic identity by these black-dominated—yet open
to all—celebrations of democracy and freedom.

Atlanta was now the most visible manifestation of the disruption of the Old South. Unlike rural areas, where many black people were relegated to sharecropping status, the city was a new and dynamic terrain open to subversion of various social, cultural, and political conventions. Many whites were coming to terms with the new social order. Some worked with blacks, hired them, and even courted them to vote for the conservative politics of the Democratic Party. Often using the terms *Conservatives* and *Democrats* interchangeably, one member of this group enjoined a group of African Americans in 1868: "We are all creatures of one good Being. We are all brethren, children of one Father. He has made us differently—we to work in one part of the vine yard—you, in another. But all to receive the wages of our work."[85] Rhetorical intimations of interracial friendship and community were not unknown. Still, the great majority of black voters refused to support the conservatives; instead, they remained loyal to the reformers of the Republican Party, which had effectively protected voting rights and educational opportunities.

Atlanta had been a small town before the war, but it expanded considerably in the years to follow. And the influx of black and white people forced into being profound ruptures in the racial order. Black people, unfettered by enslavement, moved about the streets, rode streetcars, peddled goods, opened churches and businesses, and built homes. They forged a new sense of collective self in the city: free black citizens in a world that only recently considered the concept to be an affront to law and nature. Despite the promise of Atlanta, the vast majority of Georgia's black population remained in rural areas. Some, however, with no promise of refuge, employment, or even greater justice, struck out for the Gate City in hopes that they, too, would find a wider sense of freedom, community, safety, and opportunity.

The rise of the Redeemers meant that black political power, which had unevenly developed across the South, was attacked on various fronts. Scores of former Confederates, from Senator Benjamin H. Hill to Vice President Alexander Stephens, were elected to office. By

1876, the power of the Redeemers had become so strong that the South brought the presidential election to a disputed tie between Republican Rutherford B. Hayes and Democrat Samuel Tilden. The leadership of both parties reached a compromise in 1877 that gave the presidential election to Hayes, ensuring that the GOP maintained control of the White House, but the compromise also pulled federal troops from the South, ending Reconstruction. The removal of federal troops essentially allowed white-supremacist terror groups to thrive unchecked by authorities, granting the political ascension of conservative officials who would pass a series of laws disenfranchising black voters.

In 1890 Mississippi emerged as one of the first states with disenfranchisement laws, which including poll taxes, literacy tests, and residence qualifications. In 1894 Douglass captured the essence of this vast reduction of black civil rights. The process was intimately tied to the rise of Confederate Redeemers, those recalcitrant, unrepentant defenders of the Old South. "The cause lost in the war is the cause regained in peace," he argued. "The cause gained in peace is the cause lost in war." The Confederacy's reprise was "the defeat of emancipation . . . the determination of slavery to perpetuate itself, if not under one form, then under another," and, Douglass explained, "the folly of endeavoring to retain the new wine of liberty in the old bottles of slavery." And although the conservative forces of the former Confederate states had been the architects of these schemes, Douglass believed that the "cowardly proposition of disfranchisement has been received by public men, white and black, by Republicans as well as Democrats." Indeed, the outrages perpetrated against black people across the South, while the federal government proved either antipathetic or apathetic to their suffering, infuriated Douglass: "The Supreme Court has surrendered. State sovereignty is restored. It has destroyed the civil rights Bill, and converted the Republican party into a party of money rather than a party of morals, a party of things rather than a party of humanity and justice."[86] In regard to the true motives of Redeemers, some were more explicit about their intentions. As James Vardaman, who would later serve as Mississippi's governor, clearly confessed in 1900, "There is no use to equivocate or lie about the matter. Mississippi's constitutional convention was held for no other purpose than to eliminate the nigger from politics. Not the 'ignorant and vicious' . . . but the nigger."[87] Even with the erasure of black rights and the swift return of former Confederates to office across Georgia, Atlanta proved to exemplify the power of cities to present opportunities and resources for refashioning space, freedom, community, and identities, even in the face of such rigid and formidable forces of retrenchment.

Although most African Americans never received permanent ownership of forty acres, the initial effort was as inspiring for the formerly enslaved as it was terrifying for the former slaveholders. The attempt to redistribute lands as a form of reparations was potentially transformative to the freed people along the coast, but Sherman made an indelible imprint on the very character and identity of the city of Atlanta as well. In fact, although he was essential to the city's history and its narrative of a determined and industrious spirit, the general also meant something different for Atlanta's white citizens and its black citizens. Much like the Battle of Atlanta, Sherman's meaning was drawn from subjective positionality. For some he was a leitmotif of Union aggression and war crimes, but for others he was a harbinger of freedom, justice, and even righteous vengeance.

Through Sherman's aggression, black people found the freedom that had been denied for generations in America. And for many, no doubt, there was a catharsis in witnessing their cruel captors—who had caused them unfathomable injury—flee, cower, and be defeated in battle. In the end, black people, though denied the promised forty acres, founded small communities that attempted to realize the dream for land. At the start of the Civil War, only twenty-five free black people lived in Atlanta; by 1865, hundreds had poured into the town. They amassed near the camp of federal soldiers and formed a desperate yet hopeful community named in honor of the most immediate agent of their new freedom, Sherman. Shermantown became the nucleus of Atlanta's first free black community.[88] It was in this whirlwind of progress and retrenchment that black people formed a hub of freedom in Atlanta and established an arena for worship, commerce, education, and leisure. Although most inhabitants would remain in poverty, the community eventually became known as Sweet Auburn, named for its main avenue. It would be home to much of the heart of the history of black Atlanta and its own notion of black self-determination, collective confidence, and pride in black institution building. It was here where Afro-self-determinism matured and became institutionalized in profound ways. Indeed, the fealty to Atlanta's Confederate heritage and ideals required that black advancement could happen only with such self-determinative action.

In many respects, the Civil War forged a New South that was cast in the likeness of its predecessor in regard to the racial order—only updated to accommodate the modern requirements of wage labor. As John Hope Franklin explained, the process was "Reconstruction, Confederate style."[89] Poor whites remained the majority, and the vast majority of black people were politically isolated: denied access to due process, equal education, health care, and civil rights. Like the slaveholder elites of the Old South, but under a new name, a small minority of white southerners enjoyed considerable wealth, power, and influence. More importantly, they enjoyed the fealty of poor whites who, like their lot a generation earlier, had been invested in a racial order that offered them little material comfort. No city in the region was as central to the rhetoric of a New South as Atlanta, and no person was more essential to that boosterism than Henry Grady, as Chapter 4 will demonstrate.

4 | Redeeming Atlanta
Neo-Confederacy and Political Power

[The] very last [Confederate] survivor will go down to his grave worshipping
at the shrine of Lee and Jackson, and loving the memory of Grady.
—CONFEDERATE SOLDIERS HOME OF GEORGIA BOARD OF DIRECTORS,
EULOGY FOR HENRY GRADY, 1890

In the mid-1880s the American Panorama Company in Milwaukee
commissioned a group of German immigrant artists to paint an ambitious homage to the Battle of Atlanta. Called "Atlanta Cyclorama," it
depicted an exact moment in the historic battle that shaped the outcome of national history: 4:45 p.m. on July 22, 1864. At that moment,
as thousands of troops clashed in the Gate City, the fate of the battle
remained unknown. Rebel brigades had succeeded in capturing Yankee
artillery and had broken through a Union line. The picture was a massive panoramic view of that historic 1864 summer evening, filled with
a mix of charging, flailing bodies and the smoke of assorted weaponry.

It invited the viewer to imagine the howls and screams of men killing and being killed, layered on top of the sounds of rifles, cannon bursts, and the whinnying of horses. The color painting, meant to be dramatically speculative, featured Union general John Logan charging against Confederates with reinforcements. There was no clear victor and no obvious loser. If the story had followed to the day's conclusion, it would have shown a Union victory over Confederates, but it captured only a moment in time where the tide could have gone in either direction. That was the story of the Cyclorama. The artistic capture of that single moment provided an opportunity for Atlanta's boosters to tinker with history. For some, it was a way to rewrite the past to meet contemporary emotional, civic, and political demands. Paul Atkinson, a native Georgian, purchased the Atlanta Cyclorama in 1892 and set out to retell the famous Battle of Atlanta: the boys in gray were transformed into dominating troops who pushed back scattering federals. The original painted scene was "all right to the son of a federal soldier. . . . But it don't sit so well with the son of a Confederate."[1] He, like many others in the capital of the New South, felt that when the actual history proved inconvenient, an alternative one could be crafted to meet the needs of the day.

A promoter of various entertainment venues, Atkinson initially took the Cyclorama to Chattanooga, Tennessee, before he established its permanent home in Atlanta. He ordered gray uniforms to be repainted blue, and he changed Confederate POWs into Union prisoners. The Cyclorama's nod to the Union's impending defeat was underscored by the addition of fallen and mangled American flags on the ground. The locals in Atlanta loved the alternative history. The plaudits rolled in from the *Atlanta Constitution*, which called it "wonderful" because "it is the only one in existence where the Confederates get the best of things." Another promotional flyer exclaimed that it was "the only Confederate victory ever painted."[2] In many ways the Atlanta Cyclorama embodies the contested memories of the Civil War and the efforts of local boosters to cultivate and promote a civic identity that simultaneously celebrated its Confederate history and reified its social, cultural, and political steadfastness. This steadfastness, of course, was connected to an old racial order that found democracy, racial equality, and justice for all to be anathema. It was an expression of white southern nationalism that had space for black people—in fact, demanded it—but only as subordinates. Moreover, the monument itself was one of many public attempts to reorder historical outcomes to meet the convenient needs of boosters who claimed that the Confederacy was a righteous, honorable, and just experiment in nation building. Although the government was "defeated," the rebel cause was never fully buried or forgotten. Indeed, as many Confederate sympathizers would make known, the defeat of the Confederacy meant only that its cause would adapt to any political circumstances that might appear. As an emerging icon of the New South, Atlanta moved into the new century with a clear-eyed sense of purpose and a Janus-faced look to the future and modernity accompanied by a reverent gaze into its antiquated quasi-industrial recent past.

Late nineteenth-century Atlanta saw the development of political forces that ultimately repressed the advancement of legally sanctioned racial equality by using a range of codified measures. When those measures proved insufficient, extralegal forces, mob violence, terrorism, and simple quotidian affronts to human dignity were exercised. More often than not, however, the pawns of these machinations—poor whites—fell in line as supplicants to the elites, much as their yeoman predecessors had submitted to planter elites in the antebellum era. Poor whites in Atlanta and across the state had received little in material benefit for their loyalty to the rich. In fact, millions of white voters (overwhelmingly poor) had been disenfranchised across the South as measures were taken to deprive black men of the vote. In Georgia, about one-third of white voters were removed from voting rolls during the late nineteenth century.[3] The rise of Populists such as Tom Watson

in the 1890s caused brief disruptions to poor whites' collective obeisance to the ruling class. Still, the racial solidarity promulgated by the
wealthiest of whites almost always enjoyed a receptive audience in the
region's white poor. This is what W. E. B. Du Bois, in *Black Reconstruction in America*, referred to as a "public and psychological wage" for
whites of all classes. Elevated social status was granted to all whites,
but the poor, in particular, craved it. And though "otherwise exploited
by the organization of capitalism," most whites understood that "the
value of whiteness depends on the devaluation of black [people]."[4]

In Atlanta the challenges of upholding the myth of white racial
confraternity remained a feat that could be accomplished only with
hardened legal divisions that affected every facet of life. It was in this
oppressive environment that African Americans, out of necessity,
cultivated new institutions and self-determination that would prove
foundational to an incredibly vibrant and dynamic center of black
exceptionalism. Meanwhile, universal whiteness, which transcended
ethnicity, nationality, and religion, continued to benefit the ruling
class, but for it to have the greatest utility, it had to provide a space for
poor whites. It helped consolidate power in the hands of the wealthy,
staving off reformist and racial threats and social movements that
addressed issues specific to the working poor. In many instances, the
proto-fascistic appeal of the Confederacy militated against radicalism,
reform, and social justice. It provided an almost mythic ideal of southern nationalism that, by design, embraced universal whiteness and the
subjugation of black people. To challenge it was to challenge southern
identity and its narrow constructs of patriotism.

In 1886, three days before Christmas, Henry Grady, the famed
journalist and editor of the *Atlanta Constitution*, addressed the New
England Club in New York City. Grady was perhaps the first and
most famous booster for the city of Atlanta and for the New South.
He celebrated Atlanta as the capital of the South and as a center of
great industrial promise in a somewhat bold and prescient promotion.

In fact, Atlanta was not the largest city in the South. New Orleans was more than three times its size, and forty-one US cities were also larger, including Fall River, Massachusetts; Toledo, Ohio; and Allegheny, Pennsylvania. Still, Grady tirelessly promoted Atlanta as a major city that deserved attention as a locus of economic, cultural, and even educational activity for the New South. It was the embodiment of the hope, drive, spirit, and determination of the region.[5]

In contrast to its former primitive economy, based on enslaving millions of men, women, and children, the New South, as Grady described it, was a forward-looking, industrious region unburdened by prejudice, hatred, or sloth. As he told the crowd,

> The old South rested everything on slavery and agriculture, unconscious that these could neither give nor maintain healthy growth. The new South presents a perfect democracy, the oligarchs leading in the popular movement; a social system compact and closely knitted, less splendid on the surface, but stronger at the core; a hundred farms for every plantation, fifty homes for every palace; and a diversified industry that meets the complex needs of this complex age.[6]

Grady, known for his charisma and wit, measured his audience and referred to the sectional conflicts that had arisen around slavery twenty-five years earlier. As fate would have it, General Sherman decided to attend Grady's lecture. There, perhaps curious about this famed Atlantan whose father was killed in battle while fighting for the Confederacy, Sherman attentively listened when Grady recognized him in the audience. Not to stoke any bitterness, Grady quickly stated that people of Georgia thought Sherman an effective military leader, "though some . . . think he is a kind of careless man about fire."[7] The crowd immediately laughed. Grady's humor and his praise of Abraham Lincoln as the "first typical American, the first who comprehended

within himself . . . all the majesty and grace of this Republic," put the
crowd at ease and demonstrated a magnanimity that promoted efforts
at reintegration of the South into the fabric of the United States. However, Grady did not fail to take subtle jabs at his northern compatriots
or veer too far from extolling the virtues of the Confederacy.

The New England states, he explained, eventually outlawed
slavery—years before a bloody war would force the collapse of the practice in Grady's South. Yet, understanding the economic imperative of
New England's decision, Grady noted that New Englanders were "not
to be blamed for parting with what didn't pay—sold their slaves to
our fathers—not to be praised for knowing a paying thing when they
saw it." The crowd was perhaps reminded of their forefathers' pecuniary interests at the expense of moral outrage. Moreover, many of those
assembled on that day may have similarly appreciated a shared interest
in profit at the expense of justice or equality for all. But Grady understood a general concern that some in the audience may have had about
the white South's ability to overcome its inveterate hostility to racial
equality, fairness, and justice.

Grady did not equivocate. This New South was not the South that
fought to defend slavery:

> We understand that when Lincoln signed the Emancipation
> Proclamation, your victory was assured; for he then committed
> you to the cause of human liberty, against which the arms of
> man cannot prevail; while those of our statesmen who trusted to
> make slavery the cornerstone of the Confederacy doomed us to
> defeat as far as they could, committing us to a cause that reason
> could not defend or the sword maintain in the sight of advancing
> civilization.

Grady was clear that the New South had to move beyond racial
subjugation, tyranny, and hatred. The audience was captivated, and it

applauded when the Atlanta-based journalist insisted that the New South had been inspired, in part, by the example of the forward-thinking, industrious North. He even implied that notions of racial justice had grown in southern soil, perhaps sown by northern efforts:

> Let the record speak to the point. No section shows a more prosperous laboring population than the Negroes of the South, none in fuller sympathy with the employing and land-owning class. He shares our school fund, has the fullest protection of our laws and the friendship of our people. Self-interest, as well as honor, demand that he should have this. Our future, our very existence depend upon our working out this problem in full and exact justice.[8]

Even with his pronouncements of racial goodwill, he described black people as not actual southerners—even those native born for generations on southern soil. The term *southerner*, much like the terms *northerner* and *Yankee*, unless otherwise qualified, was tacitly reserved for whites in those respective categories. When Grady discussed southerners, he was discussing white people exclusively: "The relations of the Southern people with the Negro are close and cordial." It is in this context that black citizens in this region were, even in the aftermath of the Civil War, not understood to be full citizens but quasi-citizens, an alterity, intended to be mere accessories to the landscape and part of the human capital for white enterprise—whether enslaved or free. Black people were no more expected to be southerners than they were expected to be leaders in the political, social, cultural, or educational institutions across the region. Inasmuch as "all men are created equal" in the Declaration of Independence did not extend to all men, "southerner" did not capture all those who were southerners. Therefore, it is important to understand that when Grady extolled the virtues of justice, fairness, and equality, his rhetoric must be understood in the context of his day. It excluded the application of those very virtues to all people with the same brazen assumption that any proclamations for freedom and justice for all were to be understood as freedom and justice for "most white men."

As Grady constructed the initial tale of Atlanta exceptionalism, three themes emerged as descriptors: (1) a progressive, business-friendly city; (2) a city that had disavowed the cruel practice of slavery; and (3) a city that endorsed racial cooperation and justice. Perhaps it was Grady's measure of his audience of northeasterners, whom he may have assumed to view the Confederacy and slavery as anathema, but the master of boosterism made no effort to rewrite the legacy of the Confederacy and its investment in white supremacy and slavery. And back in his hometown, neither did lawmakers, but for very different reasons.

Although Henry Grady was the most prominent promoter of Atlanta as the capital of an industrial New South, dozens of people traversed the country in the late nineteenth century touting the attractive qualities of the Gate City. The railroad industry, which had been the cornerstone for the development of Atlanta and the core of its importance during the war, was swift to rebuild. Within a generation after the war, all four lines had been rebuilt and were better than before. Of course, the city's boosters were apt to extol Atlanta's advantages as a hub for railroads, but even visitors from across the country and abroad were impressed. An Englishman who was traveling across the southeastern US explained that the city was notable. A "Yankee" told him to "get to Atlanta." From there, "you can get anywhere on God's airth."[9] Businessmen and representatives of the city promoted the city for conventions, even employing classic hyperbole in the process. In 1893, the same year that Chicago hosted the World's Fair and was on its way to being the fastest-growing city on Earth, some of Atlanta's most zealous celebrants went as far as to compare their hometown to the Windy City. Insisting that the city had moved past sectional acrimony and crude, inefficient business practices, Thomas Peters, vice president of the National Association of Life Underwriters, promoted the city as ideal for future conventions and investment. In the insurance group's annual meeting, Peters, on behalf of Atlantans, explained that "we know nothing now, but the ways of peace. You will find your battle-fields smiling with crops of grain and scarcely a vestige of war." He went on to laud the remarkable work ethic of the city, which "never does things by halves." In fact, "we are the Chicago of the South."[10] The rebuilding and development of Atlanta as the de facto capital of the New South was a result of resilience and determination. The fact that boosters could uphold Atlanta with its 1890 population of 65,533 as a veritable Chicago of the South may have appeared absurd to most. But the comparison to a city seventeen times its size was noteworthy for multiple reasons. In addition to being quintessential hyperbolic promotion, it drew subtle attention to the fact that Atlanta, like Chicago, had resurged from destruction. Chicago had been largely destroyed by the fire of 1871. Yet in a span of twenty years, Chicago had grown from being the fifth-largest city—smaller than St. Louis—to being second only to New York City. Despite more than a hundred thousand people losing homes and the destruction of more than 73 miles of roads, 120 miles of sidewalk, 17,500 buildings, and $222 million in property, Chicago famously rebounded.[11] It was an internationally known story of determination and grit. Atlanta, its promoters boasted, was cut from a similar cloth of resilience.

Grady's 1886 speech to New Englanders is often referenced as a major national message of white southern magnanimity and evolving notions of justice, democracy, and freedom, but it was not the first such expression. Seven years before Grady's famous speech, Georgia governor Joseph E. Brown provided his own recounting of the motivation to secede. In an 1879 letter to a New Englander who lived in the South, Brown addressed the racial landscape of his home state and noted that the racial order had mutated in ways that few had fathomed a generation earlier:

While speaking of the feeling that exists between the two races,
I might here remark that hundreds of thousands of Southern men
laid down their lives during [the Civil War] to sustain their view
of the Government, and especially to sustain slavery. And hundreds of thousands more would have made the same sacrifices if
it could have resulted in success, so earnest and strong was the
conviction on our part that we were right, and that it was best
for both races that slavery exist. And experience of a little over a
dozen years under the new order of things, which we supposed to
be insupportable, has shown us that we were mistaken in many of
our most cherished ideas. While the abolition of slavery has been
a terrible loss to us in a pecuniary point of view and has resulted
most distastrously [sic] to many . . . families, we are led now to
conclude that it was the will of Providence that it should occur,
and that in the future our children and their posterity will be a
more prosperous, self-reliant, useful, and happy people than they
would have been if the institutions had been maintained.

Brown concluded by speculating that "probably not 1 in every 500
[whites] in Georgia . . . would vote to re-establish slavery, or would
consent to have it re-established, under any circumstances."[12] Here,
Brown, who had earlier offered a defiant full-throated defense of white
nationalism, white supremacy, secession, and slavery, showed that he
had evolved on many matters in the postbellum years. And although
he retreated from defending slavery as a divinely sanctioned right, he
did not reimagine secession without slavery as a primary cause. His
letter may have been tempered by his sense of its intended reader, yet
Brown appears not to have offered a revision of recent history or offered
any effort to expunge slavery from the raison d'être of the Confederacy. Instead, he magnanimously offered a declaration of newfound
clarity on the issue of slavery. However, other southerners argued that
the Civil War was a "lost cause" that destroyed their idyllic antebellum

world, where wealthy white enslavers were kind, warm, just, and honorable in their rule over joyfully enslaved black people.

It has long been said that history is written by the victor. However, the Union's victory in the Civil War almost immediately proved to be a contested event in historical memory. Unlike subsequent wars involving the United States (World War II, for example), the defeated army was not a foreign power. And unlike Nazi Germany, the victors did not immediately outlaw the symbols and ideology of the defeated. The great majority of the enemy's leadership was not convicted of war crimes, or executed for other crimes, up to and including treason. Instead, its leadership found itself back in power and authority throughout the South. There was no southern disavowal of the ideology that caused the war. The provincial nature of state governments, and their autonomy with public-school curricula, allowed for disparate narratives of the Civil War, its causes, and its consequences. The Lost Cause rhetoric formed immediately, but it was not an entirely static one. It evolved and adapted to various audiences over time, reflecting shifting values and meanings of democracy, patriotism, race, and slavery.

Following the collapse of the Confederacy, the South—and then the nation—witnessed the resurrection of its spirit. "When the idea of a southern nation was defeated on the battlefield," David Williams argues, "the vision of a separate southern people, with a distinct and noble cultural character, remained." Some historians, such as Karen Cox, have called this "Confederate culture," which captures the romantic cultivation and practice of rituals, ideas, myths, and symbols of the Old South. The Atlanta white elite broadly embraced this sentiment and conspicuously tried to make it inherent in the development of an Atlanta civic character. Williams notes that a "Lost Cause religion sought to maintain the concept of a distinct, and superior, white southern culture against perceived attacks. Major components of religion include myth, symbol, and their expressions through rituals. The Lost Cause culture religion manifested all three."[13]

The southern belief that the defeat by the Union was a "lost cause" was documented shortly after the collapse of the Confederacy. Virginia native Edward A. Pollard published a book only two years after the war that popularized the phrase. *The Lost Cause: A New Southern History of the War of the Confederates* offered a clear celebration of southern nationalism. Those who took up arms against their own country in a bloody campaign that laid waste to more than three-quarters of a million American lives were transformed into noble and—ironically—patriotic figures. As Pollard argues, the dignity in fighting for "tradition" and "freedom" inspired Confederates. But, as he explains, the protection and defense of slavery were not incongruent with these ideals. In fact, he did not equivocate on the "shameless" efforts of the federal government to end slavery. He insisted that the federal government's evolving position on abolition was based on rhetorical "deception" and a "crooked path . . . attended with marks of perfidy." The aggression of northern "invaders" and their "odious flag" only provoked Confederate military reprisals.[14] Years later, Clement Evans, a Confederate veteran from Georgia, explained the essential nature of slavery relative to the Civil War: "If we cannot justify the South in the act of Secession, we will go down in History solely as a brave, impulsive but rash people who attempted in an illegal manner to overthrow the Union of our Country." But Evans argued that Confederates should not fear the "verdict of history." As John C. Calhoun of South Carolina in the antebellum era argued, the Constitution protected the right of secession. Those who opted to leave the United States were legally able to do so, Evans insisted. In an argument that avoided the moralistic justifications for human trafficking, the case had shifted to a legal one.[15]

Over time, the Lost Cause muted the importance of slavery in secession. As slavery grew to be more widely understood as a barbaric practice, the more noble principles of "tradition," "honor," and even defense against "invaders" moved to the center as the primary justifications for the Confederacy. These were subsumed in a vague yet utilitarian term: "states' rights." No one disputed that the federal government and the southern states had fought over the issue of slavery. Scores of southern politicians from John Calhoun to Jefferson Davis openly discussed their defense of slavery in Congress and elsewhere in the years leading up to the Civil War. They had long perceived slavery as threatened by the power of northern states and their influence in federal government. But what had once been openly and boldly discussed as the foundational cause for debates over states' rights had been only nebulously referenced in subsequent decades. Slavery slowly became marginally important to the secessionist cause in the decades after the war. But any scrutiny of the argument that protecting states' rights was foundational to the Confederacy demands a central question: right to do what, exactly? For slaveholding states, their right to enslave was threatened by a Lincoln administration, as detailed in Chapter 1. The argument that protection of "states' rights" animated the Confederate cause conveniently ignores the South's hostility toward northern states' rights. For example, southern states fought against the right of a state to protect the freedom of anyone who had escaped from slavery and found refuge in a northern state. The right of Massachusetts to grant freedom to someone who escaped slavery in Virginia was nullified by the Fugitive Slave Law of 1850 and the infamous Dred Scott case of 1857. Therefore, "states' rights" had never been more than a rhetorical ploy, not a principled application of law. Regardless, as rhetorical devices evolved, the useful catchall "states' rights" gained traction in the Confederate culture campaign.

By the late nineteenth century, the Lost Cause narrative was not only a corruption of actual history; it was also a way in which white southern culture found some redemption in its reframing of the past. It allowed defenders of the Confederacy a morally acceptable perspective that assuaged any collective sense of moral, religious, and even patriotic guilt. It helped mitigate notions that they, or their parents, had suffered from grave moral turpitude. It reconciled ideas of southern identity, regional pride, familial pride, provincial dignity, and sacrifice.

On a very intimate level, millions of southerners could honestly and intimately speak to the kindness, affection, love, and service that they witnessed from fathers, brothers, sons, uncles, and others who served in the Confederacy. Many of them suffered unimaginable loss from amputations, death, financial devastation, and other trauma. In many ways the Lost Cause was a much-needed psychological and cultural palliative tool that granted white southerners a way to provide a rejoinder to the country's master narrative of the war.

In Lost Cause retelling, human traffickers who brutally pried crying babies from their mothers' arms gave way to kind patriarchs who oversaw peaceful plantations with happy slaves. Sexual predators of women and girls were supplanted by chivalrous men who doted on their families. Sadistic masters and cruel mistresses were transformed into civilized and moral heads of sophisticated high society. Lost Cause advocates created provincial master narratives where "leading characters in this fiction were elite, white, and wealthy, the planters and plantation mistresses. The Old South was recalled as a region led by benevolent masters who were supported by genteel women, both of whom were rewarded by the faithfulness of slaves."[16] The mythic archetypes of the Lost Cause and Confederate culture had as much a therapeutic role as a practical one for maintaining the old racial order. Additionally, these narratives subverted the Union victory in their very hagiographic retelling of Confederate history. They heralded the southern nationalist past and demanded that contemporaries make the South great again with the political resources at their disposal. In Atlanta, Redeemers emerged as the agents of that effort to revisit the glory of the Old South.

By the 1880s, as Redeemers affirmed control of the South, the revitalization of the Confederacy and its symbols vigorously unfolded as celebratory homages to a proud heritage of white southern nationalism.

Across the South, streets, schools, hospitals, parks, and neighborhoods were named after Confederate leaders. With a near-fanatical verve, Atlanta's leaders moved rapidly to celebrate the city's Confederate heritage. Various streets were named in honor of Confederate national and local leadership. Hardee Street was named after General William Joseph Hardee, and Gordon Place was named after General John Brown Gordon. Lee, Jackson, and Ashby Streets were named after generals Robert E. Lee, Thomas Jonathan "Stonewall" Jackson, and Turner Ashby Jr. General Patrick R. Cleburne, who fought at Shiloh, Chickamauga, and in the Atlanta Campaign had two locations named after him, Cleburne Avenue and Cleburne Terrace. Collier Road and, later, Collier Hills were named for the Collier family, which owned an Atlanta-area plantation and had multiple members serve in the Confederacy. Many of the honors were explicitly tied to the Battle of Atlanta. Manigault Street was named in honor of Brigadier General Arthur M. Manigault, who commanded soldiers against Union troops. Holtzclaw Street was named after Confederate general James T. Holtzclaw, who led rebel forces against US soldiers during the Chattanooga and Atlanta campaigns.[17]

Perhaps the most audacious disregard of any pretense of postwar magnanimity was naming a major downtown Atlanta thoroughfare in honor of Nathan Bedford Forrest, a reputed war criminal who later became the first grand wizard of the Ku Klux Klan. His grandson, Nathan Bedford Forrest II, became grand dragon of the Klan in Georgia during the Second Klan.[18] For city leaders, the Confederates' dedication to the principles of white southern nationalism justified their reverence for the rebels. Moreover, the establishment of these honorific gestures to a pantheon of rebel heroes throughout Atlanta helped enshrine them in the city's landscape in the most conspicuous ways for visitors and locals alike. And as in any city, these namings recognized and honored the past, which simultaneously reflected the values of those who erected them. Finally, they were meant to be permanent testimonies to the character of the city of Atlanta, not mere ephemeral and sentimental plaudits of a passing generation.

Many other Confederates were honored in various ways across Georgia. In fact, several counties, including one honoring Jefferson Davis, were named for Confederates.[19] Sheffield Hale, director of the Atlanta History Center, explains that "southern white communities used monuments to preserve their version of the Civil War. . . . A statue of a Confederate general . . . is not about loss or grief. It is about power."[20] The assertion of power was, in some respects, meant to be directed not only at black Georgians, who were forced to see these everywhere, but also white northerners. Nonsouthern whites consumed images of a romantic Old South in novels, songs, cartoons, and traveling shows. And, of course, these efforts erected a nearly Edenic Old South that was, as C. Vann Woodward details, "one of the most significant inventions of the New South."[21] These artifacts helped form a narrative that affirmed white dominance and rewrote history in the most convenient terms for the social, political, and economic landscape of the day.

The ascendancy of former Confederates and the revision of its history alarmed not only African Americans; many whites were likewise struck by the reframing of the most immediate past. Some Confederates, in an attempt to challenge the moral failures of a cause so devoted to enslaving millions, had begun arguing that the Lost Cause was actually fought for "equality" and "freedom." A former Union general, George Henry Thomas, detailed these efforts at creating a new history of the recent war in an 1868 report:

> The greatest efforts made by the defeated insurgents since the close of the war have been to promulgate the idea that the cause of liberty, justice, humanity, equality, and all the calendar of the virtues of freedom, suffered violence and wrong when the effort for southern independence failed. This is, of course, intended as a species of political cant, whereby the crime of treason might

be covered with a counterfeit varnish of patriotism, so that the precipitators of the rebellion might go down in history hand in hand with the defenders of the government, thus wiping out with their own hands their own stains; a species of self-forgiveness amazing in its effrontery, when it is considered that life and property—justly forfeited by the laws of the country, of war, and of nations, through the magnanimity of the government and people—was not exacted from them.[22]

The efforts to adhere to the fundamental principles of the Old South gave rise to the Confederate culture being promoted in hagiographic public campaigns involving statuary; the naming of schools, streets, towns, and counties; and public-school curricula.[23] Few actions were as visible as the creation of the new Georgia state flag. In 1879, just two years after federal troops were pulled from the South, marking the end of Reconstruction, Georgia state senator Herman H. Perry, a former Confederate major, introduced a bill to celebrate the CSA and its veterans, and, not insignificantly, to express this in a new state flag. What became the state's first official flag was largely derived from the first national flag of the Confederate States of America, known as the Stars and Bars. Like the Stars and Bars, the new flag included two horizontal red bars separated by a white one. It also included a vertical blue band at the hoist, which differed from the square blue union with stars on the upper left on the Confederate flag. On October 17, 1879, Governor Colquitt approved the first official state flag. Raising a neo-Confederate flag immediately after the fall of Reconstruction was a powerful affirmation of the retrenchment of Old South ideals.[24]

Like any flag, this one, hoisted above the state capitol, had no actual authority in and of itself. The flag, like the streets, schools, parks, and counties named for Confederates (or anyone, for that matter), were gestures with no power independent of the decoded meanings embraced by those who engaged with them.[25] The flag was beautiful or ugly, inspirational or terrifying, only through a subjective familiarity with it as a metonymic device. Its meaning was relative only to what people had inscribed in it. For those who paid the flag any attention, it was clear that it was a homage to the Confederacy. And, coupled with the vast set of laws, policies, regulations, and public-sector appointments, the honorific gesture to the rebel government was incongruous with the expansion of black people's freedom or civil rights. The flag was a marker of a very special set of politics, and informed observers understood what it meant. It reminded regional and national audiences of the esteem in which the Confederacy was held. Clearly, the new flag bound the identity of the state of Georgia with the Lost Cause of the Confederacy. It was a not-so-subtle way of publicly asserting this heritage and simultaneously offering a defiant rebuke of the authority of the federal government and its Reconstruction efforts.

W. E. B. Du Bois, the famous historian and civil rights activist, discussed the creation of monuments to the Confederacy in the decades after the war. The onetime Atlanta resident wrote of

> the awful things that we are compelled to build in order to remember the victims [of war]. In the South, particularly, human ingenuity has been put to it to explain on its war monuments, the Confederacy. Of course, the plain truth of the matter would be an inscription something like this: "Sacred to the memory of those who fought to Perpetuate Human Slavery." But that reads with increasing difficulty as time goes on. It does, however, seem to be overdoing the matter to read on a . . . monument: "Died Fighting for Liberty."[26]

With sardonic commentary, Du Bois draws attention to the inversion of facts regarding Civil War history. In flagrant irony, those who rose to defend enslavement were the great defenders of freedom. Indeed, the Lost Cause had morphed into a veritable social movement with its own set of morals, gnosis, and unifying principles that centered on a narrative of regional honor and values that could never be disentangled from race. The Lost Cause became an important reminder of the fundamental ideals shared by huge swaths of the white South, who organized against any disruption to the racial order. To that end, public statues evolved as panoptic testimonies to the enduring ideals of the Confederacy. They celebrated a victory of the ideals of the rebels—even if political capitulation at Appomattox signified military defeat.

The Lost Cause and its composite elements—Confederate culture and its culture religion—were endemic to the character and development of Atlanta for generations after the Civil War. Atlanta had emerged as a locus of frenetic energy for the New South. Like many cities across the industrialized West, the chasms that separated the worlds of the haves and the have-nots were palpable. And much like the Old South, there was a gaping chasm between wealthy and poor whites, despite rhetorical and symbolic gestures that suggested interclass white confraternity by the late nineteenth century. Cloistered in dilapidated shanties in the Fourth Ward, in Shermantown, Buttermilk Bottoms, and Cabbagetown, white and black poor carved out racially separated spaces for survival in a tough, dirty, insalubrious landscape with very little in the way of genteel philanthropic munificence. Unpaved streets, outhouses, diseased-filled neighborhoods, and the attendant dangers of people living in desperation marked these communities. Wealthy whites, in contrast, basked in their excess along Peachtree in Midtown, Grant Park, or north toward Buckhead: expansive homes, servants, paved roads, sewage, indoor plumbing, and access to the best hospitals and schools that money could afford. The Atlanta newspapers brought attention to the expansion of new enclaves for the wealthy throughout the city. In 1896, the same year that the US Supreme Court legally upheld racial segregation in public spaces, local newspapers covered the new suburb of a planned neighborhood in Inman Park. The *Atlanta Constitution* gushed over the community:

High up above the city, where the purest breezes and the brightest sunshine drove away the germs of disease, and where nature
had lavished her best gifts, the gentlemen who conceived the
thought of Inman Park found the locality above all others which
they desired. It was to be a place of homes, of pretty homes, green
lawns, and desirable inhabitants. And all save those who would
make desirable residents have been excluded. . . . It's the prettiest,
highest, healthiest and most desirable locality I ever saw. Everybody is friendly and neighborly.[27]

Like new homes and communities across the country, these homes
were available only to whites. Newer southern cities were more likely to
be segregated. By the time Inman Park opened, "The vast majority of
blocks in Atlanta, Richmond, and Montgomery were either all-white
or all-black." Racial segregation was acute, of course. Class segregation,
however consequential to quality-of-life outcomes from infant mortality, education, and life expectancy, did little to disrupt poor-white
affinity for the economic interests of wealthy whites. However, the rub
was that these homes were nearly as inaccessible to poor whites as they
were to wealthy black people.[28]

The world of the ruling class (mansions, plantations, servants—free
or enslaved) may have been nearly impossible to reach, but there was
always just enough of a possibility of doing so that the white poor did
not want to destroy the order of things. Its destruction would deny any
chance of achieving that dream—no matter how improbable it was.
Poor whites were historically loath to imagine casting their lot with
black people facing similar class-based struggles. Universal whiteness
always had a certain appeal, and the visibility of black marginality was
always important to that appeal.

The Confederacy's defeat was immediately made less traumatizing to large swaths of the South because of the generous conditions
of amnesty that President Andrew Johnson offered. In addition to

regaining seized lands, the overwhelming majority of the leadership avoided persecution for treason. Most significantly, they regained the right to vote and to elect former Confederates to office across the South. In Georgia, the defiance was so great that the former vice president of the Confederacy, Alexander Stephens, was elected to the US Senate, although he was refused a seat. Former Confederates were elected to local, county, and state positions. In Atlanta, Confederates and pro-Confederates were elected to the city council and the mayor's office, as Mayor James Calhoun was succeeded by James E. Williams, an avowed secessionist. Across the country, nine officers from the Confederate military were elected to the US Congress. Nearly sixty former Confederates were sent to Congress by 1871. Georgia's Confederate governor, Joseph Brown, served in the Senate from 1880 to 1890. These were not simply reformed politicians. In general, they remained deeply committed to white nationalism.

Importantly, the former Confederates, reconstituted as Redeemers, did not concede that surrender in defeat meant disengagement from the political halls of power or acceptance of racial equality. Indeed, Stephens's famous cornerstone speech resonated in the aftermath of the war. When the federal government considered intervention to repress the tide of terrorist acts against advocates of democracy, many Atlantans mocked the effort as mere political spectacle even as people were beaten and murdered. Refuting white-supremacist organizations as a threat, pundits argued that President Grant, in forming the Department of Justice and maintaining Reconstruction, was chasing a phantom problem that existed only to keep his name in the news. The *Atlanta Intelligencer* exclaimed that congressional witnesses "manufacture for [officials] a 'tale of horror'" about the Ku Klux Klan.[29] Local officials largely refused to pursue terror groups. There was no retreat from the driving principle of white supremacy.

A confluence of fear and antipathy prompted the unwillingness of witnesses to testify against terrorists and other criminals. One federal agent explained that such fear also affected well-meaning southern whites. A law-abiding white man "is fearful, timid and trembling" in the climate of vast hate and indifference to law.[30] For years after the end of the Civil War, the barbarity of racist terror raged undaunted by law or social scorn. A privileged white woman, Eliza Andrews, documented the murder of an elderly woman near Washington, Georgia. The old woman attempted to leave her former enslaver and live her final days in freedom. Two white men stopped her, yet she persisted. One beat her, breaking her ribs, while the other, apparently finding no use for a woman who demanded to be free under the protection of the law, shot her. Her skull was crushed with a stone and her body left unburied. When the white men were arrested for the murder, Andrews echoed common white southern antipathy about black life, focusing on the "poor wife" and "poor old father" of the two killers. As for the violence directed at black Georgians, Andrews echoed the refrain of doubt: "There is only negro evidence for all these horrors, and nobody can tell how much of it is false."[31]

The antipathy to equal protection under the law is but one facet of the neo-Confederate impulse of white nationalism. Black people, whether free or not, would remain outside of the protective elements of citizenship if Redeemers had any control. The denial of citizenship meant that civil rights might or might not be enforced in the case of black people. Beyond the lack of protection from violence, this white nationalism also affected every element of life for black people in Georgia.

For a brief period, the forceful and ambitious efforts of federal authorities, black and white Republicans, and some local whites expanded access to education, health care, and food for all Georgians. The new state constitution created public education in 1868. Public schools had operated throughout the Northeast since the early nineteenth century, and by 1871 several southern cities had created public schools. Even the Georgia cities of Savannah and Augusta established public schools before Atlanta. The first public schools in Atlanta were planned to open in 1872, amid fierce debate about black enrollment. Adhering to the position of a white nationalism that provided exclusively for a white citizenry, many neo-Confederates argued against black education, even within segregated, underfunded schools. The 1870 census found that there were 6,474 prospective students in Atlanta; 48 percent were black. City Councilman Charles W. Wells of Atlanta's First Ward rejected any effort to fund a system that educated black children in any capacity. Of course, any absolute codified denial of a public education would invite further federal attention and intervention, many argued.

Mayor William Henry Husley, a former Confederate officer, endorsed a policy also supported by the president of the city's new board of education, former Confederate-era governor Joseph E. Brown. The plan endorsed a school system that granted three new schools for white students only. These were initially grammar schools and high schools combined, separated along age. Two private black grammar schools were absorbed into the public school system in an effort to offer black Atlantans a meager level of public education. African Americans were denied access to any public high school for decades.[32] The realization of a full-throated white-nationalist project had its limitations, but it was still an effective implementation of the fundamental ideals of the Confederacy and granted a degree of agility when circumstances demanded it.

As noted earlier, throughout the South and in Georgia in particular, the Confederates witnessed their loss at war as a catastrophic defeat and a fundamental threat to their existence. Over the subsequent years of Reconstruction, however, resistance to black advancement and to a range of liberties gave way to a creative "compromise" of sorts between the economic, social, and cultural traditions of the Old South and the ambitious freedoms of the postwar landscape. In Atlanta the notion that the Confederacy's legacy was inextricable to the city's identity was bolstered by a number of factors. It was the new state capital and a seat of public as well as industrial power for the region. It was also one of the most important cities for the Confederacy during the Civil War. Within two generations following the war, the city's boosters crafted an image of Atlanta as the veritable capital of the New South. Simultaneously, as the city assumed the distinction in this role, it amplified its Confederate heritage as a virtual natural fit to its municipal identity. No men were as essential to this process as Joseph E. Brown, Alfred H. Colquitt, and John B. Gordon. Brown, of course, had served as the fiery Confederate governor of Georgia, and the last two were major generals during the war. As three of the most powerful ex-Confederates, these men forged a political base that sought neo-Confederate policies throughout the state.

As governor, Brown was a fierce opponent of Confederate president Jefferson Davis and the growing power of the CSA central government. He futilely scrambled for help when Sherman marched into Georgia and bitterly opposed Davis's desperate late-war plan to fight the Union forces by augmenting Confederate troops with enslaved black men who could achieve freedom through their service. Following the Civil War, Brown was arrested, but like many high-ranking Confederate officials, he was freed shortly thereafter. He was paroled but received a full pardon from President Johnson in September 1865.[33]

The Farmers' Alliance, a national movement of agrarian workers, made demands, from banking reform to direct elections of senators, that met deep resistance from both major political parties. And despite the decline of the alliance, the move toward a third party crystallized with the People's Party, popularly known as the Populist Party. In 1892 it ran a presidential candidate, James B. Weaver, and various other candidates in state and local elections across the United States. The party took an especially strong hold in Georgia, where William L. Peek ran for governor and Thomas E. Watson, a congressman who had defected from the Democratic Party, ran for reelection as a Populist. The vast majority of the white vote in Georgia adhered to the Democratic Party, but the new upstart political party understood the critical need to expand its odds with black voters, who were locked out of any meaningful voice in statewide politics following Reconstruction.[34]

The challenge of attracting black voters to a party dominated by people who had been intractably hostile to black suffrage was self-evident. Many (if not most) older Populists in Georgia had fought for, among other things, keeping black people enslaved, as had many Democrats. It was widely known that some Populists, in addition to being former Confederates, were also members of the Ku Klux Klan. William Pledger, a black Republican in Georgia, argued that "the men who lynched colored people in the past; the men who shot and robbed colored people; the men who precipitated the 'Camilla Riot,' and the men who marshaled the red shirter and night rider" were the Populists of the 1890s.[35] But in a generation that saw the tremendous transformation of the country from one that openly regulated the enslavement and sale of babies to one that outlawed slavery and then codified universal male suffrage, some African Americans were willing to accept that these men had morally, ethically, and politically evolved. There was evidence that this was true.

The Populist Party was an ideologically distinct organization from the Democratic Party of the New South. In fact, whereas the southern Democrats provided ideological continuity between the Old South and the New South, the Populists were discontinuous with the old racial order in many ways. The southern wing of the Democratic Party was home to secessionists Robert E. Lee, Benjamin Hill, Alexander Stephens, and Jefferson Davis: a rebel government and a rebel military. As a postbellum conservative party, it continued to provide cover for the most recalcitrant and barbaric forces that resisted the expansion of democracy. It was the party of the former Confederates who attempted to adjust white supremacy to—ever so slightly—accommodate the demands for the Constitution while simultaneously militating against rights for black people. The Populist Party, in addition to advocating for black voting rights, agreed with the demands of black leaders in the state, such as Tunis Campbell and Henry McNeal Turner, to terminate the convict-lease system. The system infamously and disproportionately held black people as quasi-slaves to be leased as labor for private companies. As mentioned above, Campbell, one of the most powerful black politicians in the state, had even been arrested, neutralized, and sent into this system. Populists went further, denouncing lynching, a practice that had emerged in the aftermath of emancipation to fortify racial domination in the most brutal, lawless, and public ways.[36]

One of the most charismatic leaders of the Populist Party, Tom Watson, emerged as a powerful advocate for common rights for black and white Georgians. Born into a wealthy family of southern nationalists in 1856, Watson was part of a household on a thousand-acre plantation in McDuffie County that enslaved forty-five people. His father had volunteered to serve in the Confederacy and was wounded twice in the war. And although Watson, who became a lawyer and landowner, did not advocate for social equality between whites and blacks, he did depart substantively from his Confederate legacy by calling into question the justness and efficacy of the southern ruling elite and its postbellum designs for a New South by arguing for political and economic equality between blacks and whites.[37]

Founding editor of the *People's Party Paper*, Watson ascended through the ranks of the Populist movement and went as far as to demand full voting rights for all men in the state, regardless of race. He supported black delegates to the party's state convention and endorsed black participation in the state campaign committee in 1894. He not only emerged as the most popular Populist in Georgia; by the mid-1890s, Watson was also the leading Populist in the South and had become a critical figure in forging a New South that was a fundamental disruption of its old cast. It is true that the Republicans had dismantled slavery, realized birthright citizenship, and expanded democracy in the region, but the Populists offered a critical examination of economics in a way that the GOP did not. The intraracial class cleavages among whites across the country were never a primary concern for Republicans. In the South the party of Lincoln did not address gross economic inequality any more than Democrats had. Alternatively, the Populists provided an organic, provincial expression to the ideological scope of their party. Although it was a national organization, the local Populist Party, being so new, was decidedly Georgian in its demands, mobilization, and fundamental political expression.[38] And the role of race was central to the viability of this movement. Watson was clear that the Populists were the actual Redeemers of the South; he tried to present "a platform immensely beneficial to both races and injurious to neither."[39]

Writing and delivering speeches in a language that was part Radical Republican and part socialist, Watson drew upon the recent history of his country, his state, and the divisions of race. The rhetoric of white supremacy did not serve the interests of the mass of southerners. In the attempt to perpetuate the morally corrupt system of domination through concentrated power and wealth, racism did not empower most whites; instead, it functioned as a "keystone arch of financial despotism that enslaves . . . both [races] and a money system that beggars . . . both [races]."[40] His appeal was powerful, and it drew African Americans into the Populist fold by the thousands. Watson rejected the old conservative Democratic notion that black voters were "straw men": pliant and easily manipulated tools of Republicans. Watson understood that black voters were driven by substantive issues and concerns about their political, economic, and social conditions. Therefore, ensuring their turnout and support was crucial for making a strong case. And in a Georgia political context where many African Americans could still vote, he understood that terror and intimidation were not effective tools to expand the appeal of the Populists.

Justice, economic reform, and civil rights for all made a good case. For whites, however, notions of racial equality—regardless of how strongly that appeals for economic justice resonated—could undermine Populism. To that end, Watson made his case to African Americans: "I pledge you my word and honor that if you stand shoulder to shoulder with us in this fight, you shall have fair play and fair treatment as men and as citizens irrespective of color." But when allegations were made that Watson endorsed "social equality," his rhetoric tempered anxious whites: "They say that I am an advocate of social equality between the whites and blacks. THAT IS AN ABSOLUTE FALSEHOOD. I have done no such things." Watson reiterated that he believed that the races, though fighting for economic and political equity, should be "apart in our private affairs."[41] And given African Americans' own social, religious, and cultural institutions, they were not clamoring for interracial social intimacy either. In many ways, Watson's calculated argument against social integration reflected a familiarity with what black people held as their most essential demands. Afro-self-determinism was already a dominant ideological expression among African Americans. Critically, Watson reflected this sentiment, perhaps extending his appeal to black voters.

Even though Watson did not endorse racial integration in schools and many social spaces, the movement he led was widely viewed as an existential threat to the racial order and to white southern nationalism. Racial confraternity, where whiteness was not exclusively afforded the vote or economic advantage, was effectively treasonous to the neo-Confederate cause. Watson's belief was that regardless of race, rural people—farmers and sharecroppers—shared similar economic circumstances and exploitation. As Populists asked, "Why is not the Colored Tenant open to the conviction that he is in the same boat as the white tenant; the colored laborer and the white laborer?"[42] For many, this was racial heresy. Populists were called "race traitors" and worse. The campaign to destroy the Populist movement was also one to protect neo-Confederacy. And in many ways, the memory of the Civil War was evoked to stoke anti-Populist sentiment.

In 1892 the Populist Party presidential candidate, former Union General James B. Weaver, visited Georgia and was met with wildly hostile crowds that had been primed with stories in the press describing him as a veritable war criminal. He was booed, pelted with eggs (one hitting his wife), and forced off stages. When Tom Watson spoke in Atlanta, hostile crowds jeered and caused such a ruckus that police had to escort him from the premises. The *Atlanta Constitution* did not equivocate on the Populist threat of racial equality to its vision of the New South. Economic justice for poor whites was more repugnant than white supremacy if that economic justice was tethered to equal benefits with black workers. After years of Confederate retrenchment, "The old issue of sectionalism is confronting the South and White Supremacy is more important than all the financial reform in the world."[43] The backlash from the conservative Democrats was swift and, in many instances, violent.

There were black and white coalitions before the 1890s, but conservatives measured Populism—and its demands for reform—as a significant threat to the racial order.[44] Accused of being secret Republicans who wished to reinvigorate Reconstruction and therefore undo what Redeemers had accomplished, Populists were targeted for economic reprisals, public shunning, and physical attacks. The level of violence directed at black Populists was, as expected, more virulent. It is estimated that at least fifteen African Americans were murdered in Georgia during the election of 1892. Several whites were also killed. Watson, despite whatever shortcomings he displayed regarding social integration, offered full-throated protection for his black party members. When a black minister, H. S. Doyle, emerged as one of the most visible black Populists in Georgia, white supremacists targeted him with death threats. On one occasion shots were fired in Doyle's direction, killing a white Populist standing near him. In response, Watson invited Doyle to his estate and called for armed reinforcements from his followers. An estimated two thousand men provided protection.[45]

Conservatives assiduously and aggressively campaigned against the Populists with a range of tactics from violence to actual courting of poor black and white voters. Despite beatings, arson, economic pressures, and food giveaways to poor people, the reasons for black and white support for the Democrats varied almost as widely as the tactics used to undermine the Populists. The most conservative elements of the Democratic Party pandered to white Georgians' racial anxieties and fears, as well as their sense of southern nationalism. They accused Populists of "endangering white supremacy" and joining forces with former slaves. This rhetoric tapped into the regional and racial politics that had not moved far from the Confederate experiment. In fact, Watson's challenger, James C. C. Black, was a former Confederate who referenced his service in the 9th Kentucky Calvary as evidence of his devotion to southern nationalism. Yet the appeal of the incumbent Democratic governor, another ex-Confederate, William J. Northen, was more than paternalistic, courting with free food and drink.

Earlier, Grady, who had endorsed Northen for governor, insisted that he outflank the Populists by appealing to black people while simultaneously reassuring whites that he endorsed white supremacy. Northen took heed and joined the Populist candidate for governor in denouncing lynching, although the rates of lynching in the state suggest that Governor Northen offered few state resources to prevent it. Northen, as governor, also pushed for prison reform, which appealed to African Americans, given the biased carceral policies directed at the black community. In the end, the Democrats carried the governorship and most seats in the 1892 election. Corruption was widespread, and Populism appeared to be defeated.[46]

Two years later, Watson ran for Congress and lost amid extensive corruption and some violence. For the governorship, the Populist James K. Hines lost against W. Y. Atkinson but did garner a respectable 45 percent of the vote. The People's Party also captured five state senator seats and forty-seven representative seats. Watson's losses in Georgia did not deter national supporters from endorsing him in 1896 as the vice-presidential candidate on the Populist fusion ticket with Democrat presidential candidate William Jennings Bryan. Following this loss, Watson retreated from politics altogether for years. The Populist movement dwindled in the second half of the decade, weakened by several factors, including racial politics that continued to sow division between the white poor and the black poor.[47]

The "Atlanta Ring," a group of men of considerable power and wealth, emerged at this time and sought to center the state's cultural, economic, and political power in Atlanta. The Atlanta Ring and its Democratic Party elites organized considerable resources to prevent the spread of the Populist Party, fearing the threat to one-party rule in Georgia. They had long argued that Republicans and "black dupes" would strip power from native white southerners.[48] In the aftermath of the 1894 election, Populist leadership reassessed its strategy amid widespread reports of voter fraud, intimidation, and violence. Because the black vote had been split between Populists and Democrats, many of the former had come to view overtures to black voters as a liability. It drove potential whites away from the party and, despite the efforts, could draw only roughly half of the black vote.[49] Moreover, the black vote, like the Republican Party, had been widely viewed through the prism of white southern nationalism. It was a veritable foil to the spirit of southern independence and a Confederate legacy. And although this rhetoric of appealing to white southern nationalism had its utility in an age of hagiographic memories of the Confederacy, it is too facile to suggest that anti-Populist activity was inextricably tied to pro-Confederacy politics. In fact, as noted above, huge swaths of the Populist leadership and rank-and-file membership in Georgia had Confederate ties. If the Farmers' Alliance membership—which partially overlapped with Populists—is any useful measure, it is notable that in the 1890 state legislature, 60 percent of alliance members were Confederate veterans, and another 30 percent were sons of Confederate veterans. In total, alliance members were 58.3 percent of the state's house members.[50] Indeed, it was difficult to separate native white Georgian politicians from previous Confederate activity, but it was not as difficult to separate them from the ideological fealty to the Old South. Moving away from white southern nationalism was another matter. And the People's Party provided that vehicle for this transition away from the Confederacy's narrow notions of democracy, freedom, and opportunity. However, the task of discrediting and rejecting the politics of white supremacy proved more daunting than many may have expected. The recalcitrant forces of retrenchment prevailed. During the last decade of the nineteenth century, conservative Democrats dominated state governments throughout the South. In Georgia, they exploited racism among the white poor subverting Populists to maintain control of the political apparatus. As Barton Shaw notes, "racist claims drove many whites from the People's Party movement, and [political contests were] marked by fistfights, shootings, and several murders."[51]

Despite the power of neo-Confederates, their political spaces were not without internecine conflict in the late nineteenth century. One of the most dramatic conflicts emerged over debates to establish a publicly supported home for aging Confederate veterans. By 1890, every other former Confederate state had established such a facility. Even the Union states California, Kentucky, Maryland, Missouri, and Oklahoma created these. In Georgia the effort to establish one was met with controversy, indifference, and outright hostility, even from many Confederate veterans. The story stands in stark contrast to the overwhelming fealty to the Confederacy endemic among white Georgians. It is also a portentous indication of the extent to which white southern nationalism could not always appeal to the great majority of whites on one narrow political goal. The one-party rule of the state, which largely sublimated the class interests of poor people for ones that putatively centered on white racial interests, revealed its own frailties and vulnerabilities.

Grady, the leader of New South and Atlanta boosterism, was a key advocate for the Confederate Soldiers' Home. On April 6, 1889, Grady wrote in the *Atlanta Constitution* that southerners should not go to the North soliciting contributions for any philanthropic agendas intended for Confederate veterans. In "Shall We Go Begging for Them?" Grady argued that efforts to raise funds from the North, as former Confederate Joseph M. Stewart had done, were a "painful spectacle" and appeared as "begging." The white South had a "sacred duty" to provide for the "poor and helpless heroes" of the war.[52] To that end, Grady joined a group of Georgians to campaign for the Confederate Soldiers' Home to be established in the state's new capital, Atlanta.

In August 1887 the Atlanta Young Men's Library hosted representatives of the Atlanta Ladies Memorial Association and the Fulton County Veterans Association to discuss the need for a home for the indigent Confederate veterans in the state. Former governor Colquitt, former mayor W. Lowndes Calhoun, Samuel M. Inman, and other notables from politics and business attended. Inman, a close ally of Grady, was a cofounder of the largest cotton business in the city and an investor in a range of other industries, from banking to transportation. In many ways Inman, a former lieutenant in the Confederate Army, was the embodiment of the New South. At the start of the Civil War, his family owned a seventeen-hundred-acre plantation in eastern Tennessee and held twenty-five people in slavery. Samuel and his brother John served in the Confederacy, and when the family relocated to Atlanta after the war, they transitioned into new industries, acquiring extraordinary wealth. Owning successful firms involved with insurance, railroads, banking, real estate, and streetcars, the Inman family (particularly Samuel and John) emerged as the apotheosis of New South energy, vision, and industrialization. In founding this new home for Confederate veterans, Inman's efforts to pay homage to the past agreed with Grady, who insisted that the "'New' would always honor the 'Old.'"[53]

Despite the near universal praise and adoration of the Confederacy among white Georgians, the attempts to establish the Confederate Soldiers' Home remained unsuccessful for years. Grady was not a veteran but had lost his Confederate father in the war. A champion of the Lost Cause, Grady enjoyed an honorary membership in the Fulton County Veterans Association. Membership included around two hundred people, including many well-heeled and influential Atlantans, such as Inman and former mayor Calhoun. When Grady saw an opportunity to play kingmaker, he swiftly asserted himself and enjoined John Brown Gordon, a former Confederate major general and former Georgia senator. Like many others in power, Gordon's family were enslavers at the start of the war. Indeed, the powerful Georgia planter class crafted a near-seamless continuity of power and control in the transition from a slavery-based economy to a waged-based one, despite the catastrophic loss of wealth when slavery was outlawed. Land tended to stay in the same families, and control of the political economy enabled the (re)accumulation of wealth. Even with the extraordinary loss of wealth from war, the elites largely reemerged at the top of social, political, and cultural circles in the postbellum era.[54]

Grady tirelessly used his clout in the Democratic Party to establish the Confederate Soldiers' Home, just as disgruntled farmers—black and white—were organizing to subvert one-party rule in the state. In his efforts to stave off threats from any third party, Grady and others framed loyalty to the Democratic Party as loyalty to the state's Confederate heritage. The Confederate leadership had almost exclusively belonged to the Democratic Party. To that end, the local Democratic Party had to be repositioned not only as heirs to the rebel experiment but also as caretakers of the "common [white] man," not solely focused on the interests of elites, as alleged by alliance members. Grady used the *Constitution* in a "massive campaign to convince farmers that the 'Ring' was the farmers' friend. For three months Grady set aside a full page of Sunday editions and scattered dailies to discuss the farmers' troubles and reassured them that the future looked bright."[55] Grady even recruited Northen to run for governor with a political platform that would be sympathetic enough to farmers to stifle the growth of the Farmers' Alliance in Georgia. These efforts, and Grady's role at the *Atlanta Constitution*, demonstrated the power of the Fourth Estate. Like its predecessors, the *Southern Confederacy* and the *Gate-City Guardian*, the local press exerted incredible influence over the local and regional political, social, and economic landscape. As with Gordon, Grady's efforts were successful; Northen won the governorship in 1888. The following year, Grady pushed for the Confederate Soldiers' Home and experienced the expected plaudits but also steep resistance, particularly from the growing number of Georgians who were allied with the Farmers' Alliance.

Throughout the decade, the Georgia Farmers' Alliance, affiliated with farmers' alliances active in states across the South and Midwest, emerged as a major challenger to one-party rule. Advocating labor rights, wage increases, and financial reform, the alliance was a fundamental threat to the New South elites who sought, in many ways, to replicate the class strata of the Old South, which they intended to update for the industrial economy.

The Colored Farmers' Alliance was founded in Troup County in 1884. This county is sixty-five miles southwest of Atlanta, and more than 60 percent of the residents were black. From Troup County the Colored Farmers' Alliance began an arduous task of drawing black farmers into its fold from around the state—even in the most hostile and violent corners of Georgia. Eventually, its membership reached ninety thousand, although not all of them were registered voters. In fact, many were disenfranchised by poll taxes and literacy tests, and many others were women. Their connections and links with white alliance members provided some degree of protection, for the black alliance members were likely voting for white politicians, not forming any black political force dedicated specifically to black rights. The races attended rallies together and had black speakers and white speakers at the same events.[56] They had emerged a clear threat to the conservative Democratic Party, which had earlier removed the Republicans from any political viability.

On April 7, 1889, Grady published his appeal for the Confederate Soldiers' Home in the *Constitution*. He enjoyed financial support from members of the Atlanta Ring and many others, including public foes such as Charles C. Jones Jr., who derided Grady's promotion of a New South. The former Confederate apparently disliked the emphasis on *New*. Jones argued that this "sacred obligation has too long been neglected." Others called the home a "holy duty," and funds exceeding $30,000 poured in from across the state, although roughly half came from Atlanta alone.[57] Still, months passed, and the state lawmakers expressed tepid interest in supporting such a home. The state already provided a pension for rebels, and many thought the home redundant. Eventually, the mayor of Atlanta, Tom Glenn, argued that "if the state can't or won't sustain it, Atlanta will!" With Grady at the helm of the board, and funds raised, the construction for the three-story mansion to house poor and elderly Confederate veterans was underway when Grady died two days before Christmas in 1889.[58]

When the home was complete, in 1890, the state had not agreed to assume control of it. Lawmakers voted against it in lines that refracted acute class and regional differences within the state. By 1891, arguments against the home insisted that its advocates—the Atlanta Ring included—had personally benefited financially from the construction, maintenance, staffing, and general financial support. Appeals to deference to the Lost Cause fell flat for many observers. In fact, many of the most outspoken critics of the home were former Confederates who were also affiliated with the Farmers' Alliance. Their own political lens led them to view the "deference appeal" as a crude and exploitative exercise in pandering to sentimental ties rather than a genuine program for the poor.

Given the Atlanta Ring's general hostility to economic reform, its excitement about needy veterans was suspicious. One lawmaker, Representative Humphries of Brooks County, pointed out that Georgia was exceptionally generous with former Confederates: "No state has provided a pension for widows of [Confederate] soldiers except Georgia." Far from parsimonious, "We have provided well and shown full our full gratitude to the soldiers who fought for us."[59] Among the alliance of state lawmakers who were also Confederate veterans, one argued that veterans "never asked for [the home]," and another demanded that fellow lawmakers "don't let sentiment" cloud wise judgment. In the end, the August 26, 1891, vote was ninety-four to sixty-two against state support of the home. Nineteen abstained. Outrage sprang from the pages of the *Constitution*. "Old Soldiers Repudiated," read one headline. Former Confederate colonel William D. Ellis argued that the hostility toward the home was less about any concerns about a ruling class with disproportionate power and more to do with the location of the home in Atlanta. The "Alliance members," Ellis fumed, "fight every measure that would benefit Atlanta." Others lambasted the anti-home lawmakers as "unpatriotic" and "niggardly."[60]

The vitriol was powerful and widespread in newspapers across the state. The *Athens Daily Banner*, from Grady's hometown, criticized the act as disrespectful to veterans. The *Americus Times Recorder* devoted space to pro-home state representatives who were also former Confederates, William A. Huff of Bibb County and A. S. Cutts of Sumter County. Huff had been a colonel assigned to the Confederate Commissary Department at Macon during the war. Cutts was described as "a gallant confederate soldier who stood at the front line of battle from Georgia to Appomattox." Though providing this glowing coverage of why the home was needed, the paper refused to mention the opponents of the home or their rationale.[61]

The Farmers' Alliance had emerged as a viable third party and potentially disruptive to one-party Democrat domination. Consequently, the conservative Democrats made conspicuous efforts to undermine their alliance challengers, charging them for the failure to secure funding: "This is what we might expect of the third party should it get into power." Although some insisted that they were "traitorous," allegations of betrayals to white supremacy were intimated as well. Some referred to the ninety-four lawmakers who opposed the home as "93 men and a nigger," with a racist reference to John M. Holzendorf Sr., from the overwhelmingly black low-country Camden County. He was one of two black men in the Georgia Statehouse. The other, Lectured Crawford, of MacIntosh County, abstained. Both men, who were Republicans, were vestiges of Reconstruction-era black political participation.[62]

The lawmakers who opposed the home vociferously defended themselves and their positions. William Atkinson, assemblyman from Coweta County, insisted that his opposition to the home had "nothing against Atlanta" and was based on sound reasoning about resources for veterans. Despite the outcry about the vote, Atkinson suggested that he was very confident that any revote would be similar. Perhaps to demonstrate that he was not prone to any subversion of the racial order, Atkinson enjoined the other ninety-three lawmakers to stand against any reconsideration of the vote, but he openly referred to Holzendorf as a "nigger" colleague who would stand by his vote with the other "men."[63] Atkinson's evocation of racial contempt did two things: first, it dismissed any notions that black lawmakers were above the quotidian racist indignities that other black people experienced. They were not truly accepted among the body of white lawmakers but were more of a mere nuisance that technically had to be tolerated. Second, it dismissed any implications that the anti-home vote was a challenge to the southern white nationalism for which the Confederacy fought. Finally, an analysis of the vote found that alliance members were heavily ex-Confederates and were on both sides of the vote. Notably, ex-Confederates made up 65 percent of the ninety-four legislators who voted against the home. Despite the vote, the effort to establish a state-supported home for Confederate veterans would not subside.

Lawmakers introduced another bill in 1892 to provide state support for the Confederate Soldiers' Home. Bill Smith, a Confederate veteran from Gwinnett County, evoked Grady, demanding that the state pass the legislation in his memory. Smith noted that the legendary booster of the New South paid great homage to the Old South and to those who had fought and sacrificed for it. He also aimed to "disabuse" critics of the notion that the placement of the home was an attempt at "any speculative scheme of the citizens of Atlanta." Smith, who did not live in Atlanta when the home was proposed, first suggested that the Gate City would be a proper place for it. This home was a gesture to honor "patriotism and loyalty."[64]

Another surprising supporter emerged from overwhelmingly black Liberty County, where Tunis Campbell had organized and fought for the forty acres allocated freed people after the war. William H. Styles, one of only two black members of the Georgia assembly in 1892, was a former camp slave of a Confederate soldier. He made an appeal to his fellow representatives that the *Constitution* determined to be "especially interesting, because not only was it on the right line it was a good speech." Styles explained that "I was never a confederate soldier, but I was a servant of a confederate soldier . . . who fought . . . under General Philip Cook." Fully aware of the nearly universal acceptance of the Confederacy as representative of white southern sentiment, he noted that they "fought for principles which you now hold [to be] right." And despite the very irony of his position as a Georgia lawmaker, Styles professed his "love" for the veterans, pointing out that he had carried books to school for some of them when they were all children. Though avoiding the fact that he was enslaved as a child, Styles insisted that "there was no difference except that I was not allowed to study from [the books I carried for] them." Finally, he pointed out the federal government denied pensions and homes to Confederates but provided those very benefits to "hundreds of colored soldiers" who fought for the Union.[65]

Appealing to the racial sensibilities of the legislators, Styles's argument struck a chord. How could any well-meaning, self-respecting white Georgian vote against providing a home for former Confederates when their black Yankee former enemies enjoyed such beneficence? Styles helped push the soldiers' home bill through a gauntlet of amendments. For his enthusiastic support of the home, the Fulton County Confederate Veterans Association gave the black lawmaker a gold-headed ebony cane. Sam Small, who was so racist that even fellow white southerners described him as a "negrophobe," made the presentation. Former Confederates' cheers for Styles's acceptance speech "shook the roof til the pictures of Lee and Davis on the wall bowed." The *Atlanta Constitution* described the excitement as so great that the "old Confederate flag quivered."[66]

After years of compromises and revisions, the Confederate Soldiers' Home was finally opened to veterans in an elaborate ceremony on June 3, 1901: Jefferson Davis's birthday. Governor Allen Candler recognized the assiduous work done to realize this home from many corners of the state, including the United Daughters of the Confederacy, the Sons of Confederate Veterans, the Order of Robert E. Lee, and the Children of the Confederacy. The memory of Grady, who had been one of the most visible advocates, was celebrated in the presence of his family members, including his aged mother.[67]

The effort to establish this home in Atlanta reveals how the capital of the New South had reconciled its legacy and struggled over notions of history, sentimentality, race, and honor. It was simultaneously a test of the limits of the devotion to the Lost Cause, which had taken root with near fanaticism. The ordeal also speaks to how one-party rule faced challenges from southern-based agents who were often dedicated to the enterprise of white nationalism but were also unwilling to blindly follow it to economic ruin and the hyperexploitation of the white poor. Although they were not often deeply invested in challenging racism, many Farmers' Alliance members did not see white supremacy as the cornerstone of their politics in the same way as had the most conservative elements of the Democratic Party. Rhetoric from the Atlanta Ring, the *Constitution*, and Democratic Party elites attempted to exploit the sentimentality of the Confederate cause and the aging and needy veterans, even as they expressed little concern for the wider fundamental economic concerns of the rising tide of third-party advocates in the state. Race was used to drive a wedge between voters and the alliance members, who opposed the creation of the home, but race was not always understood in the most conventional ways. Although Styles was an advocate for civil rights for all, his fealty to the Confederate Soldiers' Home invited unusual praise. The neo-Confederate adoration of a black lawmaker reveals that there were evolving spaces for black political expression, as long as it was aligned with the southern white-nationalist cause. According to racists, black people in neo-Confederate Georgia were safe, as long as they were conservative. White nationalists tolerated black lawmakers (and could even endorse them) if these black politicians were ideologically nonthreatening. And despite the deep pull of this white southern nationalism, it was not without threats and challenges from white southerners themselves. Although the Farmers' Alliance soon fell out of favor across the state, challenges to one-party rule were not gone. Few movements proved a greater threat in the postbellum era in Georgia than the rise of Populism.

As the nineteenth century came to its end, the New South and its veritable capital were substantively transformed. In many ways Atlanta was the industrialized city on a hill, with invigorated people imbued with a sense of possibility and progress. But, as usual, the notions of progress and possibility were tied to subjective positions that were rarely in agreement. For most of Atlanta's white citizens, the city was a proud heir of the Confederate past. That past was prologue, as Shakespeare wrote. But, as found in various Shakespearean plays, characters from the past, though dead, have a curious way of communicating with, and influence, the living. The ghosts of the Confederacy animated every aspect of the development of the city in the decades after the war. The Civil War generally affected the city in nearly every way, but it was the experiment of the rebel government in particular that provided ideological direction, a resilient new provincial nationalism, and a durable resistance to the expansion of democracy.

For the majority of Atlanta's black citizens, the Confederates' defeat brought liberty, helped to realize prayers, and opened new possibilities for the United States to be closer to its idealistic self-image as just and free. The adoration of the failed southern nationalist cause was more than just a nuisance for black Atlantans. It was more than cultural artifacts that invented new histories that placated guilt or moral quandary. For African Americans, the endurance of Confederate principles meant that freedom was always constricted and access to the basic amenities of citizenship was elusive. And in the public sphere—where power existed—the Democratic Party most closely represented these neo-Confederate principles.

From the Farmers' Alliance to the People's Party, the possible viability of a third party frightened elites: Redeemers, Bourbons, the Atlanta Ring, and the New South industrialists. Across nomenclature, organizations, and descriptors, these groups had long feared political alliances between poor blacks and poor whites. Disenfranchisement, violence, and widespread corruption proved to be effective tools to repress these challenges. Throughout these campaigns to suppress the audacious political upheavals, the hegemonic pull of sentimental Confederate obeisance proved to be a reliable and persistent tool to drive wedges between white and black alliances and pander to nearly universal adoration of beloved family members who had committed themselves to the Lost Cause. The sense of community—on the family and civic level—was an enduring and formidable one. The loyalty to the Confederate war duty of fathers, brothers, uncles, and sons—and, of course, to the South itself—was a powerful tradition. It meant something meaningful, and elites used that force to consolidate power, neutralize threats, and accumulate resources.

Under these circumstances, African Americans forged a new and expanding sense of autonomy that became necessary under neo-Confederate domination and federal apathy. They built schools, continued to politically organize—even without the vote—and carved out oases of respite in the storm of racial subjugation. The New South, as Grady had long said, was modern, was energetic, and continued to look fondly to its old cast for inspiration. This was the world in which most African Americans functioned and lived lives marked by poverty and hardship. Yet some, against incredible odds, became remarkable examples of success and resistance, as Chapter 5 reveals.

5 | The New South Mecca
Atlanta, Race, and Self-Determination

The hundred hills of Atlanta are not all crowned with factories. On one, toward the west, the setting sun throws three buildings in bold relief against the sky. The beauty of the group lies in its simple unity:——a broad lawn of green rising from the red street with mingled roses and peaches; north and south, two plain and stately halls; and in the midst, half hidden in ivy, a larger building, boldly graceful, sparingly decorated, and with one low spire. It is a restful group,——one never looks for more; it is all here, and intelligible.

—W. E. B. Du Bois, 1903

Neither the Republican nor Democratic Party can do for the colored race what they can do for themselves.

—Bishop Henry McNeal Turner, 1884

n late October 1864 in Madison, southeast of Atlanta, the town's
mayor, Joshua Hill, who had been an outspoken critic of secession and
Governor Brown's wartime leadership, was grappling with the tremendous losses of war. He had recently lost his eighteen-year-old son, a
Confederate soldier, in the Atlanta Campaign. Yet despite the desolation of Atlanta and the devastating rebel defeat, many in rural Georgia,
like Hill, maintained operations on plantations as usual. They remained
faithful, irrationally hopeful, or perhaps pragmatic about the prospects
of a Confederate victory and the circumstances before them. Nearly
two years after the Emancipation Proclamation, Hill had recently sent
nine-year-old William Edward away for slave training. Enslaved by
Hill, the child was being trained to "chop, hoe, and pull fodder, corn
or anything else to be done on the plantation." It was a process that
had gone on for generations in America. Babies were enslaved at birth
and forced into labor as children with no hope of a future with freedom, democracy, or any semblance of what was popularly understood
as justice. In addition to being taught how to be an effective slave, the
child was aware that violence, and the threat of it, would control his
labor and every other facet of his life. His mother, Ellen, had also been
enslaved at birth. Her labor had been used to enrich Hill, a lawyer and
planter who had ascended to the US House of Representatives before
the war.[1]

Ellen, like four million others across the South, was a victim of an
intergenerational practice of cruelty that had been passed from mother
and to child through no fault of their own. It was not a natural, biological process despite whatever language, religion, or pseudoscience
had been used to exculpate those who protected slavery. Little William
had known only the freedom, authority, and power of Joshua Hill; the
powerlessness of those enslaved; and the inevitability of a rigid system
of slavery that shaped his world. Only white men like Hill could vote
for and occupy public office. Democracy itself was constricted to über-
citizens, like William's enslaver. However, shortly after he returned

from his weeklong slave-training process, William came to realize that few things were fixed and natural about freedom and slavery.

On November 19, 1864, four days after Sherman's troops left Atlanta on their March to the Sea, little William scrambled with other children to bear witness to a momentous unfolding of history. He and other children ran across a large plantation and pressed against the fences, peering through the railings to take in the incredible spectacle of thousands of men in blue uniforms marching through town. Because of their carts, horses, weapons, Stars and Stripes flags, and general authority, the boy was aware that these were the enemies whom his captors had so feared and cursed. However, the river of marching bodies was not entirely military. William noticed nonuniformed black men, women, and children in the amorphous mass. This struck William as a remarkable and indelible sight:

> The soldiers . . . that passed with Sherman carried provisions, hams, shoulders, meal, flour, and other food. They had their cooks and other servants. I 'member seeing a woman in that crowd of servants. She had a baby in her arms. She hollered at us chillun and said, "You chilluns git off dat fence and go learn [your] ABC's." I thought she [was] crazy telling us that, for we had never been 'lowed to learn nothing at all like reading and writing.[2]

The admonishment to read came as a surprise to the curious child. He knew that reading could result in violent punishment from his enslavers. Educating black people—free or enslaved—had been anathema to the most basic principles of the southern nationalist cause. There were no schools for black people anywhere in the South, and enslaved people were legally barred from being taught to read in many states. In fact, among states, Georgia was second after South Carolina to pass anti-literacy laws when, in 1829, it made instructing black people to read a

crime, punishable with imprisonment and a fine for whites. Black people could be beaten and tortured as punishment.[3]

In this context the black woman's call to education was brave,
subversive, and simultaneously a conspicuous affirmation of the new
freedom. In a society that held deep hostility, fear, and contempt for
educating black people, she inspired black children to prepare for a
future where literacy and education could be transformative and uplifting. Their futures, she immediately understood, could be full of great
possibility. That nine-year-old child remembered the directive for the
rest of his life. His very first moments of freedom included a call to
be *educated*. This was more than being *trained* to labor without freedom. Education and literacy were incongruous with slavery. They were
broader and more ambitious; they had possibility. William; his parents,
Ellen and George; his friends; and everyone that he knew, loved, and
respected were suddenly free.

Declarations of freedom came from many circles—federal soldiers
and the newly freed alike. Perhaps as an effort to maintain some semblance of order and authority amid the disintegration of the slave system that governed her life, the mistress of his plantation, Mrs. Emily
Hill, soberly informed the people that they were liberated. William
remembered the moment she made her announcement:

> My master [was] a Senator from Georgia, 'lected on the Whig
> ticket. He served two terms in Washington as Senator. His wife,
> our mistress, had charge of the slaves and plantation. She never
> seemed to like the idea of having slaves. Of course, I never heard
> her say she didn't want them but she [was] the one to free the
> slaves on the place befo' surrender.
>
> The next week after [federal troops] passed through Madi-
> son, Miss Emily called the five women . . . that [was] on the place
> and tole them to stay 'round the house and attend to things as
> they had always done until their husbands come back. She said

they were free and could go wherever they wanted to. . . . She meant that they could rent from her if they wanted to.[4]

William, and his family, like scores of thousands across the state, were positioned to exercise their new freedom in all sorts of ways. Some immediately disappeared from plantations, homesteads, and shops. Some negotiated new terms of paid employment with their former owners. Others ventured into cities and towns seeking employment and safety, and still others, as noted above, sought those same things by following Union soldiers. Some joined white soldiers and civilians in looting the businesses and homes of slaveholders, Confederates, and others. One thing was clear: the fate of the Confederacy was sealed.[5]

The meaning of freedom has always been contested in the United States, especially so in the South. Inasmuch as the Founding Fathers conceived and realized a nation that found no incongruence with calling itself free and democratic while most of its citizens were not allowed to vote and many people—deemed unworthy of citizenship—were enslaved, the leaders of the New South offered similarly myopic notions of freedom. Citizenship—in the full application of civil rights—had always been used with qualification. Some enjoyed greater citizenship than others. Wealthy white men in the New South had crafted a region in their own interests.

What did freedom look like for *black* citizens in a country, region, state, or city that explicitly limited full citizenship to white people and legally sanctioned discrimination against people of color? What did rights look like for Georgians who worked hard, paid their taxes, provided for their families, and were black? Could they depend on the law to be fair? Justice to prevail? Did citizenship have a qualification for them? Georgia was central in articulating a New South identity with a tenuous representation of black citizenship. In its state capital the strength of a biracial democracy was tested in the immediate aftermath of the war and in the decades to follow. In the process, this test formed the contours of the city's identity, spatial mapping, laws, culture, and social and political character. For many, the role of educational institutions proved to be an important subversion of the racial order. Schools effectively uplifted freed people and their children while simultaneously equipping the wider black community with the tools to build and lead institutions. The process drew people to Atlanta to its concentration of educational opportunities. Consequently, they built on the success of this process, highlighting the value of self-determination.

Little is known about how young William and his family carved out their first years in freedom, but they remained in Madison. Perhaps, like many others, they worked as sharecroppers on the property of their previous owners. The relationship between the Hills and William's family is unclear, but Joshua Hill did have a direct impact on the fate of all freed people in the state. His story is deeply entangled with the denouement of the Old South and the rise of its new iteration.

By the time Reconstruction came to an end, in 1877, the child whom Hill had formerly enslaved was a twenty-two-year-old who, with his family, moved thirty miles north to Athens, then a relatively small town in Clarke County. Under the family surname Evans, William, his father, and his younger sister appear in the 1880 census as living in a duplex adjacent to a white Athens merchant named J. R. Matthews on Lumpkin Street. By that point, William Edward Evans worked as a brick mason, and his father was a tailor, which could be a relatively lucrative profession for black men. Delia, William's sister, was only sixteen and was listed as a "servant," which was the most common employment for black women for decades to come. It is unclear when and how William Edward learned to read, but he did become literate, heeding the advice that he received on the day he learned that he was emancipated. Education for black people was very difficult to secure in the neo-Confederate landscape. This was especially conspicuous in his new hometown.

Home to the University of Georgia, the state's flagship university, Athens was the repository of an expanding enterprise of higher education. Students from privileged families across Georgia sent their sons to the university. Some even moved to town to provide easier access for their children. Professors, university administrators, and staff populated Athens, giving it an inflection of cosmopolitanism rare for a small town in the Deep South. The Evans family, like all black citizens in the state, supported the university through their taxes but were also denied entry, given its whites-only policy.[6]

In the spirit of neo-Confederate principles, black people were also denied access to public high schools and primary schools across the South. In fact, no public high school in Georgia was available to black children until after World War I. In the years after the Civil War, however, the determination to follow the admonition to "learn their ABC's" drove black people to do for themselves what the state refused to do. With help from white and black missionaries, black churches held basic literacy classes. Attended by all ages of the community, from young children to the elderly, the insatiable demand for education inspired organizers to establish a brick-and-mortar school in Athens. With assistance from the Freedmen's Bureau, African Americans opened the Knox Institute and Industrial School in 1868, which served as a private primary and secondary school for black children in Athens. Because of the dearth of educational opportunities for black children across the state, some parents sent their children to Athens, where they lived in dormitories. Education, as noted in earlier chapters, took a fast hold in black communities. Throughout the South, small black schools and colleges became essential incubators and later became anchor institutions for the black middle class and wider black leadership. Athens was no exception.

Although less than a fifth of the size of Atlanta, Athens had a small black middle class during William's time there. The town was even home to two black newspapers, the *Blade* and the *Clipper*, reflecting the degree to which literacy had expanded in the black community, as well as a palpable push for Afro-self-determinism. The black press employed black journalists and other professionals to inform, educate, and help shape the worldviews of its readers. Newspapers hosted advertisements for black-owned businesses: physicians, tailors, and grocers, for example. The press also played a critical role in providing communication with black communities across the region and country. News from Atlanta was common. Perhaps it was the lure of greater opportunities in a much larger city that drew William Edward to the Gate City in August 1880.

Within a decade of Evans's arrival in Atlanta, the small city was home to more black schools and universities than any other city in the country. It is difficult to overstate how critical these colleges were to forging a new black professional class, as well as providing opportunities for working-class African Americans. "No force in the city," Maurice J. Hobson explains, "had more political, social, cultural, and historical significance for blacks than the founding of these institutions of higher learning."[7] They employed scores of cooks, groundskeepers, clerical workers, and a range of craftsmen who could not be employed by white businesses. Evans was a direct beneficiary of the extraordinary opportunities that black laborers had in Atlanta.

People were drawn to the bright lights, the hum of energy, and the ever-resurrecting efforts in the city of Atlanta for many reasons. Since the end of the Civil War, the city prided itself on its phoenix-like rebirth from the ashes of war. The city's promoters boasted of its railways, access to other cities, modern conveniences, hotels, office buildings, commerce, and higher education. The state opened the Georgia School of Technology in 1888 (later renamed the Georgia Institute of Technology).[8] The new school offered a clear demonstration to the country that the New South was modernizing and that it viewed technological advancements and industrial growth as critical to the effort. The all-female Cox College was located in the town of Manchester (renamed College Park), adjacent to Atlanta. Agnes Scott College, another all-female school, was located in Decatur. Because these schools, like all majority-white schools in the South, prohibited black attendance, African Americans endeavored to support, form, and lead their own schools, mostly with the help of northern-based white religious groups.

These black colleges, some built upon Civil War battlefields, were anchored in a very special mission, broader than that of their white counterparts. Like white colleges, black colleges assumed the task of building minds, spirits, and communities and encouraging thoughtful engagement with the world around them. However, black schools were more capacious in their missions. They insisted, against all manner of expectation and intention from the wider society, to expand freedoms and opportunities for all people. Their very existence was subversive. Against the ambitions of a centuries-old white-nationalist project that viewed black education as anathema, these schools inspired and demanded intellectual, social, cultural, and spiritual development from their students. They offered them spaces to thrive and imagine possibilities of greatness and significance in a broader society that expected neither from them. They would be the most consequential institutions in black Atlanta for generations to come.

Like thousands of others from rural Georgia and even other towns in the region, George White, born in 1857, was drawn to the possibilities that the Gate City offered. Atlanta was the state capital, with exciting entertainment and several educational institutions. With his light skin, straight hair, and European features, George, it would appear, could, with enough effort, forge a successful life, unfettered by the legal constrictions faced by black citizens. The New South with its white nationalism—if not much of the world—would be his oyster, at least at first glance. Across social, political, cultural, and religious arenas, whiteness afforded its beneficiaries open pathways to all spaces of power and influence because it centered them as normative. Yet despite his appearance, White was legally black.[9]

White was the physical representation of the horrors of sexual predation faced by generations of enslaved women. Across centuries,

countless women were forced to give birth to the children of powerful, cruel, and depraved men. Some of these children were given special privileges. Many others were treated no differently from others in
shackles. Yet in freedom, hundreds of thousands of people across the
United States appeared closer to white than black. Many simply passed
into whiteness, moving into new towns and reinventing themselves.
Despite whatever moral quandaries or ethical dilemmas, "passing"
unburdened them of racial oppression.

For White, reinvention was central, but not reinvention as a white
man. He simply wanted to create a better life for himself and his
posterity—without passing. By passing as white, he could access any
public high school, find employment in any industry, and ascend to
any level that his talent and ambition would allow. He could become
a police officer, a firefighter, or a soldier and climb through to the
highest ranks. He could run for office. There were no limits to being
a white man named George White. His other option was, of course,
to seek a better life as a "Negro" in some other town. He chose the
latter option. No city seemed to offer that option as conveniently as
Atlanta. George's hometown, Augusta—like all cities and towns in
Georgia—barred black children from high school. A foundational
component of the rhetoric of white supremacy had insisted on black
inferiority in all matters, mental and physical. There was, perhaps,
some degree of insecurity about the immutable truth of this inferiority.
In every way there were assiduous efforts to prevent the provision of
any modicum of resources—especially educational—to black people.
Formidable barriers were erected to stop, limit, or otherwise curtail
their educational opportunities. If black people were as intellectually
hobbled, incurious, or lazy as racists had argued, surely antieducational
efforts need not be so strenuous, costly, or ambitious. The likely explanation has less to do with intellectual capacity and more to do with
the function of white nationalism. The denial of educational opportunity followed the same line of thinking that denied black people

access to parks, sidewalks, voting, health care, and running water. The white-nationalist state reserved its resources for white citizens. And although Atlanta was enveloped in the neo-Confederate traditions of the South, it was also a large enough space for Afro-self-determinism to found independent black educational institutions. White intended to take advantage of them.

Described by his son as "exceedingly poor," White packed up his meager belongings and settled near Atlanta University to attend its high school. Although they were in poverty, his parents sent whatever resources they could to help their only child pursue an education. He finished high school and one year of college before financial calamity caused by his parents' deaths forced him to quit school. With a year of college, he had already achieved more education than most Americans—black or white—of his day. George was equipped with enough professional training to expand his employment opportunities in one of the few spaces for black people in the public sector: the US Postal Service. After passing the civil service exams, he became a mail carrier. Ambitious, dedicated, and with an eye toward long-term goals, be began saving money from his small pay of $100 per month—a salary that was stagnant for several years.[10]

During the tumultuous years after the collapse of Reconstruction and the rise of the Populist movement, White met Madeline Harrison, a relatively well-to-do widow and graduate of Clark University, which was also in Atlanta. Six years his junior, Madeline, who was also light enough to pass as white, was the daughter of Augustus Ware, a wealthy planter from La Grange. A fierce Confederate, Ware had moved into the Joseph Poythress household in the 1850s, where nearly forty people were held in slavery. One of them was Marie, believed to be the child of the ninth US president, William Henry Harrison, who gave several of his own enslaved children to his brother when William decided to run for the presidency. Harrison's children, born from Dilsia, a woman whom he had enslaved, were ultimately sold to Poythress. When Ware arrived at the plantation, he began impregnating Marie, who had four of his children, including Madeline, who was born in 1863, after the Emancipation Proclamation but two years before the end of slavery.

Enslaved at birth, Madeline eventually joined her mother and siblings near the residence of Ware, who, like many antebellum enslavers and sexual predators, maintained a white family and a marriage. In many cases the white fathers of enslaved children provided some material benefits. Some of these children were sent away to receive educations in the North or in Europe. Some were bequeathed land and other resources. Perhaps more often than not, they received little special treatment, money, or privileges.[11] In Madeline's case, however, there appears to be what Kenneth Janken calls a "transfer of wealth" to Ware's formerly enslaved children. Even an avowed white nationalist like Ware saw the need to come to terms with the circumstances before him in the Civil War's aftermath. Although not much is known about the extent to which he endorsed education for black people at large, his daughter was able to secure an education at Clark University, one of the city's handful of schools for black people.[12] She became a schoolteacher before marrying George White.

As the couple established their own family, they joined the First Congregational Church, one of the most prominent black churches in the city. They eventually purchased a home at 101 Houston Street in the city's old Fourth Ward. The neighborhood was a diverse one with respect to the occupations of the black residents and the small pockets of whites as well. Although racial segregation banned black people from all sorts of spaces—political, economic, social—the world of poverty or economic precarity had never been the sole space of black people. Poor and working-class whites in Atlanta and throughout the South found themselves not only in similar material circumstances as black people; they were, at times, also in close residential proximity. Redlining and residential zoning had not yet fully developed in the late nineteenth century.[13]

Throughout history, cities have been loci for forging intellectual, social, political, and cultural innovation and subversion. This held true even in the New South. The larger the city, the riper it was for these subversions. Newer cities, like Atlanta, provided even more opportunities for reinvention, subversion, and social climbing. As Edward Ayers notes, although smaller southern cities had "antebellum leaders and representatives of local planter families [who] often played leading roles for generations," booming New South cities were different: "Cities with shallow or nonexistent antebellum roots, such as Atlanta . . . saw the men of greatest position come from outside the city and more common backgrounds."[14]

Some of these men and women who rose to social and economic prominence in Atlanta were formerly enslaved. William Edward Evans was one example of the unique opportunities for black people in the state of Georgia in an era and region known for its special hostility to blacks. After moving to Atlanta, Evans established himself professionally by working in the bricklaying and plastering business. He found no respite from racism there, but he also found more opportunities than in other places. The new schools for black higher education in the swiftly growing city were central to his own professional development, as they were to the cultivation of a broader African American community. White missionaries and philanthropists from the American Missionary Association founded Atlanta University in 1865. Others founded Morehouse College in 1867, which moved to Atlanta in 1879. Clark College was formed in 1869, and Spelman College was founded in 1881. The African Methodist Episcopal Church founded Morris Brown College in 1881, the only school in the Atlanta University Center founded by black people and named for one.

Black and white missionaries, and other advocates for black advancement, not only built schools for African Americans; they also employed hundreds of them in various capacities. Northern missionaries helped form the Storrs School for black people exactly a year after

Sherman's capture of Atlanta. In a city with no public school system at all, it was a critically important space for the newly freed people, who were overwhelmingly illiterate. Like many communities across the South, the Storrs School was multipurpose: it was simultaneously a center of worship, education, and social services. Established on Houston Street near Piedmont Avenue, it became a site where the possibilities and aspirations of the newly freed could be pursued and supported. In May 1867 the First Congregational Church, United Church of Christ, was formed when black parishioners established an autonomous black-led congregation. Through these efforts toward self-determination, members and missionaries poured their meager resources into the Storrs School, which was eventually absorbed into the Atlanta Public School system when it was formed in 1872, becoming one of two public primary schools available to black students. Atlanta University expanded its mission and granted its first bachelor degrees in June 1876.[15]

The critical need for the development of black schools, from primary level through higher education, was apparent to all who paid attention: both whites and blacks. For black access to higher education, no institution was as significant as Atlanta University at the turn of the century. It attracted scores and then hundreds of students. Professors, studious young adults, laborers, professional staff, and high school children filled its buildings. W. E. B. Du Bois, one of the most prominent scholars in Atlanta in the early twentieth century and a faculty member at Atlanta University, argued that the mission of education was discursive and broadly important to the black community. It was tasked with wider black uplift, beyond intellectual exercise. Du Bois explained that the American Missionary Association sent agents "not to keep Negroes in their places, but to raise them out of their places where the filth of slavery had wallowed them."[16]

In 1881 the school began efforts to build its largest building, Stone Hall, intended to be a central feature on campus, holding classrooms, professors' offices, and administrative space. In line with Du Bois's description, the university officials sought black workers who, by the scores, worked to craft the important structure, which was a testament not only to the university but also to the spirit, industriousness, and skill of black people, most of whom had been formerly enslaved. They worked as masons, painters, managers, and supervisors. It was, in many respects, a visible affirmation of the calling and efficacy of Atlanta University and of the many missionaries, educators, and eager parents who cobbled together resources to expand educational and professional opportunities for black people.

Evans was one of many black contractors who worked on Stone Hall, a three-story red-brick Queen Anne–style building with Romanesque Revival elements, completed in 1882, two years after he arrived in the city.[17] Although whites generally refused to hire black building contractors, the opportunities for Evans as a plasterer and building contractor in a city that had such a broad-based need for these services in the black community afforded him an exceptional chance at success. Perched upon Diamond Hill, one of the tallest points of Atlanta's natural landscape, Stone Hall opened its doors seventeen years after the end of slavery. Using the talents of black people, as well as those of whites—from the North and South—Stone Hall was an iconic display of the most optimistic possibilities and promise of Atlanta and the New South. It would eventually host the office of Du Bois, when he arrived as a professor in 1897. Stone Hall was where the venerable scholar wrote many of his early classics, including *The Souls of Black Folk*.[18]

Clearly, the academic buildings, the university's intellectual space, and the wider city were fundamental to Du Bois and his development. In fact, he writes that it was his time in Atlanta that deeply shaped him for life. He arrived with a PhD from Harvard, years of global travel, fluency in multiple languages, and experience in teaching and researching at different institutions, but he was still not yet thirty years old. Most

Stone Hall, flanked with North Hall and South Hall, Atlanta University, circa 1900. Stone Hall, constructed in 1882, housed classrooms and administrative and faculty offices. The university hired many black contractors, including W. E. Evans, for its construction. W. E. B. Du Bois celebrated the significance and aesthetics of Stone Hall, which housed his office where he wrote his seminal book, *The Souls of Black Folk*. CREDIT: ATLANTA UNIVERSITY CENTER ROBERT W. WOODRUFF LIBRARY. CONTACT ARCHIVES@AUCTR.EDU

Americans—white or black—of his day had not finished high school. The vast majority had never left the country. Yet, as he writes of his time at Atlanta University, "Here I found myself. I lost mannerisms. I grew more broadly human, made my closest and most holy friendships, and studied human beings."[19] Of course, the transformative experience of Atlanta was broader than the bucolic academic oasis. The city—and the people who animated it—shaped his development. Laypeople, professionals, vagrants, strivers, churchgoers, hustlers, whites, and blacks all exposed him to the diversity of the human experience. When he "studied human beings," he was not solely attentive to what he found in government data. He was interested in the random passersby whom he encountered. Everyday people, such as William Edward Evans, added to the richness of the city and its generative possibilities.

Evans was proud of his contributions to Stone Hall. This was striking testimony to the resilience and the educational and industrial aspirations of black people. He was thankful for the opportunities to practice his craft and earn a decent living: "I [was] never idle, as there [weren't] so many brick layers and plasterers at that time. I kept quite busy."[20] It is notable that black employers securing contracts with black-controlled institutions offered Evans employment, although employment was not always certain. Despite the project at Stone Hall, Evans had experienced discrimination upon his arrival in Atlanta. He initially found work under a white contractor, yet it was tenuous at best: "No matter how good a Negro [was,] he [was] the last to be hired and then he [was] given some minor job. I saw that even if a Negro [was] a better brick layer, all the white workers [were] given the first jobs and after they [were] all supplied, then the Negro workers got what [was] left." Eventually, Evans worked for one of the leading black-owned construction companies in the state, Alexander Hamilton and Son. Hamilton, who was enslaved at birth, served in the Union Army during the Civil War and settled in Atlanta in 1877, eventually becoming a contractor. In 1890 he formed his own company, securing work with the expanding institution building by the city's African American population. There were many construction projects, from family homes to large public buildings. Evans eventually launched his own construction company and, hiring his own sons, became a competitor to Hamilton. Yet in a growing city, with expanding black educational and religious institutions, there was enough work for more than one black-owned construction company.

The sense that race enterprises would be the foundation for black advancement was common throughout black communities. This was especially acute in spaces where African Americans were rigidly denied amenities and services. The unique concentration of institutions of black higher education offered even more opportunities for black leadership to rely on race enterprises. No other city in the United States had as many black colleges as Atlanta. The largest southern city, New Orleans, similarly had a relatively large black entrepreneurial class. Unlike Atlanta, its black elite had strong antebellum roots in a unique social

class of racially liminal mixed-race people known as Creoles. In the postbellum era they were, for the first time, barred from public accommodations, hotels, restaurants, and even large swaths of the French Quarter.
There were three black colleges in New Orleans, which similarly formed
a nucleus of black leadership and Afro-self-determinism. Atlanta had
five black colleges. They were all a consequence of the neo-Confederate
policies and laws that emerged in a "redeemed" South.[21]

The outright exclusion of black people residentially, economically,
religiously, politically, and socially from white spaces meant that parallel black spaces provided training grounds for black leadership across
professional arenas. This new leadership, in turn, cultivated a social and
cultural world upon itself, which was linked to the wider, impoverished
black community in nearly every way but the social. In fact, the black
leaders, even more than their white counterparts, relied on their own
community for their livelihood. The mass of black people populated
their churches, medical practices, schools, apartment buildings, rented
houses, and businesses. Several people emerged as visible leaders from
this class. Few would ever touch so many across so many spaces as the
New England native Du Bois. One of the most important early efforts
with which Du Bois was involved was anchored in Atlanta University,
the Atlanta Conference of Negro Problems, which attracted national
attention to Du Bois and the city.

Launched in 1896, the conference assembled a cross section of
academics, ministers, and others to systematically gather data on the
state of African Americans, measuring their progress and challenges.
The conference was forced to strike a balance between discussing the
evisceration of civil rights and celebrating the extraordinary progress
that hundreds of thousands of black people had made only a generation
away from slavery. It was clear that the conference would not be useful
as a source for hagiographic narratives of black progress, yet that progress demonstrated to the world how determined and industrious black
people were, despite the powerful forces of repression. The conference

also had to simultaneously address the horrors of what Rayford Logan called the "nadir." This era in African American history was marked by the rise of terrorist organizations, disenfranchisement, debt peonage, quasi-enslavement in convict-lease systems, and the legal sanction of racial exclusion, called Jim Crow laws. These were the consequences of widespread and brutal revanchism.

In the conference's inaugural year, the US Supreme Court ruled in *Plessy v. Ferguson* that separate-but-equal facilities were constitutional. Of course, the actual application of the law—establishing equal facilities—was in practice dismissed across the country. Black people were denied access to employment in public and private sectors as state and local police, municipal clerks, train conductors, firefighters, hospital staff, and the management class in corporate America. Every flagship university in the former Confederate states banned black students, as did private white colleges such as Duke and Tulane, along with hundreds of others. In Kentucky, a border state, Berea College opened its doors to all who qualified, regardless of race. Lawmakers, hostile to the notion of such displays of fairness and opportunity, legally forced the school to ban black students, forcing it to join all other schools in the state as well as those in the former Confederacy to codify the practice of racial exclusion and oppression.[22]

Of course, some of the southern states created black public schools and colleges, but they were universally grossly underfunded in comparison to their white counterparts. The excessive differences between resources at the whites-only flagship University of Georgia and the state's only black public university in 1900, the Georgia State Industrial College for Colored Youth, were obvious. The state allocations for UGA were several multiples per student higher than the allocations for black students at GSICCY. This was in many ways emblematic of how the state, under Redeemer control, navigated a world where black people were in practice quasi-citizens. The Georgia General Assembly approved the only public college available for black people in the state on November 20, 1890. A mandate from the federal Second Morrill Act for Land Grant universities required that if black citizens were barred from the flagship university, a separate college be made for their use. GSICCY lacked the facilities, salaries, physical plant, or any other qualities of a major university, whereas UGA had all of them. In fact, the state provided public funding from black taxes and white taxes to support UGA's law school, medical school, and dental school, among other graduate programs, but no Georgia state university provided black opportunities at such professional schools.[23]

Had black citizens not been explicitly denied access to education, there would not have been a need for institutions of higher education with exclusive missions to educate black people in the United States any more than in other countries in the Americas where slavery had existed. Brazil, Cuba, and Colombia never developed black colleges or universities. This does not mean that racism did not persist after slavery in those countries but that the cultivation of independent black institutions such as universities was not necessary.[24]

The demands and endurance of neo-Confederate politics were, of course, antimeritocratic and antidemocratic. By design, they rejected racial equality in education. However, the needs and demands of the black community forged and cultivated Afro-self-determinism as a response in every arena. These essential institutions satisfied needs, lifting African Americans out of the greatest depths of poverty and illiteracy. They simultaneously formed a nucleus for social, intellectual, economic, and cultural activity in the black community. The black leadership class was nearly totally tethered to these schools. Ministers received their educations there, as did schoolteachers, medical doctors, lawyers, and other professionals. Black leaders sent their children to these schools, and these young people increasingly joined fraternal and sororal organizations there. These organizations remained important anchors of the social networks of elite black leaders throughout their lives after college.

Although William Evans did not attend college, education influenced him throughout his career. It is remarkable that he appreciated the call to become educated at the moment he learned of his emancipation. "Learn your ABCs!" That nine-year-old child eventually built a life that continuously reflected his own intimate connections to education. When Evans arrived in Atlanta, in 1877, Morehouse had not yet relocated to the city. Morris Brown and Spelman had not yet been founded. As a member of Friendship Baptist Church, which was also the original Atlanta home for what became Morehouse and Spelman colleges, he witnessed these schools in their inauspicious efforts to build something beautifully ambitious for black people, as he had for himself.

In Atlanta, nothing was certain about his future; yet, with a courageous vision and, perhaps, an unreasonable optimism, Evans found a path forward. By 1900, forty-six-year-old Evans had expanded his plastering and masonry trade and had established his own business. He had also purchased a home with his wife, Sarah. Together they had seven children, ranging from six to eighteen years of age. Sarah was a schoolteacher in Fulton County. His two daughters, Ethel and Delilah, also became teachers, and two sons, Alpheus and William E. Jr., followed their father into bricklaying and contracting work. By the turn of the century, Evans had also witnessed the two small schools housed at his church mature impressively. [25]

Two white teachers from Massachusetts, Harriet E. Giles and Sophia B. Packard, with the support of the Women's American Baptist Home Missionary Society, founded the seminary for black women. However, the seminary's survival was dependent on local efforts from black churches and civic organizations, and gifts from black families. There, young women, most of whom had parents who were once enslaved, eagerly sought an education in a city that scoffed at the idea of education for black children. The landscape had remained wildly hostile to the concept of black people enjoying a range of "civic rights," which were, as Jay Driskell explains, "benefits attached to urban citizenship such as libraries, parks, and schools, sidewalks—all of which arise alongside the modern city."[26] Therefore, these newly established private schools became essential, providing secondary education as well. At the seminary, black women and girls learned the fundamentals of education, then more advanced subjects such as chemistry and literature in the church's basement.[27]

By 1882, the founders of the Atlanta Baptist Female Seminary had purchased nine acres of land that had once been a military base for General Sherman's troops. In 1884 oil industrialist John D. Rockefeller visited the campus and was impressed by the determination of the local black community to sustain this educational mission. He satisfied the remaining debt on the new campus and donated additional funds to support the growing school. His wife, a former abolitionist, Laura Spelman Rockefeller, was an enthusiastic supporter of her husband's philanthropy. Later that year, Giles and Packard renamed the school Spelman Seminary in her honor. Within a generation, Spelman College became one of the educational pillars of the nascent black elite in Atlanta and the greater South.[28]

These black educational institutions were disruptive to the old racial order in sundry ways. The quotidian relationships between the races were subverted by coworkers who shared responsibilities, discussed and debated intellectual work, and instructed black students to thrive, excel, and be more than just servants to whites. There were simple acts of kindness, laughter, and collegiality among administrators, teachers, staff, and students. The travails of teaching black students in a city and state that held such work—or the comfort and humanity of the students—in contempt was not lost on many of the white instructors.

Walter White, born and raised in Atlanta, attended Atlanta University, where he later remarked that the university was a veritable oasis of hopeful, civilized people in a sea of intolerance. White, who became the executive secretary of the NAACP and one of the most revered

The 1898 graduating class of Spelman College. Founded in 1881 and built on a former Civil War Union Army camp, Spelman educated students who were often daughters of the formerly enslaved. It would eventually emerge as the most-selective and highest-ranked historically black college in the country, with a per-student endowment higher than all other HBCUs and most white colleges. CREDIT: SPELMAN COLLEGE

civil rights leaders, was "indebted . . . to the unselfish and brilliant men and women who had forsaken their homes in New England to go south to teach in [a] school like Atlanta University. They had been subjected to ostracism and sometimes insult from Southern whites for teaching and associating on a basis of complete equality with Negroes."[29]

The employment of black professionals was a resistive act that served these schools. The class of people who could send their children to these schools widened as the schools created an ever-expanding universe of educated and professionally trained African Americans in the city. Although for many it was inspirational to witness the expansion of black professionals in such a short time after slavery, others viewed these efforts with hostility. For them, an uneducated black population was immensely more appealing. "The Negro's ignorance, superstition, vice and poverty do not disturb and unnerve his enemies so much as his rapid strides upward and onward," wrote one supporter of Du Bois's work at Atlanta University.[30] Despite such hostility, the beacon of higher education in the city continued to draw hundreds of black people each year for both education and employment.

Like others of the city's growing black middle class, William Evans found work in this orbit of higher education and black professionals' needs for businesses, churches, and homes. Members of his social and professional circles could both refer and request his work, which intersected with the wider political sensibilities of Afro-self-determinism. In fact, many members of the black elite and leadership class made conspicuous efforts to funnel business into the black community, forging economic development. Throughout the city, but concentrated along Auburn Avenue, black barbershops, hair salons, doctors' offices, and bars emerged. By 1905, there was an identifiable stratum of wealthy black businessmen who used their resources to meet needs denied the black community by its parsimonious government, especially the state and local authorities.

Of course, education had been central to the aspirations and measure of black progress. In addition to William's business connections to colleges and universities, Sarah's position as a teacher helped secure their family's solid position among the black middle class in the city. Sarah Evans used education for racial uplift. She was part of a wider community of black women who were at the vanguard of aggressive and ambitious work to educate black children. When middle-class women across the country forged reform movements and philanthropic efforts for the most desperate and poor, elite black women proved essential in identifying the needs of black communities that were generally overlooked by white women. In Atlanta, Lugenia Burns Hope, the wife of John Hope, Morehouse College's first black president, spearheaded efforts to address educational and health deficiencies among the city's black children. As chair of the fund-raising committee of the Gate City Kindergarten Association, formed in 1905, Hope used her networks among the city's black elite to provide essential resources. The heads of the Atlanta Life Insurance Company (Alonzo Herndon) and Standard Life Insurance (Heman Perry), along with the city's most prominent black mortician (David T. Howard) and various educators, donated thousands of dollars to establish and maintain kindergartens in the city. The church was also critical to the schools. The First Congregational Church, a home to many of the most visible members of the city's small community of well-heeled African Americans, covered the costs for one school on Cain Street. Atlanta University provided office space for the staff of the schools' operators, and Heman Perry bought a building for the association, even as black people were also taxed to fund whites-only schools. The thrust of Afro-self-determinism was so strong that despite the intractable forces operating against black institutional development, black organizations across professions and class were unequivocally committed to fill the voids created by an indifferent and often antipathetic government that continued to see black citizenship as a nuisance. The association raised nearly $200,000 in the early twentieth century, and as Driskell notes, "Nearly all of [it] came from black sources."[31]

Evan's business as a brick mason was growing enough for him to add to his home's size as his family grew.[32] They owned a house in the Vine City section of southwest Atlanta, at 610 Parsons Street. It was close to the Atlanta University Center as well as to downtown and other critical institutions in the community, notably less than a mile away from the Friendship Baptist Church at the corner of Haynes and Mitchell Streets, which he joined. Evans would eventually become an active member of Friendship, which had been the home of both Morehouse and Spelman colleges before they secured their own campuses. It was at Friendship that Evans would have regularly witnessed the exceptional talents and expertise of the city's black leadership. In fact, Rev. Edward Randolph Carter, senior pastor of Friendship, was one of the most prominent leaders in the city.[33] The church had emerged as a significant center of black leadership in the city, shaping Afro-self-determinism across generations through Carter's pastoral work. Black churches in the city—as they had been elsewhere—emerged for African Americans as "the bulwark of their economic and political lives," according to Alton Hornsby Jr.[34] Providing education, political organization, and social activities, the black church was the most critical institution for African Americans. Pastor Carter's leadership at Friendship led to a broader reputation far beyond Atlanta.

As vital as the schools were to the cultivation of a black middle class, the church was also essential for these educational institutions. And no churches were as important as Friendship Baptist Church and the First Congregational Church.[35] As was the case with many of the earliest black institutions in the city, the first churches were formed from larger white ones. In slavery, black people had been forced to attend white churches and be instructed in a theology that directed the enslaved to be obedient to their captors in hopes of being slaves in Heaven. Georgia laws that governed black assembly—religious and otherwise—constricted and exerted control over black religious expression. Henry Wright, who had been enslaved in Decatur, said that antebellum black church services explicitly inveighed against black freedom. In black religious gatherings, in the presence of white chaperones, there were demands that people express piety through their joy as slaves. However, Wright notes that "none of the slaves believed in the sermons . . . but [for the white gaze] they pretended to do so."[36] Of course, there were efforts to subvert these interpretations, but independent black churches were rare and in many cases were outlawed in the South.

After the Civil War, numerous black churches provided spiritual guidance for local people while simultaneously meeting many other needs, from hunger to education. An early black church, Wheat Street Baptist, founded in 1869, was a meeting place for one of the most significant cases of labor organization by African Americans in the city. In 1881 thousands of poor black washerwomen went on strike over dismally low pay for laborious work. Hundreds of women met at Wheat

Street in the sweltering heat of August to discuss their demands and the logistics of organizing in a city with such an inveterately hostile local government. With the intersectional forces of sexism, class, and race organized against them, they faced great opposition but pushed forward. The Atlanta City Council threatened new taxes on the women, and strikers were harassed by police and fined for random crimes. Ultimately, Mayor James W. English worked with the city council to help establish new regulations, which included a washer license fee of $25 to protect the workers' rights to demand higher wages. As Tera Hunter notes, the results were mixed in the long term, but they inspired other poor black workers in the city and region. The strike also exhibited an audacity among the poorest to demand some semblance of economic justice and reform. The use of black institutions—the union, the Washer Society, and the church—underscored Afro-self-determinist work in the early years after slavery.[37]

No institutions spawned from the local churches were more significant than local black schools. Frank Quarles founded the First Colored Baptist Church with twenty-five members, when the congregation separated from the white First Baptist Church of Atlanta in 1866.[38] The church started on its own in the most inauspicious way. Lacking any building or wealth, Pastor Quarles arranged to hold church in a boxcar, and then, after a handful of relocations to bigger spaces, his congregation purchased property on West Mitchell Street and established Friendship Baptist Church. When Quarles died, in 1881, Friendship Baptist Church had more than fifteen hundred members and had emerged as perhaps the most prestigious black church in the city, substantially shaping the educational, political, and social world of black Atlanta. Following Quarles's passing, Rev. Carter became senior pastor of Friendship.[39]

Like Evans and many other prominent African Americans in town, Carter was enslaved at birth, in 1856. The promise of education drew him from rural Georgia in 1879 to enroll at Atlanta Baptist Seminary, housed at Friendship. He later enrolled at Atlanta Baptist College, renamed Morehouse College, in 1913.[40] Within a decade of his graduation, he became pastor at the church that had once housed his alma mater. From 1882, he led the oldest black church in Atlanta and navigated its membership through generations of resistive and generative organization in the wider community. At Friendship, Evans found not only a spiritual home but also a locus of exceptional black people who excelled under extraordinarily difficult conditions. In a landscape that was inexorably hostile to black advancement, scores of the members of this church proved especially resilient and resourceful. The membership comprised some of the most affluent members of Atlanta's black community: physicians, morticians, small businessmen, and educators. The church was a staple for well-heeled African Americans. Morehouse College's first black president, John Hope, as well as the future first black president of Howard University, Morehouse alumnus Mordecai Johnson, called the church home. Devoted to his alma mater, Carter joined the board of trustees of Morehouse College in 1898; he was elected secretary two years later.

Indicative of the ways in which African American leaders viewed their struggles as connected to those of a wider African diaspora, Carter established and fostered institutional linkages across the United States and abroad. In 1905 he was a cofounder of the Baptist World Alliance, which was established in London. He served as a member of the organization's executive committee for decades.[41] From his extensive connections beyond Georgia, Carter was able to highlight the struggles of his hometown while also learning about shared struggles and challenges faced around the country and abroad. This undoubtedly gave him some sense of how Atlanta measured up against other cities, big and small, in the first years of the twentieth century.

On September 19, 1895, Atlanta, as a city with an eye toward its past and one toward its future, opened the Cotton States and International

Exhibition. President Grover Cleveland proudly opened the event, highlighting how significant the gathering was as well as its host city. Drawing thousands from the region and from the country as a whole, the four-month-long exhibition, based in Piedmont Park, intended to highlight in classic form how advanced and modern Atlanta had become just three decades after its wartime destruction. It was not a backwater, primitive town overrun with racial conflict, corruption, and retrograde worldviews. To that end, the exhibition invited the head of the Tuskegee Institute, a black college in Alabama, to be a featured speaker.

A relatively unknown African American leader in 1895, Booker T. Washington had ascended to the stage eight months after the death of Frederick Douglass, the most consequential and influential African American of the century. Whether Washington initially planned or not, he was primed to fill the important void left by Douglass's death. On the opening day of the exhibition, Washington offered to the nation his philosophy on race, social justice, and economic advancement. Speaking to a mostly white audience, Washington argued that black people should avoid politics and essentially accede to disenfranchisement in exchange for mutual economic advancement with white people. By every measure, Washington's speech outshone all others, including that of President Cleveland.

Given his putative capitulation to Redeemer efforts to purge black voters, but retaining his argument that the entire South would suffer without black economic opportunity and support for education, the speech became known as the "Atlanta Compromise." It became one of the most famous speeches in the country, especially by a black person. White leaders—civic, political, and otherwise—consulted him and donated to his school. Even black leadership found his approach initially compelling. Du Bois, then a twenty-seven-year-old professor at Wilberforce University in Ohio, sent Washington a telegram lauding his "word fitly spoken."[42] And although he seemed to capture the adoration of many, some openly expressed disagreement. At Nashville's

Roger Williams University, another twenty-seven-year-old, Ivy League–educated black professor, John Hope, opposed the Atlanta Compromise. A year later, Hope, a Georgia native, made it clear in a speech that Washington represented dangerous and "cowardly" sentiments. Many, he argued, wanted nothing short of full freedom, liberty, and justice. No compromises could be made on citizenship: "Let us not fool ourselves nor be fooled by others. If we cannot do what other freemen do, then we are not free. Yes, my friends, I want equality. Nothing less. I want all that my Godgiven powers will enable me to get, then why not equality?" Not wanting to constrict the scope of equality, Hope did not waver: "Now, catch your breath, for I am going to use an adjective: I am going to say we demand social equality."[43] Ultimately, the discussions and public disagreements about engagement with neo-Confederate politics presaged the ideological tensions over the advancement of democracy and race. The basic notion of black advancement being inseparable from social integration with whites was never a dominant demand or expression in black leadership. However, access to the vote and to the same civil rights guaranteed by the Constitution had been salient demands. Therein lay the discordance between Washington's rather innocuous support for "economic cooperation," education, and "mutual progress" and his insistence that black people avoid politics. The cheers and celebratory cries from Washington's mostly white southern audience evinced the problematic nature of his speech.

Although Washington did not advocate activism, he did support institution building and black professional networking to advance the wider community. Several black physicians who attended the exposition, perhaps inspired by their visit, formed a professional organization of black medical professionals. The all-white American Medical Association barred black membership, and the critical need for black health care demanded some systematic organization of black talent to address black communities' needs. In Atlanta several black doctors founded the National Medical Association in 1895. Atlanta's H. R. Butler was elected the chairman of the executive committee, and Nashville's Robert F. Boyd was elected president. Famed surgeon Daniel Hale Williams of Chicago was elected vice president. The NMA's first meeting was held at Atlanta's First Congregational Church.

By 1898 both Hope and Du Bois were professors in the same city but at different colleges. Hope accepted a position at Morehouse that year, and Du Bois had begun his career at Atlanta University nearby a year earlier. For many people, such as Du Bois, Hope, Carter, and Herndon, Atlanta had emerged as a promising home in spite of its neo-Confederate sensibilities. The rise of a small class of thriving, confident, and visible class of black professionals in this city in the Deep South attracted others there. Soon, black people across the country were reading about Atlanta: its black schools, its businesses, its hustle. Among other notable institutions in 1905, the city was home to the *Voice of the Negro*, which was the largest black-targeted periodical in the country. Edited by John W. E. Bowen Sr. and Jesse Max Barber, the magazine provided a space for literary expression and political agitation from a range of black writers, including suffragist Mary Church Terrell and poet Paul Laurence Dunbar. The magazine was prominent enough that even the most powerful African American, Booker T. Washington, published his writings there, as did Du Bois and Hope.

Amid the vitiation of black rights during the nadir, the *Voice of the Negro*, which started in 1904, emerged as a visible national advocate for Afro-self-determinism. Although its founder was a white manager, Austin N. Jenkins, from the publisher J. L. Nichols and Company, full control of the magazine rested with its black editors.[44] Because African Americans found solace in black institutions that cultivated black leadership, advocated for resources and rights, and determined their own politics and needs, the *Voice of the Negro*'s editors used their publication to popularize the critical value that Afro-self-determinism offered for black advancement.

In 1904 Bowen and Barber argued that African Americans had learned three fundamentally important points from white Southerners: (1) "love of [one's] race" was more important than a generalized love of humanity; (2) "high esteem" should be placed on the value of women of their race; and (3) "social equality" would not be achieved in law. The editors insisted in unequivocal terms that black people, confronted with the hostile forces of white nationalism, would be best served by adopting a clear-eyed politics of self-determination that was openly affirming of black people, black women, and the essential wholeness of black society. In other words, there was nothing deficient about black people. Their schools, churches, homes, and fraternal organizations were not inherently inferior to white ones. Whatever deficiencies that existed were a direct consequence of the vast and sweeping efforts to deprive black people of any semblance of justice or equality. To that end, Bowen and Barber firmly believed in and advocated for black people and white people having equal access to resources and opportunities. It was immoral and unethical to deny black citizens access to hospitals, libraries, the vote, and equal protection under the law. But they rejected the notion that freedom meant being in close proximity to whites in churches, in schools, or in spaces of social intimacy.[45] This was not a black-nationalist position. Unlike Martin R. Delany of decades earlier, or Marcus Garvey of decades to come, Bowen and Barber did not advocate for a black nation-state. They did not disavow allegiance to the United States or insist that African Americans emigrate to some other country. They fundamentally echoed what black leaders told General Sherman in the waning months of the Civil War: black people would be best served by determining their own destinies and controlling their own institutions as *American citizens*. Afro-self-determinism had developed in Atlanta and elsewhere as critical to black advancement in the generations after slavery. In Atlanta there was a firm institutional codification of this idea as the black community emerged in the post-bellum era. Its leadership class openly endorsed black people building self-sustaining institutions, demanding equal resources between races, and offering little in the way of demands for integration.

The rise of a small yet persistent class of black strivers helped shape the growing black population of the Gate City. They provided a broad selection of services that were often denied them by the white population. For example, African American morticians were common in large and small cities across the South. White funeral homes often refused to prepare black bodies for services, or did so with inferior service or in segregated and lower-quality facilities. In Atlanta, several black funeral homes had emerged by the start of the twentieth century.

Black medical doctors were barred from white private practices and even from the public hospital in Atlanta. Private black practices provided spaces for independent black health care, but these were grossly insufficient when compared to full-service hospitals, such as the largest in the city. On June 2, 1892, the city celebrated the opening of Henry Grady Hospital. Located at the center of Atlanta's black community near downtown, the hospital boasted quintessentially lofty ideals of fairness and equity in its mission statement: "It will nurse the poor and rich alike and will be an asylum for black and white." Six years later, on March 24, 1898, the state chartered the Grady Hospital Training School for Nurses. These health-care workers—all women—were trained to provide services for those in need. In the early twentieth century, however, the nurses and the physicians at Grady remained exclusively white. Despite the rhetoric for equal treatment, much like the rhetoric around "democracy for all," the largest public hospital in the state refused to train or employ black physicians or nurses. An all-white staff treated black patients in segregated facilities with inferior treatment and equipment. The hospital was so widely understood for offering two distinct health-care options that it was known as "the Gradies" rather than "Grady." Black patients who were light enough to pass as white were expelled from the superior sections if found to be black, even if it meant that such a sudden movement would be dangerous to the patient's health. The antipathy that African Americans experienced in health care affected all, regardless of class.[46]

When Du Bois's young son fell terribly ill in the spring of 1899, the Atlanta University professor "rushed out in a futile search for one of the two or three black physicians." Du Bois biographer David Levering Lewis details that in many instances, "white physicians refused to treat even desperately sick black children." Du Bois's frantic search for a physician to treat his child went unfulfilled. His only son, Burghardt, died from nasopharyngeal diphtheria a month after his second birthday.[47] The cruelty of a health-care system that disregarded human life was compounded when Du Bois and his mourning wife, Nina, walked behind a horse-drawn cart with their son's body en route to the Atlanta train station. Some peering racists, perhaps incensed by the spectacle of well-dressed black people, or simply eager to be hateful, turned to the couple and called them "niggers." The pain that Nina experienced in Atlanta was so great that she associated the city with misery and suffering. Du Bois wrote that after their son's passing, "in a sense my wife died too. Never after that was she quite the same in her attitude toward life and the world." The city and region were so unforgiving that it had become "a poisoned well" so acute that the eminent scholar suffered a nervous breakdown.[48]

Atlanta's devotion to the principles upon which the Confederacy rested meant that the construction of a tangible white southern nationalism had integrated itself into the social, cultural, and political fabric of the city. Of course, white nationalism was not unique to the Confederacy. As noted in earlier chapters, it had been ingrained into foundational institutions and laws of the United States as a whole. But the US notions of democracy and citizenship had been remade during and immediately after the war. Citizenship became capacious enough to include black people, including the right to vote, testify in court, attend public schools, secure passports, and even serve in Congress. In the neo-Confederate landscape of the later South, however, the rigid forms of white supremacy meant something else. The ascension of a neo-Confederacy meant that in Atlanta there was a concentration of black people in an urban space enveloped by an intractably oppressive and hostile state and region. To thrive under these conditions required an especially acute self-determinative spirit.

A personification of that spirit was Atlanta's first black millionaire, Alonzo Herndon. Herndon experienced a path to success that in some ways ran parallel to Evans's journey, deeply shaped by the fundamental principle of Afro-self-determinism. Herndon's story began on a plantation in Walton County in 1858. Like Evans, he was enslaved at birth and was a child when he was freed by the Union victory. He lived in poverty before making his way to Atlanta in 1883, drawn by its prospects of opportunity. Within a year he purchased half-ownership of a Marietta Street barbershop that had been owned by William Dougherty Hutchins. Hutchins operated the shop as a free black man before the Civil War, survived the Union siege, and rebuilt his shop after the war, catering to white men. As discussed earlier, the occupation provided well for black men such as Solomon Luckie, Robert Webster, and Hutchins, who all enjoyed material comfort that proved elusive for most Georgians, black or white. A generation later, Herndon owned multiple barbershops and promoted his flagship shop at 66 Peachtree Street as the largest and most extravagant one in the region. He purchased real estate in Georgia and Florida, expanding his business empire and visibility.[49] Herndon's marriage to Adrienne Elizabeth McNeil, one of the two first African American professors at Atlanta University, helped solidify his place in the black elite. His wife, a graduate of Atlanta University who also attended school in New York City and Boston, was a talented director of dramatics and instructor of elocution at AU. Through her, Alonzo cultivated friendships with the most privileged classes, learning social graces and befriending stalwarts of Atlanta's black leadership class and social elite, to which money alone would not have afforded access. Among those with whom he consorted was

Adrienne's colleague and friend Du Bois, Morehouse College president John Hope, civil rights activist and national NAACP leader Walter White, magazine editor-in-chief Jesse Max Barber, various journalists, and other intellectuals. Together, the Herndons and their cohort proved to be the nucleus of the black leadership class in Atlanta.[50]

This leadership class represented what Henry L. Morehouse, executive secretary of the American Home Baptist Mission Society, called the "talented tenth." Seven years before Du Bois expanded upon the concept, Morehouse, a prominent Baptist minister for whom the Atlanta college would later be named, argued that "in the discussion concerning Negro education we should not forget the talented tenth man. An ordinary education may answer for the nine men of mediocrity; but if this is all we offer the talented tenth man, we make a prodigious mistake." Morehouse argued that the black community most effectively challenged the conditions of racial oppression not by the sort of accommodation proffered by Booker T. Washington months earlier in his famous Atlanta Compromise speech: industrial education and capitulation to economic demands of white supremacy were no panacea for the erasure of civil rights and the expansion of terror. Instead, by cultivating "the tenth man, with superior natural endowments, symmetrically trained and highly developed, [he] may become a mightier influence, a greater inspiration to others than all the other nine, or nine times nine like them." Skilled individuals, by way of their professional training, could effectively lead and uplift the mass of black people. However, an important qualifier was that formal education was not a criterion for membership in the talented tenth. Morehouse explained that "sometimes these are 'self-made' men whose best powers were evoked by rare opportunities."[51] Herndon, who lacked a formal education, appeared to be the apotheosis of this "self-made" man who managed to be secure within the ranks of the city's black elite by almost any measure. His connections to educators, ministers, physicians, lawyers, and journalists, as well as his beneficence toward the black community, afforded him a prominent perch in black Atlanta. And it was in this ecology that the value of black institution building thrived. Across class lines, African Americans understood how critical social, religious, educational, and economic institutions were to the wider black community. Afro-self-determinism was a dominant expression across vocations.

When the Atlanta Benevolent and Protective Association (ABPA), a struggling black mutual-aid society, appeared moribund in 1905, a group of black ministers approached Herndon. The ABPA, which had helped provide insurance for poor people while employing others, needed a new owner and new leadership. Herndon purchased it for $140 and incorporated it as the Atlanta Mutual Insurance Association. By 1922, renamed the Atlanta Life Insurance Company, it operated in several southern states and was one of five black-owned insurance companies in the country with legal reserve status. Part of its growth was premised on its notion of black economic independence, which had long resonated in black communities, even as they advocated for voting and other civil rights. The Atlanta Life Insurance Company purchased smaller, struggling mutual-aid societies in black communities across the South. Its success helped Herndon become the city's first black millionaire.[52] He was a dominant black businessperson in a city with black-owned construction companies, physicians, morticians, restaurants, and other race enterprises.

In a country that denied black people from occupying leadership or sales jobs in any industry, well-dressed black salesmen fanned across the South and secured policies for black families, churches, and schools. At the company's headquarters, in the heart of the black community in what was once Shermantown, African Americans rose as managers and executives in ways not allowed in white corporate America.[53]

Du Bois, who witnessed the expansion of black businesses (and some wealth) in Atlanta, was impressed. The scholar even argued that a systematic organization of black business resources could, in effect, advance civil rights activism. The drive for economic development was not mutually exclusive from any demands for civil rights. In fact, attention to economic conditions was inextricable from the attention of the general conditions of black people. Using his platform and resources at Atlanta University, Du Bois organized a two-day conference, "The Negro in Business," held on May 30–31, 1899. Devoted to exploring the steady growth of black business enterprise, as well as the constrictions imposed upon African Americans in business, the conference assembled dozens of attendees from the region, many of them white and black academics. John Hope, future president of Morehouse College, presented at the conference, exploring the effects of industrialization on black labor among other topics. Ultimately, in endorsing the basic principles of Afro-self-determinism, the conference resolved that African Americans were best served by the establishment and support of black-owned institutions. Black people should create and patronize black businesses, which, in turn, would employ and support the black community, "even at some slight disadvantage." The larger scale of white-owned businesses might allow them to offer lower prices, but the indignities and the coarse and vulgar behavior of white establishments toward black customers could not be ignored. The conference called for the organization of "Negro Business Men's Leagues . . . in every town and hamlet" across the country. The meeting was consequential. The most powerful black person in the country, the Wizard of Tuskegee, Booker T. Washington, "paid Du Bois the compliment of appropriating the Negro Business League idea the following year."[54]

Further evidence of the significance of the meeting was the presence of Georgia governor Allen D. Candler, who addressed the attendees. Openly sympathetic to Redeemers and hostile to black people, Candler was nevertheless sensitive to his audience of academics, but he still provided some insipid and condescending observations. For example, in an offensively supercilious manner, Candler offered what he implied to be a compliment by recognizing that there were as many "God-serving

and God-loving" blacks as there were whites in the state. The statement was about as far as the governor could go in terms of recognizing
or affirming the tenacity and ambition of a people recently freed from
hundreds of years of slavery. It was also about as far as he could endorse
any notion of racial equality. Perhaps, as he implied, Christian confraternity had benefited black people in at least some way. However, Du
Bois made it clear that for whatever advances these devout Christians
had made since slavery, the terrible forces of racism had rendered most
black people as "serfs, bound to the soil or house servants."[55]

In case Redeemers had any doubt of his fidelity to neo-Confederate
politics, two months following his address, Governor Candler wrote
a clear-eyed, explicit letter defending and endorsing white supremacy.
On July 26, Candler responded to editorial questions about "race conflict" in Georgia. Writing to the editor of the *Chicago Inter Ocean* newspaper, he addressed the professional work and activism against racial
oppression, like that presented at the AU conference. But the governor
insisted that "one race must dominate the other." Without explicitly
referencing the Confederacy, Candler alluded to the famous "Cornerstone Speech" of CSA vice president Alexander Stephens, which
argued that white supremacy and slavery were natural, just, and good
for the enslaved and enslavers alike. Before the collapse of the Confederacy, the black person "was a slave, he was well contented to occupy
that subordinate place in society, to which his nature and condition
assigned him." The current discord, violence, lynching, and reports of
instability in the region were a consequence of the northern "carpet
baggers calling themselves Republicans . . . [who] falsely taught the
negroes that the southern white men were solely responsible for their
enslavement and were their worst and only enemies." In what may be
interpreted as an attack on projects like the AU conference and the
efforts of Du Bois, Candler argued that advocates for social justice
and civil rights were liars, con artists, and grifters who sowed seeds
of dissent and chaos. White southerners, he implied, were civilized,

fair-minded, and devoted to the principles of democracy; however, black people "call town meetings and discuss imaginary wrongs . . . and denounce the southern white people for crimes they have not committed." He blasted "mulatto adventurers of the Ida B. Wells stripe who impose on the credulity of the ignorant for the money they get out of it." Although he did not mention Du Bois by name, he inveighed against the "incendiary letters to turbulent negroes" written by black people in Georgia who used their writings in newspapers and elsewhere to depict the southern white man as a "conscienceless tyrant and demon of darkness." The truth of the matter, Candler concluded, was that "the greatest crime ever perpetrated . . . against American ideals . . .[,] human liberty . . .[,] and the southern negro was when . . . he was clothed with . . . the rights and privileges and responsibilities of citizenship."[56]

Ultimately, Candler redoubled his commitment to neo-Confederate politics. As he saw it, citizenship had been "criminally" given to black people, who remained as unfit or unworthy of it as they were under slavery. For him and other white nationalists, the institution of slavery was but one—albeit critical—facet of the old racial order. By itself, being held in slavery did not deny the possibility of citizenship for black people. Roughly 10 percent of black people at the start of the Civil War were, in fact, free. Most lived in the South, but wherever they lived, they were, at best, confronted with liminal citizenship. They were denied many rights, as previously discussed. However, citizenship in the postbellum era was infused with a more expansive notion of equality and justice after the Reconstruction amendments. African Americans were no longer subjected to simply being nominal citizens with racial constrictions. But Candler and others worked assiduously to prevent the expansion of civil rights, creating rigid forms of racial segregation that inadvertently provided opportunities for Afro-self-determinism in nearly every arena. For African Americans, under these conditions the fortified spaces of racial segregation fomented black institutional development. Driven by the fundamental principle of Afro-self-determinism, black leaders carved out opportunities for their community across industries, with economic development being one of the most critical ones.

Inspired by Du Bois, with whom he still shared professional respect and amiable relations, Tuskegee Institute president Washington organized the National Negro Business League in 1900. Intended to foster the cultivation of black business, it resonated with the self-determinative spirit of the black community. Herndon served as a founding member of the group.[57] At its first meeting, in Boston, businesspeople from across the country organized around the fundamental principle of black economic development: *black power* in business. The organization explicitly understood the limitations of simply advocating for integration with white-dominated institutions. Economic development was foundational to black uplift. As Washington explained, "At the bottom of education, at the bottom of politics, even at the bottom of religion itself there must be for our race, as for all races an economic foundation, economic prosperity, economic independence."[58] The organization sought to help black businesses network with one another for marketing, trade, and mutual economic development. Organizing a cross section of professionals—doctors, pharmacists, dentists, lawyers, and newspaper publishers—it quickly formed scores of chapters across the United States, further establishing the reach and influence of Washington as the undisputed leader of black America. However, his cautious politics, which avoided demands for civil rights, riled many of the black professionals active in his new organization, including Herndon and others in Atlanta's black leadership class, such as Barber and Du Bois.

Unapologetically capitalist, Herndon did not constrict his notions of black development to the sphere of economics. As noted above, the relationships between black business and academic and ministerial leadership were not only derived from the necessities of codified racial segregation; these leaders also found themselves intimately tied to common spaces of shared interest. Fighting for black economic development and fighting for civil rights and education were essentially complementary.

Nearly a hundred thousand black men registered to vote in Georgia during Reconstruction, electing thirty-two black lawmakers to the state legislature, one African American to Congress, and others to local positions across the state. There were black deputies in law enforcement, blacks serving on juries, and, as noted earlier with Tunis Campbell, justices of the peace, who had the authority to order the arrest of white criminal suspects. In Atlanta, a growing city with a visible and dynamic black community, African Americans represented 10–39 percent of registered voters between Reconstruction and 1889.[59] Black men were elected to office across the South as well, with more than twenty African Americans elected to Congress in the late nineteenth century. The rise of black political activity, though immediately facing resistance, was a mildly tolerated inconvenience for most whites and a foundation for greater freedom for black Georgians learning to navigate the new post-slavery landscape. Some Redeemers even attempted to court black voters into the Democratic Party, as discussed earlier. But the withdrawal of federal troops and the collapse of Reconstruction provided an opening for retrenchment and the rise of Redeemers. Furthermore, as the Republican Party—largely made up of freedmen and white northerners—withered in Georgia, the one-party state concentrated white power in a smaller cabal of men. The process of codifying a neo-Confederate vision for the state had begun in earnest by 1877, but Atlanta's retreat from democracy started even earlier.[60]

In 1870, when Radical Republicans held power in the city and state, William Finch and George Graham were elected to the Atlanta City Council in ward-based elections, whereby residents elected council members only from their own ward. The majority-black Third Ward and Fourth Ward sent them to office. When Democrats regained control in the early 1870s, citywide votes determined city council membership. As long as the city was majority white, it would be nearly impossible to garner enough support for a black candidate to be elected to city council, neo-Confederates reasoned. White voters would never endorse and support black candidates in significant numbers. The efforts to eliminate black voters and officials from the political process were virtually secured by 1900. Despite political diversity in whites divided among Democrats, Republicans, and Populists, "the white ranks," according to Eugene Watts, "closed and effectively disenfranchised the black minority." In fact, despite African Americans being the majority in multiple wards of the city (and nearly half of the population), it was not until 1953 that any black person was ever again elected to a citywide office in Atlanta.[61]

To the great majority of Americans, voting was essential to the exercise of real citizenship for any man. In a patriarchal society, with the assumption that men would dutifully protect and provide for their families, the denial of suffrage was simultaneously a denial of manhood. Voting meant having the power to determine access to employment, equal protection, political office, education, housing, and life itself. The citizen stripped of voting was no real citizen—or a real man. Disenfranchisement rendered freedom hollow and compromised manhood. Douglass argued that "by depriving us of suffrage," the guardians of the democratic process "affirm our incapacity to form an intelligent judgment respecting public men and public measures." Framing this argument in a broader context for an international stage, Douglass insisted that such attempts to constrict democracy "declare before the world that we are unfit to exercise the elective franchise, and by this means lead us to undervalue ourselves, to put a low estimate upon ourselves, and to feel that we have no possibilities like other men." He concluded that the United States famously boasts of its love of freedom and the election of its leaders as a heralded, enlightened right: "I want the elective franchise, for one, as a colored man, because ours is a peculiar government, based upon a peculiar idea, and that idea is universal suffrage."[62]

White supporters of black suffrage also enjoined others into action
to ensure the vote and protect the integrity of American democracy.
Radical Republican Charles Sumner argued that freedom without
suffrage was oxymoronic: "There was no substantial protection for the
freedman except in the franchise." This was essential "(1) For his own
protection; (2) For the protection of the white Unionist; and (3) For
the peace of the country." Like Abraham Lincoln and many others,
Sumner reminded Americans of the role of black men in protecting
their country against treasonous forces. To extend rights to former traitors while denying rights to patriots was an affront to the hollowed
ideals of America itself: "We put the musket in his hands because it was
necessary; for the same reason we must give him the franchise."[63] By
the collapse of Reconstruction in Georgia, however, a loud demand for
a new democratic process erupted.

The Democratic Party–controlled state legislature passed a bill
in 1877 that called for a new constitutional convention. Many whites
in the state resented the way in which the 1868 state constitution had
been "imposed" on them. That people once enslaved were full citizens
with access to democracy—even elected to office—proved nightmar-
ish for most former Confederates. Meeting in Atlanta on July 11, 193
delegates began crafting a new constitution, which they completed in
August. Voters ratified their 115-page document in December, herald-
ing a fundamental change in the political landscape and marking the
ascent of neo-Confederate power. A new poll tax levied on voters was
designed to be particularly effective in removing black men from the
polls. Of course, many poor white men struggled to provide the $1.00
tax (about $29.00 today) to vote. For subsistence farmers and share-
croppers who were often without cash, it was nearly impossible to pay.
However, the amendments to the new constitution provided a loophole for poor men: if they or their ancestors served in the Civil War
(either side) or if they or their ancestors could legally vote before the
war, they did not have to pay the tax.[64] Of the more than 120,000

white Georgia veterans from that war, more than 95 percent had served on the Confederate side. Around 3,500 black men from Georgia served in the Union; obviously, none were in the Confederate military.[65] This exemption proved to be an effective maneuver for Redeemers. The new Constitution also curtailed tax money in Article 7, which allowed for expenses for injured Confederate veterans. Where the federal government did not cover the expenses of its enemy veterans, governments like Georgia's stepped in with resources. Among other expenses, taxes would be used to "supply the soldiers who lost a limb, or limbs, in the military service of the Confederate States, with substantial artificial limbs during life." Former Confederate soldiers rejoiced at the provisions and protections afforded them by their Redeemer government. The new constitution not only restricted political advances from the newly freed people; it also reaffirmed ex-Confederate access to the critical means of establishing power from the creeping democratization of the state's landscape.[66]

However, there was criticism from some native white Georgians about voter suppression and the extent to which racism also hindered white voters. Tom Watson, the onetime Populist advocate for poor black and white Georgians, insisted that the mass of white voters had been bamboozled by white elites to adhere to racism and not consider their actual best interests. They would vote against measures such as reforms that would benefit poor whites in education and wages because these measures would also help black citizens. He argued that conservatives' allure for white voters "boiled down to one word—nigger." By pandering to racism, poor whites fell in line beyond the ruling class while preventing the rise of any independent reformist political movement in the South.[67] At least they were better off than "the Negro," poor whites reasoned. Being barefoot, being nominally literate, living in dilapidated housing, and facing chronic food scarcity were made more tolerable for poor whites if they knew that they shared a racial *civic equality* with wealthy whites. White nationalism had its practical utility, and eventually even white reformers celebrated it. The appeal of racism as a means to undermine free elections was so formidable that many of the neo-Confederacy's opponents capitulated to its power.

By 1904, Watson had rejected a robust commitment to democracy. Instead of losing to the conservative Democrats who pandered to white fear of black political power, Watson exclaimed that "nothing can be done as long as the South is forever frightened into political paralysis by the cry of 'negro domination.'" Watson offered an explicit call for neo-Confederate white nationalism, removing black people from elections legally. He demanded a "change in our Constitution which will perpetuate white supremacy in Georgia."[68]

The neo-Confederate landscape of turn-of-the-century Atlanta provided ample opportunities for black people to forge agendas to subvert and challenge the racist recalcitrance of their hometowns. The forces of retrenchment had also forced black leaders to address, more directly and systematically, the superstructure of racial oppression in a way that rejected the accommodationist style of Booker T. Washington. Although Herndon had been a collaborator and supporter of Washington, working with the Negro Business League, he also supported Du Bois, who was growing critical of Washington in the early twentieth century. Du Bois directed the Atlanta businessman to consider a more direct challenge to white supremacy and invited him to the first meeting of the organization that the scholar had hoped would upend and supplant the Wizard of Tuskegee. Another important figure in shaping the political landscape of black Atlanta was Barber, managing editor of the *Voice of the Negro*. A forceful voice of hope and resistance to oppression, the publication fit squarely in the ideological frame of the new movement's major architects, Du Bois and his Boston-based, fellow Harvard alumnus William Monroe Trotter.[69]

In 1905 Du Bois, Trotter, and others organized a meeting to discuss the crises in the black community and the need for a new organization. Herndon joined the organizers in Niagara Falls as a cofounder of the Niagara Movement, which famously presaged the National Association for the Advancement of Colored People in 1909. Following the gathering, the men organized local chapters of the movement, founding twenty-one chapters within five months.[70] As they had in other cities across the country, the black elites in Atlanta formed the bulk of the leadership class in no uncertain terms. They had the professional expertise, the resources, and a sufficient economic buffer between them and the white power structure to enjoy some degree of independence and freedom from economic reprisal such as job termination or expulsion from land.

At the turn of the century, Atlanta witnessed the maturation of its black elite. The term *elite*, as it applies to any community, is always subjective, and it requires some degree of qualification. It identifies the top echelon of the community, but exactly how that "top" is defined is not always exact. In general, the term captures the top tier of the black community in terms of income, wealth, and social status. However, some people who may have wealth may not be fully welcomed into any generally understood elite spaces. For example, a popular minstrel entertainer known for coarse, buffoonish, and offensive racist caricatures of black people may earn more money than a lawyer or physician but never be invited into the closed spaces of the established elite. However, someone like Du Bois would circulate easily within African American elite spaces across the country, given his critical role in a range of visible black institutions: leader, author, activist, and academic. In addition, given the profound constrictions imposed on black life, the most talented, industrious, ambitious black person would have been denied access to the levers of power commensurate with a white counterpart in any industry, including entertainment, business, academia, politics, and professional sports.

Given the nearly universal hostility to anything close to a racial meritocracy in the country (a hostility that was especially acute in the neo-Confederate South), black success was necessarily limited by the parameters of racism. The highest stratum of African Americans enjoyed wealth and luxuries out of reach of most whites yet would be nowhere near the industrial-level wealth, power, and access of the highest stratum of the country's exclusively white robber barons or even of the richest local families, who owned railroads, large banks, swaths of real estate, and manufacturing industries. The industrial-level economy was a space controlled by whites and closed to blacks in Atlanta and beyond. Indeed, the comparative scale between black elites and white elites reflected the superstructure of white supremacy and its inherent limitations on black success.[71] The fact that the term *elite* captures, perhaps, the top 10–15 percent of black people as measured by wealth, education, and family pedigree necessarily underscores its scale in relation to whites: simply working as Pullman porters or domestic servants for wealthy white families afforded some degree of status in this small pocket of black privilege in the first generation after slavery.[72]

Atlanta's postbellum black elite evolved differently from those in cities such as Charleston, New Orleans, Washington, and Savannah, each of them having relatively sizable communities of free black people in the antebellum era. Some free black people in these other cities owned upscale hotels, restaurants, barbershops, and real estate, among other businesses. Atlanta's late nineteenth-century black elites were relative upstarts. But by the last decade of the century, Atlanta had morticians, grocers, physicians, ministers, teachers, a pharmacist, and a lawyer who all relied almost exclusively on providing services to the black community. They were the leaders of a self-contained sphere of black entrepreneurial work that exemplified the self-determinism of the wider black community. Interestingly, however, some of the black elites accrued wealth much as their counterparts had in the aforementioned antebellum communities: by providing services exclusively to whites. In fact, the city's premier barbershops for white men were owned and operated by African Americans. Atlanta's leading shoemaker was a black man. Two black realtors had exclusively white clients.[73] By the dawn of the twentieth century, Atlanta saw fundamental shifts in terms of how white clientele patronized black businesses.

Multiple factors precipitated a shift toward the cultivation of Afro-self-determinism throughout the black community. The emergence of new economies and the decline of some trades—such as blacksmithing—meant that some reorganization of the black small-business class was inevitable. However, neo-Confederate ascendance proved to be an essential driver of these changes. The toxic racial politics in Georgia during the nadir—its extraordinarily high rates of lynching, disenfranchisement, open exclusion of black citizens from municipal and state employment, and generally coarse and hostile behavior directed at them—pushed black people into more rigidly segregated business communities.[74]

By the end of the nineteenth century, the black community in the Gate City managed to carve out an island of well-to-do people amid a sea of poverty and deprivation. Some of the elite lived in large homes, had servants, and established social circles that were accessible only to those of similar social ranking. Like African Americans and white Americans elsewhere, the elite carved out separate social spaces for leisure and civic engagement. They belonged to several exclusive social clubs. Two of the most prominent women's groups were the "Twelve," a social club, and the "Chautauqua Circle," a literary society formed around 1900. Although family pedigree was noted, it was not the sole criterion for access to these exclusive spaces, nor could occupation alone guarantee membership. Some wealthy people expressed a lack of interest, but others were "excluded on the basis of personal characteristics." The upper echelon of black Atlanta included members of select churches, primarily the First Congregational Church and Friendship Baptist Church. They formed a geographically contiguous community around Auburn Avenue in Northeast Atlanta. Financial institutions such as the Atlanta Life Insurance Company and, later, the Citizens Trust Company provided a professional space for black white-collar workers that intersected with their social arenas as well.[75]

Black and white migrants from rural areas continued to pour into the city in patterns similar to cities across the country. The influx of black people provided an expanding demographic of customers for black small businesses from grocery stores to the expanding class of physicians, morticians, pharmacists, and lawyers. This group of black professionals organized their resources for the advancement of black people in Atlanta and across the state.[76]

The expansion of the black middle class and a visible cohort of black leadership would foment two things in the coming years in the city: (1) a horrifying display of racial terror in one of the most notorious racial massacres in United States history, and (2) a shift toward greater militancy and broader acceptance of Afro-self-determinism as a central ideological motive for that leadership. The wave of violence that swept the city targeted black people, their businesses, their homes, and other institutions. The successes in achieving so much against so many obstacles only inflamed the most economically marginal members of the white community, who widely viewed black success as a threat to their advancement. An heiress to a large antebellum plantation who lived through Reconstruction fumed at the rise of educated black people. An educated black person, she complained, "does not fit in with our natural order, and for this reason no distance is so wide as that between the people of my class and aspiring, wronged, intelligent, vindictive negroes."[77] It was long argued that the most vicious among the agents of racial terror were poor whites, who were, as one contemporary noted in 1866, "at the bottom of nearly every assault and battery on the freedmen."[78] But this convenient foil obfuscates the ubiquity of racist retrenchment across the South and the country itself. Wealthy lawmakers, local elites, local journalists, and law enforcement enabled or excused murder, rape, and various other cruel and savage acts to ensure the subjugation of millions. The culpability transcended class.

The new century's hopeful start was quickly disrupted by a horrifying display of violence, which would itself reshape the physical landscape of black Atlanta and also change many black leaders' faith in the ability of local whites to ever be fair, democratic, or humane to their black neighbors. More than anything, black leaders scrambled to secure a greater freedom, safety, and security for their community, all things that neo-Confederates opposed even in the New South. The challenges to black freedom took creative forms and simultaneously influenced black social, political, and cultural spaces as African Americans galvanized to avoid conflict with whites. Freedom—or, at least, greater freedom—could be achieved only by retreating farther away from the gaze of whites and forging black institutions to meet the needs of the people.

Like states across the South, for a short period after the Civil War Georgia was enveloped in a profoundly disruptive reconfiguring of the racial landscape: millions of freed people and their children who had never experienced the indignity and horror of enslavement slowly moved closer to full citizenship, real freedom, and some semblance of power. They acquired hundreds of thousands of acres of land; established churches, schools, and small businesses; and voted and held office. But every step toward greater freedom was immediately met with a creative and agile campaign to restrict progress. Few sites offered clearer examples of this progress than the Gate City. As Lewis explains, "It was . . . the turn of Atlanta, the capital of the New South, where black men and women were accused of setting terrible examples for their country cousins by throwing off three hundred years of servility" by their striking achievements in business, education, theological autonomy, and political action.[79] Atlanta, in small but measurable ways, had become a visible rejection of the most hostile notions regarding black ability, social mobility, industriousness, and self-determination. Black Atlantans were striving and achieving against incredible forces. This advancement was fueled, in many ways, by the emergence of the city as the new state capital and the base for local federal agents, including the military.

However, the power of the Redeemers was daunting. Neo-Confederate power asserted itself in the most conspicuous ways. White nationalism virtually eliminated African American access to voting. Through terrorism, poll taxes, literacy tests, and whites-only primaries, African Americans in elected office nearly disappeared in the South. By the time of the founding of the NAACP in 1909, Congress was again completely white.[80] Thousands had been beaten, sexually assaulted, hanged, seen their homes burned, or removed from their jobs and lands for attempting to vote or otherwise politically organize black communities. As Du Bois explained, black people emerged from slavery, "stood brief moment in the sun; then moved back again toward slavery." This "move" was not their will, of course, but a consequence of cruel measures of legal and extralegal forces that, though strongest on southern soil, were met with mild indifference in other regions of the country.

There was no doubt that black people had the capacity to be university professors, college presidents, physicians, editors of newspapers, magazines, or executives of corporations. Even if the majority of white Americans were not yet willing to entertain these possibilities, Atlanta provided visible refutation of the racist myths. More specifically, the rigid neo-Confederacy sensibilities in that city produced a climate that was conducive to the rise of Afro-self-determinism.

Even as boosters for the city of Atlanta inveighed against the Old South and exclaimed their determination to create something more just, modern, and forwarding looking in the state capital, Georgia's neo-Confederate forces were fiercely dedicated to forging a new order that could, as best as possible, approximate the one that preceded it.

Much like any other facet of how segregation operated, the function of white nationalism provided state power and resources to be collected, organized, and pooled from all citizens for the exclusive use of whites only. The laziest, most untalented white person would enjoy resources denied the most industrious, gifted black citizen. The state demonstrated that all lives did not equally hold value, from the moment of birth forward. Unquestionably, race trumped class, individual merit, patriotism, and religion as the key denominator for access to civic, civil, and human rights.

6 | To Ashes, Again
The Desolation of Black Atlanta in 1906

A city lay in travail, God our Lord, and from her loins sprang twin Murder and Black Hate. Red was the midnight; clang, crack and cry of death and fury filled the air and trembled underneath the stars when church spires pointed silently to Thee.

—W. E. B. Du Bois, "A Litany of Atlanta," 1906

On an unusually mild summer day in Madison, Georgia, not far from the Joshua Hill plantation where William Edward Evans was born, Hoke Smith, the editor and owner of the *Atlanta Journal* newspaper, held a major and auspicious event. There, on June 29, 1905, Smith delivered his very first gubernatorial campaign speech to a festive crowd of 3,500 people. The people enjoyed a brass band, barbeque, and other activities organized by the Morgan County Hoke Smith Club. Smith, the son of a University of North Carolina professor and publisher, centered his campaign on the theme of "Justice and Civic

Righteousness," arguing that he had the strength, vision, and integrity to ensure that democracy and justice would thrive under his rule as governor. Smith presented himself a savior for a state suffering under the rule of a cabal of New South industrialists, heirs of the Bourbon elites, who used banking and railroad industries to exploit the working poor. Politicians, loyal to big business over all other interests, had failed to serve the people. He argued that he was a progressive reformer who sought control over big business, increased regulation, increases in educational expenditures, stronger child-labor laws, and popular election of US senators. The cabals of powerful Bourbon industrialists that controlled the New South economy had to be destroyed.[1]

Given his progressive reformist agenda, Smith reasoned that tapping Populist icon Tom Watson—the most popular reformist political leader in the South—for an endorsement would be a significant asset to his campaign. The progressive foundation of his campaign overlapped with Watson's Populist Party demands fifteen years earlier. Watson, who had later emerged as a virulent white supremacist, demanded that Smith would have his support only if the candidate could eliminate black citizens from voting altogether. Smith did not equivocate: if elected, he would create an amendment to the state constitution to eliminate black men from the vote. This, Smith argued, was his vision of democracy, justice, and electoral integrity.[2] Over the next several months, many others would emerge as candidates for the Democratic nomination for governor. In what was essentially a one-party state, whoever won the nomination in the Democratic primary was guaranteed a win in the general election. Among the other candidates, Smith's most bitter rival would come to be Clark Howell, editor of the *Journal*'s rival newspaper, the *Atlanta Constitution*. Together, Howell and Smith, through the power and influence of their newspapers, would add fuel to a cauldron of hate and racial animus. In the contentious, divisive race for governor, the two men's campaigns and newspapers would make an indelible imprint on the statewide politics and catapult

Atlanta into international notoriety for a violently brazen expression of neo-Confederate white nationalism.

By early 1906, the campaign was in full swing. On a cold January evening in Barnesville, about fifty miles south of Atlanta, five hundred people assembled to listen to a discussion between the congressman of Georgia's Tenth District, Thomas Hardwick, and Sam W. Small, a popular journalist. Small, a former Confederate volunteer, wrote a series under the nom de plume of "Old Si" for the *Atlanta Constitution*.[3] Old Si was a popular character in a minstrel-type persona of an old black man. Once enslaved, but finally freed, Old Si told stories (in a horrid approximation of African American vernacular) of his life and experiences. He waxed about the genteel and kind people who once held him captive. His simple, childlike fascination and misunderstanding of the quotidian elements of life reflected his basic unfitness for the responsibilities of democracy and full citizenship. The stories were popular beyond Atlanta, eventually giving him a national following.[4] The minstrel show, along with all of its archetypes, emerged in the antebellum era and was of northern provenance. Eventually, the minstrels, enjoyed by everyone from Abraham Lincoln to Mark Twain, spread across the country.[5] In an era of romantic memories of the Old South, a character like Old Si made perfect sense. At this meeting, however, Small was not operating through some blackface performance for excited crowds, thirsty for plantation-based amusement. This meeting was about the fate of democracy in the state of Georgia—and how to suppress or eliminate black voters.

As the new year started, the state of Georgia was already in a very contentious stage of the gubernatorial race. Citizens were concerned about the role that the state government would have in regulating a range of issues, new laws, and resources for the people of the largely rural, poor, and undereducated state. At the Madison meeting, people ventured out in an unusual snowfall to listen to Hardwick and Small. Debates raged about the right to vote being extended to African

American men. Even after a series of efforts to purge black men from the polls, there were still pervasive fears that African Americans would participate in elections, undermining the integrity of a sacred civil rite/right for white men. Small did not waver, stammer, or stutter when he offered his own full-throated opinion on the issue: "Giving the Negro the ballot was the most monumental crime against the nation."[6] His screed fell on sympathetic ears. Hardwick, for his part, confirmed his support of a white-nationalist project that denied the vote and other rights to black people.

Most histories of the 1906 Atlanta Racial Massacre center on the city's newspapers whipping up racist fears of black male criminals as the most salient theme in the months leading up to the rampage.[7] However, the *Constitution* and the *Journal* conspicuously focused on a threat of a different type: the black male voter. Although the *Constitution* endorsed Howell and the *Journal* supported Smith, both papers were unified in trying to secure the repression of black voters, if not their complete removal.

The debates in the earliest days of 1906 portended the dire circumstances of African Americans in the state of Georgia and in the state's capital. The gubernatorial race evolved into a contest between conservative Democrats who wished to prove that their opponent was not as committed to white domination. Of course, inextricably connected to their commitment to white supremacy, each candidate proffered a strong-willed desire to suppress or eliminate the black vote. In newspapers, in large and small public rallies, and in smoke-filled back rooms, people openly debated the effort to disenfranchise black men. Georgia's Democratic Party established a white primary in 1900, granting only whites access to the statewide primary voting. Before that, Democratic primaries were local, and some counties had no racial exclusion. The total exclusion of black men (and any men of color) had, in effect, eliminated them from the democratic process of a one-party state. Yet for Tom Watson, poll taxes and the white primary were not strong enough:

citizenship and democracy itself were to be enjoyed by white men only. Much like Confederates viewed freeing the enslaved as an abrogation of white freedom, neo-Confederates viewed extending democracy to black citizens as a fundamental threat to white democracy. And although the black voter was the most dominant bogeyman in the press, there were other nefarious black images that the press called upon to influence voters.

The months leading up to the election witnessed an increased use of virulent antiblack rhetoric. The case was being made in Atlanta's two leading newspapers: black men were not only a danger to the democratic process; they were also a threat to civilization itself. Black men were a monolithic criminal class, prone to theft, violence, and every manner of misanthropy. Alternatively, they were Old Si: minstrel versions of kindly old uncles who were content to remain in their place. These archetypes dominated US popular culture in a host of ways, and they operated with a very specific utility to popularize the notion that black men—whether prone to criminality or infantile indolence—were unfit for democracy. To politically empower a group too feeble to grasp the complexities of life was a fundamental threat to the integrity of democracy. Yet by 1906, another specter had emerged: the educated, industrious, politically sagacious black striver. The business leaders, physicians, lawyers, professors, and even college presidents were walking black refutations of the most ingrained and hostile stereotypes of the capacities of black people. These black men were, according to neo-Confederates, as much of a threat to white nationalism and the racial order as were their lazy and criminally inclined cousins. The only proper place for black people in the Gate City—and the New South at large—was a subordinate place in every respect: socially, culturally, economically, and politically. Much to their chagrin, Atlanta had become an oasis of black resistive energy of various sorts. African Americans constituted more than 40 percent of the city. They were visible in a way that they were not in northern and western cities, where the average black population (including New York, Chicago, Detroit, San Francisco, and Los Angeles) was 2.4 percent in 1900.[8]

For Atlanta, the proportion, density, and visibility of black people were exceptional. As noted in Chapter 5, no other city in the country had as many black centers of higher education. The city hosted the most widely circulated black periodical. African American leaders hosted ongoing national conferences, drawing hundreds of participants to the city each time. In the religious and financial regions, the city was already a distinct space for African Americans. For those in the capital city who witnessed the growth and vitality of the black community, responses ranged from pride and optimism to fear and rage.

The city also had a notoriously racist police force, even when measured against other southern cities. In fact, among twelve cities across the South, Atlanta had the highest ratio of black arrests—about 300 per 1,000 between 1890 and 1903. Only one city, St. Louis, exceeded 200 arrests per 1,000. Also, during that same era Georgia exceeded all but four states in the number of lynchings.[9] Given the deep-seated investment in racial subjugation, the gubernatorial campaign was certain to pander to those who feared black advancements in education, economics, and politics.

Therefore, 1906 proved to be a significant year for the most recent convulsions against the expansion of democracy in the state of Georgia. Of course, the state did not operate in a vacuum. It was more than simply the Deep South. It *was* the South. It was an essential expression of the neo-Confederate politics of white nationalism. To that end, the Redeemers and their allies in power organized around the most potent tool at their disposal: the vote. The election of officials who could form policies to grant Georgians uniform access to the benefits of citizenship hung in the balance. Therefore, the election and its consequences were closely followed by African Americans—from the elite to the poor.

Howell's supporters, such as Sam Small, were clear on their support of white nationalism and white supremacy. Yet they opposed

Smith, editor of the *Atlanta Journal*, who had allied with former Populist Tom Watson on a new scheme to disenfranchise black voters. The contest for governor had become a contest over who could be the most vitriolic racist. Smith declared that he would go further than Howell in restricting the vote to white men by demanding literacy tests to purge the remaining black voters from the voter rolls.

However, Small protested that the literacy test would be terrible for whites. He maintained that the "Smith-Watson combine" would not disenfranchise black voters. Its plan to establish an educational requirement, rather than the current cumulative poll tax, would instead reduce the number of white voters while increasing the number of black ones. In fact, the *Constitution* argued that when educational requirements had been enacted in Virginia, the effect was disastrous for whites. According to the newspaper, when literacy requirements were implemented in Virginia, scores of thousands of whites were disenfranchised. Rev. W. W. Landrum reported from Virginia, warning that when the former cradle of the Confederacy attempted to return suffrage to white men only, the effort was foiled by literacy tests. The new state constitution, "designed to eliminate the negro as a voter, as a matter of fact takes away the ballot from eighty thousand white men." There should be, Landrum argued, universal outrage among whites, but "strange to say nobody objects to it." He insisted that "the law must operate universally. If we wish to get rid of the negro in politics we must be willing to part company with the illiterate white men." Ultimately, the whites of Georgia, if true to the tradition of civic equality among white men, had to reject new proposals to disenfranchise black men. Such efforts would be disastrous: "If the majority favor taking away the ballot from eighty to one hundred thousand white men, let them say that such is their purpose."[10] The opposition to putatively antiblack literacy tests was significant and came from various political corners of the state. Of course, these efforts were not intended to safeguard access for all Georgia voters.

In many ways, Howell appeared to have the bona fides of a proper son of the South, as imagined by most Georgians. The son of a former Confederate artillery captain, he was born in South Carolina, educated at the University of Georgia, and had deep roots in the state. In 1876 his father purchased a half-interest in the *Atlanta Constitution*. Among his significant efforts, the elder Howell hired New South visionary and legendary Atlanta booster Henry Grady. He also added writer and story-teller Joel Chandler Harris to the team. Howell purchased the paper in 1901 and secured his role as someone with profound influence on public opinion. Politics appeared to be his calling.

In 1906, after years of various schemes to prevent black men from voting, gubernatorial candidates Smith and Howell both argued for the need to prevent any reprise of interracial political equality. At the encouragement of Watson, Smith amplified his racist bona fides. Watson believed that a progressive agenda would never win if it was associated with racial democracy or equality. His experience over the last twenty years convinced him that the mass of white Georgians wanted policies that reformed and limited the abuses and power of big businesses, like the railroads. He was convinced that many white Georgians would appreciate infrastructure and new schools: an approach that gave more resources to working people. He also argued that white Georgians would sacrifice all of those things if they believed that black Georgians would also benefit. At the very center of his experience lay the belief that racial animus remained the "keystone" of the arch supporting the exploitation and oppression of common people in Georgia. Because most whites were racist to the extent that they would suffer tyranny rather than enjoy interracial justice, Watson insisted that black voters should be removed from the democratic process. He seemed to conclude that the only remedy was the elevation of white supremacy into a Populist platform.

Democrats, Republicans, and Populists had all made appeals to black voters since Reconstruction, even if racial equality was an elusive component of their platforms. And despite the ubiquity of corruption in white-controlled political spaces, there was a pervasive notion that black voters tainted, or outright undermined, the integrity of the democratic process. Through bought votes or fraud, the black electorate had become a liability to a secure democracy, Redeemers and others argued. More importantly, the allusion to the neo-Confederate principles affirmed central tenets of white nationalism, where black suffrage was anathema. Despite one-party domination by corrupt conservatives in the Democratic Party, "nothing can be done," Watson argued, "as long as the South is forever frightened into political paralysis by the cry of 'negro domination.'"[11] Disenfranchising black voters, both Howell and Smith argued, was required, but Smith insisted that new measures be enacted, whereas Howell claimed that the poll taxes and the white Democratic primary had already secured white supremacy. Alternatively, Smith viewed the literacy test as critical to disenfranchisement.[12]

Howell used his many allies across the state in the difficult campaign against Smith. One of his many supporters included Congressman W. G. Brantley, who represented Georgia's Eleventh District. Brantley, mirroring Howell's platform, openly and proudly upheld the principles of white nationalism and simultaneously denounced the possibility of literacy tests in Georgia. Brantley argued that the disenfranchisement efforts directed at African Americans would actually "take the ballot from many white men and give it to the negroes." He dismissed concerns that his actions would defy the Fourteenth Amendment protection of equal rights or the Fifteenth Amendment protection of male suffrage. He instead insisted that Smith's scheme to purge black voters would not hold up against Supreme Court challenges. To great cheers from the audience, he said that "the white people of Georgia are [a] unit on the question of white supremacy. There is not a white man in Georgia worthy of the name, who does not believe in the supremacy of the white race." If literacy tests were the only legal pathway to the vote, calamity would follow. He warned that "young men coming of age who have neither education nor property, although the blood of Anglo-Saxon courses through their veins, can neither register nor vote."[13]

Consistently, Howell and his supporters warned that any educational requirement would advantage black people. "Enforce an educational test," fumed Small, "and you will disenfranchise more white men and enfranchise three times as many negroes as are going to the polls today."[14] Ultimately, Small argued that Smith—with the help of Watson—wished to gain political power by expanding democracy to black citizens. Howell's supporters drew connections to Watson's earlier support of white and black voters. Although Watson had denounced his belief in a fair and democratic process open to all eligible men regardless of race, the implication that literacy tests were actually going to increase access to the ballot proved a curious argument in the campaign to be the most racist candidate.

In various ways, the campaign to disenfranchise black men found allies in Confederate heritage organizations that saw their work as tied to the white nationalism of their forebearers. The United Daughters of the Confederacy had been the most successful organization in erecting Confederate monuments across the South. Of course, its female members could not vote, but they weighed in on the issue of democracy. Leadership did not equivocate in their stance that white nationalism was foundational to their efforts to celebrate and honor Confederates. As Jane Dailey notes, "The vast majority of Confederate monuments were erected after the turn of the twentieth century [to proclaim] the heroism of Confederates and their cause." Essential in this effort "was the disenfranchisement of nearly all African Americans and a significant number of white southerners, too."[15] These statues were also part of very specific agendas to extol and maintain the old racial order. In 1905 Martha Gielow cofounded the Southern Industrial Education Association (SIEA), which was dedicated to "neglected Southern white children." She argued that the extraordinary advantages (access to schools, student expenditures, teacher salaries, literacy rates, textbooks, quality of schools) that white children had were still insufficient. The excitement among African Americans to acquire education was outrageous to her and a fundamental affront to white people. A visible member of the Daughters of the Confederacy, Gielow endorsed the prolific creation of shrines to rebels but argued that they were more than just symbolic odes to veterans. In her campaign to raise funds for the SIEA, she made appeals that referenced Confederate memorials as hollow gestures unless the work to erect them was tied to an agenda that in a tangible way honored the Confederate legacy: "What good will monuments to our ancestors be . . . if our Southland is to become the land of educated blacks and uneducated whites?"[16] Even in defeat, these rebel generals and politicians were venerated because of their dedication to a specific cause, an ideology that resonated deeply with those who established the monuments for their posterity and their contemporaries alike.

African Americans, though not silent on the erection of Confederate monuments, were confronting the more pressing needs of securing the right to vote. They faced inexorable and hostile forces. Thomas Hardwick endorsed Smith and did not equivocate on expelling black citizens from the vote: "Until the south is finally rid of the negro even as a political potentiality she will never again have either freedom of thought or independence of action. Every Georgian who loves Ga. . . . ought to . . . rid the state of this curse."[17] This cry for the repression of democracy in the name of "freedom" rested at the cornerstone of neo-Confederate nationalism.

The effort to outlaw the black vote was challenged by the African American community, which mobilized in 1906 to defend what little political power it retained by forming the Georgia Equal Rights Convention (GERC). Its membership included several members of the Niagara Movement. These leaders had a focus on protecting and securing basic rights in both national and local contexts. They strategically used their professional resources and networks to advocate for civil rights.

Morehouse College's cofounder, Rev. William Jefferson White, called people to gather to defend civil rights. More than two hundred from around the state heeded his call, arriving in Macon in February 1906. The GERC had assembled an impressive body of black leaders. Many whites may have been shocked to see how privileged the GERC was. From AME Bishop Henry McNeal Turner to the first black lawyer in the state, Judson W. Lyons, the achievement of black progress against revanchist forces was notable. Among the 265 signatories of the appeal to white Georgians were Ivy League–educated black people, including John Hope, W. E. B. Du Bois, scores of ministers, twenty-five educators, seven physicians, and three lawyers.[18] They were disproportionately concentrated in the capital city, evincing the arrival of Atlanta as Georgia's most prominent site of black political power and influence.

The conference included workshops, lectures, and panels to discuss the forces organized against democracy in their state. The attendees grappled with the charged nature of the gubernatorial race and the hostile rhetoric around the "menace" of the black vote. They understood that their very existence was a challenge to the propaganda that black men were lazy, unfit, and unworthy of democracy. Yet they simultaneously understood that the antidemocratic forces did not need the "lazy Negro" archetype to justify their efforts at voter suppression. When convenient, the rhetoric against black men voting accused black elites of disrupting the natural racial order by attempting black rule over whites. The GERC made little effort to explain away the rabble or uneducated among the ranks of black people. Theirs was not an approach that rested on what has been called "respectability politics": the idea that if black people appealed to whites with certain ("respectable") cultural attributes (speech, dress, credentials, etc.), whites would soften their hostility to black people. They were under few illusions about the challenges before them: white nationalism had no space for the equal rights of anyone other than white people. Whites, from the wealthy to the poor, barefoot, unlettered dirt farmer, enjoyed civic equality in white nationalism. No manner of attire or education would subvert this fundamental tenet of neo-Confederate politics. The GERC argued that all black men, including bootblacks, sharecroppers, and unskilled laborers who languished in poverty, deserved the rights afforded them by the US Constitution. The organizers offered a cogent denunciation of the gross inequities and deprivation that they faced. In the spirit of Afro-self-determinism, although they demanded desegregation, they did not demand or request integration or social intimacy with whites.

Despite the presence of several prominent leaders who had once been open supporters of Booker T. Washington, the GERC did not ideologically cohere to the "separate as the fingers" in "all things that are purely social" that Washington had promoted at the Atlanta Cotton Exhibition a decade earlier. John W. E. Bowen, who was the second black person to earn a PhD in the United States, endorsed the GERC and had distanced himself from Washington, with whom he shared a stage at the 1895 exhibition. Bowen was the first black professor at the Gammon Theological Seminary and had become, by 1896, its acting president. A member of the Niagara Movement, Bowen argued that it was critical that black people have more than an industrial education and also that they must have full access to rights and equal protection. Washington's approach, which did not demand equal access to public accommodations or offer challenges to white nationalism, was not in step with this historic gathering.

As the signatories in Georgia made clear, having equal access to public accommodations, such as paying for and using first-class tickets for trains, was different from insisting that whites and blacks be "forced together" in all manner of social spaces in order for equality to exist. There was nothing special about the presence of white people. However, there were distinct differences in the quality of resources afforded white spaces, and these were regulated by current law.

Equality of access, not integration, was central to their call: "We do not desire association with anyone who does not wish our company, but we do expect, in a Christian civilized land, to live under a system of law and order, to be secure in life, and limb and in property, to travel in comfort and decency and to receive a just equivalent for our money." Public institutions were generally the focus of the declaration. The signatories revealed the stark differences in resources afforded white children over black ones: "The white and black student populations are nearly equal and yet out of every dollar of that state school money 80 cents go to the white child and 20 cents the Negro child." The state offered no pretense of equity for its citizens: "White teachers receive over a million dollars a year and Negro teachers less than three hundred thousand." At a time when black men were lynched for appearing "insubordinate" to whites yet white males assaulted black women and girls with near impunity, the collection of black male leadership demanded defense of black womanhood. They wanted black men to "look to the care and protection" of black women and girls from abuse and "degradation" by white men.[19]

Even as the convention outlined a history of enslavement, post-slavery exploitation, and institutional and legally sanctioned oppression, black advancement, they argued, could not be obstructed by formal laws and policies any more than by informal and de facto practices: "We must agitate, complain and protest . . . we must besiege the legislature." But just laws alone were not a nostrum for black people's miserable conditions. Black people, the signatories made clear, needed to "buy land and homes" as well as establish businesses.[20] Given that this leadership class was fully dependent upon black-controlled institutions and had personally witnessed how essential they were to the survival and uplift of the black community, the emphasis on self-determination was no surprise. Afro-self-determinism shaped and grounded their message, organizing, and basic principles.

Despite efforts at moral suasion, patriotic appeals, and practical application of the principle of a greater good, the African American leaders who met in 1906 were well aware that most white Georgia voters endorsed some form of racialized voter suppression. Logic, morality, ethics, and even an appeal to their Christian faith made little progress in this conservative white-nationalist space. Redeemers were openly promising various plans to suppress and restrict black voting and outright defy the Constitution. African Americans' citizenship and its essential power to participate in shaping law, policies, and justice were being dissolved in Georgia. The irony, of course, is that blacks were intractably loyal to the country, as these leaders made clear.

The organizers demanded that blacks be allowed to serve in the state militia. Echoing the position that black ministers explained to General Sherman in 1865, black people pledged fidelity to the United States. Moreover, in declaring that "we have fought for this country in four wars," they underscored that they, unlike most of the Redeemers, had not fought any treasonous war *against* the United States. African Americans were loyal not only in words but in deeds as well. In fact, they were so loyal that they wanted to realize the promise of the Constitution itself rather than defile it with gross abuse and corruption: "We ask this nation therefore the enforcement of the 14th and 15th Amendments." African Americans did not want to be deprived of access to any basic component of rights that whites expected from their own citizenship. In the end, the conveners called for interracial cooperation and goodwill: "Let us strive together, not as master and slave, but as man and man, equal in the sight of God and in the eye of the law, eager to make this historic state a land of peace, a place of plenty and an abode of Jesus Christ."[21]

Despite such pleas for human decency, the popularity of white nationalism was obdurate, powerful, and ingrained into the conservative identity of most Georgians. Whether white conservatives were ignorant of or indifferent to the appeals to aspire to a greater civic and moral good, the Georgia Equality Rights Convention gained little traction or consideration in the election. If anything, it provided evidence that a class of black people had become too ambitious, educated, and industrious for the greater good of the racial order.

African American calls for racial reconciliation and realization of the greater good notwithstanding, Smith wished to prove himself a bigger racist than Howell. Smith, eager for Watson's support, campaigned for the absolute removal of black men from the polls, arguing that a potential black voter was also a potential agent of crime and "miscegenation."[22] In doing so, during the months leading up to the election Smith and Howell used their respective newspapers to advance their campaigns and pander to racist fears of black men. Smith's newspaper claimed that black voter suppression was necessary "because we are the superior race and do not intend to be ruled by our semi-barbaric inferiors."[23]

On June 10, 1906, the *Atlanta Constitution* reported on its front page in bold print, "White People of Georgia Are Being Threatened by the Educational 'Disenfranchisement' Fraud Fathered by Hoke Smith–Tom Watson Combine." Quoting Congressman William Charles Adamson, one of Howell's supporters, the newspaper's headline reflected its own position against Smith while affirming the idea that "the real disenfranchisement has already happened in Georgia, the only state in which it was done effectively and constitutionally." Viewing Georgia as a standard-bearer of white nationalism, Adamson encouraged "other southern states to adopt Georgia's policy at once." It was unwise to fix what was not broken, Adamson reasoned. In a society that believed in the intellectual inferiority of black people, it appeared immediately incongruent that neo-Confederates insisted that black people would be at an advantage with the application of literacy tests. According to Adamson, however, the fear was based on a bizarre mix of racist theories grounded in surreal illogic and pedestrian ignorance. Black people, according to the congressman, "can go naked and live on nothing and go to school all the time." On the other hand, Adamson argued, "white men—no matter how illiterate, having both pride and energy, having to keep up appearances, clothe their families—are compelled to allow some of their children to work." He lamented that

"all of the money from all our enemies at the disposal of the negroes"
to seek an education will "abandon our advantage" in Georgia.[24] Of
course, racism rarely follows consistent lines of logic. What was evident
in the public debates about voter suppression in Georgia was a peculiar
desperation that was discursive as it was illogical. Black men were at
once lazy, childlike, unambitious, incurious, and ignorant yet also zealous about education—even more so than whites were—and politically
ambitious and cunning. As a political class, they were a thoroughly
active and fundamental threat to the racial order and thus a threat to
neo-Confederate nationalism.

Although the campaigns against black men as voters were constant
throughout the year, a shift toward trafficking in tales of black male
criminality dominated the press in the weeks leading up to the primary
election in August. False reports of black men sexually assaulting white
women circulated on the pages of the newspapers, culminating in acute
white vigilance and simmering racist hostility by the late summer. The
integrity of democracy in the state of Georgia had always been tenuous
at best. It was, after fall 1906, a pipe dream, a wishful state of nearly
dystopian hardship for many, and a world with a rapidly eroding sense
of common good. But the increasingly inhospitable social, cultural, and
political landscape encouraged greater emphasis in the black community on channeling resources and talent into black institutions.

In the months before the fateful days of late summer, African
Americans in Atlanta had emerged as important figures in casting
light on a new, invigorated stage of struggle for freedom and justice. On
August 17, 1906, the men of the Niagara Movement assembled again
with new members, including women this time. They met at Storer
College, a black school in Harpers Ferry, West Virginia. There the congregants recognized the historical legacy of the 1859 John Brown raid
while underscoring the continued fight against racial oppression. AME
bishop Reverdy C. Ransom, a radical religious leader based in Boston,
offered a powerful speech on the model of John Brown's spirit.[25]

The meeting at the site of the John Brown raid was symbolic. The raid was a major catalyst of the sectional tensions that would erupt in civil war within two years. The sense that the conditions of 1906 were dire, along with the idea that a meeting at Harpers Ferry was associatively subversive, reflected the militancy of the organizers. They were fully aware of the daunting undemocratic forces before them. Georgia's efforts at disenfranchisement were not unique to that state but were endemic to the former Confederacy states. These disenfranchisement efforts posed a sectional threat to the integrity of the Constitution and to American democracy itself. Perhaps something as bold as meeting at Harpers Ferry would highlight the seriousness of the national efforts that were underway.

Niagaraites made a case for a new movement that stood in stark contrast to the accommodationist politics of Booker T. Washington. Like John Hope, who argued immediately after the Atlanta Compromise speech, "Why not equality?," they refused to prostrate themselves before the forces of white nationalism. They would not obsequiously ask for mutual economic advancement at the expense of dignity and full citizenship. As David Levering Lewis explains, Du Bois had grown to believe that "compromise was the cousin of cowardice" in matters of justice. Du Bois had also "polite contempt" for those who embraced Washington's belief that "silence . . . was frequently the optimal means to gain an advantage."[26] The demise of black rights, seemingly all but certain by 1906, would not be passively accepted. A national network of black activists—Chicago's Ida B. Wells, Boston's William Monroe Trotter and Josephine St. Pierre Ruffin, and Washington's Mary Church Terrell, Anna Julia Cooper, and Charlotte and Francis James Grimké—offered exceptionally talented and resourced people poised to systematically raise a new standard of protest for civil rights.

The Niagara Movement declared that "in detail, our demands are clear and unequivocal. . . . We would vote. With the right to vote goes everything; freedom, manhood, the honor of your wives, the chastity of your daughters, the right to work and the chance to rise, and let no man listen to the liars who deny this. We want full manhood suffrage. We want it now, henceforth and forever." Continuing a theme common among black leadership since Reconstruction, the group called for widespread education for all people: "We want the National Government to wipe out illiteracy in the South." But all forms of education were not acceptable or equal. In an allusion to the industrial education that the Wizard of Tuskegee promoted, the Niagara Movement insisted that "we want our children trained as intelligent human beings should be, and we will fight for all times against any proposal to educate black boys and girls, simply as servants and underlings, or simply for the use of other people."[27]

Events like this undoubtedly inflamed efforts to fully remove black men from the voting rolls in Georgia and elsewhere. The neo-Confederate leadership in Georgia dismissed any notions that democracy was either compromised or being altogether dismantled in their state by their efforts. Local journalists simply refused to cover the Niagara Movement meeting. Although newspapers across the country reported on the gathering, the *Atlanta Constitution* ignored it altogether. Even southern papers hostile to the notion of equal rights provided coverage, such as the *Sentinel* of Grenada, Mississippi. That paper derisively referred to the organizers as "misguided negroes largely from Northern states." Maryland, according to the paper, "was the only Southern state with any representation there at all." And it had "largely lost its Southern identity."[28] In truth, however, attendees arrived from across the country, including every former Confederate state.[29] Only a week before the meeting, on August 10, the *Constitution* reported that Hoke Smith's "discourse upon the negro in politics" had lost him support among the "conservative citizens" of Macon. Again, the emphasis on excluding the black vote remained dominant in nearly every issue.[30]

On the eve of the Democratic primary, it appeared that Smith's campaign, despite reports to the contrary by the *Constitution*, had been a success. Among those who promised white supremacy, the one who promised white supremacy and reform had the greatest appeal. Poor whites had always been positioned to significantly benefit from progressive reform through safer working conditions, expanded infrastructure, increased resources in health care and education, and child-labor laws. Since the Populist movement, however, any reformist efforts had been undermined by conservatives who argued that Populism enabled "negro domination," "racial amalgamation," and "social equality" or otherwise weakened white domination. Any effort to benefit Georgians suffered as long as white Georgians believed that blacks would also benefit. They were willing to deny themselves resources as long as it also kept resources from black people. Any biracial political coalitions had been tenuous and short-lived. It appeared that Smith found the right path to progressive reform against conservative rule: promise to deny resources to black people. Therefore, reform in the context of a neo-Confederate white-nationalist construct had the perfect appeal. Many in the white political leadership in the state fully understood the power that Smith held. Hardwick explained to Watson that Smith could "mentally, physically, and financially beat Clark and 'the boys.'" Smith had the appeal, resources, and political platform to provide a "square deal" to the (white) people of Georgia.[31]

As the Niagara Movement gathering was ending at Harpers Ferry, Georgia's Democratic primary was held on August 22. After a grueling, bitter, and intensely race-baiting campaign, Smith, who promised to remove black men from the ballot, won in a landslide. In a field with five major candidates, he won more than half the votes cast.[32] Indeed, the reformist who promised to use the state constitution to deny one-third of Georgia's potential voters the ballot rejoiced after an overwhelming victory. The fact that so many white Georgians were so eager to support the most outrageously antidemocratic candidate was not lost on African Americans.

Only a week after the primary, the National Negro Business League (NNBL) started its meeting in Atlanta, its first national meeting in the

Deep South. Although the idea for the NNBL emerged from the 1899 Atlanta University conference "The Negro in Business," organized by Du Bois, it was Washington who founded the league, in 1900. His conciliatory politics granted him a wide range of favors and benefits in the Gate City. During the Atlanta meeting, various powerful and influential whites supported the endeavor and general mission, including the acting mayor, J. H. Harwell, and the head of the Atlanta Chamber of Commerce, Sam D. Jones. The city's leadership even granted black people and white people equal access to trolleys during the meeting as a demonstration of the city's openness to black investment and capital development. Africans Americans were also granted access to the city's public parks for the duration of the conference.[33]

In a rousing speech at Big Bethel AME Church, the participants cheered Washington as he spoke on the cornerstone principles of African Americans at large. The optics could not be overlooked. The conference centered its focus on the establishment and support of black businesses. It was made possible by a black leadership class tied to black institutions, educational and religious. Big Bethel was connected to Morris Brown College, the only college in Atlanta formed by, named for, and led by black people. Afro-self-determinism was the cornerstone of the general meeting. The cheers and accolades resonated because Washington struck a chord with the sensibilities of the mass of black people in the city who witnessed the value of black-controlled spaces.

The response to the NNBL from some white power brokers in the city reflected the degree to which the white community, much like the black community, was not ideologically monolithic. The more moderate elements of the black community—particularly as expressed by the accommodationist style of Booker T. Washington—appealed to some elements of the local white population. These white leaders, such as Jones and Harwell, understood that business development was critical to the advancement of Atlanta. Given that roughly a third of the state and around 40 percent of the city was black, education, employment, and commerce among African Americans could be beneficial to the city and state. This was also good for the national image of a city unburdened by race hatred, as Henry Grady famously insisted. Moreover, there was always a popular notion that whites of any sort—white nationalists, white progressive reformers, or even white conservatives—believed that they did not *hate* black people. More often than not, the general white sentiment sought control over the fate of black people and the general continuing of a racial order that kept whites in a dominant role. To that end, some whites advocated for varying degrees of resources (electoral, educational, employment, etc.) for black people. As long as whites still controlled the major economic institutions and wielded political power in all things that mattered, many black people could enjoy some semblance of comfort and collective advancement. Putting on an accommodating show of tolerance in the city was worth the resources to court black investment. Of course, these relatively progressive ideals were in direct contrast to the hostile diatribes that dominated the local press. The *Constitution* argued that "the willingness of the southern negro to work is fast dying out." And much like its treatment of the Niagara Movement, the newspaper largely ignored the NNBL's meeting, even as the league received national media attention.[34]

Despite the opening of parks and trolleys to African Americans, Washington was keenly aware that the racial climate in the Gate City was terribly charged. On the heels of Smith's victory and his promise to disenfranchise African Americans forever, there were reports of black assaults on whites that alarmed the Wizard of Tuskegee. These reports, generally unfounded, had been so common that one newspaper, Washington noted, demanded that there be a resurrection of the Ku Klux Klan. He presciently observed that the racial tensions, in the wake of Smith's Democratic primary victory, brought the city "almost to the breaking point."[35] Perhaps sensing that some form of violent racial conflict was imminent, white shops had refused to sell firearms to black people in the past several weeks.[36]

Washington hoped that the NNBL's meeting and its showcase of black industriousness and quiet self-determination would mollify white rage and challenge hostile stereotypes of indolence and criminality. Like other black leaders, he denounced black criminality. However, Du Bois and other activists had made it clear that white criminality was also a problem. In particular, they had long protested sexual assaults against black women and girls. For his part, the more conservative Washington sought appeals to editors of the four largest white newspapers in Atlanta. Washington believed that his appeal to southern whites would help calm racist yellow journalism, but his influence "was waning." He shared his NNBL speech with the white newspapers in an effort to demonstrate to the largely hostile presses that black people "have self-reliance, patience, sagacity, and thrift."[37] The degree to which his appeals affected white public opinion is uncertain. Yet what is clear is that the simmering rage was about to explode in a very public and tragic way.

The political landscape leading into the fall elections was shaped by an especially acute antiblack chorus from the candidates. The newspapers that were respectively associated with each candidate offered a sedulous campaign to appeal to the most base, white-nationalist principles. By default, southern newspapers identified the race of a criminal suspect only when he or she was black. Front-page reports of every type of black misanthropic riffraff highlighted the danger that black people posed beyond the ballot box. Articles covered attacks on police officers and on civilians, and "dives" overrun by black vagrants and loafers. One article insisted that even "respectable negro citizens of Atlanta as well as all white citizens" stood against these dives. The implications that loafing and vagrancy were domains exclusive to black people were clear, given that "all whites" objected to such examples of ill repute.[38]

Newspapers in the state capital and beyond assiduously pushed antiblack hysteria in late September. As noted above, the press provided space for the condemnation of the loafer, the criminal, and the ambitious Niagara Movement crowd as well. They represented the dangers of "'uppity' Blacks [seeking] equality with whites."[39]

Yellow journalism maximized the moment. Satisfying appetites for more sordid tales of black danger, papers produced special editions "with lurid details and inflammatory language intended to inspire fear if not revenge."[40] Some representative headlines were "'Extra! Third Assault on White Woman by a Negro Brute!,' 'Extra! Bold Negro Kisses White Girl's Hand!,' and 'Extra! Bright Mulatto Insults White Girls!'"[41] Sensing that the city was on the precipice of civil unrest, Mayor James G. Woodward attempted to mitigate fears. He visited the streets downtown, enjoining people and addressing the angry groups, demanding they go home to their families. It was too little too late. "The honor of Atlanta before the world is in your hands tonight," Woodward told the hostile crowd. The chief of the city's police department, James English, joined the mayor in the effort to calm the mob. Incensed, the defiant mob accused the officials of being "nigger lovers."[42]

As the sun began to set on the warm late-summer day of September 22, crowds shared news of more assaults on white women: the city authorities were doing little to nothing about it; whites were the victims; blacks were the villains. Finally, they began screaming at black passersby and pushing, spitting on, and hitting them as they attempted to pass through crowds seething with anger and resentment. Then the attacks escalated. Packs of frothing, red-faced, screaming men and boys began moving into black areas, including Wheat Street and the current Auburn Avenue, pulling black people from streetcars and out of shops, and attacking black homes and businesses. Black people were pulled outside and chased along streets and sidewalks. Innocent people with no connections to any alleged attacks against anyone were stoned, kicked, and stabbed. Forty-two years after Sherman first expelled Confederate troops from Atlanta, the black community—in its entirety—was met with extraordinary wrath and violence.

Starting at the corner of Pryor and Decatur Streets, barbarous handfuls of hoodlums snowballed into groups of dozens, then hundreds.[43] The *Atlanta Constitution* reported in bold headlines on September 23 that "Atlanta Is Swept by Raging Mob Due to Assaults on White Women: 16 Negroes Reported to Be Dead." The paper provided graphic coverage of the violence sweeping the city. At Alonzo Herndon's barbershop across from the post office downtown, a mob assembled screaming, "Get 'em! Get 'em all!" The pack, "armed with heavy clubs, canes, revolvers, several rifles, stones and weapons of every description, made a rush on the negro barber shop." After breaking the windows with bricks, the horde rushed inside, finding two startled barbers who offered no resistance. One of them, perhaps intending to calm the crowd, stepped forward with both hands in the air as if to surrender. A white journalist described the scene: "A brick caught him in the face, and at the same time shots were fired. Both men fell to the floor. Still unsatisfied, the mob rushed into the barber shop leaving the place a mass of ruins." The ferocious pack attacked the bodies, kicking and mauling them. After tearing cloth from the men's corpses, the hooligans waved the bloody fabric in the air to wails and cheers. With blood-stained cloth souvenirs, members of the murderous group dragged the bodies across the street to form a small mound of corpses. The pile of the dead expanded with another victim, emerging as a horrifying public spectacle at the base of the statue of Atlanta's biggest New South booster, Henry Grady. It was a vivid demonstration of the utter barbarity and lethality of a city in civil collapse. It was also a sobering example of the consequences of neo-Confederate white nationalism.[44]

Property across the city was attacked as well. Trolleys and store windows were smashed. Victims were taken to Grady Hospital. From Marietta Street to Auburn Avenue, black people were found killed by mobs. Three men were murdered on a trolley car along Georgia Avenue.[45] Tying in neatly with the wider narrative of the unfitness of black men as citizens in the body politic, the press centered its focus on black people as the culpable party for the violence. According to the *Constitution*, the marauders who terrorized the city were simply reacting to the violence posed against innocent whites. The riot was the "culmination of crime" that had been targeting blameless white victims, the paper insisted. Targeting innocent people, including women and children who had no connections to any alleged attacks, seemed logical to the writers at the esteemed newspaper. The murders, arson, and assaults, the paper reasoned, were not a consequence of a deeply ingrained system of racist subjugation and continuous propaganda against black people. The violence was "caused by assaults on white women in last few months and four attempts yesterday." That anyone who may have assaulted a woman was not counted among the scores of black victims—including women and children—was immaterial to the rampage itself. The violence was otherworldly in its depravity. One horde that had been scouring the streets found a small black child and decided to use the child for target practice.[46]

Thugs roamed the streets with near impunity. Even people in their workplaces—regardless if they were white controlled or not—were victimized: "The post office, train station, and white-owned businesses had been pillaged whenever the marauding mob ferreting out its prey like a huge bloodhound, sniffed terrified black employees in hiding."[47] An estimated mob of ten thousand whites—the size of the entire population of Atlanta at the start of the Civil War—assaulted black people in various spaces in the city. For more than two days, the violence raged as racists attacked black men, women, and even children. In addition to being shot, some people were pelted with rocks and bricks, beaten by packs of hoodlums, and even hanged from lampposts: "Rioters crucified several bodies on utility poles and expressed contempt for the New South's concession to racial progress. . . . They also chased blacks into traditional refuges: homes of paternalistic whites, recreation areas, suburbs, and campuses of black schools."[48]

The police attempted to temper the roving bands of looters and rioters, using varying degrees of effort. Many people reported that the police worked hard to stop the violence, but others insisted that their efforts were tepid at best. Governor Terrell met with Colonel Clifford L. Anderson of the Fifth Infantry and other military officials on the first night of violence. They decided to mobilize the militia, which was called out shortly after midnight on the morning of September 23.[49] In Brownsville, Mechanicsville, the Bottoms, and other black sections, as the state called in reinforcements, black people witnessed military units of white men with rifles, handguns, and even a Gatling gun. It appeared as if they had been transported to another battle of Atlanta.

The event has been thoroughly explored by historians, sociologists, and others, and a veritable who's who of black Atlanta left documentation of the event.[50] William E. Evans, who had achieved so much since he scrambled to the fences to bear witness to Union soldiers offering freedom to him and his family in 1864, was one of those who recorded what he saw in 1906. By this time, Evans was a married father of several children and a successful businessperson. Despite the year's extraordinary racial tensions, he had recently celebrated the college graduation of his daughter Ethel, who earned a degree from Atlanta University's normal department in 1906.[51] Amid elation and pride at the arc of his family's accomplishments achieved in the Gate City, he also became overwhelmed by the violence around him. Although many had hoped that Governor Terrell's mobilization of the state militia would put down the mobs, Evans explained otherwise. The troops, he observed, often joined in racist attacks:

> I saw the toll of the riot—hatred, prejudice, and murder. I [was] working out on what is now Highland Avenue at the time. Soldiers had to be sent out and they [were] supposed to protect everyone but some of them didn't uphold the law. There [was] a gang of soldiers. . . . They [were] acting like ordinary, revengeful people, pouring

out their hatred for the Negro. Those soldiers came down the streets shouting and singing: "We are rough, we are tough, We are rough, we are tough. We Kill niggers and never get enough." That gang of soldiers went right on their marching and when they got to McGruder Street they killed a Negro. . . . They seemed bent on showing their wrath against the Negro. That [was] a pitiful time.[52]

As with Evans, 1906 provided a grand moment of celebration for John Wesley Dobbs, who married Ophelia Thompson that year. Years before he would become the unofficial "mayor of Auburn Avenue," however, the twenty-four-year-old loaded his Colt pistol and stood watch at his home at 446 Auburn Avenue as civil society appeared to collapse around him. With ammunition stacked nearby, he stayed vigilant every night of the unrest and remained so even after order had been restored.[53] George White, who had migrated to Atlanta for opportunities elusive to him in Augusta, had achieved some degree of comfort in the city. As noted in Chapter 5, he finished high school at Atlanta University's secondary school, then completed one year of college before leaving school for financial reasons. He became a postal worker, married a schoolteacher, and established himself as a middle-class parent of several children. The ironically named White family could pass as Caucasians yet were absolutely enveloped in African American social and political spaces. They were members of the First Congregational Church with the Dobbs family and, of course, attended black schools. They lived in a black community on Houston Street, a few blocks from the Candler building, in an area with poor, working-class, and other middle-class black families.

George's youngest son, Walter, left a harrowing record of their experience during the unrest. Walter, who was a twelve-year-old with blond hair and blue eyes, enjoyed the benefits of racism by passing as white and even secured whites-only employment as a youth. But despite whatever ephemeral crossings over the racial line he experienced, the racial massacre taught him that "there was no isolation from life" for a black family in a racist society. George and Walter were on a mail truck in downtown when the massacre unfolded. They cautiously navigated the mayhem, weaving in and out of groups of assailants who did not recognize them as potential targets of a veritable racial pogrom. They were traveling through downtown Peachtree Street when

> we heard the terrifying cries, this time near at hand and coming toward us. We saw a lame Negro bootblack from [Alonzo] Herndon's barber shop pathetically trying to outrun a mob of whites. Less than a hundred yards from us the chase ended. We saw clubs and fists descending to the accompaniment of savage shouting and cursing. Suddenly a voice cried, "There goes another nigger!" Its work done, the mob went after new prey. The body with the withered foot lay dead in a pool of blood on the street.

Later they witnessed an older black woman running as fast as she could from a mob. George steered closer to the woman until they hoisted her to safety from the hooligans.[54]

African Americans, vastly outnumbered and outgunned, courageously armed themselves and systematically defended their community. Luther J. Price, the postmaster general in the Brownsville community, was one of the black leaders who sprang into action. He passed guns to people to protect their families. According to Walter, George handed him a shotgun. In a somber and direct tone, he instructed the boy to protect his mother and sisters. If terrorists stepped on the lawn, George told him, "go on shooting as long as you can." They both perched at the windows of their home as gangs roamed the streets seeking victims:

> A voice which we recognized as that of the son of the grocer with whom we had traded for many years yelled, "That's where

that nigger mail carrier lives! Let's burn it down! It's too nice for a nigger to live in!" In the eerie light Father turned his drawn face toward me. In a voice as quiet as though he were asking me to pass him the sugar at the breakfast table, he said, "Son, don't shoot until the first man puts his foot on the lawn and then—don't you miss!"

The mob moved toward the lawn. I tried to aim my gun, wondering what it would feel like to kill a man. Suddenly there was a volley of shots. The mob hesitated, stopped. Some friends of my father's had barricaded themselves in a two-story brick building just below our house. It was they who had fired. Some of the mobsmen, still bloodthirsty, shouted, "Let's go get the nigger." Others, afraid now for their safety, held back. Our friends, noting the hesitation, fired another volley. The mob broke and retreated up Houston Street.[55]

Generations before the black community and its leadership would be inspired to embrace notions popularized by Martin Luther King Jr. regarding nonviolence and the refusal to use firearms, black people practiced every option: evading the threat, peacefully attempting to neutralize the threat, and finally meeting that lethal threat with lethal self-defense.

In the oases that the black college campuses provided the community, professors, students, and administrators were overrun with uncertainty and fear. There was an obvious anxiety, given that the community was a veritable city on the hill for black people and a point of intense jealousy for a certain segment of whites. "All of these institutions by the turn of the century had started gaining momentum, intellectually and physically," argues Rodney T. Cohen. The achievement of these institutions had become "a problem for the so-called establishment."[56] It was also a problem for the most marginalized in the white community, for poor whites often viewed black success as the most flagrant betrayal of the utility and purpose of white nationalism.

Many black people near the campuses armed themselves. On September 22 and 23, with the violence at its peak, John Hope, the president of Morehouse College, organized faculty to protect the campus. He provided some with guns. Perhaps they never imagined that a professional pursuit of intellectual and scientific inquiry—as well as the special mission of social justice—would call upon them to carry firearms. They rose to the challenge, patrolling the acres of buildings, offices, classrooms, and dormitories carved out of the woods and red-clay landscape.

The land had been barely two generations removed from the blasts of cannon and the cries of wounded men. On a site that had once been part of the battlefields of the Civil War, these faculty found themselves called to action in another violent struggle over the fate of freedom, democracy, and justice. The highly educated, refined elite had always understood that racial subjugation generally made little distinction regarding class. Even when they could enjoy comfortable homes, fine clothes, and gainful employment, they were at all times reminded that they could not send their children to public high school. In their hometown, they could not enter hotels, restaurants, cafés, or hospitals. None of them could join the ranks of law enforcement or political office. White nationalism had always made it clear that black citizenship was liminal at best. They could not expect the state to be fair, to be just, or to protect all people equally. Again, class did not matter. They were well aware that their lives were at risk.

As the violence intensified, racist mobs grew and seemed to develop the intention to destroy the most privileged of the black community. Brownsville was a largely black area around Clark University and Gammon Theological Seminary. The other cluster of black schools (later known as the Atlanta University Center), which housed Atlanta University, Morehouse, and Spelman, was a few miles north. In those days, Morris Brown College was farther away, yet no area was free from danger.[57] The areas housed bucolic and stately buildings for teaching, research, and administration. Libraries held vast numbers of books. Dormitories housed the hundreds of young people filled with the promise of a better life. The whole area had a unique sense of optimism and hope. It was also largely new. The campuses had been constructed within the last generation. In many respects, it represented what Du Bois called the greatest threat to white supremacy: black aspiration, industriousness, intelligence, and community.

On September 23 a mob invaded Brownsville. Even with the threat of mobs and militia, indiscriminate police invasions and violence to households in Brownsville would not happen: the area was not racially homogenous. Whites lived there as well. Wanton destruction of homes could mean white lives lost. For their children's protection, local whites moved them into the local white public schools. White militia were later sent to protect the white school grounds. The black defensive forces assembled therein surprised the invaders.

Although the only images of black people in popular culture vacillated between cowardly, shiftless Negroes and criminals who scurried and plotted in dark shadows, the African American elite had formed groups of armed defenders. The community, called "an armed camp," turned back a mob that attempted a raid. Groups of black men with rifles, shotguns, and handguns scoured the streets for potential threats from terrorists. They (perhaps more likely than their working-class and poor counterparts) were able to exploit subversive networks to secure firearms. Amid the threat of police sweeps, firearms were smuggled to people in bundles of dirty clothes. From porches, on rooftops, and at street corners, vigilance swept the community. Brownsville's inhabitants knew that they could not expect help from a notoriously racist police force that refused basic protections under ordinary conditions. Lugenia Burns Hope, wife of the Morehouse College president, noted that even though white gun-shop owners had denied black people access to firearms in the weeks leading up to the massacre, out-of-town friends brought them guns: "We had enough to feel secure."[58]

The city's most famous intellectual, Du Bois, was one of those who had no illusion that his visibility, class, or status would offer special protection for him or his family. Du Bois was researching in Lowndes County, Alabama, when he learned that the racial massacre had erupted. He referred to Lowndes as a particularly vicious, oppressive area. He noted that of his years of living and researching in the South, "and outside of some sections of Mississippi and Red River Valley, I do not think it would be easy to find a place where conditions were more unfavorable to the rise of the Negro."[59] Yet it was from there that he had to flee to attend to the safety of his family in Atlanta, under lethal threat from an unfolding racial massacre. He swiftly boarded a train for Atlanta and hurried to his young wife, Nina, and daughter, Yolande. The violence left him shaken. He joined his colleagues in armed vigilance. The young scholar sat with his "Winchester double-barreled shotgun and two dozen rounds of shells filled with buckshot. If a white mob had stepped on the campus where I lived I would without hesitation have sprayed their guts over the grass."[60]

Although African Americans accounted for nearly all of the victims of the rampages, police officers and state militia arrested white and black people by the dozens. State authorities appeared throughout black communities on the morning of Sunday, September 23, ostensibly to establish order. Yet the presence of hundreds of armed white men brought little comfort to the traumatized citizens there. As the sun rose on Sunday, an eerie and discordant silence settled across the city after several hours of fires, shootings, assaults, and screams punctuated the ambient sounds of the city. Uncertain about the state of security and order, many were wary of venturing outside. "The church bells tolled the next morning for Sunday service," Walter White recalled. However, the people of Atlanta were sure that "the hatred and lust for blood" had not dissipated: "Like skulls on a cannibal's hut the hats and caps of victims of the mob of the night before had been hung on iron hooks of telegraph poles. None could tell whether each hat represented a dead Negro. But we knew that some of those who had worn the hats would never wear any again."[61]

Through their resources, the privileged class of black people defended themselves while simultaneously attracting attention from white militias determined to concentrate their focus on the black people with guns. On Sunday night, officially sanctioned troops from the state mobilized in the city. When word spread that black folks had dared to arm themselves and shoot at marauding whites, militia members—in full uniform—"joined the white mob, which headed toward Brownsville, the city's middle-class black college suburb, and attacked its black residents." The beloved institutions of higher learning had long been a refuge from ignorance and the hostile world around them. On Sunday night, they were literal refuges for those seeking safety from misanthropic hordes. While men armed themselves with every manner of weapon, Clark University and the Gammon Theological Seminary opened buildings to house hundreds of women and children. Gammon president John W. E. Bowen soberly reported that the women and children huddled "in terror" while fires, looting, and general lawlessness unfolded.

The following day, after authorities learned of a gathering of heavily armed black men in the Brownsville area, police raided the community, and shots rang out. An officer, Jim Heard, was subsequently shot and died from his wounds. The officer's death would not be taken lightly. Many anticipated a violent, even indiscriminate, response against the community. They were right. The heavily armed militia aggressively pushed into Brownsville with three companies of troops. They swiftly killed four black men "in cold blood." Two unarmed men, Sam McGruder and Wiley Brooks, were "shot to pieces" by a mob of "unknown" whites who suspected that they may have been part of the killing of Heard. These four killed that night were a shop owner, a veteran of the Civil War, a carpenter, and a mason.[62] In many ways the local white press reflected in print the racist animus that the mob expressed in the streets. On September 25 the *Atlanta Constitution* implied that black people had been the dominant architects and per-petrators of the violence: "Riots end all depends on Negroes." Suggest-ing that black people might provoke their own mass murder, the story headline stated that it was "Their Power to Stop Trouble or Bring on War of Extermination."[63]

The state made no pretense of providing equal protection under the law. The contrast between the white communities and black commu-nities and their relationship to the state is manifest in the memories of Margaret Mitchell, author of *Gone with the Wind*. She was a child at home with her family when her father, who did not own a gun, grabbed an ax and stood at the front door prepared to defend his family. She recalled the moment when she peered into the street to see armed white militia; she was elated. Years later, as a grown woman, she explained that "no sight has ever been so sweet to these eyes."[64]

The unrest captured global attention in newspapers. The *Hartford Courant*'s front page reported that "Atlanta Mob Kills 10 Negroes." The *Chicago Tribune* described the "savagery" of the mobs that were "after all negroes because they were negroes." Even the newspapers and magazines in Europe graphically detailed the event. On October 7 the French publication *Le Petit Journal* provided a graphic drawing of the murderous rampages in Atlanta on its cover, with the title "The Lynch-ings in the United States: The Massacre of Negroes in Atlanta." The *New York Times* reported on the violence, the black resistance, and the massive invasion of the black middle-class community.

Contrary to the minstrel archetype, actual black men were not the sloth-footed cowards of children's books and the vaudeville stage. Local country sheriff agencies, augmented with 300–400 newly deputized white men, invaded homes, stripped people of weapons, and arrested around 300 black men. Three large military wagons were filled with confiscated weapons: "The negro men took their arrest in a solid way, and some even joked about 'the scared white folk.'" Authorities were especially keen to arrest postmaster J. L. Price, who had distributed guns. Among those arrested were "a number of Negro professors and students at Clark University." Given Price's prominence and visibility in attempting to arm and defend the black community, he was forced, at gunpoint, to lead the columns of arrested men in a march through the streets of Atlanta "for the effect on other negroes." With troops and a machine gun pointed at these men, the display of white-nationalist authority was unmistakable. Price was the only man in actual hand-cuffs.[65] Police arrested other prominent black professionals, including the acting president of Gammon Theological Seminary, Rev. Bowen, who had provided refuge for hundreds of women and children.[66]

The white-nationalist establishment was, by definition, hostile to the concept of equal justice, and there were many whites—often people of means—who saw the violence as reprehensible and anathema to the spirit of the city. Several white people actively intervened during the chaos. As noted above, there were prominent white patrons of Herndon's luxurious barbershop who notified the barbers of the increasingly threatening mobs encroaching the area. Others left their own homes and businesses to help black friends and colleagues. Gregory Mixon details that "some whites during the riot literally dashed to their places of business just in the nick-of-time" to protect their black workers. The head of the Bijou Theater, J. D. Belsa, arrived at the theater just as a horde of rioters approached. Belsa, a white man, "locked these black employees in a safe place, armed himself with a shotgun and stood guard over his charges the rest of Saturday." Other whites vouched for innocent black people who had been cornered, arrested, or were otherwise under threat. One white woman in the West End community, near Brownsville, provided refuge for a man fleeing a mob estimated at a hundred strong. Ms. F. S. Cox invited Walter Hicus, who was "hard pressed," into her home for safety. After locking Hicus inside, Cox courageously faced the throngs of seething brutes panting for breath outside her house: "This man has worked for me for a number of years. He may be guilty, but he ought to have a chance for his life and not be put to death on suspicion." The crowd relented when Ms. Cox requested that Hicus be safely turned over to police. White ministers and other members of civil white leadership publicly condemned the violence. For many, the collapse of authority and the destroyed homes, businesses, public buildings, and human life were not things that fed into the narrative of Atlanta's boosters.[67] One prominent white member of the city, Charles T. Hopkins, faced a biracial crowd of one thousand at the Fulton County Courthouse on Tuesday, September 26. In a "ringing speech" punctuated with interruptions from applause, Hopkins insisted that before the massacre, "the races were at peace with each other." However, the spectacle of violence "put us on a plane of criminality with the most disorderly city in America."[68]

In a sober assessment of the violence, Lugenia Burns Hope observed that despite the death and disproportionate suffering experienced by black people, there was also the bravery and defiance of armed black defenders. White people, she noted, "knew how they had treated the Negro all the while, now they feared retribution. The Negro man went home, sat in the door with his gun across his knees and was prepared to die protecting his home and family. . . . Not until then did the good Christian white people care what happened to the Negro."[69]

The violence of the Atlanta Racial Massacre was shocking and horrifying in its rapacity. For people who had always been aware of the community rampages that could cull black people from small rural towns, there had been a sense that Atlanta—as a modern city—offered some semblance of law and order. Even in a municipal and state governmental structure that viewed black citizenship as an oxymoron, there was a pervasive notion that a collapse of civil order and a wanton disregard for law were unlikely in the Gate City. Although the final count remains disputed, the municipal government reported that twenty-five black people were killed, in addition to two whites, including a woman who had a heart attack when she saw a mob roaming the streets. Some organizations put the black death toll closer to one hundred people. The event was so traumatizing that the veritable oasis that offered so much hope and promise to black people had turned into a place of hate and malice. Estimates report that more than a thousand African Americans left the Gate City.[70]

Jesse Max Barber's periodical, the *Voice of the Negro*, the largest circulated black magazine in the country, was targeted by mobs. The offices were destroyed, forcing Barber to relocate to Chicago, where he resumed publication until the magazine collapsed in 1907. Other institutions fared better over time as black businesses relocated into more concentrated black spaces in the city around Auburn Avenue. This process significantly reshaped the physical landscape of the city while simultaneously hardening the social and physical distance between whites and blacks there.

The deadly rampages did not emerge out of a vacuum, nor were they unique. There were veritable pogroms of black people in small towns and cities across the South. Wilmington, North Carolina, had perhaps the most dramatic, brazen, and destructive explosions of Redeemer violence in 1898, when a horde of conservative extremists protested the results of an election. Refusing to accept the results of the democratic process, they stormed government buildings, took hostages, murdered civilians and black and white lawmakers, and assumed power of the local government. The federal government did not intervene.[71]

In an era that Rayford Logan named the "nadir" for its terrible rise in terrorism and lawlessness, hundreds of people were murdered by mobs across the South. Black people accused of offenses—legal ones or social ones—were attacked, beaten, or murdered by packs of lawless criminals. Disregard for the court system—already fully controlled by whites—typified communities across the former Confederacy. In 1904 a mob invaded a courthouse in Statesboro, Georgia, to kill two black men accused of killing some white people. There were outbursts of mob violence in Brownsville, Texas, and lynchings throughout the country, primarily in the South.[72]

There were several factors simultaneously at play in fomenting Atlanta's violence. The inflammatory and reckless yellow journalism of the local press primed white Atlantans to grow even more resentful of black people. As noted above, the gubernatorial race, with its overt white-nationalist rhetoric centered on constricting suffrage to white men, was central to the propaganda. African American men were fundamental threats to white voters and therefore to white freedom, white democracy, and white supremacy. Black men were simultaneously lazy, shiftless, politically ambitious, and studious. Racist narratives vacillated between competing images of pathos: the Negro who was too smart, too industrious, and too successful against the Negro who was ignorant, idle, and criminal. Of all hostile stereotypes, the lurking threat of black male sexual predation gained traction in the weeks and days leading up to September 22. Not to discount the power of yellow journalism in whipping up white public opinion into a violent frenzy, one cannot dismiss another influence in popular culture: the runaway popularity of Thomas Dixon Jr.'s novel *The Clansman* and its subsequent stage production. It functioned as a perfect interlocutor between competing narratives of black male threats.

The second in a trilogy, Dixon's novel, published in 1905, offered a grossly ahistorical narrative of Reconstruction that neatly fit into the Lost Cause rhetoric of neo-Confederates. Although the story was a flagrant departure from historical accuracy, Dixon insisted in its prologue that "I have merely changed their names without taking a liberty with any essential historic fact."[73] The novel and the stage play were part of the cultural nationalist wing of neo-Confederacy. The Lost Cause rhetoric embedded itself into the fabric of white southern popular culture. *The Clansman* praised Confederates and their cause, and it vilified the US government and the Radical Republicans who oversaw Reconstruction. It aligned with the race-baiting 1906 gubernatorial campaigns, which trafficked in tales of black men savagely assaulting white women, the fictional work simultaneously romanticizing white mob violence, especially that of the Ku Klux Klan.

In the summer and fall of 1906, throngs lined up to see the neo-Confederate fiction that Thomas D. Clark said "opened wider a vein of racial hatred which was to poison further an age already in a social and political upheaval." After the unrest, southern and northern cities banned the stage play. From Savannah to Montgomery to Washington, local leadership did not want to repeat what Atlanta witnessed. The *Washington Post* panned the drama: "The play does not possess even the merit of historic truth. It is as false as Uncle Tom's Cabin and a hundred times more wicked, for it excites the passions and prejudices of the dominant class at the expense of the defenseless minority. We can imagine no circumstances under which its production would be useful or wholesome, since it disgusts the judicious and the well-informed." Joel Williamson argues that Dixon's fiction helped ignite the Atlanta Racial Massacre.[74] As a propagandistic expression of neo-Confederate revanchism, it celebrated Old South nationalism while pandering to the basest elements of ignorance and fear. It was an artistic complement to the political debates, fears of economic competition and social equality, and conspicuous threats to the racial order. Its power was not lost on anyone who paid attention: culture mattered. Controlling the narratives of history mattered; these narratives had powerful implications.

In the aftermath of the Atlanta Racial Massacre there were profound transformations in the city's racial landscape. The violence forced the black community to geographically shift, forming a more contiguous black community that swept across Mechanicsville, Summer Hill, Darktown, and Auburn Avenue, moving toward Vine City and the Atlanta University Center. Also, the racial rampage proved important to agents of white nationalism. The threat of violence and, significantly, the reach and force of the white-controlled state revealed the overwhelming power of neo-Confederates. The limitations of black power fomented a keen sense that the very survival of the black community depended on acute organization and support of black institutions.

Immediately after the violence, evidence confirmed that the reports of the four cases of black sexual assaults of white women on September 22 were unfounded. The *Atlanta Georgian*, a white paper, reported that "none was a case of real criminal assault."[75] Globally, people expressed horror and condemnation. The *Evening Star* (Washington, DC) wrote that "nothing more hideous had occurred, or could occur in a country with laws and officers to execute them." It compared the massacre to Russian pogroms against Jews. The most recent pogrom, in October 1905, resulted in the deaths of hundreds of Jews in the city of Odessa (now in Ukraine), then part of the Russian empire. Similarly, editorials from newspapers from St. Louis to Indianapolis made comparisons to Odessa. The *Philadelphia Record* called Atlanta "disgraced." The mobs "hunted down negroes much as a Russian mob hunts down Jews."[76]

Above all, the massacre revealed the virulence of unleashed white nationalism, separated from the most basic principles of civilization. For black people, class was no protector. Being internationally cosmopolitan and multilingual, having the highest level of education attainable in the Western world, and wearing a tailored tweed suit, spats, and a walking cane did not shield one from the indignities of racist rage. Individual achievement, an industrial education, a working-class job, waking up early for work or leaving work late, or being an elderly woman or a child made no distinction to the savage agents of racist mob violence. Conservative accommodationist politics did not work. More than anything, the horrors of the riot hardened the idea that black people would be best served by securing their rights, not hoping that white nationalists would be fair, nice, moral, or humane. Black people needed to have access to the vote. They needed to have access to municipal employment: the police, the state militia, and all other elements of the public arena that shaped their lives. Accommodating neo-Confederate demands to sublimate dignity, decency, and their humanity was anathema for most black people.

For white Atlantans, the violent rampages meant different things. Many whites argued that the massacre "quieted the negroes" and was "ugly, but necessary." For example, John Temple Graves, conservative editor of the *Georgian* newspaper, infamously reported the sentiment that the slaughter would stop black criminality for at least "five years." Other white Atlantans were appalled at the barbarity of their cousins, neighbors, friends, and coworkers. The looting, mayhem, and destruction were not part of the capital of the New South they envisioned. It was not the modern, forward-facing city on a hill. Even in the context of an old racial order that rejected racial equality, many whites could not approve of the collapse of law and order. For local leadership, the massacre offered an opportunity to forge, at the minimum, a facade of interracial cooperation.

Black leaders and white leaders convened in public spaces soon after order had been restored. William F. Penn, a prominent Yale-educated physician, shared the stage with white politicians in a demonstration of racial reconciliation. Another black Yale alumnus, Hugh Proctor, the senior pastor of the First Congregational Church, joined white lawyer Charles T. Hopkins to found the Interracial Committee of Atlanta. Hopkins was not just any white lawyer; he was the legal counsel for Atlanta University. He personally and professionally saw value in black institutions and their missions. It would be hard to work so closely with the African American community and be dispassionate about the horrors that its members witnessed. He spearheaded a relief fund that collected more than $4,400 (more than $127,000 in today's dollars) for victims.[77] An acolyte of Booker T. Washington, Proctor was palatable to many local white moderates who wanted law and order without disrupting the racial order. In the patriarchal tradition, the Interracial Committee—unlike the Niagara Movement—was strictly male. The group had forty members, evenly divided between white men and black men.[78] Hopkins continued to make efforts to mitigate the racial hostility that pervaded the city with useful, meaningful, and effective

Cover of *Le Petit Journal,* October 7, 1906: "The Lynchings in the United States: The Massacre of Negroes in Atlanta." The massacre made international headlines and destroyed black businesses, homes, and lives. It revealed the lethality of neo-Confederate politics, but it also strengthened notions of Afro-self-determinism and underscored the need to demand civil rights. CREDIT: PUBLIC DOMAIN

institutions that worked toward "racial cooperation." On Thanksgiving Day 1906, he announced the formation of the Civic League and invited thousands of Atlantans—black and white—to join.[79]

Despite the rise in visibility of Proctor, Washington's accommodationist philosophy appeared impotent to the most prominent black Atlantans. However, Washington used the massacre to galvanize support for greater social responsibility and accountability among black people, and he encouraged white benefactors to help eliminate the "ignorance and social destitution of the lower classes" of black folk. Du Bois, the Hopes, Barber, the Herndons, and many others all became more conspicuously involved in civil rights work. The Niagara Movement seemed more critically needed than ever. Its mission had a national and even international audience, and a sense of urgency that it did not have before the unrest.[80] Twelve-year-old White, who could pass for white, had been irrevocably changed: "After that night I never wanted to be a white man." He would not do what thousands had done before him and pass into the white fold: "I was sick with loathing for the hatred which had flared before me that night and come so close to making me a killer. . . . I was glad I was not one of those made sick and murderous by pride."[81] More importantly, he decided to devote himself to the cause of justice and civil rights. Within a generation, he would align himself with Du Bois and eventually become one of the most celebrated civil rights leaders in the country, known as "Mr. NAACP."

The threat of virulent hostility from racist mobs strengthened the generations-old idea of Afro-self-determinism. There was safety in numbers, and there was greater security in a larger, more protected community that relied on its own membership for survival. The rampages forced black businesses into a larger contiguous black space for safety. African Americans, traumatized but not broken by the barbarity of September 1906, rebuilt and consolidated resources in black areas. Notions of racial solidarity intensified, as did the funneling of support to black institutions: "After the race riot, [Auburn Avenue] saw increased building of offices for black professionals, like the Atlanta Life Building. Alonzo Herndon built Atlanta Mutual, [and] the grandest of all was the Odd Fellows building, with its grand theater." Called "Sweet Auburn" by Odd Fellow, Mason, and political leader John Wesley Dobbs, the community would erect restaurants, churches, beauty salons, barbershops, the only daily black newspaper in the country (the *Atlanta Daily World*), and various nightclubs and bars.[82]

African Americans were also motivated to "retreat into their highly stratified social enclaves." In particular, the visibility and importance of black colleges and universities grew. These became centers of hope, of training, and of leadership incubation in nearly every professional arena. Moreover, they offered critical and often overlooked cultural and social functions. From fraternities through professional associations, African American college graduates enjoyed a rich space for leisure and pleasure in ways that few other cities could offer. Though enveloped in the Deep South, Atlanta offered what Los Angeles, Chicago, Philadelphia, New York, or Detroit did not: a large community of private black colleges and a concentration of extraordinarily talented African American college students, faculty, and staff. They were respites from the unwelcoming space in Atlanta and beyond. The black colleges in the city educated hundreds each year. Many of the graduates returned to their hometowns across the country, but many others stayed local, where they poured their talents into local institutions.

With smoldering buildings and bodies in the city morgue, Hoke Smith, for his part, reveled in his victory. When he was inaugurated in June 1907, he tried to realize his campaign promise to introduce an amendment to the state constitution to remove African Americans from the ballot. He also visited Europe on a recruiting trip for immigrants to supplant black labor and simultaneously help increase the white population.[83]

Atlanta, despite all of its modern ambitions, was also a standard-bearer of the neo-Confederate sensibilities that pervaded the South. Being progressive, reform minded, and socially and culturally conservative were not incongruent impulses to white nationalists. Access to democracy, power, and most levers of authority and influence across industries had been restricted to white men only. Through terror campaigns, basic intimidation, and various laws, including poll taxes, literacy tests, and eventually a white primary, black men were excluded from the body politic. They were purged from voter rolls, denied political appointments and municipal and state employment, and relegated as quasi-citizens who were legally bound to pay taxes for services and resources denied them. In Atlanta, some African Americans maintained access to voting, but at-large elections meant that the city council would remain exclusively white as long as an overwhelming majority of voters were white. Citizenship was more than voting. It was also access to public space, to public institutions. Through control of municipal and state governments, the city provided many amenities—roads, running water, electricity, paved streets, sidewalks, public schools, and parks—to white citizens only. Yet despite these deep-seated and inexorable forces, Afro-self-determinism forged a remarkable space of black achievement in the heart of Dixie.

Afro-self-determinism was shaped by the direct interactions and collective experiences that black people had with whites. It inspired black people to establish and support black institutions and to nourish black spaces as refuges from a wider hostile society. This racism simultaneously forced the most talented and resource-rich black people to cast their lots with other black people and their communities. Race, more than class, mattered. There was no greater catalyst for the growth of this idea in Atlanta than the 1906 Racial Massacre.

7 | The Second Resurgence
Atlanta, the Old South, and the New Negroes

Atlanta is herself again; business activity restored and the riot is forgotten.

—*ATLANTA JOURNAL*, 1906

In 1895, six years after Henry Grady died at age thirty-nine, Ivan E. Allen, another son of a Confederate soldier, moved to Atlanta from small-town Georgia. Like Grady, Allen was raised by a mother who adored and celebrated the memory of her late Confederate husband. In fact, when Allen was three years old, his mother changed his birth name from Isaac Anderson to Ivan Earnest to honor his deceased father, Earnest. Like Grady, Allen had originally intended to study law but was drawn to working in commerce, which would position him to make a remarkable name for himself in his adopted hometown. In the ever-expanding and bustling capital city, Allen found wonderful business opportunities. In 1900 he founded Fielder and Allen, an office-supply store. By 1910, he was known as a leading figure in the city's business circles. He was the first president of the Atlanta Convention Bureau, a new marketing organization for the city, founded in 1913. By 1917, he was president of the Atlanta Chamber of Commerce, the most visible and ardent booster of the Gate City. Throughout his career, Allen operated with an eye to local philanthropy, civic duty, and maximizing profit in his company. To those ends, promoting Atlanta as a center that was good for business and its citizens was important.

After African Americans demanded access to a public swimming pool, the chamber of commerce enjoined the Fulton County Board of Commissioners to provide one. After a series of high-profile incidents of civic discord in the city, the chamber reasoned that such a facility would be a strong demonstration of racial goodwill to visitors and local residents. To show that it was fully committed, the all-white chamber offered to provide partial funding. When white residents of the Sixth Ward, where the pool was to be constructed, protested, the plans collapsed. Public pools would remain for the exclusive use of whites for the foreseeable future.[1]

Considered the "New South descendants of Henry Grady," the Atlanta Chamber of Commerce organized businesses and coordinated campaigns to improve the political economy. Working with county and city governments, the chamber was a powerful agent in promoting investment in Atlanta. Under Allen's leadership, the chamber adopted the New South rhetoric of Grady, promoting the city as welcoming and tolerant. Atlanta was both modern and industrial, yet southern and not too far removed from its agrarian surrounding areas. Still, the massacre of 1906 left many people across the country shocked at the unfettered barbarism. However, Atlanta's boosters swiftly diverted attention away from the horrors and highlighted the city's racial benevolence instead. Despite the white nationalism, black people had, the chamber insisted, thrived *because* of white paternalism.

In a country where most Americans of any race did not complete high school, few examples better represented black success than

Atlanta's black schools. In 1917 the chamber's official publication, *The City Builder*, promoted local black colleges and universities: "Could it be true that these people, these earnest students are but one or two generations removed from the darkest jungles of Africa?" Boasting of the extraordinary work of these schools, the magazine asked, "Where is the mother college which produced this negro culture? Is it Africa or Asia? No, it has grown on Atlanta soil." Lauding the "Christian spirit of Atlanta," the chamber, without any sense of irony, offered a model for settling the "vexed problem of race."[2] Of course, these schools, unlike the University of Georgia, were private schools. They were supported largely by tuition from black people and philanthropy from black and white (mostly northern) private institutions. The fact that white southerners largely disregarded these schools (as they had black education in the public spheres) did not stop Allen from staking a claim in their successes.

Allen, through the chamber of commerce and several other organizations, left a remarkable imprint on the city of Atlanta. His modern vision was aligned with that of Grady, from whom he took clear inspiration. Like Grady, he found no incongruence with modernity and a racial order that excluded black people from the halls of power or from full citizenship and the basic conveniences of a modern city. Only one generation removed from the Confederacy, Allen understood the foundational values of white southern nationalism. Although the South had been defeated in war, the efforts to maintain the old racial order were constant. These efforts were also being repeatedly revised. In the midst of war, Confederates fought to maintain their right to enslave people. In their defeat and in the war's aftermath, the mission had evolved into controlling the labor and civil liberties of the newly freed and their descendants: an updated white nationalism. To that extent, the mercurial neo-Confederate landscape adapted to pressures from the black community, the federal government, and local whites. Because federal law required the white-nationalist state to provide some resources to black citizens, Atlanta's boosters attempted to display how benign their racial order was.

Far from benign, the city was not unique in its exclusion of black people from rights, privileges, and accommodations. What was unique was having the sprawling complex of black institutions of higher learning. That community continued to attract black people by the hundreds and ultimately thousands each year. And many of these black newcomers would leave indelible imprints on the capital of the New South.

Newcomers and native Atlantans forged urban spaces with overlapping and discordant politics across the city. What occurred was much more than a Dickensian tale of two cities. Variegated by race and class, Atlanta also witnessed intraracial ideological cleavages as fiercely fascistic racist groups vied for power against old-line racist conservatives and more moderate whites. Simultaneously, the largest black movement in history found a foothold in Atlanta. The Universal Negro Improvement Association, a black-nationalist group, surged in the interwar years, appealing to a huge segment of the black community while causing considerable clamor among black leadership both locally and nationally. All of these events unfolded in the long cast of the Confederacy's shadow. For their part, African Americans were inspired to redouble their politics around self-determination, given the intensified racial hostility in the aftermath of the 1906 massacre. Together, all these groups, with their disparate interests, would leave an ineffaceable legacy, making Atlanta one of the most significant cities for black people anywhere by the 1930s.

When the riot's embers cooled and residents started to rebuild the city anew, Atlanta began another resurgence that would be fundamental to the trajectory of the city's development over the next several decades. Of course, the desolation of the city under Sherman's assault was foundational to Atlanta's identity. However, the Atlanta Racial Massacre of 1906 deeply scarred the black community and pushed African Americans inexorably toward Afro-self-determinism.

Additionally, for many members of the city's black community, the experience wrought from the massacre would intractably shape their political, social, and cultural lives. Walter White would forever reference it as a key factor in shaping his commitment to civil rights. Many of the city's leadership class became more fervent than ever in their civil rights work. Instead of cowering in fear of racist vengeance, the Niagara Movement, led by W. E. B. Du Bois, expanded its reach and mission. The young and venerable scholar was permanently changed by the explosion of savage violence in Atlanta. It not only hardened his gaze on racism and all of its cruel manifestations; it also proved critical in radicalizing the patrician academic, who in some ways still believed that personal human interaction could effectively challenge the bitterness of conventional racism. Du Bois biographer David Levering Lewis observes that his subject was perennially disturbed by the incivility and common disrespect that he experienced in the city. The most prominent scholar in the state, Du Bois was barred from—among many things—the largest library in the South, a whites-only ornate public Carnegie library in downtown that opened in 1902. He petitioned the city to allow all Atlantans access to a public library supported by their taxes. His attempts at basic principles of civic fairness and decency were for naught. These many indignities also tested his wife, who would walk downtown rather than ride segregated transportation: "Along the route, there was not a single water fountain or park bench lawfully permitted [for her use]." The riot stunned and awed Du Bois. In "A Litany at Atlanta" he expressed sentiments ranging among sorrow, faith, pain, and anger:

How long shall the mounting flood of innocent blood roar in Thine ears and pound in our hearts for vengeance? Pile the pale frenzy of blood-crazed brutes who do such deeds high on Thine altar, Jehovah Jireh, and burn it in hell forever and forever!

Forgive us, good Lord; we know not what we say![3]

Like the effect on the city itself, the massacre changed Du Bois. Dominic Capeci and Jack Knight argue that "in coded language, classical idiom, and religious imagery, [Du Bois] disclosed that southern racism inflicted massive damage on his own double consciousness—that troublesome intersection of racial identity and national citizenship in a white-supremacist country that he described so poignantly in *Souls*."[4]

Simultaneously, white supporters of democracy and equality in law viewed the veritable pogrom of 1906 with shock and horror. They knew that the bitter treatment of millions of Americans, subjugated to the will of white nationalism, would not relent on its own. They were also inspired to systematically organize. Francis Garrison, the youngest son of famed abolitionist William Lloyd Garrison, reached out to black leadership to learn more about the events of September 1906. Although he thanked his accommodationist friend Booker T. Washington for his insight, Francis embraced the activist politics of the Niagara Movement and Du Bois. So did antilynching crusader and black journalist Ida B. Wells-Barnett, who openly opposed Washington.[5] Many others banded together, overwhelmed by the spate of violence and systemic racial oppression. Within two and a half years, Oswald Villard (Francis Garrison's nephew), Wells-Barnett, Mary White Ovington, Mary Church Terrell, and others joined Du Bois in founding the National Association for the Advancement of Colored People. The NAACP, with resources from white philanthropists and thousands of dues-paying black people in nearly every state, would mount the most effective, well-crafted struggle for civil rights in the United States. Du Bois left Atlanta University for NAACP headquarters in New York City in 1910, working full-time as director of publicity and research and editor of the organization's official organ, *Crisis*.

Locally, some elements of the white community also found ways to systematically organize against a repeat of the unrest. Motivated by different forces, they found themselves in conversation with one another over the tarnished image of the city, a disruption of law and

The Niagara Movement delegates, Boston, 1907. The Atlanta Racial Massacre, a year earlier, had laid bare the critical need to protect civil rights. Many members of the Niagara Movement, including W. E. B. Du Bois, Alonzo Herndon, and Jesse Barber, intensified their work for social justice. CREDIT: PUBLIC DOMAIN

order, moral outrage over the violence, or a mixture of all three. Some white leaders and black leaders established the earliest interracial civic groups in Atlanta.

After his gubernatorial victory, Hoke Smith declared that his efforts had opened the door for voting integrity: "For generations to come white supremacy will be preserved in Georgia without the necessity for intimidation or violence, and even though the white voters may be divided, there will still be no danger at the ballot box from the ignorant and purchasable negro voters."[6] The mobilization for voting rights appeared daunting for black people throughout the South. In Georgia the various mechanisms that made voting even more difficult only grew in the first years of the twentieth century. Its remarkable record of Afro-self-determinism and collective resources notwithstanding, the black community in Atlanta lagged behind other southern cities in numbers of registered black voters. Statewide, 4 percent of African American men were registered to vote by 1910. The Democratic white primary disempowered the utility of a black vote: in the one-party state, the primary winner was also the winner in the general election.

Therefore, any votes that blacks cast in the state of Georgia would be of little consequence in advocating for justice and equality of resources. For the city of Atlanta, however, there were moments when the small voting bloc of African Americans could have an effect. One such case was when there was a popular referendum.

One area where black people would have some direct benefit from Governor Smith's reforms affected only a small portion of the community: those in the penal system. Incarceration rates were relatively low compared to the extraordinary rates to which they would rise by the civil rights era and thereafter. When Sherman captured Atlanta, fewer than ten black people were imprisoned in the entire state of Georgia. (Of course, more than 99 percent of black people in the state were enslaved.) Numbers of imprisoned black people jumped three years later, but there were fewer than fifty prisoners (both races) incarcerated in 1868. By the start of the new century, however, African Americans, 46 percent of the state population, represented more than 85 percent of convicts in state prisons. This was a sharp contrast to antebellum prison demographics.

Until the end of slavery, about 80 percent of the state's prisoners were white. Most were white Anglo-Saxon protestants who, like Samuel W. Whitworth from Jones County, were met with very punitive punishments up to execution, even for nonviolent crimes. Whitworth, described as a "blond and blue-eyed cotton farmer," was charged with the crime of "mayhem" in 1817. Likely for "some drunken violence," he was given a ten-year sentence but escaped three years into his punishment. Authorities later captured and hanged him in South Carolina.[7]

Thomas Ruger, the provisional state governor, decided to turn punishment into profit for the state and began the convict-leasing program in 1868 with a one-year lease of one hundred black laborers to the Georgia and Alabama Railroad. The state received $2,500 for the laborers, who were forced into brutal conditions worse than slavery. Unlike slaves, who were a valuable commodity, these convicted prisoners offered no major commercial value to the businesses that exploited their labor. They were mistreated and abused to such an extent that sixteen of them died in the first year, a death rate exponentially higher than during slavery.[8]

Between 1900 and 1908, the numbers of annually incarcerated people sent into forced labor increased by a factor of eight: 396 blacks and 58 whites. But between 1868 and 1908, the numbers of black convicts remained low relative to the entire population, never representing more than half of a percent of black people in the state. Various investigations over the years found the deplorable and abusive conditions, including "inadequate food and physical accommodations" and the gross exploitation of inmates, to be "immoral." Despite an astonishingly high mortality rate of 16 percent in the first year of operation, the private companies to which convicts were leased continued to beat, torture, and even kill prisoners in their possession with near impunity. As Dewey W. Grantham explains, this was an "evil" system, and "there was no getting around the fact that the state was trafficking commercially in criminals."[9]

Although convict leasing had been profitable for Georgia, Smith was able to abolish it in his first year of office, something that Du Bois must have appreciated. In fact, at the first meeting of the Niagara Movement in 1905, its declaration of principles demanded the end of "the dehumanizing convict-lease system" as well as the establishment of "juvenile reformatories for delinquents."[10] Not limiting criminal reform to convict leasing, Smith also established the juvenile court system and a parole system. The state adopted a new, less brutal form of convict labor, chain gangs, which were employed for state public-works projects, especially for work on road construction. The Georgia Prison Commission reported that by 1911, "135 of the state's 146 counties utilized convict labor on road projects."[11] This may have been the only area where the most abused of the black community experienced some meaningful benefit from reform; whites in the state enjoyed a broader benefit, particularly in education.

The absurdly low level of state support for black education saw no substantial change of circumstances under Smith's tenure as governor (he had actually campaigned on expanding resources for education). For those who measured his policies, Smith was regarded as "no friend of Negro education," even as he offered "a paternal type of manual and moral training" for black people.[12] It is notable that for huge swaths of the state, white school-age children were also exposed to poor educational resources by the standards of the day. White teachers were paid poorly and "habitually paid in arrears." Particularly in rural areas where white and black sharecroppers were tied to the land and relied on entire families to work on farms, public schools were closed for most of the year. Black children and white children worked for wages or on family farms across the state.

Pressing poverty, low wages, and the absence of child-labor laws allowed children to miss school to work in various industries—including labor-intensive crop picking. Big business benefited from low-wage child labor and pushed against regulation or progressive reform. The one-party rule of conservative Democrats had for generations made reform immensely difficult. As discussed in Chapter 4, the New South Bourbon industrialists in Georgia secured and concentrated resources in the hands of those who were heirs of the antebellum planter class. Much like their antebellum counterparts, they used white nationalism to prevent any solidarity between the mass of black people and the white poor. Populists attempting to forge interracial solidarity in a common party found that the appeal of white nationalism was too strong for the majority of poor whites in Georgia. The fear of racial equality—politically, economically, or socially—had been so great that reform efforts never achieved success. However, the Smith campaign divorced progressive reform from any element of racially progressive politics. Instead, it beat the conservatives by advocating a particularly aggressive form of white nationalism that pushed the outright elimination of black men as a voting group. Outflanking the establishment conservative Democrats on racism finally allowed for some degree of reform in Georgia, even if black people were largely excluded from its benefits.[13]

The regulation and ambitious taxation of the railroad industry, as well as other big businesses, was a meaningful achievement. It was so significant that the loss of convict-leasing revenue was more than compensated for by the regulations on big business. The progressive administration "showed the largest appropriations in the state's history." The growth of revenue into the state's coffers was passed on to public schools, which in 1909 saw a 30 percent increase over the funding received two years earlier.[14]

The public school system in Atlanta, established during Reconstruction, had always applied the concept of universal whiteness to its management of educational resources. The Atlanta City Council had established two whites-only high schools by 1880. No public high school was open to African American children, but all white children, regardless of ethnicity or religion, could attend any white public school. Although there were black public primary schools, the gap between white and black student expenditures was vast. In 1910 black students received twenty-nine cents for every dollar that white students received. In 1914 the Atlanta Board of Education terminated eighth grade for African Americans (the highest grade available to black students in the public school system) to provide more funding to white schools. Politically weak, outnumbered, with few options, and perhaps unwilling to offer too much criticism of the white power structure, the black community offered no substantive challenge. Perhaps emboldened, the school board two years later decided to limit public education of black children to the sixth grade to create more funds to build a new school for whites. This ignited a renewed passion for organizing among African Americans, fundamentally changing the racial political landscape for decades.

Black education, despite white antipathy for it, had expanded significantly since the end of the Civil War, when an estimated 95 percent of black people were illiterate in Georgia. By 1920, less than a third were illiterate. Still, black public education in Atlanta was dismal, and it was cruelly neglected. A population of more than 75,000 black people used fourteen grammar schools; all but one were small, old wooden structures, terribly deficient in every manner of modern convenience. They were so overcrowded that the schools had to create double and triple sessions to accommodate the need. One black school was a sturdier brick building. It had originally been a white school until the school board erected a new one. There was a deep irony here: the city was home to the dynamic consortium of private black higher education, which, along with a handful of private Catholic schools, offered the only high school options for black students. Of course, poor black families could rarely afford to pay tuition for a private education.

A group of exceptional black leaders—all tied to the black higher-education establishments in the city—wrote a 2,500-word appeal demanding investment in black public education. Not satisfied with children being limited to seven or even eight years of education, the letter demanded resources equal to those of white schools. Notably, the leadership did not demand integration with whites or desegregation of the schools. That request was not only too radical for whites; it was also probably not particularly popular in the black community of Atlanta. Quite logically, black parents likely feared for the safety of their children in white schools. White administrators, teachers, and students—like the wider white community—viewed the education of black children with contempt. Given the fact that black children were banned from equal access in health care, public libraries, protection under the law, and every other meaningful facet of their lives, there was little faith that a black child would be safe, nurtured, or taught with care or compassion under any institution under local white control and administration. Instead, the spirit of Afro-self-determinism informed the demands to the Atlanta School Board in 1916. The writers argued that "we should demand high schools, both regular and technical, new and modern grammar schools, and every other facility given to white students."[15]

William F. Penn, who moved to Atlanta in 1897 after graduating from Yale Medical School, served as one of the most prominent African American leaders in the city. Although he had many options regarding where he could have served as a surgeon, Penn found his professional home as physician to the local universities and colleges, including Atlanta University, Clark University, and Gammon Theological Seminary. Penn offered the petition to the school board. Other signers of the petition included John Hope, Harry H. Pace (insurance executive), Walter White, and Benjamin J. Davis Sr. (newspaper publisher and chairman of the state Republican Party Committee).

Surprisingly, there was a sympathetic voice among the board members. James L. Key, upon hearing the powerful testimony, remarked, "We should be derelict to our duty if we did not grant their demands." However, Mayor Asa G. Candler protested. The chief executive of Coca-Cola, Candler was a very powerful figure in local politics. "Let us not give way to hysteria," he responded to Key.[16] After deliberation, the board decided against eliminating the seventh grade for black students and opted to raise a bond fund for education, but there would be no black high school. The bond money would be used exclusively for whites. The struggle was far from over, but the small victory of restoring the seventh grade inspired many.

Although he was no longer in the city, Du Bois was critical to these events. He knew the signatories of the petition to the school board. Pace had been Du Bois's student at Atlanta University, graduating as valedictorian. Amid the battle over the elimination of the seventh grade, White reached out to Du Bois's new group, which had been an ideological heir of the Niagara Movement. Though still a very small organization, with fewer than nine thousand dues-paying members and a handful of full-time workers, it offered resources, and it ultimately formed a chapter in Atlanta with Harry Pace as its first chapter president. White was elected as its first secretary. Other leaders included James Weldon Johnson; Dr. Louis T. Wright, an alumnus of Clark University and Harvard Medical School; and Adam Daniel Williams, the senior pastor of Ebenezer Baptist Church, who had elevated the membership of his church from fewer than twenty, when he first became pastor in 1894, to hundreds by 1906.

Eventually, the local NAACP discovered that the bond had to have the approval of two-thirds of registered voters—not two-thirds of the votes cast. This essential point was critical to the efforts to demand resources from the Atlanta School Board. The way to block the bond was to increase the number of registered black voters. "Our major hurdle was the poll tax," recalled the new secretary, Walter White. The group fanned out across the black community, where people pulled together their meager resources and paid back taxes. One man, wealthy enough, agreed to pay back taxes with interest going back thirty-two years. The turnout was so great that the NAACP instructed black people to stagger their trips to pay their taxes at city hall so as not to alarm whites or tip their hand about the efforts underway. Finally, when the election took place, there were not enough votes among the registered population for the bond to pass.[17]

Amid incredible voter suppression, the achievement offered an important strategy for the local political landscape. No referendum was likely to pass as long as black people voted as a bloc in their interests. The mayor and the school board, bitter about this loss, sought a compromise. If most black voters supported a new bond, the funds would be shared with black schools. Between 1923 and 1924, two schools were built for black children, one of them constructed on land donated by one of the city's wealthiest black businessmen, mortician David T. Howard. The city opened a grammar school that would eventually be named for Howard. A year later, the Booker T. Washington High School opened to great fanfare, becoming the first black public high school in Georgia. For comparison, schools in cities across the South, including Houston, New Orleans, Memphis, Charleston, and even Birmingham, had black high schools before Atlanta did.

The virulence of the white-nationalist cause in Atlanta was remarkable. Although the schools were a victory, they were immediately overcrowded and underfunded. White students had had access to at least two high schools since the nineteenth century. They had several by 1924. In a city that was nearly half black, the disregard for black education would be a prolonged obstacle.[18] Between 1910 and 1935, the money spent on black students dropped from twenty-nine cents to twenty-seven cents for every dollar that white students received. Just as private citizens accepted and practiced discriminatory behavior in their everyday lives, they used the state to support white nationalism regarding resources in various public spaces, including education.[19]

In the first decades of the twentieth century, the political landscape shifted closer to the neo-Confederate white nationalism that Hoke Smith promised. African American men, who had already struggled to protect the right to vote despite poll taxes, were purged from voting rolls and denied the ballot through new legal maneuvers. Georgia had long led the way in establishing a neo-Confederate form of government. Although it became the seventh state to create a constitutional amendment to prevent black men from voting, it was the first state to use the poll tax to suppress the black vote, adopting this measure in 1877.[20] The disenfranchisement efforts were, for many, an affirmation of the state's core values. Georgia voters poured into voting booths across the state on October 8, 1908, to ratify the voter-suppression amendment, which had been modeled after an identical Alabama measure from 1901. Of course, in trying to circumvent the US Constitution, which ensured that adult male citizens could not be denied from voting based on race, the new amendment was not explicitly racial. It included a state residency requirement, a poll tax, and literacy tests. As previously noted, although many poor whites, particularly sharecroppers, lost the right to vote, as they had across the South, there were common loopholes for white men. For example, white men could secure the ballot if they attested to having served in the Civil War or being a descendant of a Civil War veteran.

With Smith as the new governor of Georgia, a wave of reform had come to the state. His victory over the heirs of the Bourbon elites was consequential in many ways. Smith's administration ushered in increased regulation of railroads, education, roads, and infrastructure. Although the reforms were not directly targeted at them, African Americans were able to benefit from some of the improvements to commonly used roads and transportation. Smith's efforts expanded those already enacted in Atlanta. Progressives built new sewer lines and streets, parks, and sidewalks. Electricity and public transportation were expanded into various neighborhoods. Of course, the constricted notions of citizenship did not make these improvements accessible to all people. These new amenities—including paved streets—almost always stopped at the start of black neighborhoods in Atlanta. Most black communities were cut off from trolleys. The city's southeast was served by only two east-west lines. Affluent whites had easy access to city services, but black working-class and poor residents in Summerhill had to walk long distances to make track transfers to reach various amenities. In addition to lack of access to public transportation, "many of Summerhill's streets remained unpaved decades into the 20th century, [whereas] white Southsiders prevailed upon the City Council to regrade and repave Georgia Avenue, then a white residential street, so it might serve as a major artery moving people from Grant Park to the West End."[21]

Many other basic public amenities were denied black people. For example, black children were lawfully barred from playing in any park in the city. Lugenia Burns Hope, who had been active in the women's club movement for social reform in Chicago before she married John Hope, initiated efforts to expand resources for black people in her new hometown. Through the Neighborhood Union, which she cofounded, black women reformers provided a day care for black children and negotiated with Morehouse College for the school to grant land for a park. By instructing mothers on health care, parenting skills, education, and civic awareness, the union expanded its reach as the first social reform organization in the city led by black women.

In 1915, as a critical agent of Afro-self-determinism, Hope expanded her national visibility when she demanded that black southern women have "self-determination" over the affairs of black YWCAs in their communities. At the national meeting of the Young Women's Christian Association, the group's leadership discussed plans to extend black YWCA clubs beyond college-based branches. (In essence, black YWCA branches would be treated as white ones had been.) However, the national leadership wanted to have white southern women decide where and how these new branches would operate. As her biographer, Jacqueline Rouse, explains, Hope was driven by the basic principle that institutions guided by capable black leadership served African Americans most effectively. For a host of reasons, white southern women could not be entrusted with the fate of black people, even in ostensibly progressive reform. Instead of demanding integration into white spaces, she wanted "Blacks [to have] the right of self-determination over their branches. Hope asserted that Black women should demand outright independent branches, responsible only to the National Board."[22]

In a patriarchal society that relegated all women to the sidelines, African Americans, though also operating within patriarchal norms, elevated women into political, social, and economic affairs more prominently than did the wider white society. Historically, black male leadership—for example, Douglass, Du Bois, Washington, and Hope—had openly endorsed suffrage for all women.[23] Black women were essential to reform and civil rights work in Atlanta, and few were ever as visible as Lugenia Burns Hope. In the 1920s she became the first vice president of the Atlanta chapter of the NAACP. With other privileged black women, she petitioned the local, state, and federal governments to provide equal resources and protection for all citizens. Elite women, often the highly educated spouses of the black male leadership class, formed exclusive social clubs, but they also tirelessly organized around reform. Rouse writes that Hope's clubs, from the National Association of Colored Women to the National Association of Colored Graduate Nurses, shaped black Atlanta and beyond: "Black women instituted the services needed by their communities: . . . kindergartens, medical clinics, reading rooms, libraries, settlement houses."[24]

Through the 1930s, none of these endeavors ever focused on what was called "social equality" with whites. African Americans in Atlanta had never placed integration as a foundation for their struggles for justice. Instead, the rhetoric and tactics were centered on access to similar resources (properly funded black high schools and parks, for example) or, at most, desegregation of institutions such as the public libraries or the primary elections. In the aftermath of the 1906 Racial Massacre, black political organization only intensified, even as black newcomers continued to arrive in the city.

Despite the dangers that the threat of mob violence posed, it was not unique to the Gate City. In a country with little promise of equal protection under the law or great economic opportunity, there was no mass movement of black people anywhere in the first decade of the century. People stayed close to where they were born. But Atlanta, more than most cities, held the prospect of higher education. Hundreds of young, promising African American students continued to enroll at the cluster of black colleges in the city. The schools, in turn, continued to recruit African American faculty and professionals. As they had for decades, they continued to hire black men and women as staff on all levels. These schools employed black contractors and even physicians. They would remain the most significant institutions in the black community, indelibly shaping and influencing the broader community.

In 1910 nearly 75 percent of African Americans were rural. About 90 percent still lived in the South, where most were in poverty, poorly educated, and faced with legally codified oppression. However, the Great War (1914–1918) affected nearly every corner of modern life. In addition to the human toll of war, geopolitical landscapes were altered, as were economies, immigration, laws, and demography across the United States. It precipitated the largest peacetime migration of people in history.[25] The movement was stunning, and it was widely discussed by newspapers, civil rights organizations, churches, and lawmakers.

With rigorous recruitment from labor scouts, black newspapers, and familial networks, more than a half million African Americans left the South between 1910 and 1920. Another 903,000 left the South in the following decade. Most moved to the Midwest and the Northeast, and some southern cities also saw increases. Between 1910 and 1920 the black population of New York City increased by 66 percent, and Chicago's jumped nearly 150 percent. Philadelphia's black population increased fivefold, and Detroit's went up more than 600 percent. Yet among these cities in 1920, the proportion of black people ranged only from New York City's 2.7 percent to Philadelphia's 7.4 percent. All these northern cities still remained over 90 percent white. Even after these staggering increases, Atlanta's black population, as a proportion of the city, stood at 31 percent—multiples higher than any of these northern cities. In New Orleans, the only Deep South city larger than Atlanta, African Americans were higher in raw numbers than in Atlanta but made up only 25 percent of the population, similar to Washington's percentage.[26] No major northern city in the country had a higher proportion of black people than Atlanta by the so-called Harlem Renaissance or New Negro movement of the 1920s.[27]

Atlanta saw a surge of black newcomers seeking employment in various industries, such as carpentry, drafting, and construction. William Edward Evans, who had found some success working with the black-owned construction firm Alexander Hamilton and Son, helped build the expanding footprint of black Atlanta. For the construction of private homes, churches, and educational and civic structures, African Americans funneled work to black firms. An especially notable project was the Butler Street YMCA. Built in 1907–1908, it became one of the most important centers for black life in Atlanta. Evans worked on the building, located in the heart of Sweet Auburn, which became known as "Black City Hall" for its prominence. The brick building provided remarkable space for a deprived community: forty-eight dorm rooms, a swimming pool, a gymnasium, a basketball court, classrooms, and an auditorium. Schools in the Atlanta University Center also contracted with Alexander Hamilton and Son for construction projects. In 1916 Morehouse College used the company to erect Robert Hall, a modern dormitory with multiple floors.[28]

Even the wealthiest among the African American community tapped black talent to build their homes. The most celebrated of these homes is the Herndon family mansion. Atlanta University professor of drama and elocution Adrienne Herndon, wife of the city's first black millionaire, Alonzo Herndon, oversaw the building of their stunning classical revival brick mansion, adjacent to Atlanta University. As with any massive home, it provided for entertaining and family gatherings: "Among its unique features was a terraced roof garden where Mrs. Herndon planned to stage plays and entertain university colleagues and her husband's business associates. The showpiece of the mansion itself would be the magnificent frieze, which she had placed in the library. Located near the ceiling, the frieze contained a series of panels depicting the life of Alonzo Herndon from slavery to freedom." Years later, researchers confirmed that the extraordinarily talented Adrienne undertook years of research and careful study to conceive the bulk of the design for the home, even the "complicated mechanical systems." The Herndons tapped Will Campbell, a black developer, as the lead builder. All contractors, except for the electrical and plumbing systems, were black firms.[29]

For all intents and purposes, by 1920 the capital of the New South had already achieved the distinction of being a disproportionately black city with unusual opportunities for black success. In a landscape where most black people were rural and cities had single-digit proportions, black Atlantans in the 1920s were witnessing an unusual social, economic, and cultural flourishing. The city's black business class was centrally organized in the Atlanta Negro Business League, which met monthly at the Butler Street YMCA.

In August 1921 Atlanta hosted the twenty-second annual meeting of the National Negro Business League, which had been inspired by work that Du Bois completed at Atlanta University decades earlier. People from across the country poured into the city to promote, network, develop businesses, and advance the economic health of the black community. An estimated five thousand people attended the meeting, including many whites who opted to promote business, industrial products, and more with black businesspeople. Mayor Jason L. Key welcomed the throngs of participants at the city's auditorium-armory, which was opened to both races. In typical Atlanta fashion, Mayor Key lauded the city's hospitable business climate for the "Negro as well as the white man." Emmett Scott, Booker T. Washington's former secretary, as well as Tuskegee Institute's new president, Robert R. Morton, were among the speakers. Local leaders, including R. H. Singleton and John Hope, also spoke, stressing the critical need for black empowerment in the "industrial, commercial and financial world." Not to limit black economic power to domestic spaces, the event also had an international component. Liberian president C. B. King addressed the attendees and promoted transnational investment in development between African Americans and Liberia, then one of only two independent countries in Africa.[30] The meeting was headquartered at the Odd Fellows Building, and attendees stayed at the Butler Street YMCA, at the black-owned McKay Hotel, and at private homes. For all the attention paid to Harlem in this decade, Atlanta was experiencing its own explosion of artistic, cultural, and intellectual expression while making steady economic achievements.

In Atlanta, newcomers found a city profoundly separated by race, as were other American cities. For example, scores if not hundreds of cities in the North and the South had whites-only policies for public accommodations and schools. However, the distinction in Atlanta was the extent to which black people had established their own institutions: economic, educational, religious, and social. Although the language of the day claimed that black folk wanted "social equality" with whites, little evidence suggests that African Americans ever considered social spaces without whites (fraternities, sororities, social clubs, nightclubs, churches, etc.) as lacking anything of substance. To the contrary, black people formed a rich social ecology along the lines of class, leisure, and professional interests, much as whites had. Moreover, there was no notable agitation among local blacks to integrate themselves into white social spaces: clubs, churches, and so on. African Americans were erecting their own social institutions with aplomb.

In the interwar years, the eight major black Greek-lettered fraternities and sororities all established chapters in Atlanta. Additionally, several private social clubs brought people together for social events, semiformal dinners, annual banquets, fund-raisers, black-tie galas, and casual gatherings throughout black Atlanta. Although membership in the Greek-lettered organizations generally required, at a minimum, some college, the Prince Hall Masons and the Order of Eastern Star had members who had never attended college along with others who had advanced degrees. Dozens of social organizations occupied the lives of people in an era of no television, limited radio, and few modern diversions, such as constant access to professional sports or movies. In various religious denominations, the Utopian Literary Club, the Junior Matrons, and the Twelve Club, black women and men found that the city offered almost something for everyone. The social gathering spaces for black Atlantans, who were excluded from downtown hotels, included the Butler Street YMCA and the famed Odd Fellows building, erected in 1912 and 1914, respectively.

The Odd Fellows building, in addition to providing office spaces for black businesses and various organizations, had a 1,300-seat auditorium. There was a rooftop club and the Paramount Theater, which offered movies as well as space for live performances. Even local black universities provided ornate spaces for weddings, receptions, and conferences. At a time when most hotels in northern and western cities allowed whites only, blacks in Atlanta were able to enjoy an exceptional world of accommodation and mobility, one that outstripped most cities by far. Of course, this was not a result of local whites being more open or racially progressive. It was the consequence of the local black population's ability to build institutions.

Black folks did not necessarily express hostility toward any white presence, but there was rarely any expressed sense of deprivation at their absence. If anything, the notion of "social equality" privileged a white gaze that centered whites in ways that black people did not. Moreover, there was an acute sense of emotional and physical safety that black people experienced in all-black spaces. James Weldon Johnson, an alumnus of Atlanta University, NAACP leader, US ambassador, and coauthor of the de facto black national anthem, "Lift Every Voice and Sing," described the Atlanta oasis of black higher education as "a spot fresh and beautiful, a rest for the eyes from what surrounded it, a green island in a dull red sea." Similarly, Dr. Clarence Bacote, a noted AU historian and civil rights leader, remarked that despite being in the Deep South, "You could live here, at any of these schools, and not suffer the injustices that the person who had to make his living in the city did. You didn't have to face Jim Crow; you had your own group right out here."[31]

Notably, Johnson and Bacote belonged to collegiate fraternities, Phi Beta Sigma and Alpha Phi Alpha, respectively. Each provided these men a rich social and professional network throughout their lives. They were also fraternity brothers through Sigma Pi Phi ("the Boulé," further discussed in Chapter 8), which was arguably the most exclusive African American social group in the country. Through conferences, dinners, and a host of social gatherings, these fraternities provided spaces for fellowship, conversations, and levity. In all, Johnson and Bacote were not unlike other African American leaders whose lives were enveloped in a diverse world of black churches and social clubs. Of course, colleges and universities were the critical foundations of much of what meaningfully anchored their lives and the lives of their friends, families, and colleagues. Importantly, these schools proved to be essential to the resurgence of black Atlanta after 1906. Black leadership, which was closely tied to the colleges and universities, operated with special intimacy with the black business and religious leadership as well. Though traumatized by the 1906 riot, the community was not broken.

Most cities boasted no black insurance companies, but in the 1920s there were several in Atlanta, including Alonzo Herndon's Atlanta Mutual Insurance Company, which amended its charter in 1922. It increased its capital stock to $100,000 and was renamed the Atlanta Life Insurance Company. This restructuring made it more agile. Within three years, it had broadened its operations into Florida, Kansas, Kentucky, Missouri, Tennessee, and Texas. The Mutual Federal Savings and Loan Company was formed in Atlanta in 1925. In 1913 business titan Heman Perry formed Standard Life Insurance, which was the first black-owned and black-operated legal reserve company in the state and only the third in the country. By 1915, Standard Life had $2 million in insurance policies and $245,170 in assets. By 1922, it had more than $20 million in insurance policies and $2 million in assets, with an all-black workforce of 2,500 people, making it one of the largest black-owned businesses in the country. Perry's ambitions did not stop there. He expanded into real estate with his Standard Realty Company as well as construction.[32]

In a city with a Klansman as mayor and no black public high school, there were multiple black construction companies, from Perry's Service Engineering and Construction to Alexander Hamilton and Son in the early 1920s. Of course, W. E. Evans had established his own construction firm as well. When Theodore "Tiger" Flowers, the first black middleweight boxing world champion, built his expansive mansion, he contracted with Aiken and Faulkner Real Estate, Building, Loan and Construction, which completed it in 1926. Some others, like Perry, diversified their portfolios, venturing into a range of businesses.

David T. Howard, who was enslaved at birth, found a critical need for mortuary work in Atlanta. Processing the bodies of the deceased had been one of the most rigid racially drawn lines in the skilled professions. Across the country, nearly every town with a sizable black population had a black mortician. Many whites simply refused to process black bodies or proved to lack the sensitivity expected from the grieving black family. Howard eventually purchased a number of properties through the city, becoming one of the wealthiest African Americans there. He donated money and resources to a number of charities and causes, including public education for black children. Howard's success in Atlanta was an obvious example of the popularity and resilience of the principle of Afro-self-determinism. Surveying the landscape of his hometown, he applied it throughout his life. He purchased land and homes, and in 1913 he established a bank. His Atlanta State Savings Bank emerged as the first chartered black-owned bank in the state. The wider black community had an immediate appreciation of this achievement. Black-owned companies poured in deposits. Its board comprised some of the giants in business in the city, including Herndon, who had been a charter member of both the National Negro Business League and the Niagara Movement. Atlanta Mutual and Pilgrim Health and Life Insurance companies were among the clients of the new financial firm, headquartered on Auburn Avenue.

The same year that Howard's bank opened, Perry's Standard Life Insurance Company moved its accounts there, contributing to a promising synergy of bold black economic power in the city. Perry was remarkable for his business success but also for his lack of a formal education. Unlike many others who had studied or operated in or around the universities and colleges, Perry was educated through "various work experiences," not college. After spending time in Houston and New

York City, he was drawn to Atlanta, where he arrived "penniless" only two years after the racial massacre. Inspired by the idea that race enterprises were key to the advancement of black people, Perry thrived in the unique business community of the capital city. Following the success of his insurance company, he formed Service Enterprises in 1922. This consortium included a farm bureau, an engineering and construction company, a philanthropic arm, a pharmacy, and a printing company.[33]

Throughout the 1920s the reputation of Atlanta drew national meetings of several black organizations: National Negro Insurance Association (circa 1920), NAACP (1920), Phi Beta Sigma (1921), Omega Psi Phi (1921), National Medical Association (1928), and Alpha Phi Alpha (1929). Not only did professionals from across the country spend money in the city; they must also have marveled at what African Americans had accomplished. Especially in the business arena, the examples are notable: on Auburn Avenue alone, there were more than seventy black-owned businesses. Atlanta had popular black chroniclers of the people who gave life to the city. Paul Poole and Andrew Kelly opened photo studios in the Auburn area and documented weddings, graduations, family portraits, and the beautiful range of black social life: smiling children, teasing teens, and proud parents. Numerous morticians operated across the city, including Jesse Hanley, Henry Ivey, the Seller brothers, and the Cox brothers. None was as prominent as the philanthropist Howard, who opened a new construction building on Piedmont Avenue. His Atlanta State Savings Bank operated from 1913 until 1922, when the newly formed Citizens and Trust Company, founded by Perry, supplanted it.

From small hamlets and cities, the children of hardworking, poor, working-class, and wealthy people entered the ivy-covered brick buildings in southwest Atlanta to be educated by black and white scholars who were deeply invested in the possibilities of black achievement. As they had in the nineteenth century, these schools affirmed their utility and purpose by extending employment to black professionals in ways unavailable at any college or university outside the South. Regardless of how many more black people lived in New York City, the universities and colleges there did not employ black professors, administrators, secretarial staff, lawyers, physicians, or security at all or beyond a paltry handful. The same applied to Philadelphia, Chicago, Los Angeles, or any nonsouthern site for black migration in that era. It is no coincidence that Washington, DC, a segregated southern city and home of Howard University, would rival Atlanta for its concentration of black professionals and large black middle class throughout the century and into the next.

The appeal of these Atlanta schools had extended far beyond Georgia. Despite the presence of a black college in every southern state, some parents and prospective students were inspired by the growing reputation of the Atlanta schools or of the city itself. This was especially the case if families were tied to a particular denomination. For example, members of the AME church might be more partial to Morris Brown, whereas Morehouse or Spelman might have had greater appeal for Baptists, given those colleges' origins. Others, motivated by purely secular metrics, were drawn to the academic reputation of the schools. The educational complex was not the only draw for transplants. Many, like W. E. Evans, had no formal ties to the schools except as a parent of alumni. However, they did find that their professional and/or business success was almost always related, in some part, to those schools.

By the time that William Alexander Scott II arrived to attend Morehouse, the city of Atlanta was in full bloom, especially along the storied Auburn Avenue. John Wesley Dobbs, a native Atlantan who had dropped out of Morehouse but ascended to the heights of the black social world nonetheless, called the street "Sweet Auburn" for its sublime offerings to those who traversed it. Newcomers like Scott witnessed a unique oasis of ease, success, independence, and racial pride. Arriving from Mississippi as the Great War was coming to an end, Scott was taken by the rush of activity and the energy of the state capital. No other city looked like this one. Although all black people were not prosperous by any means, he witnessed well-dressed black men and women at lecterns, at pulpits, and as shopkeepers throughout the areas near campus. Along Auburn Avenue, he saw a marvelous cluster of businesses: a theater, a hotel, insurance companies, the six-story Odd Fellows building, and medical offices. This was a testimony to the tenacity and industriousness of the local community. After graduating from Morehouse, Scott traveled and worked in Washington, DC, and Florida, before returning to the city that offered Sweet Auburn.

Building upon the principles of Afro-self-determinism, Scott crafted a means for people to easily identify black-owned businesses for patronage. The community needed something more than the city directory, so Scott created the first known directory for African Americans in Atlanta. He later founded the city's newest newspaper, the *Atlanta World*, in August 1928. He was only twenty-six years old. Along with the *Atlanta Independent*, the city had two black newspapers until the *Independent* stopped printing in 1933. Scott's mission was clear: "The publishers of *The Atlanta World* have felt the need of a Southern Negro Newspaper, published by Southern Negroes, to be read by Southern Negroes." In 1931 it became the only daily black newspaper in the country and one of the most widely read black newspapers in the South. It employed black journalists, office managers, newsboys, and photojournalists. There, on Auburn Avenue, the street that left him awe-inspired when he arrived as a student at Morehouse, he established his office. When the New Negro movement was in decline and the Great Depression made lives inexorably more difficult, Scott's media empire expanded to include the *Chattanooga Tribune* and the *Memphis World*. Atlanta was home to the first black newspaper chain in the country. It eventually grew to a portfolio of fifty newspapers. By the following decade, the city also became home to the first black-owned radio station (WERD) in the United States, making Atlanta a black media powerhouse.[34]

In the course of his tenure as publisher, Scott helped shape public opinion, influencing the worldviews and politics of thousands each day across the country. Scott's newspapers covered critically important civil rights cases, including the infamous Scottsboro Boys case in the 1930s. Additionally, its pages drew readers eager to learn about the diverse activities of the black community and the wider world. International affairs, including the Italian invasion of Ethiopia in 1935, as well as coverage of black musicians, athletes, and authors, explored a fullness of black life wholly absent from any white newspaper. Readers could read about the latest scores of the Atlanta Black Crackers games, a baseball team in the Negro Southern League. Originally known as the Atlanta Cubs, the team later joined the Negro American League and, like many black teams across the country, shared the same stadium as the local white team, in this case the Atlanta Crackers, a high-level minor-league team. The field was located at Ponce de Leon Park. If both teams had a home game, the Black Crackers played theirs at Morehouse College, Morris Brown College, or the black amusement park, Joyland.[35]

Enveloped in a society that dismissed the capacity of black people to thrive in professional spaces—let alone appreciate full citizenship—Scott's media empire demanded both. His story intersects neatly with those of many others who migrated to Atlanta for opportunities, fortunes, and a better life. Although Scott was a contemporary of Ivan Allen, with whom he shared a passionate devotion to their hometown, civic duty, and business success, the natural ecology of the city did not provide opportunities for their respective worlds to interact. Moreover, there were vast barriers against Scott's success that did not exist for Allen. Scott's rise is even more remarkable given these daunting institutional forces. That larger communities—New York or Philadelphia, for example—did not have daily black newspapers speaks to the market that black Atlantans created. The reach of Scott's newspaper empire, and its ability to highlight Sweet Auburn, Atlanta's remarkable institutions, and advertisements for black insurance companies, banks, physicians, and more, helped draw attention to the Gate City. Given that no part of the United States was free from the burden of racism, the systemic oppression endemic in the capital city was a price to pay for the opportunities to live in a veritable oasis of black success.

In 1921 African Americans even established their own amusement park, one of the first of its kind. In fact, it is the first black-owned amusement park of this scale to open in the United States. Although various amusement parks operated in Atlanta, including Ponce de Leon Amusement Park, White City, and Lakewood Fairgrounds, they restricted admission to whites only. Undaunted by the familiar practice of mean-spirited stinginess, black leadership started Joyland, which debuted to considerable fanfare on May 16. Later that month, Suburban Gardens in Washington, DC, was the second black-owned amusement park to open. Located in southwest Atlanta, Joyland welcomed an awe-inspiring five thousand people on its opening day. Speeches from local leaders, including Rev. Dr. R. H. Singleton, Rev. Dr. P. Jason Bryant of Wheat Street Baptist Church, and Dr. William F. Penn marked the occasion. Even Mayor Key visited and delivered an address celebrating the opening of the city's first black amusement park, which featured rides and a diverse selection of amenities. There was even a (traveling) big top featuring large animals. The park became a locus for a range of black leisure activities from picnics to civic events, as well as serving as the occasional home field of the Black Crackers. Black boxing promoters with black professional fighters held bouts at the park as well.

The Gate City, in the midst of the audacious New Negro movement, produced what very few other cities had ever done. As the name implied, Joyland offered levity and pleasure to African American families in ways that were denied in the wider hostile city. Situated in a city that disregarded simple accommodations like public parks, public benches, public libraries, and public schools, the amusement park had become a wonderfully defiant oasis. African Americans could enjoy the park with their families without facing racial indignities. This was rare anywhere in America.[36]

The New Negro movement was known for its ability to boldly destroy conventional old stereotypes of timid Negroes who were quick to bend to racist demands. Popular culture played an important part in this refutation of the old Negro archetype, as well as simply highlighting black artistry that was not always explicitly counter-hegemonic. Atlanta was not short on black popular entertainment. Chicago's Bronzeville boasted the Regal Theatre, Harlem had the Apollo, and South Central Los Angeles hosted the Club Alabam, but Atlanta enjoyed the 81 Theatre as well as the 91 Theatre. Both, in the Sweet Auburn district, hosted the biggest names in blues and jazz. Bessie Smith, Ma Rainey, Thomas Dorsey, Ethel Waters, and many others came through the city. The record-breaking Broadway musical *Shuffle Along* was performed in Atlanta in 1924. In the realm of public intellectuals, a veritable who's who of academics, novelists, and other literati visited the campuses for talks, conferences, and symposia. Iconic literary figures from the Harlem Renaissance, including James Weldon Johnson, Walter White, and W. E. B. Du Bois, had only recently lived in Atlanta. Additionally, poets such as Thomas Jefferson Flannigan and Welborn Jenkins published in nationally read journals, including the famed *Crisis* and *Opportunity*. The great educator and activist Mary McLeod Bethune delivered Spelman College's Founders' Day speech on April 11, 1928, and Langston Hughes taught a literature course at Atlanta University years later.[37]

Despite the notable achievements of so many African Americans in Atlanta, they, like their well-dressed and chic counterparts in Harlem, Los Angeles, or Chicago, were outliers in almost every way. Thousands in the city, such as W. E. Evans or Alonzo Herndon, had once been enslaved. There was no doubt that African Americans had made remarkable advancements. Most saw improvements to their lives, but each step toward democracy, decent housing, education, or justice was met with strident resistance. Most black people in Atlanta were poor, uneducated, and exposed to extraordinary deprivations in every way. They faced underresourced and overcrowded schools, racist and corrupt law enforcement, dilapidated housing, and slum conditions in diseased areas without running water. No force was more crude and atavistic in its vulgar display of racism than the KKK. Beyond the Klan, however, city politicians, white business leaders, and city bureaucrats invested in and protected white nationalism with vigor. They were, by any measure, more lethal to black life than the Klan. They controlled access to health care, water, sanitation, police, and employment.

In 1922, in the midst of the New Negro movement, the Atlanta City Planning Commission hired nationally celebrated urban planner Robert Whitten to design a zoning ordinance for the city. His plan demanded that "home neighborhoods had to be protected from any further damage to values resulting from inappropriate uses, including the encroachment of the colored race." The city passed a new zoning law that established an "R-1 white district" and an "R-2 colored district." Of course, desired resources, such as schools, parks, sidewalks, public sewage, and streetlights, were concentrated in white residential areas. Paved streets stopped where black communities started.[38]

From the cultural pride of Confederate southern nationalism to the local tradition of maintaining an exclusive hold on power, the landscape of the capital city was punctuated with forces hostile to black advancement. Yet in the same city, the exceptional community of black colleges and universities offered unique arenas for black success to unfold in spite of the wider forces at work. These race leaders were essential parts of the most important movement for social justice in the country's history.

In every way, Atlanta ranks as a center of the New Negro Renaissance. Only one major city in the Deep South, Birmingham, had a higher ratio of black people in 1920. Even among those cities with numerically larger black populations, none had exceeded the concentration of black businesses—newspapers, banking, higher education—in Atlanta. Many members of nationally prominent African American leadership were based in or had recently lived in the city. It was a touchtone and beacon of the New Negro Renaissance in conspicuous ways.

In many respects, as this chapter reveals, the exclusions fostered by the "Christian spirit of Atlanta" fomented more sophisticated and resourceful ways to dismantle the white-nationalist project that brought them into existence. The schools were the most important institutions for training generations of leaders who would ensure the demise of white nationalism, expanding democracy and opportunity for all. More specifically, the Atlanta black colleges afforded some of the most talented, ambitious, and gifted students the opportunities to excel in ways not available in most other cities. They attracted students, faculty, and staff from across the country. In turn, by the thousands, these people patronized and were employed by a community of black businesses, churches, and civic organizations across every sphere of life. By the end of the 1920s, Atlanta had already become, at least for the South, a Black Mecca, long before that term would come to be widely associated with the city.

Tiger Flowers, the boxing champion who was raised in Philadelphia, could have lived anywhere, but he selected Atlanta to erect his mansion. (Tragically, he died after a surgery in New York City in 1927.) His choice of Atlanta reflects the appeal that the city offered African Americans, even in a hostile racist climate. There was essentially a protective space for black people of means. For the mass of black people who were too poor to afford private school, education was cut short after spending no more than eight years in grossly neglected and overcrowded schools. Living in abject poverty in Buttermilk Bottoms, Summerville, or the Beaver Run's shanties in the shadows of Atlanta University was not any easier just because some black folks managed to financially succeed. For the poor, the glow and promise of Atlanta was an elusive and dim prospect that was far from reach. The Great Depression only made conditions more miserable, at least until liberal reform provided some relief.

W. E. Evans, who had settled in Atlanta in the late nineteenth century and immediately found work in contracting work with the black colleges and universities, lived long enough to see his legacy. By the mid-1930s, his construction company had helped shape Atlanta. The father of nine children built an impressive residence, which had grown to "ten or twelve rooms." He remembered when Spelman College was initially founded and housed at his church, Friendship Baptist. Evans lived to see both Spelman and Morehouse leave Friendship and build campuses on acres that had been former sites of Confederate military camps and Civil War battles. In fact, the skulls of Confederates were said to have been uncovered in early construction efforts.[39] By the 1940s, Evans had witnessed local colleges and universities acquire impressive campuses and graduate generations of black men and women. The opportunities in the Black Mecca paid off for him. Multiple daughters had been taught at local black schools and had become educators, and his sons worked for his construction company. As Evans stated, "My house now is somewhat larger than Colonel Hill's house where the family lived who owned us as slaves."[40] When he died at age eighty-eight, in February 1944, the *Atlanta Constitution* announced his passing and his funeral services, to be officiated by the legendary E. R. Carter and D. T. Babcock at Friendship Baptist Church, where he had been a loyal and active member for more than half a century. Rev. Carter passed away only four months later, also at age eighty-eight.[41] His successor, a year later, was another Morehouse College alumnus, Maynard H. Jackson Sr., from Dallas, Texas.

Evans and Carter, like thousands of other black Atlantans, were interred in South-View Cemetery, which had been incorporated in 1886. Founded by African Americans when many black people were shunned or mistreated by white cemeteries, South-View offered black people "a dignified resting place to honor their loved ones." Officially, the history of South-View accounts how black people "had to enter cemeteries through back gates, and even wade through swamps to conduct funeral services. They were told 'If you don't like it, start your own cemetery.' And so they did."[42]

8 | Black Nationalism in the Klan's Sacred Kapital City
The New Era and Neo-Confederate Revival

A branch of the reorganized Klan . . . should be in every community in the nation. Its need to-day, when fourteen million people of the colored race are organizing . . . cannot fail to be apparent to the thinking man.

—EDWARD YOUNG CLARKE, IMPERIAL KLEAGLE OF THE KKK, ATLANTA, 1920

The Gate City had drawn white people from across the North and South for decades. Black southerners were also attracted to the prospects of this dynamic city, in spite of its crueler traditions. It was not the most industrialized city, but it had many industries—mills and various factories—that employed newcomers without many skills. Additionally, managers, executives, and other skilled professionals were hired. In 1908 Leo Max Frank, an Ivy League graduate and mechanical engineer from New York City, moved to Atlanta to assume the job as superintendent of the Atlanta National Pencil Company, a position he got partially because of his uncle's influence.

Like Alonzo Herndon, Ivan E. Allen, and others, Frank, though a transplant, swiftly found himself a leader in the community. His hometown had the largest Jewish population in the country, and his new hometown, Atlanta, was home to the largest Jewish population in the South. Jews were well integrated into the city's white social, economic, and political spaces. A year before Allen had become head of the Atlanta Marketing Company, Frank was elected president of the city's chapter of a Jewish fraternal order, B'nai B'rith. He and his wife were part of a "cultured and philanthropic community whose leisure pursuits included opera and bridge." However, his world was torn asunder in May 1913 when he was arrested for the rape of Mary Phagan, a fourteen-year-old white former employee of the factory that he supervised. Frank was tried and, with evidence and testimony against him from a black man, convicted and sentenced to execution. Following failed appeals all the way to the US Supreme Court, Governor John Salton reduced Frank's sentence to life in prison. Many were furious.

Tom Watson emerged as one of the most visible critics of the commutation of the death sentence. In his *Watson's Magazine* he asked if Frank wanted "extraordinary favors and immunities because of his race" while also questioning why Jews, a "great people," locally rallied around Frank. Were they, Watson asked, willing to "risk the good name . . . of the whole race" in order to protect "the decadent offshoot of a great people?"[1] Others, livid at the decision, formed a well-organized mob to remove Frank from prison. On August 16, 1915, a pack of armed men overpowered officers at a prison camp in Milledgeville and drove their prisoner more than 110 miles to Mary Phagan's hometown, Marietta, north of Atlanta.

With unmasked men, women, and children assembled to witness the killing, the mob handcuffed and hanged Frank from a tree facing

Phagan's home around 7:00 the next morning. Multiple people took pictures of the lynching. As customary, members of the horde took parts of his clothing as souvenirs. One man, Robert E. Lee Howell (related to the gubernatorial candidate Clark Howell), demanded that the mob cut Frank's body into pieces as further desecration. The lynchers collectively disagreed. Frank's body was returned to Atlanta. Authorities condemned the murder but charged no one.[2]

The Leo Frank case demonstrated, once again, that the capital of the New South was not all that it advertised. It was, by many measures, a tolerant city for Jews, who were, as noted, intimately integrated into the Atlanta white world. The *New York Sun* reported extensively on the case and argued that Atlanta was "freer" of anti-Semitism "than any city in the South." Jews, the paper noted, had been elected to office without any opposition to their religion. In fact, five Jews were members of the grand jury that indicted Frank. A Jewish attorney worked in the solicitor general's office.[3] They went to whites-only schools, were police officers, and enjoyed all of the whites-only public amenities that the city offered. Still, many in the local Jewish community viewed the lynching of Frank as an anti-Semitic act. Lynching, some had come to believe, was a measure of antiblackness, not something that targeted white criminal suspects. It was, at best, reserved for "Others" for whom equal protection or full citizenship did not apply.

Although equal protection was always denied people of color in a white-nationalist project, not all whites were safe or free from capricious legal or extralegal actions. From whites who were military officers over black troops in the Civil War (Confederates agreed to kill them rather than take them prisoner) to white abolitionists, to agents of Reconstruction, a whole class of antiracist whites could at any time be victims of extralegal violence by white supremacists. Also, as noted in Chapter 7 about the situation of antebellum prisoners in Georgia, white Anglo-Saxon protestants could be executed by the state or submitted to inordinately harsh punishment. In fact, from the end of the

Civil War to the 1950s, roughly a quarter of those lynched across the United States were white Christians who were targeted by other white Christians.[4]

The lynching of Frank did prime some of the most virulent racists to embrace the sort of new white supremacy about to sweep the country. Only months after the murder of Frank, the country was again swept up in Lost Cause mythology because of the most celebrated movie of the day, *Birth of a Nation*. Based on Thomas Dixon's infamously racist and ahistorical novel, *The Clansman* (see Chapter 6), the film offered a spectacular cinematic reimagining of the Civil War and Reconstruction. The most significant terror group of the era was heroically represented in filmic drama with huge sweeps of the camera. With stock archetypes of shiftless and rapacious Negroes and gallantly honorable white men, the movie took the country by storm. There were protests and plaudits, depending on perspective. Atlanta, more than any other city in the country, was affected by the renewed interest and celebration that the film bestowed upon the Ku Klux Klan.

Atlanta descended into one of its most volatile, dangerous eras in its history as the "Imperial City" for the largest terror organization in the country. The Ku Klux Klan ascended to new levels of popularity and appeal in the 1920s, spreading to every state and even Canada. Lawmakers, police officers, and men and women pushed the membership of the Klan into the millions. Yet even in the insalubrious landscape of the 1920s, African Americans managed to build new and more expansive black enterprises in the midst of the Klan's revival and under their noses in their capital city. Although the Klan had national popularity, its identity was inextricably tied to the southern nationalism of the failed breakaway state. Beyond the Klan, of course, many mainstream organizations, including the United Daughters of the Confederacy, found space to amplify their mission with the Klan's resurgence.

Many were so enamored by the celebration of the Confederacy, the Klan, and their legacies that an Atlanta-area man, William J. Simmons, and fifteen associates reconstituted the Klan at Stone Mountain, just outside of Atlanta, on Thanksgiving eve, 1915. Simmons, considered a failure and chronic joiner of organizations, appeared to strike the right chord with his revival of the terror group. As an act of continuity, he even included two elderly men who were members of the original Klan. With a Bible and a sword, he made some ritualistic declarations before naming himself imperial wizard of the Invisible Empire of the Knights of the Ku Klux Klan.[5]

On November 28, 1915, the *Atlanta Constitution* covered the founding of the "Invisible Empire," calling it an "impressive" event that purported to take "an active part in the betterment of mankind." The newspaper offered no comment on the original Klan's terrorist legacy or the new incarnation's commitment to a cause of white nationalism. The group was not officially chartered until July 1 the following year. All twelve charter signatories were residents of Fulton County. The imperial kleagle, Edward Young Clarke, was the brother of Francis Clarke, managing editor of the *Constitution*. Eventually, Klan membership included a wide swath of prominent Atlantans, including Paul S. Etheridge, chairman of the Fulton County Board of Commissioners of Roads and Revenues; John A. Boykin, solicitor general of the Atlanta Judicial Court; and Elizabeth Tyler, vice chairman of the Georgia Committee of the Republican Party. Atlanta had become home to the national headquarters, a mansion known as the Imperial Palace that was located in the Buckhead neighborhood.[6]

There was little doubt that the neo-Confederate legacy of the new Klan was central to its raison d'être. In fact, the first official organized public event was an Atlanta Confederate Reunion on October 10, 1919. The Klan proudly marched down Peachtree Street behind aging Confederate veterans. Nathan Bedford Forrest Klan No. 1 was established as the local chapter of the Klan (separate from the headquarters), named after the infamous Confederate general who was accused of war crimes for slaughtering black surrendering Union troops during the Fort Pillow Massacre in 1864. The revised Klan immediately found a special synergistic relationship with the most influential and powerful organization dedicated to the Confederate legacy: the United Daughters of the Confederacy (UDC). By the time the Second Klan was formed, the membership of the UDC had expanded to 100,000.[7] Given their shared genealogy, the connections between the Klan and the UDC were natural and mutually beneficial. In Atlanta the president of the local chapter of the UDC, Caroline Helen Jemison Plane, began promoting the bold vision of a massive monument to the Confederacy at Stone Mountain, where the new Klan had been established.

Plane convinced the organization to hire famed artist Gutzon Borglum for the project. Borglum "had a vision of the Klan as the instrument of a pro-farmer, anti-tariff, Anglo-Saxon progressivism . . . without foreign ideologies."[8] Not only was Borglum a talented and renowned sculptor; he was also a member of the Klan. In the same year that the Second Klan was founded outside of Atlanta, the UDC secured a lease from the Venable family, which owned many acres, including a granite mountain that shared the name of the town in which it was located. The UDC planned to carve a massive monument on Stone Mountain to honor Confederate General Robert E. Lee. A wide cross section of locals who supported the plan wanted to expand the honor beyond General Lee to include other Confederate icons.

Borglum enthusiastically accepted the job and broadened the design of the project from a proposed twenty-foot carving of Lee to a monument to Confederate generals Lee and Stonewall Jackson, along with Confederate president Jefferson Davis. Plane was pleased and perhaps inspired by his vision. Because of the groundswell of support from Atlanta society and beyond, she requested that Borglum incorporate the Ku Klux Klan into the relief as well. As the president of the local UDC wrote, "I feel it is due to the KKK that saved us from Negro domination and carpetbag rule, that it be immortalized on Stone Mountain."[9] Although he was an avowed Klansman and supporter who was "deeply involved in the national activities of the terror group," the final version of the monument did not include hooded Klansmen, as Plane and others had wanted. The resources and labor required for a massive carving that depicted Klan hordes were infeasible.[10]

Involving police, politicians, and civic and social groups, the Klan resurgence in Atlanta and its surrounding communities was endemic.[11] As a complement to codified racial policies, the group assumed responsibility of enforcing racial spaces when the law could not. For example, Klansmen ordered Lebanese and Syrian residents of Marietta, a northern suburb of Atlanta, to flee the town. Although federal law categorized Middle Easterners as racially "white," the Klan's provincial xenophobia thought otherwise. The murky nature of racial lines of demarcation among whites was always manifest. The Second Klan offered up some newer iterations of these debates.

Surprisingly, the United Daughters of the Confederacy were willing to honor Confederate veterans who were immigrants, Catholics, or Jews: three groups that the Second Klan denounced and identified as anathema to its fascist ideals of Americanism. In fact, Jews and Catholics were members of the UDC.[12] While the Second Klan was also anti-Catholic and anti-Jewish, there were local expressions of the group that still adhered to the universal whiteness of the Confederacy (and that of the United States more broadly). According to David Chalmers, "The Georgia Klan seldom directed its violence toward Jew, Roman Catholic, and Negro. They were objects of semantics, but its direct action was visited primarily on its fellow white, native-born Protestants." Yet if white protestants were their chief targets for physical abuse, the local Klan still flogged and threatened a wide range of black and white people for infractions as innocuous as "loafing," which could include being lazy, unemployed, or otherwise idle. Local expression of Klan politics varied across the country, reflecting provincial values and notions of community and race that could outweigh official Klan dogma when convenient. Just as the CSA granted whites who

were Catholics and Jews full-fledged rights, some Klansmen maintained adherence to the "big tent" whiteness of Confederate white
nationalism. None other than President Franklin D. Roosevelt insisted
that he once shared a dais in a southern chamber of commerce with an
Italian Catholic and a Jew who were members of the Klan. Surprised,
Roosevelt noted that the president of the chamber explained that both
men were members of the KKK "because everybody in the town knew
them."[13] Whiteness, in some instances, could serve as the great unifier,
above any religious, gender, or class difference. Yet despite the degree
of provincial difference in how much a white group was tolerated or
targeted by the Klan, the Klan position against black people was clear.
There were no black Klansmen; the Klan firmly saw black people as
subjugated to a white-nationalist project.

Despite the divergence of their notions of white supremacy, the
UDC valued the Klan as an agent of white supremacy's defense against
a primarily black population. Differences in ideological detail did not
stop them from uniting in spaces of shared interest. Moreover, even
as the Klan affirmed its control across Atlanta, Jews, Catholics, and
other non-WASP whites remained fully ensconced in whites-only
spaces throughout the region. They lived in whites-only neighborhoods, attended whites-only schools, golfed at the whites-only public golf courses, and enjoyed the whites-only swimming pools, parks,
hotels, and restaurants. The city's premier department store (and, by
the 1960s, the country's leading regional department store), Rich's,
founded in 1867, had a whites-only policy for its customers. Eventually,
black people could purchase goods, but they were barred from trying
on any clothes and from eating in the store's restaurant. Its founders
and owners were Jewish.[14]

In a city with rigid segregation and oppression of black people, the
modern Klan largely considered white nationalism to be secure. "White
supremacy was so widely accepted as to require no special preachment,"
explains Kenneth T. Jackson, a specialist on Klan history. Because

white supremacy had been so firmly established, there was little need to push for black exclusion from white space. However, the new group did inveigh against Roman Catholics "more vigorously" than others in at least one instance.

In 1921 the Klan led a campaign to remove Catholics as teachers in Atlanta public schools. Although pro-Klan members of the Atlanta Board of Education supported the measure, they were outnumbered, and the campaign failed. However, the Atlanta City Council, after a Klan-initiated anti-Catholic effort, passed a resolution in September 1921 condemning the Knights of Columbus as "un-American." Mayor James Key vetoed it. Despite some setbacks, the Klan remained extraordinarily powerful.

By the mid-1920s, the KKK had an estimated national membership of four million and was firmly in place in Georgia. Thomas Hardwick lauded the Klan in his successful 1920 Georgia gubernatorial race against Clifford Walker. As governor, however, Hardwick openly criticized the Klan, proving not to be the ally the group had hoped for. In 1922 Walker entered a rematch with Hardwick. The Klan denounced Hardwick, whereas Walker met with Klan leadership, praised the group, and won its endorsement. Walker defeated Hardwick, becoming the sixty-first governor of Georgia. An open Klansman, Walter Sims, successfully ran for Atlanta mayor in 1922. A moderate candidate, James G. Woodward, rejected the Klan frontrunner, arguing that "any man that makes a political plea on a platform of religious prejudices is unfit to be a mayor." (Note the absence of any comment on "race.") Even the police chief, James L. Beavers, denounced the intentions of the "Klan to control, influence, or enter into politics." Sims won the mayoral election on September 20, 1922, during a Klan sweep across Georgia.[15]

Throughout the state, the Klan exerted its power and influence, but the capital city was nearly sacred. At the height of the Klan's popularity and its "expansive foray into Washington, D.C.," David Chalmers details that "Atlanta was the capital of the order." After the election of

Sims in 1922, a cascade of Klan politicians won elections in the city and state. Within a handful of years, the Atlanta chief of police, both US senators, and three members of the Georgia delegation to the House of Representatives were members of the Klan. It is widely estimated that more than half of the police force were Klansmen. The *New York Times* accounted how firmly embedded the terror group was in Atlanta, estimating its membership at forty thousand. Although this was likely an overestimate, the Klan was central to the machinations of the city and the state, exerting far-reaching power and influence.[16] The promotion of innocuous values such as "Americanism," "freedom," "Christian morality," "patriotism," and "family" evaded the more insidious and odious elements of the group's agenda. So many had joined the group that it proved fashionable in certain circles. "Once it got to be enough of a fixture in communities, it became sort of like not being able to get into the country club," one historian explains. "If you weren't in the Klan, people sort of wondered if you were really on board with community improvement or protection of community values."[17] Klansmen even affected tourism.

In addition to all of the Atlanta politicians, police officers, and random men and women who paid Klan membership dues, the group welcomed members into the city each year. Thousands regularly took the Klan pilgrimage to the Imperial City. Klan revelers paid registration fees, packed hotels and restaurants, and attended sessions on how to protect white supremacy through "real Americanism." The hooded hordes were great for local businesses: "The hotels of Atlanta filled with Klan potentates who came to attend Klonciliums and Klonvokations."[18] Eventually, flush with cash and fully aware of the power of controlling the delivery of education, the Klan movement sought to found its own university in Atlanta.

Not to be satisfied with whites-only schools such as Emory, the University of Georgia, or Georgia Tech, the Klan attempted to create its own school when a local college went defunct: "Emperor Simmons dreamed of founding his Klan university to teach the principles of one-hundred-per-cent Americanism." Atlanta was the throne upon which the head of the congregation surveyed and preached to his flock. "Georgia," Chalmers explains, was the "tabernacle" for the Klan.[19]

The appeal of the group was pervasive: it included many white-collar members. The terror group knew very well that infiltrating the police department would provide the Klan with a particularly powerful way to wage brutal campaigns of intimidation against citizens and also to circumvent efforts to expand equality and civil rights in the city. Herbert Jenkins joined the police force in 1931 and joined the Klan almost instantly, as a near de facto process. Being a Klansman was "your ID card, your badge of honor with the in group."[20] Jenkins noted that the Klan had so thoroughly infiltrated the city's police force that "at one time most of the members of the Police Department were members of the Ku Klux Klan."[21] The violence was staggering. One patrolman alone killed more than a dozen black people. When his peers granted him a prize on killing his thirteenth person, he joked that "I hope I don't have to kill all the niggers in the South without getting some help from my brothers." Although it is unclear if the cop was a Klansman, his violence was not offensive to the terror group.[22]

The fact that the Klan was so deeply embedded in law enforcement and every other facet of white Atlanta reflected the city's importance to the group. Atlanta was called the Imperial City, but as one historian insists, it was actually the Klan's "holy city."[23] It was a shining example of a modern, industrial city under Klan control. Neo-Confederate nationalism operated, unfettered, in a way that no other major city had accepted. The symbolic value of Klan control of the capital of the New South underscored the importance of its presence.

Although many in Atlanta endured intimidation, hatred, and floggings, the moderate business class did not offer a vociferous denunciation of the Klan. The major papers were largely passive and, outside of a remarkably courageous effort from the editor of the *Columbus Enquirer-Sun*, did not draw great attention to Klan scandals or criminal activity. By many accounts, the Klan was good for business. Atlanta contained the headquarters of a massive organization with millions of members, and it offered employment to hundreds, if not thousands, of Klan members in the publishing and garment industries. All Klansmen were required to purchase their robes from the official robe producer, Atlanta Klansman W. E. Floding. One could not produce a homemade Klan garment. Using an unofficial robe was punishable by expulsion. After 1923, other local manufacturers enjoyed the robe-making boon-doggle, raking in profits. The local printers published the *Spotlight*, the official Klan newspaper, which contained ads from local and national businesses, including Coca-Cola. There were also pamphlets, books, and Klan publications produced locally and sent around the country.[24]

In a social and cultural space that offered hagiographic narratives of the Old South and the neo-Confederate agents who protected its legacy, few organizations were as admired as the Ku Klux Klan. Its original incarnation was directly tied to the Confederacy. The Second Klan attempted to refashion a modern organization in the tradition of its nineteenth-century antecedent. The cultural surge of popularity, fueled by the runaway success of *Birth of a Nation*, as well as the novel on which it was based, was a boon for the Klan. Members enjoyed appeal as politicians in ways unknown even after the Civil War: "The men and women of the Klan were more than capable of both enjoying contemporary mass culture and turning it to their own ends. . . . This was no fringe element—these were the Klansmen next door. Nowhere was this more apparent than in the Klan's 'Imperial City' of Atlanta."[25]

Politicians understood how much being a Klansman aided their political aspirations. A list of the most powerful Klansmen in the state of Georgia reads like a who's who of political leadership for nearly two decades. During the zenith of its power, city council member James O. Wood, editor of the *Searchlight*, ran against twelve other candidates in the Democratic primary for the state legislature. He declared to crowds that "I am the original Ku Klux Klansman, and I am proud of it. I belong to everything anti-Catholic I know of. I have always stood for the laboring man and for organized labor." He ended up nearly a thousand votes ahead of the entire field. This historical moment was the "apogee of its power and leverage in Atlanta."[26] Eurith Dickinson Rivers joined the Klan, openly celebrated his membership, and enjoyed success as a member of the Georgia House of Representatives in 1924. Two years later he was elected to the Georgia State Senate.

Being in the Klan did not guarantee lasting political success, of course. There were various forces at work that undermined Klan dominance. The Klan's appeal had begun to wane in the late 1920s as internecine feuds, lawsuits, arrests, and scandals destabilized the group. Julian Harris, son of Joel Chandler Harris (creator of the Uncle Remus tales), used his platform as editor of the *Columbus Enquirer-Sun* to mock, investigate, and attack the fascist group. Despite death threats, Harris published scathing pieces that drew attention to the discordant rhetoric of freedom and democracy from the elected officials who held membership in a terror group: "Is it great to be a citizen of a state whose governor is a member of and subservient to that vicious masked gang. . . . Is it great to be a Georgian?" In addition to the *New York World* and the *New York Times*, local Georgia newspapers started to turn against the Klan and report its violence (particularly against whites). Klansmen flogged, beat, and killed men, women, and children. The Indiana Klan leader David Stephenson was tried for beating and murdering a white woman in 1925. This national case, where he was found guilty, further tarnished the group, even though the Indiana Klan had separated itself from the Atlanta-based one.[27] Rivers lost his 1928 and 1930 bids for governor. In 1932, however, he was elected to the Georgia House of Representatives, where he served until he successfully won the race for governor in 1937.

Not to be constricted to just one organized expression of extralegal white supremacy, other racists, inspired by the rise of fascism in Europe, created the American Fascisti Association in June 1930. Better known as the Order of the Black Shirts, its founders included the state agriculture commissioner, Eugene Talmadge, who would later serve three terms as governor of Georgia (1933–1937 and 1941–1943) and be elected to a fourth term (1946) but die before taking office. The Order of the Black Shirts used terrorism to assert control and domination of black people but could not compete with the larger, more familiar, and more American KKK for the hearts of Atlanta's racist masses.[28]

Above all, the Klan functioned with multiple missions. Its most obvious charge was the protection of white nationalism. Like its earlier incarnation, it was a backlash to the changing social, cultural, and political world. Yet instead of newly freed black people, this new iteration was largely bound to a narrow definition of whiteness that viewed with hostility Catholics, Jews, recent white immigrants, leftists, and in many cases even white union organizers. Therefore, its ideological platform was broader than the neo-Confederate white nationalism of its nineteenth-century version. The Klan also functioned as a secret fraternal order and important social space where entire families, churches, and communities could share leisure in a homogeneous space. Politically, the Klan was active across partisan lines. Throughout the South its membership was dominated by the same single party of most white southerners since the antebellum era: the Democrats. In the Midwest, however, the Klan stronghold of Indiana was controlled by the Republican Party, which had dominated that state's politics for decades. Its broad-based appeal rested on the degree to which it resonated with neo-Confederate sensibilities in Atlanta and broader white nationalism outside of the South.

By the time that the Klan emerged as one of the largest expressions of terror and fascism ever, African Americans were organizing in their own communities to create oases of respite against the vast forces of hatred and oppression that enveloped them. In the years following World War I, a new political consciousness and militancy emerged, ushering in what became known as the New Negro era. The

New Negro movement was shaped by an explosion of black intellectual, artistic, political, and even economic works in the interwar years. In Harlem, Chicago, Washington, and Los Angeles, African Americans were mobilizing, building, and expressing themselves in ways that reflected a new militancy and self-determination. In the move to urban spaces, the innovative new music of jazz, and the visual artists, novelists, and journalistic social commentaries, the 1920s displayed a veritable New Negro indeed.

The resurgence of the Klan only amplified the need for black people to forge the meaningful institutions that would enable their advancement. As with the 1906 massacre, the massive growth of the Klan tested any faith that racial reconciliation was likely. Few places were probably as ripe for the message of the Universal Negro Improvement Association (UNIA) as Atlanta was. The black-nationalist organization opened offices in Harlem in 1916, with the goal of establishing a sovereign country in Africa free of Western imperialism. The Jamaican-born UNIA founder, Marcus Garvey, visited Georgia multiple times after the establishment of branches, first in southern Georgia and then throughout the state. Garvey found support from local mainstream black leadership, probably given his full-throated call for black self-determination and racial uplift, two generally innocuous demands that resonated with African Americans. One of the most visible black churches in the city, Big Bethel AME, hosted the relatively unknown leader on March 25, 1917. At the corner of Auburn and Butler Streets, the church was one of the religious anchors in Sweet Auburn. Senior Pastor Richard Henry Singleton was a significant figure in town, but also one whose professional work centered on cultivating independent black institutions. He sat on the board of Morris Brown College, the first college established by, named for, and operated by black people in Georgia. There is little doubt that Garveyism aligned with the politics of local people.

By 1922, the UNIA had become the largest mass movement of black

Morris Brown College faculty, 1920s. Morris Brown was the only college or university in the city established by and named for a black person. It always had black presidents, unlike most other HBCUs, which whites administered into the early twentieth century. CREDIT: ATLANTA UNIVERSITY CENTER ROBERT W. WOODRUFF LIBRARY. CONTACT ARCHIVES@AUCTR.EDU

people anywhere, with millions of members in numerous countries. A thriving UNIA branch was operating in Atlanta when Garvey met with the Klan there in June.[29] However, the meeting with Imperial Kleagle Clarke had a damning effect on Garvey's public image. African American leaders—most of whom were already anti-Garvey—unleashed a powerful campaign against the black nationalist. Some even called him a lackey for white supremacists, an enemy of black people, and a "messenger boy of the Klan." But the meeting with the leader of the largest terrorist organization in the country was not aimed to offer supplications to white supremacists. Garvey spoke about Klansmen as "honest" whites who did not lie about their hostility to justice, democracy, or freedom: "I regard the Klan, the Anglo-Saxon clubs and White American societies, as far as the Negro is concerned, as better friends of the race than all other groups of hypocritical whites put together. I like honesty and fair play. You may call me a Klansman if you will, but, potentially, every white man is a Klansman as far as the Negro in competition with whites socially, economically and politically is concerned, and there is no use lying."[30]

The UNIA proclaimed a number of basic points with which the Klan and many whites had no quarrel:

1. The US was a "white man's country."
2. Black people should not seek integration or desegregation with whites.
3. Black people should "return to Africa" to establish an independent nation-state.
4. Black people should practice self-determination in all matters.

Components that celebrated racial pride and African-descended people's history from ancient Egypt through modern Ethiopia were anathema to most whites, but innocuous enough if confined to black space. The meeting was fundamentally a strategic one that met multiple goals for the UNIA. It allowed the organization, a clearly defiant black group that conspicuously criticized white supremacy as no other organization had in US history, to operate openly in the most violent strongholds of the Klan. In a country that was deeply invested in the corruptive ideology of white supremacy and its necessary dependent—black subjugation—the UNIA demanded that black people be free. It was also potentially subversive to the state. An organization that did not insist on pledging allegiance to the United States, white people, or even a white Jesus would be able to mobilize thousands of armed black people throughout the country.

In another immediately practical way, the meeting with Imperial Kleagle Clarke focused on areas of mutual agreement, including (1) maintaining separate black and white social worlds, and (2) ensuring no race mixing. The first point had been famously endorsed by black educator Booker T. Washington in Atlanta to thousands of cheering whites less than thirty years earlier. The second, related to the first, was a significant issue of safety for black women. Since enslavement, white men had sexually terrorized black women and girls with impunity. Virtually all biracial babies had emerged from the wombs of black women. Of course, this did not mean that intraracial sexual crimes did not occur. But if the perpetrator of an interracial sexual crime was white, punishment was not likely.[31] The Klan, although it used rape in its arsenal of terror, granted Garvey and the UNIA the clearance to physically enforce any transgressions of black women by white attackers.[32]

The gravity of the outcome of this meeting cannot be ignored. On a very practical level, the UNIA was strategic in its ambition to secure the safety of its membership in a way that the NAACP, its ideological rival, did not. It was able to simultaneously defy white racists openly while celebrating black people and their humanity in ways that countered every message propagated by white society. Black people were centered in their spiritual, educational, economic, and cultural frames. The UNIA built businesses and other institutions that sustained the black community in important ways. These efforts were not ignored or forgotten, even as the UNIA collapsed under government repression, mismanagement, and squabbles with other black organizations.

At a basic level, this meeting was motivated by the cynical belief that whites could not be collectively reformed ethically and morally to be fair, just, and democratic in a multiracial society. Black people's freedom must come, the UNIA believed, by self-determinative action. Because any effort to morally reform most whites would be futile, black people's most viable option for freedom was to establish their own nation-state away from the United States. In essence, the crucible of black nationalism—that black people must be independent of whites to achieve freedom—could not exist without white supremacy. And there was no greater example of this than the Ku Klux Klan movement sweeping the country.

The black nationalism of the UNIA certainly resonated with Afro-self-determinism's basic tenets of self-determination, racial pride, and even self-defense, but the two concepts were ideologically distinct. As noted above, Afro-self-determinism always affirmed the right of black people to their American citizenship. Loyalty to the United States had been a core principle, even if blacks did not believe that most whites (particularly white southerners) would be just, democratic, or ethical in their relationship with them. Black nationalism, though reaching its peak level of appeal in the Garveyite movement, had never represented the majority belief among black people. Black leaders, whether integrationist, accommodationist, or Afro-self-determinist, had never advocated mass exodus from the United States. They had never renounced their citizenship, no matter how tenuous or elusive it was. Instead, they demanded realization of their rights as citizens. To that end, the black leadership in Atlanta grew to view Garvey with deep hesitation at best.

By 1920, Rev. Singleton of Bethel AME had become a staunch ally of Du Bois, who castigated Garvey. Singleton was the president of the Atlanta chapter of the NAACP and rose to national prominence. He was one of ten African Americans who advised President Woodrow Wilson at the Paris Peace Conference as part of a black delegation in 1919. Singleton's endorsement of Afro-self-determinism was evident. However, he did not denounce American citizenship. He emerged as part of the "Garvey Must Go!" campaign.

On April 30, 1925, Singleton hosted Prince Madarikan Deniyi from Lagos, Nigeria, a British colony. Deniyi had been traveling across the country and offering forceful criticisms of Garvey. Although Singleton had welcomed Garvey eight years earlier, his church had become a center for local anti-Garvey efforts.[33] At worst, many black leaders had come to view Garvey as an active enemy of black people's interests. Much as they had viewed Washington a decade earlier, they measured Garvey as one who made racists comfortable. He argued against black people's activism for their rights, as Washington had. Moreover, Garvey had little practical value to add to the black community in the city. Most African Americans were not willing to move to Africa.

Most wanted to realize the rights guaranteed them by law. And most believed in and practiced black institution building.

By the 1920s, all major black communities across the country had the same kinds of black institutions: churches and a range of small businesses, including barbershops, grocery stores, mortuaries, and medical and dental offices. Many had weekly newspapers. Several cities—New Orleans, Nashville, Washington, and Baltimore—had colleges and universities. But unlike most other cities where the UNIA took root, Atlanta was especially characterized by black institutional development. In addition to the usual black institutions in large communities, by the 1920s the Gate City boasted the largest number of black colleges and universities in the country. Atlanta also had a black amusement park, multiple black-owned medical and dental offices, multiple black construction companies, and two black newspapers. It had banking and insurance company executives and well-paid middle management.

These financial and educational institutions hired black women in secretarial positions at a time when white ones in every city excluded them. This is notable for multiple reasons. The gendered landscape of privilege in Atlanta was more capacious than the vast majority of cities. For example, African American women in New York or Chicago were generally denied access to what were known as "pink-collar jobs," positions such as secretaries, librarians, nurses, and teachers. Atlanta's black middle class thus had more employment options.

Although black people were universally excluded from open housing across the country, the Great Migration made overcrowded housing crises more acute in big cities such as Chicago, New York, and Philadelphia. Atlanta also suffered overcrowding in black areas but, by contrast, offered newly constructed suburban housing opportunities for black people. In 1926 Joyland Park, a black suburban housing development, was constructed in the vicinity of the black amusement park of the same name. The development boasted homes on "high rolling ground" and an "attractive lay" for all homes in the area. The *Atlanta*

Constitution reported that "the better class of colored people . . . are flocking to Joyland park." Though relatively modest homes, these were respites from the "noise and dirt of the city," drawing people with prices and mortgages accessible to lower-middle-class families. Plans included a clubhouse, a pool, and "a grove of beautiful shade trees."[34] There was no other street in the country with a higher concentration of black banks, insurance companies, medical and legal offices, and small businesses than the strip of Auburn Avenue. When one factors in the large churches and the proximity of academic leadership, even Chicago or Harlem could not compete with what Atlanta offered the world in terms of black institution building during the 1920s.

The Atlanta black leadership class could not be accused of being sycophants of whites or being too weak to forge or support black institutions. Moreover, as the well-armed black men of the 1906 racial massacre had demonstrated, the privileged classes of black Atlantans could not be charged with being passive cowards in the face of white supremacy or desperately seeking white acceptance. They valued black institutions and black people, and they cultivated black space for people to thrive in. The community was a complex social ecology of increasingly variegated class-based diversity. Fraternal orders such as the Prince Hall Masons had membership across class lines, whereas some excluded all but the most privileged.

Just as the Garveyites were sweeping the country, taking root in grassroots sectors of every major city, Atlanta chartered its newest local outpost of a national black secret fraternal order, in this case Sigma Pi Phi Fraternity. Widely known as the Boulé, the fraternity chartered its Atlanta chapter ("subordinate boulé") on January 24, 1920. Founded in Philadelphia in 1904, the Boulé was the oldest African American Greek-lettered fraternity. Membership was drawn from college graduates, not from college students, by invitation. The Atlanta chapter proved to be a significant social anchor for the city's black elite. Inductees were from among men who had already established themselves as outstanding in their respective professions. Membership included a veritable who's who of African American leadership in any city where the fraternity emerged. Atlanta's chapter, the Kappa Boulé, was an assemblage of the most powerful, influential, and educated black men in the city. Though ideologically diverse to some extent, its membership would politically align with Du Bois over the accommodationist or nationalist rivalry he had with Washington and Garvey. In fact, in 1912 Du Bois was the principal founding member of the New York City subordinate boulé (Zeta), in which nearly half of the charter members had been involved in the Niagara Movement.

The charter members of Kappa Boulé included college presidents (or soon-to-be college presidents) John Hope, Samuel H. Archer Sr., John W. E. Bowen Sr., and William J. Trent Sr. Among the medical leadership were physicians Henry Rutherford Butler, Charles C. Cater, William F. Penn, Thomas H. Slater, and the prominent dentist Leonidas C. Crogman. Attorney Austin T. Walden, Truman Kella Gibson Sr. (insurance company executive), Charles H. Johnson, and George A. Towns were also inducted. Most of these men were not only tied to the colleges and universities but were also socially and politically tethered to the local NAACP.[35] Therefore, the social world of black community in Atlanta had become nearly as layered and socially complex as the larger white one.

Along the lines of class, education, denomination, gender, and ideology, the world of black Atlanta in the interwar years was as rich and diverse as any black community in the country. Although Harlem, with its proximity to the largest publishing houses in the country, garners immense attention today as the center of black culture in the 1920s, New York was not the only signifier for the explosion of black art, culture, and political activity known as the Harlem Renaissance. Erin D. Chapman explains that "formerly known as the 'Harlem Renaissance,' the New Negro Renaissance was an era of cultural and political ferment, exhilaration, and self-generated 'opportunity' among people of African descent as they gathered . . . in the world's metropoles . . . in the decades leading up to and following World War I and continuing through World War II." Additionally, the moment was marked by "self-determined distinction from the docility and dependence on white benefactors they saw in their parents' and grandparents' generations."[36]

Atlanta, despite these remarkable strides among black people, was not, of course, Edenic. In addition to the immensely racist institutional forces at the local and state level, there were pressing conditions of poverty and extreme labor exploitation that were especially acute for black workers. By the end of the 1920s, Atlanta's black community, like communities everywhere, had begun to experience the economic challenges of the Great Depression. Although most black people in the city were already poor, the conditions actually became more desperate as low-paying jobs laid off black workers. Members of the community who owned small businesses struggled to survive. Many businesses collapsed. Families that tenuously cobbled together resources to send children to local colleges found the task impossible. Even families that were more financially secure struggled.

In 1932, at the peak of the Great Depression, around a thousand white and black leftist activists attempted to organize workers protesting for relief payments from the federal government. The scene was alarming: people of different races assembling around issues of mutual class interest. As in earlier Populist campaigns, the state swiftly arrested a young black organizer, Angelo Herndon. Although the light-skinned Herndon shared a surname with the city's first black millionaire, Angelo was from a poor family in Ohio. In 1933 an all-white jury convicted the twenty-year-old of "insurrection" for having communist materials in his possession. He was sentenced to 18–20 years of hard labor on the notorious Georgia chain gang. The draconian punishment shocked all who had not been aware of the carceral brutality of the state and its particular antipathy to leftist interracial activism.

Seventieth-birthday celebration for W. E. B. Du Bois, 1938. The Atlanta University Center was an important place for professional training, scholarly inquiry across disciplines, and the development of black leadership and activism. It was also a site for social activities, including weddings and birthday celebrations. People could gather in upscale settings and enjoy quality services. Back row left to right: Charles Johnson, Yolande Du Bois Williams, James Weldon Johnson, Ira De A. Reid, Rufus Clement, William Stanley Braithwaite. Front row left to right: (unknown), W. E. B. Du Bois, Mrs. Nina Du Bois, Joel Spingarn. CREDIT: W. E. B. DU BOIS PAPERS, ROBERT S. COX SPECIAL COLLECTIONS AND UNIVERSITY ARCHIVES RESEARCH CENTER, UMASS AMHERST LIBRARIES

Atlanta was simultaneously a space of inordinate black success and a locus of incredibly cruel antiblack repression.

The 1930s did deliver some reforms and relief from various travails. The state's Klan membership plummeted over 90 percent from a 1925 high of around 156,000 members to fewer than 1,500 in 1930. Many forces precipitated its decline: internal squabbles, lawsuits, and scandals. The flagrant hypocrisy made some disillusioned. Aligned with the Anti-Saloon League, Klansmen were nevertheless arrested for public drunkenness across the country. It became known that Edward Clarke, the imperial kleagle who met with Garvey in 1922, had been arrested in 1919 for "sexual impropriety and possession of illegal alcohol." Klansmen beat and even shot each other in violent feuds. During World War II, the group formally shuttered its doors after it was prosecuted for tax evasion. Its mansion, the Imperial Palace on Peachtree Street, was purchased by an insurance company that eventually sold it to the Catholic Church.[37]

Throughout the decade, competing narratives of freedom, democracy, and citizenship continued to circulate in Atlanta. Even as the city heralded its neo-Confederate ways, there was a slow erosion of some of the crueler traditional components. The chain-gang system that replaced convict leasing was notorious for its harshness. It penetrated the national imagination when Robert E. Burns's *I Am a Fugitive from a Georgia Chain Gang!* was made into a film in 1932. Investigations had confirmed the brutality of the system and exposed Georgia as having a particularly coarse, primitive system of carceral operation.

In 1937 the US Supreme Court ruled that Georgia's insurrection law was unconstitutional. The antebellum law stated that "if any person be in any manner instrumental in bringing, introducing or circulating within the state any printed or written paper, pamphlet, or circular for the purpose of exciting insurrection, revolt, conspiracy or resistance on the part of slaves, Negroes or free persons of color in this state he shall be guilty of high misdemeanor which is punishable by death."[38] This slavery-era law, which was used to control and oppress black people, was finally nullified. Herndon, who had been out of prison on appeal, was freed.

Meanwhile, Herbert Jenkins, who joined both the police force and the KKK in 1931, climbed through the ranks of the all-white force. He was named Atlanta's new chief of police in 1947 and oversaw the hiring of the first black officers a year later. In 1945 Governor Ellis Arnall initiated a prison-reform act, modernizing prison systems in the state and eliminating chain gangs, although convicts could work on beautification projects along highways. He also abolished Georgia's poll tax that same year.

A year earlier, the US Supreme Court had ruled that the white primary was unconstitutional.[39] A month after the decision, attorney A. T. Waldon and C. A. Scott, publisher of the *Daily World*, founded the Fulton County Citizens Democratic Club to mobilize and register black voters. Klan sympathizer and former Georgia governor Eugene Talmadge snorted that if black people attempted to exercise their rights, "blood would run through the streets of Atlanta." Undeterred, on July 4, 1944, Dr. Clarence Bacote, Virgil W. Hodges (assistant publisher of the *Daily World*), attorney A. T. Walden, and Eugene M. Martin (vice president of the Atlanta Life Insurance Company) attempted to vote in the Democratic primary. The polling officials, surrounded by local press and onlookers, claimed that the four men's names were not on the list. Though unsuccessful, these organizers, building upon the work of Du Bois, the Hopes, the Herndons, and many others, mobilized thousands and "laid the foundation necessary to take advantage of the new Supreme Court precedent," explains Tomiko Brown-Nagin. All of the architects of the voting campaign had been either alumni or faculty of Atlanta colleges and universities.[40]

The expansion of the vote was consequential. In less than thirty years, the former citadel of the Klan would be transformed by black voters into the citadel of black political power in the South.

9 | The Dixie Reprise
White Nationalism and the Modern Civil Rights Movement

The rest of the nation is looking to Georgia for the lead in segregation.
—GEORGIA GOVERNOR MARVIN GRIFFIN UPON ADOPTION OF THE NEW STATE FLAG,
WHICH INCORPORATED THE CONFEDERATE BATTLE FLAG, 1956

Few people know that Martin L. King Jr., the nation's most iconic civil and human rights leader, was once a singer. In December 1939, as a precocious ten-year-old child of a middle-class family, he joined his classmates in the biggest performance of their lives to that point. They were part of the boys' choir at Ebenezer Baptist Church, one of the most prominent black churches in Atlanta. His maternal grandfather, A. D. Williams, the former senior pastor at the church, helped establish the first branch of the NAACP in the city. Williams was succeeded as pastor by his son-in-law, Martin L. King Sr. The young King was raised in a veritable oasis of black comfort in Sweet Auburn, the area once known as Shermantown. Many of the newly freed people had gravitated to the camp, and in their search for safety from Confederate violence they formed a shantytown in the ruins of the fires that burned much of the city. Out of sheer industriousness against extraordinary opposition, these formerly enslaved people and their descendants created a storied neighborhood anchored by an array of black-owned institutions: restaurants, medical and law offices, theaters, churches, a bank, and an insurance company. In 1956, as King was leading his very first civil rights campaign, the Montgomery bus boycott in Alabama, *Fortune* magazine identified Auburn Avenue as "the richest Negro street in the world."[1] Still, on that night in 1939, King marveled at the opulence in the room before him.

Although the young King had witnessed professional black men and women, those who lived in Victorian homes (some with maids), this affair was quite different. He had never seen extravagance like this high-society gathering. The Junior League ball was a conspicuous display of wealth, not just bourgeois comfort. He peered into the crowd of well-dressed, chatting faces. There was an energy and excitement that swept the city, and it similarly pervaded the room. Even children were not immune to the sense that this was a major event.

It was a sort of self-celebratory gathering that heralded the city of Atlanta. More specifically, this ball was a celebration of the city's white population—the elite ones, at least. Most whites in Atlanta had never been rich, had never enslaved people, and had never lived in palatial plantations, but the air of pride in this very specific class of whites was on full display. The event, celebrating the world premiere of *Gone with the Wind* at Loew's Grand Theater, exalted a classically romantic view of the Old South and the Confederacy, complete with singing, cheerful slaves. Indeed, King and the other children, arranged to appear as happily enslaved, sang and received smiles and applause from the crowd. And because the event was for whites only, King and his family had to exit the premises immediately following their performance. Even Hattie McDaniel, a black costar of the film, was banned from the premiere and the associated parties because of Atlanta's racial laws. For others, however, this gala was a celebration of a glorious local history and of southern honor.[2]

The people who have controlled the popular narrative of Atlanta's identity have always been especially adept at boosterism, no matter how much the finely crafted images might have veered from reality. Atlanta, during the 1939 celebrations of the city's history, had a well-formed image of exceptionalism that went back to the late nineteenth century. Atlanta was exceptional in its progressive and even cosmopolitan view of the world, boosters argued. It was similarly exceptional as a southern city that was governed with a greater sense of confraternity, goodwill, and cooperation between blacks and whites, rising above the sectional discord that once divided white southerners and white northerners. It was the capital of the South, with an investment in industrial capitalism and "highbrow" culture. Yet it continued to pay homage to its rich past, which also demanded pride and celebration. In these narratives the Confederacy itself was inextricably woven into the tapestry that gave Atlanta's image color, depth, and value. Moreover, the Confederacy, over the course of the seventy years since the Civil War, had functioned as a leitmotif of white-supremacist recalcitrance. And although the Confederacy operated as intrinsic to the history and identity of (white) Atlanta, the shifting political and cultural landscape had forced revisions to the various meanings and significance of the Confederacy and its symbols.

On December 13, the day before the ten-year-old King's performance, the city of Atlanta had begun the first of three days of the most extravagant festivities in its history. Governor Eurith D. Rivers declared December 15 a state holiday as hundreds of thousands of people poured into the state capital for the culmination of celebrations, which included a seven-mile parade of limousines, bands, and dignitaries. Mayor William B. Hartsfield boasted to guests that the city was a gateway to the future while simultaneously enjoying a rich, southern history of plantations, red clay hills, and all the romantic clichés of antebellum Dixie: grinning slaves, "pedestalized" southern belles, and proud planters included. It was also a city that was modern, cosmopolitan, and civilized enough to host an event of this magnitude. Atlanta was proud to showcase itself to the throngs of tourists who filled hotel rooms to capacity and crowded its streets. There were dozens of parties, including debutant balls with belles in hoopskirts and parasols. Thousands of Confederate flags marked the city, clutched in the hands of partygoers, hung from walls, or hoisted above the heads of children swept up in the festivities. Future president and Georgia native Jimmy Carter, who was fifteen years old, noted that this was "the biggest event to happen in the South in my lifetime."[3] The celebrations culminated in the world premiere of *Gone with the Wind*.

Though based on a historical novel that centers the South in a generally sympathetic light, the movie version of *Gone with the Wind* provided an even broader audience with lush, visual representations of an imagined community of white southerners who pledged fidelity to a rebel cause. This cause was in clear defiance of the country of their birth, but the rebels redefined the boundaries of their native land. Theirs stopped at the Mason-Dixon Line. In reality, the Confederate States of America led millions of white southerners in a treasonous pro-slavery war that cost more American lives than any conflict before or after.

By the release of *Gone with the Wind*, there remained little explicit rejection of the CSA's raison d'être: defending slavery. Even as the city that had for decades lauded itself as the veritable capital of the New South, Atlanta's boosters did not consider racial oppression and being forward-facing proponents of modernity as incongruent concepts. In fact, in many aspects these conflicts were not uncommon across most of America. For example, most African Americans were still not allowed the right to vote or serve on juries, and they were segregated in federal, state, and local agencies, including the military, and thousands of public school districts. States across the country legally allowed whites to deny housing, undergraduate and professional school education, health care, and employment to people of color. People from Asia were barred entry into the country, but no European country had any such absolute exclusion. In most states in the country, including many nonsouthern states like Arizona, California, and Idaho, it was illegal for whites and people of color to marry.[4] Therefore, the notion that Atlanta was intimately part of the social fabric of a more cosmopolitan urbane world, rather than a backward, southern cliché of primitivism, made sense to the rhetoric of exceptionalism. Moreover, this construction of a rehabilitated southern city had taken form decades prior to the 1939 extravaganza with the ambitious vision of one of Atlanta's greatest boosters, Henry Grady, who in the aftermath of Reconstruction help forge Atlanta boosterism.

The film was wildly successful, eventually earning a larger box-office take than any other film in history. It received a record thirteen Academy Award nominations. At the 1940 Academy Awards ceremony in Los Angeles, it won a record ten Oscars (two were honorary), including Best Picture, Best Director, and Best Actress. Hattie McDaniel, who portrayed the loyal slave "Mammy," became the first black Oscar winner when she won for Best Supporting Actress.

Gone with the Wind, however successful and far-reaching, was not the first attempt to reconfigure the Confederacy in the popular imagination. In many ways the film confirms widely propagated myths of the Old South that were not restricted to the states below the Mason-Dixon Line. American popular culture itself had developed with a centered focus on blackness as an inferior Other to whiteness. From the minstrel shows that emerged in the cities of Philadelphia, New York, Pittsburgh, Boston, and beyond, there was a national construction of black people as servile, indolent, pliant, and content with subjugation. And although these hostile caricatures of blackness were often tied to the images derived directly from southern slavery, the national expression of freedom and citizenship had been constricted to whiteness since the country's inception.

Gone with the Wind depicts the Battle of Atlanta and General Sherman's conquest of the city. In the fictional narrative, the plantations of Tara and Twelve Oaks were casualties in this battle, and the city, long after Sherman's departure, would remain an important locus of symbolic value in the long shadow cast by slavery, the Civil War, and the Confederacy itself. The narrative did not refashion history. It built on the stories of former Confederates and their sympathizers. For them, the CSA was remembered as a noble struggle for a nebulous and sufficiently innocuous affirmation of "states' rights" that would, in turn, protect and defend the southern "way of life." The war made heroes of men and, at least through *Gone with the Wind*, made Atlanta into a bastion of Confederate activity, sympathy, and genteel sacrifice for southern liberty. Inasmuch as the Junior League, an all-white women's club, insisted on propping up fictive images of happy slaves, the narrative of the Confederacy as the apogee of organized white nationalism is central to how Atlanta became so important in the collective memory of that failed cause.

While the Lost Cause narrative was enjoying a renaissance in popular culture, the nation was still in the throes of the Great Depression. The New Deal introduced a liberal federal government that employed citizens; built bridges, schools, hospitals, and roads; and brought electricity and running water to communities across the country. It also provided housing, food, and general welfare, forever changing citizens' expectations of government. Atlanta proved central to the evolution of liberal governance.

Locally, two Atlantans, Morehouse College president John Hope and Charles Forrest Palmer, a white real estate developer, proposed the idea of "public housing" to the Roosevelt administration to provide for the homeless and near-homeless of both races in Atlanta. Palmer's research found dire conditions among whites in the Techwood Flats area. They were the "working poor, prostitutes, and thieves who could not afford rent in decent housing." They lived in disease and squalor, amid "pools of stagnant water near an open privy serving several families." The poorest black slums were no different. Eventually, the Federal Housing Administration founded public housing. October 1934 saw the beginning of the construction of the country's first public-housing project, Techwood Homes. A year later, President Roosevelt dedicated its opening. Techwood Homes served as a whites-only project. The first black public housing, University Homes, opened six months later.[5]

Despite the appeal of the New Deal to the city and the state's poor, Georgia governor Eugene Talmadge, a rabid white nationalist, echoed the rhetorical devices of his neo-Confederate predecessors in protecting the interests of the wealthy landowners by opposing much of the New Deal. Despite his veneer of common-man "dirt farmer" talk, the governor fought against social safety nets, such as public housing and expanded resources for education and health care. Similarly, he resisted economic regulation, which would have benefited (white) poor tenant farmers. Ultimately, Talmadge viewed public works as anathema and advocated instead for two main objectives of the wealthy conservative business class: lower taxes and less regulation. Still, he remained popular among the white poor, whose financial advancement through public education, wage increases, and health care he opposed. Like the Bourbons whom nineteenth-century Populists lamented, Talmadge pandered to racism to garner votes at the expense of poor black and white people. Another white conservative governor, Ellis Arnall, would later proclaim that none could beat Talmadge in a "nigger-hating" contest during elections.

The governor's racial politics adhered with those of the most infamous white-nationalist state of the moment, Nazi Germany. As the country neared war, Talmadge inveighed against US involvement and, instead, offered accolades for Adolph Hitler. William Anderson, a Talmadge biographer, argues that the governor's praise of Nazi Germany gave "an eerie backing" to his words, but not enough to dissolve his popularity among white Georgians.[6] Still, World War II precipitated

An artist rendering of the planned University Homes public housing to replace the slums of Beaver Slide, which surrounded the Atlanta University Center. University Homes, erected in 1938, was a segregated public-housing complex, only the second one built in the country, after the whites-only Techwood Homes had opened a year earlier in Atlanta. CREDIT: PUBLIC DOMAIN

important transformations across the country and expanded opportunities, if just moderately so in Georgia.

The wartime manufacturing industries in Atlanta attracted white and black migrants who filled openings and satisfied labor shortages. Housing expanded, as did businesses of every size. The expanding tax base and size of the city meant new schools, parks, and resources for public health. Almost all of these were unavailable to black people in Atlanta. The Klan, though a shadow of its presence from a generation earlier, was not a required tool of racial subjugation. The machinations of racial oppression functioned well without the vulgar expressions of hooded terror. In the postwar years, however, one of Atlanta's own would reluctantly assume leadership of a critical boycott in Montgomery, Alabama, inserting himself into the national spotlight and helping to inspire and lead the mobilization of the modern civil rights movement. This effort would transform the country and indelibly change his hometown in ways that he never imagined. The push for civil rights would provoke a resurgence of Confederate rhetoric, symbols, and backlash in a frantic effort to undermine black advancement. Atlanta would be an epicenter of some of the most virulent expressions of Old South–style vitriol.

Except for the early Blue-Gray Civil War reunions of the 1880s, the public display of the Confederate flag was rare until after World War II. This changed quickly as challenges to codified forms of racial subjugation accelerated during and in the aftermath of Nazism's reign of terror. In the 1940s several important legal decisions and other events helped erode discriminatory policies across the country. In June 1941, months before the nation entered the war, President Roosevelt issued Executive Order 8802, which banned discriminatory employment practices by federal agencies and all unions and companies with federal war-related contracts. The administration also formed the Fair Employment Practices Commission as an enforcement agency. Three years later, in *Smith v. Allwright*, the US Supreme Court decided that the white primary, one of the most effective bulwarks in defending white nationalism, was unconstitutional. On May 3, 1948, the Supreme Court, in *Shelley v. Kramer*, unanimously ruled that racially restrictive housing covenants were not enforceable by law. In 1947 even America's favorite pastime, Major League Baseball, was integrated with one lone player, Jackie Robinson. Despite significant national hostility, violence, and resistance to these reforms, there was little doubt that white nationalism was being fundamentally disrupted. The most significant challenges were soon to come, and they inspired white southern nationalists to traffic in the rhetoric and symbolism of the Confederacy in ways unseen since the Civil War.

There were many different challenges to the expansion of democracy and civil rights in Atlanta, often from local organizations. One of the most notorious terror groups was the Columbians, founded in 1946 as a fascist white-supremacist group. Emory Burke, a cofounder, insisted that "what the Germans have done to the Jews will be a mere tea party compared with what we are going to do with them!" The group's office in Atlanta displayed both Nazi literature and a Confederate flag. The avowed fascist organization planned to reestablish a white-nationalist government. As cofounder Homer Loomis argued, "If we want to bury all niggers in the sand, once we come to power we can pass laws enabling us to bury all niggers in the sand!" Ultimately, donning tan uniforms with a lightning bolt on the shoulder, the Nazi-inspired gang, which proclaimed a hatred for Jews as well as blacks, assaulted black people throughout the city. After he was arrested for stomping a young man on October 28, 1946, one Columbian admitted that he had attacked "a dozen or so" black people. They bombed the homes of several black families before an Atlanta jury revoked the charter of the fascist organization. In 1947 the group's leaders were convicted of a plot to bomb police headquarters, city hall, and newspaper offices. Ultimately, after learning of the horrors of Nazi Germany, many whites had little tolerance for a neo-Nazi terrorist organization, especially one that targeted white-controlled institutions.[7]

In 1948 President Harry S. Truman's executive order to desegregate the military, as well as the Democratic Party's endorsement of a federal antilynching bill and voting rights for all Americans, enraged southern Democrats. At the Democratic Convention in Philadelphia, all of the Mississippi delegates and half of the Alabama delegates stormed out in protest. In bold opposition to the civil rights plank, the remaining southern delegates turned to Georgia's senator Richard B. Russell as a presidential nominee against Truman. The efforts to expand democracy were, Russell fumed, an "uncalled-for attack on our Southern civilization." When their effort failed, southern Democrats formed the States Rights Democratic Party ("Dixiecrats") and evoked the spirit of the Confederacy in assorted ways throughout the campaign. This act bore an uncanny similarity to the 1860 fissure in the Democratic Party, when its southern wing broke away when it wanted to ensure the survival of slavery. The postwar sectional crisis was a result of a clear through line from these earlier ideological fractures.

Much as their Confederate predecessors protested the threat to slavery, the Dixiecrats protested threats to white nationalism, which they euphemistically called segregation. This more innocuous term implied, at a minimum, separate facilities (bathrooms, water fountains, etc.) that applied to black and white people equally. If a thirsty white man could bear walking a few more feet for a "white" water fountain, a black man should similarly be able to bear that burden, Dixiecrats reasoned: "We oppose the elimination of segregation, the repeal of miscegenation statutes, the control of private employment by Federal bureaucrats called for by the misnamed civil rights program."[8]

More than separate facilities, Dixiecrats did not want black citizens to have equal protection under the law, the ability to serve on juries, or the right to vote. They also wished to deny access to the basics of public resources, including electricity or running water. Like their Confederate predecessors, they framed their rhetoric as defending the legal authority of the majority of a state's voters to determine state law. If the majority of a state's voters wanted to constrict access to a flagship university or a public hospital to whites, it should be their legal right to take such steps. This "state's right," they argued, was undermined through federal intervention: "We favor home-rule, local self-government and a minimum interference with individual rights."[9]

The echo of the nineteenth-century sectional tensions pervaded the Dixiecrats' July 1948 convention in Birmingham and its second convention a month later, when six thousand participants cheered at the nomination of South Carolina governor Strom Thurmond for his presidential run. Waving hundreds of Confederate battle flags and pictures of Confederates such as Robert E. Lee, the crowd roared during Thurmond's acceptance speech when he declared, "There's not enough troops in the Army to break down segregation and admit Negroes into our homes, our theaters and our swimming pools." The Georgia Democratic Party managed to keep the Dixiecrats from being listed as the "Democrat Party" on state ballots. Appearing as a third party,

Thurmond did not carry Georgia, although he carried each state where he was successfully listed as the "Democratic" Party candidate.[10]

Locally, Atlanta mayor Hartsfield, who had ascended to power after serving on the city council and in the Georgia House of Representatives, felt pressure from the expanded access to the ballot in his city. With an eye to the national landscape, the local flexing of political muscle from black leadership, and the expanding black population in the city, Hartsfield (who was elected mayor six times) annexed surrounding white communities throughout the 1940s to dilute the black vote. This move did not work as well as he had planned. In 1940 the black population represented 34 percent of the city. A decade later, the black proportion had grown to 40 percent. Hartsfield lamented the expansion of black political access and influence, warning that the "Negro population [in Atlanta] is growing by leaps and bounds." In a 1943 private letter to residents of the mostly white suburb of Buckhead, the mayor offered them annexation in order to protect Atlanta against black control: "With the federal government insisting on political recognition of negroes in local affairs, the time is not far distant when they will become a potent political force in Atlanta." Hartsfield's plan finally paid off in 1952. Once Buckhead and other white communities were absorbed, more than a hundred thousand new residents were added to the city. The percentage of the city's black population, which had stood at 41 percent, immediately declined to 33 percent.

Despite the frantic efforts to annex white towns, the pressure for racial equity, including access to municipal jobs, grew. Few municipal jobs were more important, symbolically and substantively, than law enforcement. The demands of the Atlanta Negro Voters' League (ANVL) tirelessly pressured the mayor for black police officers. Local leaders, including the Atlanta Urban League's executive director, Grace Towns Hamilton, and A. T. Walden of the ANVL, insisted that black officers would offer meaningful progress in realizing civil rights and equal protections. However, the resistance to equal protection was strong.

The police force had long been the front line of white nationalism throughout the country, and especially so in the South. By 1948, dozens of southern cities, including New Orleans, already had black officers. In 1948 alone, Houston, Savannah, Memphis, and Atlanta hired their first black police officers. To mollify racists in the Gate City, the nine newly hired black officers were segregated from whites and had no authority to arrest white people, even if they were caught in a criminal act against another white person. Like civilians, they had to call white police to arrest white criminal suspects. Black officers were not allowed to change their clothes in the police precincts; instead, they were relegated to the Butler Street YMCA. Finally, they were allowed to patrol only designated "Negro areas." Even under these humiliating and impuissant conditions, black leadership and the wider black community largely celebrated Hartsfield.

An agile politician who reached out to the black leadership and mediated with white moderates, Hartsfield in many ways embodied the Atlanta spirit. He was a charismatic booster, like Henry Grady and Ivan Allen Sr., telling all who would listen how his hometown and its people were warm to industry and welcomed modernity. He presciently understood the power of aviation in the modern age and initiated the effort to lease Candler Speedway in the nearby suburb of Hapeville for a landing field in 1925. This was the start of a decades-long promotion of commercial aviation that would transform Atlanta as the railroads had in the nineteenth century. Still, as mayor, Hartsfield, had to grapple with the groundswell of resistance from his white residents over the desegregation of public schools. However, the bulk of the legal resistance to school desegregation came from the state, giving the mayor some political cover.

The notoriously racist Georgia governor Herman Talmadge, anticipating the intervention of the US Supreme Court to grant all children access to equal education, proposed to privatize the state's public school system. This would allow private schools to circumvent the law by maintaining segregation. Citizens, according to his plan, would be given grants to pay for education at these converted private schools. "We can maintain separate schools regardless of the U.S. Supreme Court," Talmadge insisted. Subsequent governors openly supported his plan.[11]

Of the many challenges to codified racial oppression, housing evoked the most resistance and violence in Atlanta, and the Klan and other terror groups emerged as some of the many agents of resistance to open housing, bombing homes on occasion. At an April 1947 Klan rally, a member declared that "a family of niggers has moved into an apartment building for whites at 300 Pulliam Street!" The violent horde was incensed. Stoking the anger, the grand dragon of the Association of Georgia Klans, Dr. Samuel Green, demanded a response. Looking upon his white-robed minions, he called upon "three more of your police officers . . . to go in your police car to that address at once, and report back here!" Four of the Klansmen disrobed, revealing their Atlanta police uniforms, and swiftly answered Green's demand, while another yelled that "the niggers are getting out of hand." Ambitious, striving black families had dared to move into housing unfit for them. The "Night Hawk" Klansman continued his outburst amid his brothers: "We've got to dish out some more floggings, and if necessary a few lynchings!"[12]

In the mostly white West End, whites resisted black homeowners, even beating them and setting their homes on fire. In the summer of 1947 the Klan was informed that it would have to increase its vigilance because some black folks were defending themselves. That summer a terrorist was repulsed when he attempted to bomb a black family's home and a male occupant of the house began firing his pistol at the would-be bomber. The Klan expressed "outrage" at armed black defenders.[13]

When the local Klan began to lose its appeal among whites who sought a more respectable expression of protecting the racial order, one Klansman offered an alternative, the West End Cooperative

Corporation (WECC). Its founder, Klansman Joe Wallace, insisted to white churches and civic groups that "we don't hate the nigger; we love him—in his place!" To that end, the WECC organized to prevent black families from moving into the area. The group created telephone trees to relay information about black prospective home buyers, whom Wallace or others could "visit." Wallace offered to explain to the prospective home owner that "I doubt if I can control more than a small part of the mob, and that if he does move [into the West End,] he'll be endangering his whole family." Wallace claimed that the threat almost always worked. Ultimately, the WECC claimed that it would erect a "Great White Wall" around the West End.[14] However, the wall was never built—literally or figuratively.

Despite Wallace's efforts, the Klan was nowhere as effective as local, state, and federal laws in conceiving, establishing, and protecting white nationalism. The exploding population of white and black Atlantans in the postwar era accelerated the demands for housing, and white real estate agents, racial zoning laws, banks' redlining policies, neighborhood civic groups, and federal housing policies all conspired to prevent black people from accessing housing. Whites alone could access new homes in the newly constructed suburbs that ringed the city, as was true nationally. The Federal Housing Administration, formed in 1934, prevented black families access to majority-white communities in the 1940s and 1950s by refusing mortgages to black home buyers. Simultaneously, the FHA funded developers to expand housing in all-white suburbs. By the early 1950s, nearly sixteen million homes were being constructed across the country for whites. White veterans received guaranteed home loans with little or no money down. Collectively, the FHA insured $65 billion in home value for whites.[15] It was such a massively successful federal campaign to expand white wealth that, for the first time in history, most white Americans had ascended to the middle class. However, these opportunities were virtually unavailable for black people. Because black home purchases in suburbs were *almost* impossible, local African Americans creatively navigated around the racial constrictions with a fierce reliance on black resources and institutions.

Black veterans, who in theory could benefit from the G.I. Bill, were limited by the bill's accommodation of states' racial laws. For example, black veterans might have access to a free college education but be barred from white universities (public or private) in every southern state. However, they could use the G.I. Bill to attend a college without a whites-only policy. Similarly, black applicants could not receive a federally guaranteed home loan that would disrupt the "racial integrity" of a majority-white neighborhood.[16] If, however, black people could use black banks, black real estate agents, and black developers with enough resources to develop their own black suburb, the housing "loophole" against black people could be overcome because there would be no subversion of "racial integrity" when a black family moved into a new black neighborhood. But few, if any, black communities in the United States had the resources to avoid racially exclusive loopholes in the same way that black Atlantans did.

In the early 1950s, African Americans deftly put into motion "Project X" with the help of local black leadership, including the Atlanta Urban League, to create the largest, most extensive upscale black suburban development in the country. In the postwar era, the city had two real estate boards: the white Atlanta Real Estate Board and the black Empire Real Estate Board. In 1946 the president of the former told his members that they were "under obligation not to sell to Negroes in predominantly white areas."[17] However, the black board largely partnered with its white counterparts to seek ways to make "separate but equal" more than rhetoric. The constant threat of violence when moving into a white neighborhood made the effort unattractive for many African Americans, although many took the risk. Simultaneously, the neighborhoods in which black people were forced to live often lacked modern amenities such as paved roads, sidewalks, streetlights, or access to green space. The houses were often older, smaller, and in high-density areas.

As with many other efforts in Atlanta, the black community, supported by the Empire Real Estate Board, opted to use its own resources to realize its needs. Grace Towns Hamilton, head of the Atlanta Urban League, and the group's housing director, Robert Thompson, worked with white authorities to access "Negro Expansion Areas" where black residents could obtain housing. Hamilton reported the league's analysis of "FHA 608" loans, where the federal government supplied up to 90 percent of the cost for new housing developments: "I think [that out of] the total . . . of some six thousand [loans in the Atlanta area], less than a hundred units [went to black borrowers]." This represented around 1 percent of the FHA loans going to black applicants.[18]

According to Hamilton, the ambitious efforts of black developers such as Heman Perry and Walter A. Aiken helped break the "log jam" preventing black access to FHA funds. Aiken, a World War I veteran and Hampton Institute graduate who coached football at Clark College and Atlanta University, created the most successful black construction firm in the city. One of his projects, Hunter Hills, located on the west side, had fifty-two homes across one hundred acres. He was also a developer of the nearby Dixie Hills. Perry constructed many homes in the area as well. Black developers quickly made their own cultural signposts in Dixie Hills, a former Confederate camp during the Civil War. Streets were named after the city's black iconic institutions and famous African Americans: Bethel, Morehouse, Morris Brown, Spelman, and Carver. The development of hundreds of new homes for middle-class and lower-middle-class African Americans in west Atlanta still could not keep up with the acute housing pressures.

The Atlanta Urban League, under Hamilton's leadership, surreptitiously crafted campaigns to access more housing, partly by pandering to white fears. In the 1940s and early 1950s, white residents in the working-class and lower-middle-class area of Mozley Park in southwest

Atlanta resisted open housing. If only one local family would sell to a black family, the league counted on a rapid exodus of white residents, thereby opening an entire community to African American families, who were more densely populated and faced with a severe housing crunch. In 1953 a white family agreed to sell their home to a black family, and Citizens Trust, a black-owned bank, approved the home loan. As predicted, white flight prompted a swift transition from white to black.[19] Although it represented an advancement, Mozley Park, like new developments in Hunter Hills, Dixie Hills, and West Lake, did little to relieve the pressing demands for housing, especially newer upscale homes, given the migration of thousands of African Americans into the city each year.

In the western edges of the city, Collier Heights, a sparsely populated area that had mostly been farmland, looked ideal for development. A small community of whites lived in this area. Like many sections, streets, parks, and squares in the Atlanta area, the community was probably named for former Confederates: several members of the local Collier family had served in the Confederate military. Collier Heights, seven miles west of downtown, had home prices around $10,000 in 1950. Throughout the area, advertisements for homes touted the special conditions for veterans: "FULL G.I. LOAN," "ELIGIBLE G.I. LOAN WITH 10% CASH." When the national median home price was about $7,400, the G.I. Bill allowed veterans to access homes at a record pace. In fact, national development in suburbs was ten times higher than in central cities in 1950. The scale of suburban home construction was so vast that it represented three-quarters of the country's total during the 1950s.[20]

The Atlanta Urban League's Project X sought to maximize the resources of federally insured home loans available to whites. A group assembled twenty-three investors, including physicians, educators, businesspeople, and other professionals. The process included black real estate agents, black banks, and the National Development Company, a black company. The initial purchase of large swaths of land was done without much fanfare. Yet in order to manipulate white fears and hostility about living near black people, Project X did not hide the race of the consortium of investors.

The black newcomers were generally wealthier than the whites who lived in Collier Heights. However, class proved to have little effect in mitigating anger at black families constructing "modern, gleaming new middle-class houses." The black newcomers proved to be one of the earliest waves of gentrifiers in Atlanta. Despite widely perceived assumptions that gentrification is defined by whites moving into a community of color, the term was coined in the 1960s to describe higher-socioeconomic status (SES) whites moving into lower-SES white communities in Britain. Globally, gentrification mostly unfolds intraracially: within racial lines. Class is the defining feature of the process, not race.[21] The influx of higher-SES black families raised the real estate prices of Collier Heights. The black gentrifiers (developers, home buyers, and banks) purchased a thousand acres west of a holdout white neighborhood in 1953. A local white homeowners association argued that it was "a moral issue" to resist open housing and demanded that white neighbors continue "holding the line." The white Southwest Citizens Association appealed to whites not to sell their homes to black families: "We ask you, as a fair-minded individual, to refuse to make a fast dollar at the expense of the majority . . . in this always white community." By 1954, however, all 135 white-owned holdout homes had sold, relinquishing the area to the National Development Company and making Collier Heights the largest upscale black suburb in the United States.[22]

The process of black-on-white gentrification was profound. Home prices in the area doubled as higher-SES black newcomers built in the area. By the mid-1950s, when the area was entirely black, homes averaged between $22,000 and $50,000 ($243,211 and $552,753 in today's dollars). Ultimately, the effort was successful for Project X's planners. Robert Thompson, perhaps the most central agent in the process of black influx, called the operation "both a leapfrog, and a military style pincer move." A decade later, at the peak of the civil rights movement, hundreds of modern homes occupied beautifully landscaped streets. Many of the houses had pools, recreation rooms, large yards, and patios. Some had tennis courts and basketball courts. Collier Heights had become four thousand acres of Afro-self-determinist success in black housing development, unprecedented elsewhere in the country.[23]

Despite the successes of Collier Heights, other portions of southwest Atlanta continued to push against open housing, even if it involved higher-income black professionals. The Klan never erected its "Great White Wall" in the West End, but in 1963 white residents of Peyton Forest, a middle-class community, did build a wall to prevent black citizens from having access to the area. Known as the "Peyton Wall," it was a wooden and steel barricade dug into the concrete street and designed to stop residential desegregation. When the Peyton Wall was erected shortly before Christmas, some residents wrapped it in Christmas paper and ribbon, celebrating it as a holiday gift to the white Christians in the city. One even wrote, "Thank the Lord!" on the Christmas display.[24]

The Peyton Wall immediately disrupted the boosterish Atlanta narrative of racial moderation by providing a clear, visual symbol of entrenched racial discord and active resistance to the civil rights movement, much as other southern cities witnessed. Earlier that year, Mayor Ivan Allen Jr. testified before the US Senate in favor of the Equal Accommodations Act. He was the only southern mayor to make such testimony, bolstering the claim that Atlanta was an exceptionally progressive southern city. But behind the facade of Atlanta as a model of forward-looking, progressive openness, the truth was quite different. The intractable forces of racial discrimination were not only pervasive and endemic; they had always crossed class lines, geographic spaces, and generations in the city. In various professions—health care, education, leisure, municipal work, and housing—white Atlantans created all-white domains and fought tenaciously to defend them. One such group was the white realtors' association, which used a range of methods to (1) circumscribe black access to professional realtor work, and (2) use a range of methods to limit racial residential desegregation. The organization lobbied lawmakers and created policies to fortify the racial status quo. Various local neighborhood groups formed to complement the efforts of the white realtors' association, including the Southwest Citizens Association, which tirelessly fought to prevent residential desegregation in Peyton Forest. The organization opposed the "vicious, block-busting tactics being used by Negro realtors" and saw their work as intrinsic to a wider struggle to defend racist policies.[25]

Even as civil rights activists and the media brought attention to the Peyton Wall, comparing it to the Berlin Wall or the Warsaw Ghetto, the wall's defenders insisted that it was an essential step to save white Atlanta from black people. Few local white journalists were as critical of local racists as the famed editor of the *Atlanta Constitution*, Ralph McGill. Violence, hatred, and hostility to justice and law were ugly features, McGill wrote. In his assessment of the 1963 march on Washington, McGill celebrated how white and black citizens pushed for realization of civil and human rights while simultaneously insisting that "racial prejudice is un-Christian."[26]

In the same year that the Peyton Wall was erected, Martin Luther King Jr. referenced McGill in his famed "Letter from Birmingham Jail" as one of the "few enlightened white persons" to appreciate the urgency for civil rights for all people. Though a Pulitzer Prize winner and nationally recognized journalist, McGill suffered incredible hostility from Atlantans who felt that the writer not only betrayed the tradition set forth by his historical predecessor, Henry Grady, but that McGill had also betrayed Atlanta boosterism. He pulled back the curtain from the stage of his widely read paper, showing the world how far Atlanta was from being the bastion of progressive and cooperative people who transcended the stultifying traps of racial animus.

In 1958, when terrorists bombed Atlanta's oldest and most prominent synagogue, Hebrew Benevolent Congregation (likely in response
to its outspoken Rabbi Jacob Rothchild, who advocated for civil rights),
McGill immediately denounced the attack. Careful to place the bombing in a broader context of regional intolerance and hate, he wrote that
the bombing was "a harvest of defiance of the courts and the encouragement of citizens to defy laws on the part of many Southern politicians." Readers sent threats and hostile letters, and some (suspected to
be Klansmen) burned crosses at night on his front lawn, as they did at
the King house in Atlanta. But even more than what was done to King,
attackers shot out windows and left bombs at McGill's home.[27] The
responses to whites like Rothchild and McGill were especially violent.
Like the Confederate slaughter of white POWs who commanded black
Union troops in the Civil War, southern whites who were advocates of
civil rights for all citizens faced racist retribution on par to that faced
by black civil rights activists. In fact, in Atlanta and its environs, racism
was so ubiquitous and normative that any progress toward expanding
black freedom was perceived as an ontological threat to white people.
Any end to black misery meant a net loss to whites, many reasoned.
Southwest Citizens Association officer Barbara Ryckeley argued, "If
the whites could just win once, they would have some hope for holding
out. I think the whole city of Atlanta is at stake. You realize that every
time negroes replace whites about eighty-five percent of the whites
move out of the city?"[28]

Membership in the Klan saw a resurgence during these years.
Attorney James Venable, who at age thirteen joined his uncle in 1915
when the Second Klan was founded at his family's property in Stone
Mountain, formed a new National Knights of the Ku Klux Klan in
1963. The imperial wizard defended the Hebrew Temple bombers,
burned crosses, spewed racist drivel, and denounced efforts to open
schools, public accommodations, or democracy to all citizens. A schoolmate of Nathan Bedford Forrest III at Lithonia High School, Venable

was indoctrinated in extremist white-nationalist beliefs from an early age.[29] Others who wished to defend the old racial order through more civilized means formed the White Citizens' Council (WCC) in July 1954. The WCC was an immediate response to the Supreme Court ruling in *Brown v. Board of Education of Topeka, Kansas* that outlawed racial segregation of public schools. By the early 1960s, the WCC was firmly in place throughout the Deep South. Also known as the Citizens' Councils of America, it adopted as its logo two crossed flags, the US Stars and Stripes and the Confederate battle flag from the Army of Northern Virginia, suggesting less sectional antagonism and more shared investment in the cause of white nationalism. The following year, the chairman of the Georgia Democratic Committee, John Sammons Bell, an outspoken segregationist and member of the State's Rights Council of Georgia (an affiliate of the WCC), initiated a campaign to include the Confederate battle flag as part of the Georgia state flag. Bell drafted legislation to do just this.

The effort to resurrect the Confederate battle flag was more than a mere symbolic suggestion to resist federal intervention. Like the Hammer and Sickle (Soviet Union), the Union Jack (Great Britain), and the Stars and Stripes (United States), flags, as any vexillologist will note, are not the reason that people go to war or rally and sacrifice for a national cause. Flags have no authority in and of themselves. They are metonymic signifiers of ideology, belief, or purpose. They are encoded and decoded with specific meaning. For the proponents of white nationalism, the Confederate battle flag was simultaneously evocative of entrenched opposition to threats to the racial order—federal or local—and a recognition of a heritage that could not, despite any interpretive gymnastics, be disentangled from the politics of racial subjugation.

The state of Georgia consistently affirmed its dedication to white nationalism, which necessarily established boundaries and limitations on freedom in Atlanta. In 1956, protesting the *Brown* decision, the state assembly adopted the Confederate battle flag as part of the state flag. Given that the flag was already inspired by the Confederacy's Stars and Bars, the new flag, adopted from the later incarnation of a CSA battle flag, evoked an even greater determination to stand against the expansion of civil rights. Like the battle flag in the waning years of the Civil War, however, the newest expression of resolve and rebellion to federal force would prove ultimately ineffective at preventing the widening of liberties to the citizens of the region. Still, the lawmakers made considerable effort to deny civil rights in general and integration especially. The state passed a law that would refuse funds to any public school in the state that allowed equal access to black students and white students, as mandated by the US Supreme Court.[30]

James Mackay, who was a member of the Georgia State Assembly (one of thirty-two members who opposed the flag's change), explained that "there was only one reason for putting the flag on there: like the gun rack in the back of a pickup truck, it telegraphs a message."[31] There was little doubt about the intent of the flag's redesign. Civil rights groups recognized the new flag as a powerful gesture against the expansion of democracy and various rights to black citizens. Much like other efforts to "hold the line" during the Civil War in Georgia in general and Atlanta in particular, the flag held special symbolism for the agents of racial subjugation. In fact, Governor Griffin, who presided over the adoption of the new state flag, insisted that "the rest of the nation is looking to Georgia for the lead in segregation."[32] Weeks after the adoption of the new state flag, Georgia senator Russell finished crafting a most audacious congressional protest of the *Brown* ruling. In the spring of 1956, 101 members of Congress issued the Declaration of Constitutional Principles (the "Southern Manifesto"), outlining their opposition to the attempted expansion of legal rights to all citizens. Russell was a member of the State's Rights Council of Georgia. The power and reach of this organization were daunting.

The perennial struggle over the fate of the capital of the South played itself out in scores of arenas, from the statehouse to bars, parks, golf courses, schools, and restaurants. White nationalists had long understood the utility of controlling historical narratives in schools, so advocates of the Lost Cause in Georgia adopted a white-supremacist history book. *History of Georgia* was published in 1954 for Georgia public schools by one of the most prominent historians of the South, University of Georgia professor E. Merton Coulter. In this book Coulter writes that slavery was a fundamentally benign institution where the enslaved danced, sang, and were cheerful. In his early work, Coulter had explained that the spread of freedom to black people was an unmitigated disaster. Coulter believed that the more grievous transgression was to extend civil rights to black people, who, according to him, "were fearfully unprepared to occupy positions of rulership." Black elected officials produced "the most spectacular and exotic development in government in the history of white civilization . . . [and the] longest to be remembered, shuddered at, and execrated."[33] Reconstruction historian Eric Foner notes that even as the superstructure of white nationalism was being dismantled and the intellectual genuflections to racial oppression were discredited, Coulter was "the last . . . scholar of the era" to be "wholly antagonistic" toward Reconstruction and black political involvement. Coulter "described Georgia's most prominent Reconstruction black officials as swindlers and 'scamps,' and suggested that whatever positive qualities they possessed were inherited from white ancestors."[34] In many ways, Coulter, a grandson of two Confederate soldiers, provided through his critique of Reconstruction an intellectual defense of white nationalism and a critique of extending civil rights to black people in his own era. The rhetoric of state's rights, given a veneer of scholarly weight and refashioned for his contemporaries, gave the State's Rights Council additional tools to resist civil rights. And much like the Klan a generation earlier, the council was a mainstream part of state affairs. The textbook, lauded by the White Citizens' Council and adopted by state lawmakers, remained in use until the 1970s.[35]

The Federal Bureau of Investigation opened a file on the Citizens' Councils of America and reported on the activities in Atlanta and other locations across the country. The FBI explained that "it [is noted] that officers and members of [the local Citizens' Council] include the top political and civic figures of the State of Georgia."[36] Membership, activities, speeches, and other surveillance on the organization revealed how the group fought against voter registration and black access to hospitals, schools, employment, and various public accommodations. It used intimidation and violence, and in some towns it published the names of blacks who registered to vote, instructing their employers to fire them. The councils won plaudits from the Klan, neo-Nazis, neo-Confederates, and assorted other fascist and white supremacists.[37] Despite the clear and present threat to black citizens and the explicit hostility to enforcing federal laws, the Citizens' Councils were measured as too innocuous to merit the interest of the FBI. On December 13, 1956, J. Edgar Hoover, in a memo to all field offices, noted that "these organizations do not fall within the purview of Executive Order 10450. In view of this fact, there is no basis upon which to base justification for further inquiry."[38] The notorious FBI director explained that "you are instructed to immediately discontinue inquiries concerning all citizens councils upon receipt of this letter." Any further collection of information on this group would rely on published accounts in newspapers and any information that "may be volunteered you."[39]

The local Atlanta FBI office, unable to initiate its own surveillance against the group, was reduced to following the Citizens' Council through the press. Citing the local paper, the Atlanta office reported to Hoover that on the night of February 11, 1959, "1,800 persons attended a dinner of the States Rights Council of Georgia . . . with principal speakers being Georgia U. S. Senators HERMAN TALMADGE and RICHARD RUSSELL, and Georgia Governor EARNEST VANDIER." Quoting the coverage in the *Atlanta Constitution*, the FBI memo stated that lawmakers planned to resist any challenge to the state's racial order: "Council President ROY HARRIS stated, 'Our battle is in Atlanta' in speaking of segregation. He said the $50,000.00 cleared on the dinner would be used 'to fight the battle of Atlanta.'"[40] Evoking the 1864 Battle of Atlanta was not lost on those who viewed themselves as ideological heirs of the Confederate fight against federal efforts to disrupt racial domination and unfettered white control over the political, social, and cultural landscape of their city and state. Like their antecedents, local political leadership understood states' rights to function as a surreptitious defense of the very specific right of a state to deprive its citizens of various privileges of US citizenship. No other right was as controversial as racial equality.

Resistance to the *Brown* ruling was intense throughout the region. The Georgia Ku Klux Klan emerged as the largest of several Klan groups to re-form during the civil rights movement, and it attempted to ride a wave of anger about equal access to education. It is no surprise that the Klan was especially active in Georgia and metro Atlanta. The area had been the birthplace of the Second Klan and its Imperial City in its heyday. Its defense of white nationalism continued to resonate with many in the country. However, its violence, vulgarity, and coarse arguments for white supremacy evoked archetypal images of ignorant, backwoods miscreants for huge swaths of Americans, including many whites. Still, the organization recruited new members in and around Atlanta, where many whites felt they were losing their fight for segregation. Curiously, as the civil rights movement grew, Klan members initiated contact with the fastest-growing national black group, the Nation of Islam (NOI), as a way to try to stave off integration.

In the fall of 1960, the Georgia Klan contacted Mosque no. 15, housed in the heart of Sweet Auburn in the Odd Fellows Building. Malcolm X, the national spokesman for the NOI, had established the mosque in 1955, the first one that he personally established in the South. Minister Jeremiah X relocated from Philadelphia to serve as its head minister. As the center of black Atlanta, the Sweet Auburn area was not only the business center of the city; it was also home to the community's major religious institutions. One of the city's oldest black churches, First Congregational, was there. Ebenezer Baptist, headed by Martin L. King Sr. and co-pastored by his son, and Big Bethel AME called the area home. Marcus Garvey spoke at Bethel when he visited Atlanta on March 25, 1917. He famously met with the Klan in Atlanta in 1922, forever tarnishing his image among many African Americans. The NOI was at risk of repeating this misstep.

After consideration of the invitation to meet and under the direction of NOI leader Elijah Muhammad, Malcolm and Jeremiah met several Klansmen at Jeremiah's home on January 28, 1961. Headed by W. S. Fellows, who made the invitation, the Klansmen sat in Jeremiah's living room, and the two groups discussed their mutual opposition to racial integration. However, Malcolm clarified that the NOI endorsed "separation," not "segregation." This distinction was lost on the Klansmen. Malcolm noted that the extant white-controlled system of segregation that relegated black people to inferior resources was anathema. Separation, or black nationalism, provided black people the opportunity to "do for self" and regulate their own resources without white control. As Fellows responded, "Call it whatever you like. As long as you stay over there and you're glad to be black, good. We just wish all niggras would be glad to be niggras." Despite the NOI's belief that whites were immutably wicked, they did not chasten this "devil" for his offensive words. According to the NOI's theology, Fellows was acting as his nature dictated. He could not help being an uncivilized racist.

The most outrageous part of the meeting was when Fellows leaned in to the ministers. Both sides shared a record of publicly ridiculing and denouncing Martin Luther King, but Fellows was fishing for critical information: "We know he lives around here somewhere, but we don't know where." The terror group wanted the Muslim leader's assistance in harming the civil rights leader, who was known to have an erratic schedule and personal security. Malcolm immediately rejected the prospect of harming King. He sternly explained that the NOI would not be "hurt-ing our own kind," despite whatever ideological fissures existed. Fellows explained that "you don't have to kill him. . . . We'll take care of the vio-lence." Malcolm declined the offer of any sort of lethal alliance with the "filthy cavemen" of the Klan. More than anything, for the ministers the meeting only affirmed the nefarious and wicked nature of the defenders of white supremacy. The Klan was getting desperate, and its attempted alliance with the Nation of Islam proved fruitless. However, the confab with the vulgar racists left Malcolm "unhinged."[41]

In this transition away from explicit avowals of racism, Atlanta occu-pied a tension-riddled, muddled space. It was Georgia's capital and the de facto capital of the South, and it had a relatively large and visible black middle class during the civil rights movement. City leaders, long aware of the challenges of promoting the city as good for business—progressive and hospitable—understood the utility of marketing a proper image for Atlanta. It wanted to stand in contrast to the infamous cases of racial vio-lence sweeping the South, such as Montgomery and Little Rock. Mayor Allen, a relatively progressive politician elected in 1961, argued that white leaders understood that racial violence "was not good for business." To that end, white leaders in organizations like the Commerce Club, the most exclusive group of business leadership in the state, operated behind the scenes to avoid incidents that would draw negative media attention and racial demonstrations and counterdemonstrations. Formed in 1960, its founders were well aware of the negative attention that the Montgom-ery bus boycott and the Little Rock Nine had brought to those cities.

In 1955 the slight, bespectacled activist Rosa Parks emerged at the center of the Montgomery bus boycott to protest abusive and racist policies in public transportation. Its leader, MLK, was arrested along with more than a hundred others for violating the city's antiboycott law. His house was bombed. He, Parks, and others faced death threats. After 381 days of entrenched resistance from racists, the US Supreme Court ruled that the buses in Montgomery had to be desegregated.

Little Rock captured the nation's attention in 1957 when howling mobs attempted to stop nine children from integrating Central High School. Red-faced, spitting, and cursing teens surrounded a lone girl who was supposed to join her black classmates at Central. She waited for a bus, frightened and alone, as the hostile horde offered up chants of hate. Three years later, images of vulgar and hateful racists protesting a six-year-old girl's entrance to a New Orleans school also laid bare the ugliness of racial oppression in public education. During this and other confrontations in Memphis, Houston, and Charleston, Atlanta avoided bad press. The absence of bad press did not mean, of course, that Atlanta was deserving of good press. Little Rock and New Orleans had integrated their schools years back, but Atlanta had not. Even as Montgomery was forced to desegregate its buses, Atlanta had not done so. In fact, despite the Supreme Court ruling, it was not until January 1959 that an NAACP lawsuit resulted in a federal judge ordering Atlanta's buses desegregated, nearly three years after Parks took celebratory photos of Montgomery's buses.[42] Ironically, the absence of desegregation—and the attendant racist resistance to it—fed into the narrative that the Gate City was racially progressive.

Images like those of police and firemen attacking peaceful demonstrators in Birmingham, Little Rock, New Orleans, and Nashville were to be avoided. In classic fashion, Atlanta mayor Hartsfield quipped in 1959 that Atlanta was the "City Too Busy to Hate." The slogan stuck, even as the city experienced more terrorist bombings than Birmingham, integrated its buses after scores of cities, and desegregated its schools after and at a slower rate than all but one other southern city.[43] Atlanta, despite its effective marketing, was measurably less progressive than most southern cities.

As the Cold War progressed in the years following the defeat of Nazism and fascism in Europe, defenders of white nationalism found explicit celebrations of racial oppression to be untenable. Because of independence movements in Asia and Africa in particular, the geopolitical landscape had evolved to an extent that avowed domestic racial domination had become a liability for US foreign policy. Still, on matters of local defense against civil rights, linkages between politicians and various civic organizations demonstrated a strong effort to formulate strategies that would ensure the survival of state and local laws that maintained racially discriminatory policies.

Among many, there was a pervasive sense that the death of the legal structure of white nationalism was imminent. Many were enthusiastic, but others lamented the system's demise. Fearing integration, the leader of the Georgia Klan, "Wild Bill" Davidson, offered a plan that would subvert efforts to integrate his home state. At a rally in Atlanta the day after the Klansmen had met with Malcolm X in 1961, Davidson offered three elements of his "secret weapon to the world." In addition to opposing the "brainwashing of integration" and promoting boycotts of white businesses that serve all races, the imperial wizard planned to "move all Negroes to a central location, that location being Atlanta, the black jungle of the South."[44] The Gate City, at least for the Klan, should be turned over to black people as a veritable black city-state. The inchoate Klan ethnic-cleansing plan lacked details. It was unclear if Atlanta was supposed to be turned over to all existing black people in the state of Georgia or to all of the estimated twelve million black people in the South. By any measure, the Klan proposal would have made Atlanta a "Black Mecca" before it was anointed so by the press.

In 1960 black access to the most basic of the city's public resources had not changed much since the Klan's heyday of the 1920s. Many public parks were reserved for whites across the city. Racial zoning laws mandated that parks were designated for whites or for blacks, depending on the demographics of the surrounding community. Yet in a city that was a third black, whites had twenty-two baseball fields, and blacks had three; twelve swimming pools were for whites, and three were available to blacks; forty-two parks were for whites only, and African Americans had three. The city provided whites with twenty football fields, but black people were barred from any public football field in the city.[45]

In the protracted struggle to maintain white nationalism across different fronts, nothing was as visceral an issue as integrated education. A decades-long protracted struggle against equal access to education continued with steep resistance from the city and state's white leadership. Much of this struggle was humiliating and demoralizing for black citizens. In the early 1960s, after various maneuvers to circumvent the law, the city developed innovated ways to "comply" with desegregation laws. In 1961 the Atlanta Public School Board argued that it had desegregated its system through its "freedom of choice" program, which allowed families to petition to attend a school of their choosing. In reality, 99 percent of black children still attended overcrowded, underfunded, understaffed, dated, dilapidated all-black schools. The sleight of hand was a policy that assigned black and white students to segregated schools but allowed them to apply through a cumbersome bureaucratic process at city hall for a chance to transfer across racial lines. One hundred and thirty-three black students applied through this process and were required to take psychological and other tests to determine their fitness to operate effectively among white people. Ten were accepted. Of course, no whites were required to test into the resource-rich all-white schools.[46]

In the same year as the March on Washington, where one of Atlanta's most celebrated native sons gave his iconic speech, King's hometown was next to last among southern cities in the number of students desegregated. The infamously racist cities of Birmingham, Montgomery, Memphis, and Charleston were all more integrated than Atlanta. Only the much smaller Greensboro, North Carolina, lagged Atlanta in the raw numbers of students desegregated in its schools.[47]

Mayor Hartsfield, long celebrated as a model of racial moderation, entreated calm from local whites by pandering to their reverence for the Confederacy's most beloved general. It was a curious rhetorical subterfuge used against a backdrop of neo-Confederate demands to resist open education and civil rights. As the city grappled with anticipated unrest over desegregated schools, the mayor argued that racist troublemakers would not be allowed to undermine orderly and peaceful processes: "Robert E. Lee wouldn't even spit on the rabble rousers we have today. . . . What happened in Little Rock won't happen here. We're going to ride herd on these damn rabble."[48] The City Too Busy to Hate was not going to devolve into chaos, incivility, and violence. The desegregation was miniscule in scope but did not prompt the open violence that many feared. However, the process was not smooth or easy.

For those black students who had entered white schools, the experience was cruel and traumatizing. Whether as an effort to protect them from physical and verbal assault or to uphold segregation surreptitiously, school administrators at Murphy High School put two black students, Martha Ann Holmes and Rosalyn Walton, into classes by themselves. This did not stop a barrage of hate and abuse from white students who called them "niggers" and "jungle bunnies," and told them to "go back to Africa." Antipathetic teachers emboldened the student-led abuse. In one instance, a girl was hit in the face with chalk, followed by pennies and other objects. As Kevin Kruse explains, the traumas of the two girls "were perhaps the worst experienced by Atlanta's transfer students, but they were by no means unrepresentative."[49] Across the city, the small numbers of black students entered new landscapes of hostility and abuse that in many ways disrupted their own sense of social positioning. Whatever popularity, social status, and affirmation that they received in their lives in all-black spaces were wholly undermined by their insertion into the overwhelming hatred, ridicule, and abuse of white schools throughout the city. The racist recalcitrance would not be forgotten by black citizens who struggled to open opportunities for all citizens. By the close of the decade—fifteen years after the passing of *Brown*—a full 80 percent of Atlanta students still attended segregated public schools.[50] Of course, the struggle to desegregate Atlanta stretched from public education to every other sector of the city.

In 1960 the city's most celebrated department store, Rich's, was the centerpiece of a prolonged battle over desegregation. People of color could purchase merchandise, but the store had a whites-only policy regarding customers being able to try on clothes or dine in its restaurant, the Magnolia Room. In spring 1960 the Committee on Appeal for Human Rights (COAHR) targeted Rich's racist policies. COAHR, largely composed of college students from the Atlanta University Center (AUC), formed a bridge of resistance stretching back through the AUC to the days of Du Bois. Martin Luther King Jr. and Morehouse student leader Lonnie King (no relation) were arrested and jailed. Universal whiteness had guided the company to such an extent that its Jewish president, Richard H. Rich, resisted integration on the premise that he was simply "following custom" in the city, which granted full access, courteousness, and dignity only to whites. Protests persisted, and on May 3 several burning crosses appeared in black neighborhoods in Atlanta, including a four-foot cross at MLK's home.[51] The Klan, it appeared, was stirred into action. In full display of the efficacy of a special, provincial expression of neo-Confederate universal whiteness, the Ku Klux Klan even marched in support of Rich's decision not to integrate its whites-only restaurant. The Klan and other racists praised Rich when he closed the Magnolia Room in November 1960 rather than allow integrated service.[52]

As the push to open the city to all citizens progressed, segregationists continued to use the Confederacy as an expression of white nationalism. Confederate flags were unfurled at homes and businesses across the metro area. The relatively newly designed Georgia flag, which incorporated the Confederate battle flag, was a conspicuous reminder of the legacy of racial oppression as a formal and systemic matter of public and private regulation by the state. However, the explicit celebration of racism, which had been intrinsic to the Confederacy, was becoming more of a fringe rhetorical tool: the cultural and political sensibilities of the country increasingly disavowed openly racist proclamations.

Atlanta appeared as a veritable circus, with Mayor Hartsfield mesmerizing the world with curious feats that defied reason. He was the P. T. Barnum of a wondrous spectacle of racial politics that convinced the nation that Atlanta was beyond the travails and predilections of retrograde, intolerant, ignorant, and bigoted leadership. Yet even as he touted his city as beyond the inconvenient, self-defeating, and insipid investment in racism, Atlanta's few black police officers still lacked the authority to arrest white criminal suspects, even if they were visibly committing crimes against white people. Its school district still banned black students from attending its significantly better-resourced all-white schools. The city still enforced a whites-only hiring policy with its firefighters. Convincing visitors that the city was tolerant and hospitable to all became very difficult. Local hotels, which were segregated, became flashpoints in the contest of rhetoric and reality. A decade earlier, international news focused on Atlanta when the most celebrated American in France, Josephine Baker, was scheduled to give a show in the capital city. The renowned entertainer, businesswoman, and philanthropist, who famously fought against Nazis on behalf of her adopted country, France, was banned from whites-only hotels in Atlanta. In 1951 her contract insisted that she not perform to segregated audiences, a clause that was going to be accommodated for her benefit concert at the NAACP's annual convention. The city was willing to "not insist on segregation" at the rented Municipal Auditorium. But the June 30 performance was canceled because of the segregated hotels. However, the NAACP convention went off as scheduled, with up to a thousand attendees, most of whom were accommodated by local black colleges (dorms were closed for the summer) or private homes.[53] Despite such occurrences, which would ordinarily draw some degree of embarrassment, local supporters of racial oppression generally appeared shameless.

By the 1960s, as more whites abandoned their commitment to segregation, some professional associations dropped their whites-only policies. Professional conferences that permitted black members did not necessarily confirm that members would be universally allowed to stay at hotels. These associations, either in their ignorance or intent, occasionally chose cities that denied their black membership basic accommodations. This occurred multiple times in Atlanta, frustrating various professional associations. In April 1961 some white hoteliers in Atlanta attempted to pander to the rhetoric of Atlanta exceptionalism by unveiling a new policy for the City Too Busy to Hate: black people could attend conferences in city hotels but could "have [nothing] to drink but water." Additionally, they were banned from going above the second floor of any hotel.[54] This modest step toward open accommodations was swiftly met with resistance from some hoteliers.

In 1962, only a year after the concession to allow black people to enter hotels and consume nothing more than water, the Atlanta Hotel Association reported that its members opposed open accommodation to people of color. They affirmed their rights to exclude any customers who were not white, regardless of professional affiliation. Cities across the South, including Dallas, Houston, and Miami, officially desegregated their hotels before Atlanta did. When the NAACP announced that its 1962 national convention was being held in Atlanta, some thought that the national visibility of prominent African American leaders being denied accommodations would shame the city. Instead, the Atlanta Hotel Association opted to "take no action on the matter" of desegregation, leaving hotels to impose racist policy or not. Across the city, from chain hotels like the Hilton to local ones, like the Biltmore, hotels barred black conference-goers who had made reservations. Even the acclaimed Nobel Prize recipient Ralph Bunche, undersecretary to the United Nations, was denied access to the whites-only Dinkler Plaza Hotel. For several days, activists picketed more than a dozen hotels to no avail. All of these establishments rigidly adhered to their whites-only policies, fearing that treating people fairly, regardless of race, would drive away white patrons. In all, the fiasco was another example of the illusion of Atlanta as a racially progressive city.

However, there was a glimmer of hope amid the discord. A month before the NAACP convention, a new hotel, the Americana, opened without an official whites-only policy. Built by Irving and Marvin Goldstein, local dentists, the hotel opened downtown on Spring Street a full two years before Congress passed the landmark Civil Rights Act of 1964, which outlawed racial segregation in public accommodations. Personal friends of King and supporters of the civil rights movement, the Goldsteins dared demonstrate that an "open" hotel could thrive in Atlanta. Indeed, the hotel proved beneficial to the city when, in 1963, Major League Baseball questioned the logic of moving the Milwaukee Braves to Atlanta, where black players would be barred from all downtown hotels. The head of the Milwaukee Braves owners' consortium, Bill Bartholomay, offered up the Americana: "That hotel helped us move the team here. It was a must."[55] Although the Civil Rights Act was passed as Bartholomay was making his case for the Braves' move to Atlanta, there were immediate challenges to the 1964 ruling. Not surprisingly, local Atlanta hotels emerged at the national vanguard of resistance. They were part of the fabric of a city that stridently resisted living up to its brand. On December 16, 1963, King lamented that his hometown, despite "boasting of its civic virtue," had "allowed itself to fall behind almost every major southern city in progress toward desegregation." In fact, 90 percent of the restaurants barred people of color, as did 98 percent of the hotels and motels.[56]

The Heart of Atlanta motel filed a lawsuit to maintain its whites-only policy. Owner Moreton Rolleston filed suit in federal court arguing that federal law exceeded the authority granted to Congress over interstate commerce. He curiously argued that not only was he being denied his civil rights; he was also being denied his Thirteenth Amendment right not to be enslaved. In a court of law, Rolleston insisted that he was reduced to involuntary servitude by being forced to open his 216-room motel to paying customers of any race. Additionally, he protested that the Civil Rights Act violated his Fifth Amendment right to choose customers according to his own discretion. The case made its way to the US Supreme Court, which ruled on December 14, 1964, that the motel was, in fact, in violation of federal law by denying access to black customers.

The case was joined with another Atlanta case, this one involving Lester Maddox, owner of the Pickrick Restaurant, which also had a whites-only policy. Maddox, who famously carried an ax handle to threaten anyone who challenged his policies, became a local celebrity for his opposition to integration. When three black college students from nearby Georgia Tech attempted to patronize his restaurant after the passage of the Civil Rights Act, Maddox brandished a handgun and screamed, "You no good dirty devils. You dirty Communists" to the students. Rolleston continued to operate his motel, complying with the court order to serve all paying customers, but Maddox, angry with the decision, closed his restaurant rather than open it to blacks.[57] Maddox, who was already well-known in Atlanta as a rabid racist, ran unsuccessfully for mayor against Hartsfield in 1957. And with the civil rights movement in full swing, Maddox appealed to the basest elements of racial fear and ignorance when he ran against Ivan Allen Jr. in 1961.

Allen, the dignified scion of a well-heeled Atlanta family with strong social and business ties in elite circles, understood the challenges of rejecting the coarse and increasingly unacceptable vitriol of Maddox. Allen knew the image of Atlanta, however rooted in hokum, was ultimately useful for its appeal as a city for investment, travel, and even leisure. Simultaneously, however, most whites in the city rejected the goals of the civil rights movement and did not approve of King's leadership or agenda. They stood opposed to school desegregation and equal resources for black and white students. In a racially divided election, two-thirds of white voters cast ballots for Maddox, who lost the election when a huge black voter turnout gave Allen the victory. Unde-terred, in 1962 Maddox ran unsuccessfully for lieutenant governor against Peter Zach Geer, also an ardent racist.[58]

The idea of white nationalism is much broader than the provincial Southern example found in the Confederacy, of course. But the Con-federacy's rise in 1861 and its bloody charge to defend principles of rac-ism and enslavement did not relent at Appomattox in April 1865. There have been ebbs and flows across the southern landscape and beyond, yet Atlanta long had a special relationship with both the Confeder-acy and its ideological heirs. The resilience of the Confederacy is strik-ing. Although its explicit, visceral, and forceful celebration of white supremacy and slavery may have become more socially repugnant over the years, the idea that the flag was a clear signifier of white nation-alism was what inspired assorted groups of racists from the KKK, the Knights of the White Camellia, the Dixiecrats, and the White Citizens' Councils to adopt it as a symbol. When the avowed racist Maddox chose to lead thousands of followers to protest civil rights for black citizens in April 1965, it was no surprise that a Confederate battle flag would lead the way. It resonated with local white Atlan-tans and Georgians who similarly found black political, economic, and social advancement anathema. Maddox received so much praise from Klansmen and neo-Confederates for his hard-line stance against racial equality that in 1966, with no previous experience in any elected pub-lic office, the high school dropout ran for governor of Georgia. Given that the overwhelming majority of white voters in the reputed "City Too Busy to Hate" had voted for his mayoral campaign, Maddox was convinced that whites across Georgia would vote for him for the state's highest office.

Many dismissed Maddox to be an absurd and outdated expression of white racial fear, ignorance, and hatred. Moderates and liberals dis-missed him as a clownish, ignorant caricature of southern intolerance. National media lambasted him as a "strident racist," a "backwoods demagogue out in the boondocks."[59] Moreover, the national media fully embraced the ruse that Atlanta was a moderate if not progressive city on racial matters. From the *New York Times* to *CBS News*, the City Too Busy to Hate was heralded as a model southern city despite the metrics proving otherwise. From bombings to an incorrigible municipal and state government that resisted meaningful desegregation of schools, public accommodations, and housing, Atlanta was not the bastion of tolerance touted by the mayor.

When *Time* magazine surveyed how various southern cities were peacefully desegregating in the days after the passage of the 1964 Civil Rights Act, the Gate City stood in contrast to the most infamous places, such as Jackson or Memphis. "In Atlanta, perhaps the most moderate of the South's big cities," *Time* claimed, "some of the worst flare-ups took place." The magazine covered the actions of Maddox, described as a "loud racist" who met black prospective patrons by brandishing a pistol and screaming, "You ain't never gonna eat here!" White patrons joined Maddox in chasing black would-be customers away: "Among them was a small boy dragging a 3-ft. ax handle and squealing: 'I'm gonna kill me a nigger!'" Despite arguments that Maddox was an anachronistic outlier, the resistance to civil rights was pervasive throughout the city. The day following the Maddox event, three black youths and a young white civil rights worker attempted to attend the Atlanta fairgrounds, where a "Fourth of July segregationists rally" was taking place. A horde of forty whites chased the youths into a fenced corner where they were beaten with metal chairs until police officers intervened.[60] Maddox was well aware that his political sensibilities were shared by most white Atlantans and most white Georgians, despite what the booster rhetoric suggested. In a close election in November 1966, Maddox, who enjoyed the endorsement of the Ku Klux Klan, was elected the seventy-fifth governor of the state. The election of Maddox stunned people across the country. After his election, King said that he "felt ashamed to be a Georgian."[61]

What was particularly instructive about King's observation was his increased witness to white backlash at black political advancement. The resistance manifested itself across the country in a range of ways, including the election of open racists like Maddox and Alabama governor George Wallace, as well as white flight from cities in every region. King did not deny or dismiss the significance of the progress achieved during the dozen years of his activism. Indeed, the transformations across the country were dramatic. He often affirmed and brought attention to the goodwill of the human spirit expressed across racial lines. However, he did grow intolerant of the incessant struggle to convince most whites that real racial confraternity and integration were possible and in the mutual interest of all.

With Maddox, the Confederacy continued to linger as a resonating if not mercurial expression of local white identity and recalcitrant resistance to racial equality. Even as the explicit celebration of white nationalism and open racial hate became increasingly marginalized—even in the Deep South—the vestiges of the Confederacy proved to have a peculiar durability, enough to win most white voters in two Atlanta elections. Maddox's election was demoralizing for many, as were the fights to resist integration of schools and neighborhoods.

Part of the allure of the images of Atlanta as a racially progressive city was based on two points: the relatively moderate white mayors and the visibility of black success. Despite popular rhetoric of Atlanta as a progressive, tolerant city of racial cooperation, the facts demonstrate that moderate white mayors had been elected by overwhelming black support and about a third of white voters. Most white Atlanta voters had historically opted for the Maddox types. Whatever success that black people achieved in the city, they achieved in spite of the city's racist policies, not because white people (power brokers, city officials, or random white civilians) had aided them. The fact that the city was home to the largest concentration of black colleges and universities in the country obfuscated the degree to which white Atlantans generally resisted quality access to black education and civil rights. As discussed earlier, the AUC was a private consortium that helped coalesce, forge, and support a rich social and economic landscape of visible black success. The municipal and state government had always either denied black people basic services (access to schools, parks, or libraries) or reluctantly and, often under pressure, provided the most inferior services. The private sector—hotels, shops, and restaurants—was similarly hostile to equality, fairness, or justice. The Atlanta model of black success was palpable. It largely grew from black-controlled institutions, a fact that affected King in his last year, shaping his own ideological evolution.

In 1967 Atlanta's native son offered a new take on the vain efforts to achieve residential integration in cities. Forever the believer in racial reconciliation, King began with his commitment to the principles of humanism, rejecting black nationalism:

> I don't believe in black separatism. I'm against it. . . . But I do say this. It seems that our white brothers and sisters don't want to live next door to us. . . . So . . . they're pinning us in central cities. . . . We're hemmed in. We can't get out . . . what we're going to have to do is just control the central city. We got to be the mayors of these big cities. And the minute we get elected mayor, we've got to begin taxing everybody who works in the city who lives in the suburbs. I know this sounds mean, but I just want to be realistic.[62]

The impulse of Afro-self-determinism was a clear motivator of King's political shift. Black people, King intimated, should apply the fundamental principles of self-determination, not because it was preferred but because circumstances demanded it. And if his hometown was any model, it would precipitate black economic, social, and political power.

King never framed whites as immutably prone to malevolence. He also insisted on the total humanity of all people and the ability of the most depraved to be saved by what Christians know as grace. When guided by principles of love and forgiveness, transformation and redemption are possible for even the most morally deficient. Still, in a very practical way, King could not ignore the political, social, and cultural world mutating before him. White flight, coupled with federal, state, and local housing policies, meant that whites were moving from all-white enclaves in cities to all-white suburbs, taking with them jobs and enormous tax bases, and depriving cities of services. Efforts to integrate were met with bombings, harassment, brutality, and isolation.

The self-determinative spirit of black power was itself tethered to Afro-self-determinism, which shaped King throughout most of his life. Although it was not unique to Atlanta (African Americans forged institutions in every major black community in the country), it was a particularly acute expression in King's hometown. He was enveloped in black institutional spaces from birth. He sat in no classroom with a white student until he was in graduate school. The professors, department heads, deans, college presidents, ministers, and others who shaped his life were black people. He saw black businesspeople, physicians, and lawyers throughout his childhood. They all led black institutions and achieved comfort and a rich cultural space there. He was a member of black social spaces, including three black fraternities: Alpha Phi Alpha, Sigma Pi Phi (the Boulé), and the de facto fraternity of Morehouse. They were not deficient because whites were not present. He extrapolated: there could be a practical power in black people controlling cities that whites had abandoned. Racial reconciliation was still a good thing, but black advancement did not require whites to be present in every space.

On August 16, 1967, King addressed the national convention of the Southern Christian Leadership Conference, the formidable civil rights organization that he cofounded in 1957. Its headquarters were in Atlanta, as were those of the Student Nonviolent Coordinating Committee, two of the leading civil rights groups. In what was to be his

last address to the SCLC, King, who had been resistive to the rhetoric of black power, shifted his tone. A year earlier, King had argued
that black power connoted "black supremacy and an anti-white feeling that does not or should not prevail."[63] To those who first popularized the term, such as Stokely Carmichael of the Student Nonviolent
Coordinating Committee and Floyd McKissick of the Congress of
Racial Equality, black power was simply the realization of the economic, social, political, and cultural power of black people. It was
not integration, which guaranteed no control over institutions heretofore in the hands of whites. What black people needed, McKissick
stated, "is self-determination—the right to control one's own destiny."[64]
Being beaten, slapped, and harassed during a sit-in to spend money
at Maddox's restaurant was not as empowering as establishing a black
restaurant and serving all people with dignity and respect. King, at the
SCLC convention, took a cue from Carmichael and others, telling the
membership that the successes of the civil rights movement could not
be ignored, including landmark legislation such as the Civil Rights Act
(1964) and the Voting Rights Act (1965). Scores of counties across the
South had seen massive increases in black voter registration. African
Americans had access to restaurants, hotels, hospitals, universities, and
juries. But, as King noted, economic forces often meant that restaurants and hotels that formally barred black people remained economically out of reach for most of them, who languished in poverty.

King's economic prescription was not a Marxist revolution (despite
what his enemies said). King insisted on cultivating black capitalist
development. He drew attention to the success the SCLC had in Chicago by supporting two black-owned banks that were unable to provide
loans to black customers on a scale that would be helpful to prospective
home and business owners. Because of the SCLC's Operation Breadbasket, "both of these Negro-operated banks have now more than
doubled their assets." King's operations petitioned black people as well
as whites to contract with black-owned firms, including services for

janitors, painters, masons, electricians, excavators, and exterminators. He proudly announced the increased contracts and business expansion that resulted from these efforts.[65]

King's demands grew bolder. In Cleveland the SCLC's Operation Breadbasket program targeted Sealtest Dairy, which employed more than four hundred people, 90 percent of them white. Blacks made up 10 percent of the Sealtest employees but more than a third of the city's population. Following threats of pickets and other protests, Sealtest agreed to expand employment opportunities, but more significantly, King and the local Operation Breadbasket leadership met with the executives and demanded that the company "put something back in the ghetto." King explained that "we also demand that you put money in the Negro savings and loan association and that you take ads, advertise, in the *Cleveland Call & Post*, the local Negro newspaper." There was little doubt about the relationship that black inner cities had with the wider white communities: "The ghetto is a domestic colony that's constantly drained without being replenished." After the meeting with the all-white Sealtest leadership, King reported that they had signed an agreement that resulted in $500,000 in new income for the Cleveland black community, a new corporate account in the local black bank, and ads in the black newspaper. To applause, King, concluded, "This is the *power* of Operation Breadbasket."[66]

That meeting in Atlanta drew thousands of locals. Perhaps some of those in attendance would convey the power of King's politics to those who would hold office in that city. Maybe those who would control contracts in the city were in the audience, captivated by the power of King's new strategies and programs for the development of black economic power. Whether they were there or not, the message gained traction across the national spheres of black politics.

Increasingly, King's politics questioned economic justice. It was the cause of labor rights for sanitation workers that brought him to Memphis in April 1968, where he was struck down by an assassin's bullet.

When his body was returned to Atlanta for his burial, Morehouse College (his alma mater) and Spelman College (where his grandmother, mother, and sister had attended) hosted services as mourners marched through the city. Dignitaries of every sort attended. Politicians, including the major candidates in the 1968 presidential race, Vice President Hubert Humphrey, Richard Nixon, and Senator Robert F. Kennedy, attended. The Academy Awards ceremony was scheduled for the day before King's funeral; however, many of the Hollywood elite, including nominees like Sidney Poitier, would not attend because of attending King's funeral. In an unprecedented move, the Academy postponed its ceremony. Sammy Davis Jr., Marlon Brando, Eartha Kitt, Harry Belafonte, and Paul Newman were among the many celebrities in attendance. James Baldwin, Nikki Giovanni, Aretha Franklin, Stevie Wonder, Ossie Davis, and Ruby Dee joined nearly all of the civil rights leaders at the services. Benjamin E. Mays, president of Morehouse College and mentor to King, gave the eulogy. The global media reported on the procession of more than a hundred thousand people, a number that had been matched or exceeded only by two other events in the city's history: the 1939 parade during the premiere of *Gone with the Wind* and the 1864 parade after Union soldiers captured the city. The city was as transfixed as it had been in those earlier eras. However, not all citizens were unified over these gatherings, which tended to be both unifiers and dividers for a city as tragically polarized as Atlanta.

Soon after the fall of Reconstruction, Atlanta's elite—politicians, civic leaders, business leaders, newspaper editors, and academic leaders—had begun promoting the city as an outlier among southern cities and towns. The city had risen from the ashes of Union soldiers' destruction under General Sherman's campaign and in doing so sloughed off the skin of the Old South and its investment in slavery, parochialism, and sectional vitriol. But even in the aftermath of the Confederacy, the legacy that the Civil War represented was always a touchstone for the city's promoters, who assumed the task of shaping an image that carefully addressed its more troublesome past by creative erasure, assiduous myth making, and, as later eras would show, contentious debate.

Governor Lester Maddox, who openly derided and denounced King, refused to allow the civil rights leader's body to lie in wake at the state capitol when he was slain. Two years after Maddox's second term, in 1973, his hometown elected the first black mayor of any major southern city. Maddox, and others like him, were outraged. This election was also an opportunity for the city of Atlanta to realize the curious goals set forth by King less than a year before his assassination.

Not only was the city changing; change was happening in a rapid and particularly defiant way. Black power politics, complete with an irreverent style, confidence, and boldness, characterized the era and the new mayor. In addition to making substantial changes in the politics of city hall and introducing aggressive affirmative-action policies, the new mayor did not ignore symbolic gestures either, as Chapter 10 details.

10 | "Atlanta Is Ours and Fairly Won"

The Rise of the Black Mecca

William Faulkner's South—heavy with ghostly Spanish moss, penumbral myths and morbid attachment to the past—is giving way to a South that has discovered it does not need fable to shore up its pride or the past to cloud its future.

—*TIME*, MAY 30, 1971

"The Black Mecca" leads the nation in numbers of African American millionaires; at the same time, it leads the nation in the percentage of its children in poverty.

—ROBERT D. BULLARD, *THE BLACK METROPOLIS IN THE TWENTY-FIRST CENTURY*, 2007 n 1971 the nation's largest black-oriented lifestyle magazine, *Ebony*, covered Atlanta, among other southern cities, in an issue on black quality of life in the South. Atlanta, the magazine declared, was the "Black Mecca" because "black folks have more, live better, accomplish more and deal with white folks more effectively than anywhere else in the South—or North." The article praised the Afro-self-determinism that distinguished the Gate City: the massive consortium of black institutions of higher education, black businesses, rich black civic and social organizations, black religious leadership, and even the expanse of black middle-class neighborhoods. "Evidently, Atlanta is not ready for integrated housing," the magazine quipped, even as it measured these all-black, beautifully lush residential enclaves as points of praise. The article noted the rise of publicly elected officials, such as State Senator Leroy Johnson, Atlanta Board of Education member Benjamin Mays, and the "big and bold" thirty-three-year-old vice-mayor, Maynard Jackson, who served as the president of the nineteen-member Board of Aldermen (the city council). The magazine mentioned several business leaders, including Jesse B. Blayton, Jesse Hill, the Paschal brothers, and Norris B. Herndon, president of the Atlanta Life Insurance Company. Herndon had inherited his business from his father, Alonzo, who was enslaved as a child. In 1971 Norris was worth an estimated $18 million (nearly $131 million today), making him, according to the magazine, the richest black person in the country. In a country where people of color had been denied access to quality housing, employment, and (until recently) the vote, these stories displayed social, political, and economic black excellence.

The celebration came when the city was roughly 51 percent black. Though one of the few predominantly black major cities in the country, Atlanta offered little in the way of real black political power. In addition to a white mayor, fifteen of the nineteen members of the city council were white. Whites represented the overwhelming majority of leadership positions in municipal and county departments. The disproportionately white police force, under its white leadership, had integrated its patrols only two years earlier. Two-thirds of the 160,000 Atlantans in poverty were black. Adoring nods to the Confederacy were ubiquitous. Streets, schools, and neighborhoods were named after virulent white supremacists, terrorists, and enslavers, even in the black communities of every class strata. Despite the article's copious praise of black business in the city, touting, among other things, the black-owned insurance companies and the new twelve-story office building erected by the black-owned bank, the portion of the city's contracts to black firms was about the same has it had been during slavery: less than 1 percent. In the arena of popular culture, from *Gone with the Wind* through *Song of the South* and *Tales of Uncle Remus*, Atlanta was firmly anchored in Old South tropes of genteel enslavers, civilized southern belles, joyful slaves, and grinning Negroes. Huge swaths of black people languished in shanty-like homes in pressing poverty, with dismal rates of high school completion.

As civil rights veteran Julian Bond summed it up, Atlanta "is the best place in the United States for a black if you are middle-class and have a college degree. But if you're poor, it's just like Birmingham, Jackson or any other place." Bond, a member of the Georgia House of Representatives at the time, noted that in his district of Vine City, "the average family income is $2,500 a year, and the education level is six years. This district also includes the colleges, but the professors don't live here."[1] Atlanta's newest sobriquet, the Black Mecca, was just as complicated and lofty as its previous moniker, the City Too Busy to Hate. Yet it endured.

How did a city with so few examples of real political, economic, or even cultural power come to be regarded as the country's veritable black city on a hill? Much of this can be explained by the historical moment. Only a handful of major cities had black mayors in 1971. No city with a sizable black population had a police force with black officers at parity with the city's black demographics. African Americans were, for the first time in history, entering a decade where most were not enslaved, in poverty, legally constricted from voting, living in certain neighborhoods, or denied public accommodations. In historical context, Atlanta—even though deeply burdened by the legacies of racial subjugation—had achieved a considerable amount of success. Additionally, the article was released at the height of the black power movement, which had an indelible effect on how black people viewed themselves and their relationship with whites.

The utility of black self-determination became more popularized as the black power movement emerged as a mainstream expression among African Americans by 1970. As explained throughout this book, the fundamental tenets of what became known as "black power" had been dominant among the Atlanta black community for generations. Black power and Afro-self-determinism are not opposed to desegregation. Having a desegregated, open society was fine, advocates insisted. Attending any hotel, hospital, or restaurant was desired over being barred from them. However, owning hotels, hospitals, or restaurants was preferred. Moreover, insisting that racial integration was critical to black advancement was anathema to black power agents, who argued that black control over institutions in black communities was more important than simple access to white-controlled spaces. As desegregation became law, the dominant political expression among African Americans was centered on the establishment, support, and celebration of black institutions. In the National Society of Black Engineers, the National Association of Black Journalists, and the Congressional Black Caucus, for example, black professionals who enjoyed unprecedented access to white professional organizations had established black ones between 1966 and 1975. Atlanta, in this context, was clearly on its way to become "the first citadel of black political power in the New South."[2]

Perhaps most consequential to this historical moment was the ascension of the "big and bold" young politician Maynard H. Jackson Jr., who was described in 1971 as "aggressive and black-oriented."

His mayoral administration (1974–1982) achieved what few, if any, major municipal governments had in the history of the United States. He upended racist practices in hiring, promotions, contract negotiation, and more. Jackson established a new standard for successive black administrations that built upon his legacy of aggressive affirmative action and hard-nosed policies aimed at widening opportunities for a diverse city. Although white Atlantans—from the business class to the working class—were generally hostile to his regime, Jackson was incredibly popular with black voters, who reelected him overwhelmingly into a second term. His successor, Andrew Young, the civil rights leader, former congressman, and ambassador to the United Nations, offered Jackson-like affirmative action with an eye to mollifying white fears. He openly courted white supporters, corporations, and international investment. Moreover, for the first time since Mayor Hartsfield in the 1950s, Young was able to win the majority of white voters, when he ran for reelection. It appeared that he was able to balance the ambitious and effective policies that opened opportunities for people of color without alienating Atlanta's white voters. The Jackson standard would politically survive throughout subsequent mayoral administrations, transforming the city that had once been the "heart" of the Confederacy.

Black leaders in Atlanta were on the rise before Jackson became mayor. In August 1967 the Southern Christian Leadership Conference (SCLC) hosted its annual meeting in Atlanta, where none other than its cofounder, Martin Luther King Jr., insisted that it was essential for black people to support, invest in, and promote black-owned businesses for collective black advancement. King did not argue that black people should avoid white banks, restaurants, or other institutions. They had choices. However, the struggle for freedom would not and could not stop at the vote or access to public accommodations. It meant economic advancement and uplift as well. To that end, black people needed to forge economic power on four major fronts: (1) encouraging/forcing white-owned private-sector employers to hire and promote fairly; (2) demanding that the federal, state, and local governments enforce policies that ensured fair employment for federal agencies and those that had public-sector contracts; (3) creating and supporting black-owned businesses; and (4) demanding government funding to establish economic stimulation in black communities. Among these four points, the one that could be immediately affected by black municipal control was employment and contracts with black firms. Those fundamental principles were neatly aligned with the tradition of Afro-self-determinism that had been practiced in King's hometown for generations.[3]

The effort to systematically desegregate the halls of power began years before Jackson's election. That process would prove essential to the efficacy of his future administration. Much of this process came through the incredibly sensitive and controversial efforts at school desegregation. In Atlanta, that process conspicuously decentered and "de-pedestalized" whites, which was shocking for some old-line Negroes and whites alike. In the end, though, the notion that black people could, in fact, cultivate healthy, thriving communities without whites continued to gain traction as the black power movement matured. However, this had long been the dominant approach used by black leaders in Atlanta.

By the early 1970s, after various legal maneuvers to slow desegregation since the *Brown* ruling, the Atlanta Board of Education, it appeared, was out of options. On November 27, 1972, the court of appeals ordered the board to submit a comprehensive plan to desegregate public schools within a month. Nationwide, racial tensions over equal access to schools grew more acute in the 1970s as federal judges forced busing plans on school districts that had made little progress. In many cities, black communities had also faced intraracial conflicts over school integration. In Atlanta the prospect of a black mayor, coupled with the politics of the era, made school integration a vexing issue between and within black and white spaces.

In 1969 Benjamin E. Mays, who had served as president of More-house College from 1940 to 1967, was elected to the Atlanta Public School Board. The next year, he was made president of the board. A mentor and close friend to his former student, King, Mays was an internationally known scholar, religious leader, "Dean of the Move-ment," and titan in the city. By 1970, Atlanta's school system was three-quarters black, but among its 153 public schools, 106 remained mostly segregated. Additionally, most administrators were white. Although Atlanta had a long, storied history of extraordinary black achievement in various professions, especially education, the white superintendent, John W. Letson, argued that the overwhelmingly white administration was a consequence of being unable to find quali-fied black people.[4]

Simultaneously, under court order the Atlanta public school system was in negotiations to bus nearly thirty thousand of its black students into white schools. Aware of the deep opposition among whites, black leadership, including the Atlanta chapter of the NAACP and its chap-ter president, Lonnie King, endorsed a compromise with the white leadership: only 10 percent of the original number of black students would be bused into white schools in return for a black superinten-dent of the Atlanta Board of Education and more black administra-tive control. King believed that "administrative desegregation" and a black superintendent of the 77 percent black school system was a more substantive policy to advance black educational equity than sending black children to schools with mostly white students, teachers, and administrators.[5]

On February 20, 1973, in an eight-to-two vote, the Atlanta Board of Education approved an out-of-court settlement of a desegregation lawsuit. The agreement created administrative desegregation at a higher ratio than student desegregation, realizing increased black control of the school system.[6] On July 1, 1973, amid the debates about desegrega-tion of classrooms and administration, Mays appointed Alonzo Crim as the first black superintendent of the school system. This appointment aligned with the efforts to achieve some compromise between those hostile to busing and its supporters. Known as the "Ten Percent Plan" or the "Second Atlanta Compromise," this agreement reflected the new realities of the Black Mecca: a self-assured black leadership class more concerned with black control of resources for the black community than integration into spaces where whites primarily determined how black resources were allocated.

Given that for nearly a century, black people in Atlanta had run everything from corporations to universities in the city, black control of the public school system was a feasible step. As one historian notes, "Supporters of this idea believed that if there was ever an opportunity presented itself for blacks to demonstrate the effectiveness of their administering community-controlled education, it was in Atlanta." For their part, black leadership insisted that the push for increased black administrative control, rather than busing, reflected the sentiment of the majority of black people, who preferred community control of well-funded black schools that were equipped with inspiring teachers, quality administrators, and peers who would forge amiable social spaces for education. Black parents consistently expressed opposition to busing their children to white schools, which likely led to abuse and torment of their children for the sake of an abstract idea of "racial cooperation" or a nebulously measured better education. This effort, black parents argued, "did not outweigh its detriments if it resulted in the degradation of their culture and institutions."[7]

The compromise put power into black hands before the city had its first black mayor. It was a milestone in the advancement of black equity in education, even if it sacrificed integration for black management. It mollified many white and black Atlantans, but it infuriated the national leadership of the NAACP, which had long looked askance at the local chapter for its tepid demands for integration, even calling the local branch "anti-NAACP."

Viewing the Gate City as different from most other cities working with desegregation plans, Lonnie King invited the national NAACP leadership to visit and survey the city and its people. Ultimately, the national leadership suspended King and the entire Atlanta branch because they had abandoned the core principles and mission of the organization. Legally, the organization believed that the action of the local branch would make for a troubling precedent for other cities fighting school desegregation. In his defense, King insisted, "I think Atlanta has a unique situation, one that is not present in many other cities in America. That's why I am presuming that this won't be a precedent, but it will be something which the Atlanta case with its uniqueness had to bring into focus in order to resolve this problem."[8]

King was correct. Atlanta, once known as the "heart of the Confederacy" and the "Imperial City" of the Klan, had political leadership that was so obdurate regarding school integration that it desegregated its schools later than all but one other major southern city's school system. Even the cities that had become iconic showcases for violent resistance to *Brown v. Board* were ahead of the "City Too Busy to Hate" on integrating schools. Opposition was widespread, when Imperial Wizard James Venable vowed to fight the "horror" of integration with his many silent white sympathizers throughout the metro. Moreover, Atlanta's black leadership had generations of institutional management experience. Lonnie King and others in the leadership class had been fiercely proud alumni of and members of black institutions, including colleges, fraternities, sororities, churches, and social clubs. For many African Americans, black control of schools was more attractive than greater proximity to whites, especially if that proximity came with a cost of emotional, physical, or mental harm. Although there were other majority-black cities by the early 1970s, there was perhaps no city better positioned to make this claim than Atlanta. Cities like Gary or Detroit did not have generations of black university deans, provosts, presidents, or corporate executives. The responsibilities of these positions meant that there were generations of black professionals who managed massive budgets, staff, and hundreds of acres of property while simultaneously adhering to federal, state, and local compliance, finding funding, and, in most cases, undertaking international relations. The fundamental sentiment that privileged administrative integration over social integration would guide and shape the municipal and county government for the next fifty years, transforming the city.

In addition to the unique history of black institutional control in Atlanta, the city had an unusually high ratio of black people. In the South, where black people were leaving rural areas for cities, no major city was majority black, except Atlanta. Memphis, Charleston, New Orleans, Montgomery, and Birmingham remained mostly white as late as 1970.[9] The demographic shifts were distressing for many white Atlantans: a convergence of circumstances meant not only that blacks were increasing their numbers in the city but also that traditional methods to politically neutralize them were becoming ineffective. Unlike earlier eras, under Mayor Hartsfield and others, annexing majority-white areas to dilute the power of the black vote was no longer an option when the Atlanta public school system was integrated. In fact, white communities outside Atlanta resisted annexation because of explicit fears that their children would have to attend integrated schools. As noted above, black parents in Atlanta, though not mounting violent opposition to integration of schools, expressed little enthusiasm for busing. "Community control" of schools, equity of resources, and black administrators were vastly more popular among black Atlantans. Although the sentiment of Afro-self-determinism had permeated various sectors of black America, it was most popular among the young. College students in the city were as important to local politics in the black power era as they had been during the 1960s.

In the fall of 1972, Rodney Strong entered Morehouse College, which had become an educational enclave of members of the black elite in Atlanta and beyond. The school also enrolled first-generation college students from poor and working-class backgrounds, providing a rich class diversity. In the midst of the black power era, various events mobilized students, including the November 1972 shooting at Southern University in Louisiana, the largest HBCU in the country. Police and National Guard troops fired on student protesters, injuring several and killing two. AU political science professor Mack Jones helped organize a demonstration around the shooting. Amid these circles, Strong forged connections with AUC student activists Adolph Reed, Vince Eagan, Mike Fisher, and others, ultimately forming a student group, University Movement for Black Unity (UMBU). Like most campuses, the Atlanta University Center had its share of ideological diversity, and UMBU pulled together some of this range. Some students were self-described revolutionaries, others were black nationalists, and many were liberals. UMBU closely followed current events, such as school desegregation. Of course, the prospect of a black mayor electrified the group.

Amid the Second Atlanta Compromise controversy, on March 28, 1973, Maynard H. Jackson Jr., the vice-mayor of Atlanta, declared his intention to run for mayor. Son of a prominent minister and the grandson of the venerated John Wesley Dobbs, Jackson and his entire family were intimately tied to the institutions that had been critical to Atlanta's black community over much of the twentieth century. In 1945 Maynard H. Jackson Sr., a Morehouse alumnus, became senior pastor at Friendship Baptist Church, only a year after Edward Randolph Carter died. His wife, Irene Dobbs Jackson, was a professor of French at Spelman, her alma mater. Her father, Dobbs, was the leader of a Masonic lodge and the founder of the Atlanta Civic and Political League in 1936 (which later became the Atlanta Negro Voters League). Dobbs became a father figure to his grandson when the elder Jackson died in a car accident in 1953. As a thirty-year-old vice-mayor, Maynard swiftly moved into prominence, serving under Mayor Sam Massell, a Jewish Democrat.

To raise the stakes even higher, the Georgia General Assembly had passed a law in 1971 creating the City of Atlanta Charter Revision Commission, which shifted the municipal government from a "weak mayor" to a "strong mayor" form of government. Under the strong mayor model, as chief executive of the city, the mayor had the authority to appoint and hire people, and to create more administrative policy.

When Jackson declared his intentions, many were eager to commit to the promise of the transformative power of black political leadership, particularly college students and other young people who volunteered for Jackson's campaign. Through UMBU, AUC students formally organized a mock vote to determine which of two AUC alumni, Leroy Johnson or Maynard Jackson (both Morehouse men), would receive their endorsement. Johnson, who was elected to the state senate in 1962, was the first black person elected to the Georgia General Assembly since 1907. He was the first black state senator since Reconstruction. Although he was a prominent figure with the endorsement of the *Atlanta Constitution*, he struggled to gain traction with young voters. Many felt the state senator did not take the UMBU election seriously, while the vice-mayor visited each AUC school and every dorm at Morehouse. Jackson overwhelmingly won the mock election. In turn, UMBU endorsed him, canvassing neighborhoods and donating time and money to his campaign.[10] With the support of the AUC and of black business leaders Jesse Hill and Herman J. Russell, as well as religious leaders, Jackson had a critical advantage in the election.

Many would benefit from the expansion of opportunities emanating from a mayoral administration that embraced Afro-self-determinism, but few were as well positioned as Russell. An Atlanta native who spent his childhood in poverty before cobbling together enough resources from various enterprises to attend college at Tuskegee, he built upon his family's plastering business. He followed the tradition of E. W. Evans, Heman Perry, Chief Aikens, and other black construction pioneers in Atlanta. Like many of them, Russell poured resources into social justice work, befriending Martin Luther King, Andrew Young, and many others while also donating money to the movement. In his support of Jackson's first mayoral bid, Russell introduced the young politician to white business partners and friends, who contributed to his campaign. For some, these contributions foreshadowed amiable relations between white business leaders and Jackson.

On election night, October 2, 1973, nineteen-year-old Rodney Strong was elated that Jackson had secured the most votes among a crowded field, winning 46 percent in the fall election, triggering a runoff against Massell. The sitting mayor campaigned that he should win because "Atlanta's Too Young to Die." He also released campaign ads showing Atlanta as a dystopian wasteland after a Jackson victory. In contrast, Jackson pushed themes of racial unity and forward-facing, modern movement for the city. On October 16, runoff returns came in along racial lines. Massell solidly won the white vote but not the election. Jackson carried around a quarter of white voters and 95 percent of black voters.[11] Atlanta had elected the first black mayor of a major southern city. The Jackson victory on October was "the happiest day of my life," Strong recalled.[12] The joy was national in scope, evocative of the telegram that General Sherman had sent President Lincoln 109 years earlier: "Atlanta is Ours and Fairly Won."

It was in this moment that Strong had become an advocate of a community-engaged brand of black power that reflected the sentiment of one of MLK's last prescriptions. King's message of black political and economic power was deeply interwoven with the spirit of the black freedom movement that was also evolving. Much has been said about the fissure of the movement in 1966, as black power emerged. Nevertheless, it is important to note that the civil rights movement was not ideologically static; neither was its most visible exponent, King. In many ways, upon Jackson's election the slain civil rights leader's hometown became a testing ground for the application of the mercurial notion of black power in municipal governance.

Like W. E. Evans, Adrienne Elizabeth McNeil Herndon, John Hope, W. E. B. Du Bois, A. T. Walden, George Alexander Towns, and thousands of others, Strong was attracted to the opportunities that Atlanta institutions of higher learning offered African Americans. He anticipated that in this new political moment, Atlanta would be a shining example of the possibilities of black political power. His faith was undergirded by his direct involvement in Jackson's campaign with Morehouse students and alumni such as Paul Howard and Charles "Chuck" Burris. There they witnessed, up close, the political operations of a new, more aggressive style of black politics. Many of them found work in Jackson's administration.

The new mayor agreed to meet with UMBU once a semester. Adolph Reed, a left-leaning doctoral student at Atlanta University, advised Jackson, and Burris worked in the mayor's office. Strong worked with Jackson for three years after graduating college in 1976. By the time Strong finished law school in 1983, he was firmly ensconced in the political apparatus that the new mayor had created. Jackson was, in many ways, the personification of the latest stage of the dramatic arc of Atlanta's political history. From the postbellum era onward, the city, through the persistence of neo-Confederate nationalism and the struggle for Afro-self-determinism, had emerged in its newest iteration with a new sobriquet, the "Black Mecca." The moniker had been applied to the city before it had actually earned it, but as with past nicknames, Atlanta's boosters proved more aspirational than accurate.[13]

The black power that Strong came to endorse was best expressed in the newest mayoral regime in Atlanta. It was not a politics that relegated whites into a cast of immutably corrupt hostiles. Nor did it fetishize whiteness or measure proximity to it as a solution to racial oppression. The politics of Jackson was not revolutionary, nationalist, or traditionally one that idealized integration. It was, perhaps, *the most successful example of the mainstreaming of Afro-self-determinism in the expression of municipal governance in the United States*. In this historic moment, it had become known as "black power." Ultimately, the successes of Jackson's first term were such that the subsequent administrations would be measured by what was achieved in Atlanta during 1974–1982. Scores of articles, books, theses, and dissertations have explored the example of Atlanta as a veritable beacon of black political achievement—and failure. Nevertheless, as with other narratives told by the city's boosters, the failures have always rung with a quieter resound than any successes.

Jackson's victory as the first black mayor in Atlanta was as devastating for some hardened white supremacists as had been the end of slavery itself. Jackson recalled that "for the first two years I was mayor, the [local white] press was almost hysterical."[14] Not only was the city changing; it was happening in a rapid and particularly defiant way. Black power politics, complete with an irreverent style and confidence, characterized the era and its new mayor. In addition to making substantial changes in the politics of city hall, introducing aggressive affirmative-action policies in city contracts, municipal hiring, and police reform, Jackson did not ignore symbolic gestures either. In his first term he changed the name of Forrest Avenue, which had been named after the infamous Confederate general Nathan Bedford Forrest. In addition to alleged war crimes against black and white Union soldiers during the Fort Pillow Massacre, Forrest was the first imperial wizard of the Ku Klux Klan. The first chapter of the resurrected Ku Klux Klan was named for him. With a nod toward racial reconciliation, the street was renamed for another white native son of the South, Ralph McGill, the famed antisegregationist editor of the *Atlanta Constitution* who challenged his compatriots to resist the ugliest impulses of racism and violence. McGill was once a target for Klan violence, and his house was bombed, as Chapter 9 mentions.

Jackson assiduously pushed for a broader representation of the demographics of the city with his hiring efforts. In his first term, nearly 60 percent of the appointments to the two highest job grades went to black hires. Overall, a whopping 80 percent of new hires were black people. Jackson appointed Morehouse men David Franklin, Michael Lomax, and A. Reginald Eaves as his chief political lieutenants. In 1978 the city appointed George Napper as director of police services. Jackson established the Bureau of Cultural Affairs, and young Howard graduate Shirley Franklin eventually served as its director. In all, Jackson hired more women and black people than all previous mayors combined.[15] This rapid transition was not lost on citizens of either race.[16]

Throughout the history of African Americans in Atlanta, the fundamental core principles of what became known as "black power" were rather common: self-determination, self-defense, and self-pride. These basic precepts of Afro-self-determinism had been openly advocated for generations. In the "long sixties," the degree to which one expressed this was clearly much bolder, more vituperative, and aesthetically counterhegemonic. Afros, African names, African clothes, and occasional public denunciations of white people were departures from the earlier expressions. Nevertheless, one did not need the Nation of Islam or the Black Panther Party to promote self-defense. Long before television, black elites from John Hope to W. E. B. Du Bois either distributed firearms or boasted about brandishing them against racist terrorists. "Picking up the gun," as the Panthers demanded, was not a new idea, nor were other foundational tenets of black power. Although the US Organization and its cofounder Maulana Karenga found traction with their holiday Kwanzaa, the architects of black banks, insurance companies, universities, construction companies, and seminaries did not need black nationalists to instruct them on the principle of *kujichagulia* (self-determination) or *ujamaa* (cooperative economics) in supporting black businesses. These ideals were so endemic in the city's black community that national NAACP activists complained that the city's black leadership had been palpably slow to demand integration with whites.

As it had nationally, the growth of black power unfolded locally across ideological lines. The term did not have a singular meaning that erased political differences among groups that adopted the slogan. Revolutionaries in the Black Panther Party and moderate liberals in the Urban League adopted the term. For the latter, the city under Jackson's administration was positioned to widen black power in economic, political, cultural, and social spaces in a way that had never been seen before in any American city. Central to this development was the economic opportunities afforded African American entrepreneurs. When W. E. Evans settled in Atlanta in 1880, the bricklayer and plasterer had few, if any, options to secure contracts with the municipal, county, or state government. White firms exclusively held these construction contracts, with nearly no change until Jackson's tenure. Evans did, as detailed in earlier chapters, work with the black construction company Alexander Hamilton and Son before establishing his own firm. He worked on buildings in the Atlanta University Center and on the Butler Street YMCA, as well as projects throughout the city and beyond. The Jackson administration opened up opportunities for black contractors, especially those in construction, at a scale unprecedented anywhere else in the United States.

The resistance of white business leadership to Jackson's efforts came as no surprise to the mayor. And he was prepared to respond to it. Businesses threatened to leave the city. Lawsuits were filed. Hostile exchanges behind closed doors speculated on ways to constrict Jackson's power: "If people felt that what they wanted to do was to punish Atlanta . . . because they were racist . . . then there was nothing I could do about that." Jackson answered his critics when in 1974 he more than doubled funds to black contracts: "Now, if anxiety attaches when the black community gets one percent . . . just imagine what happens when we double it to two percent."[17] As it turned out, the mayor had undersold his future success. The following year Atlanta awarded 5 percent of its contracts to minority-owned firms. In his first two years in office, he increased the percentage of monies that went to black firms by over 500 percent. He increased the portion by another 400 percent by the time that his first term as mayor concluded. Through ambitious and hard-nosed programs and policies, the city of Atlanta advocated for minority-owned businesses, sought black-owned firms outside of the metropolitan area, and promoted "joint-venture" partnerships between white and minority-owned firms to widen access to business. A quarter of the contract funds went to minority-owned (almost all black-owned) firms by 1979, one of the highest rates of any major city in the United States.[18] The consequences were not lost on national political observers. It was, according to economist Thomas Boston, "the first local program with a significant minority goal that was not tied to a federal mandate."[19] It inspired mayors across the country as a model for expanding black access to public contracts and shaping public policy and the political economy.

Not only was the local government bullishly pushing for black capitalist development; the federal government provided incentives as well. Republican president Richard Nixon famously advocated for "black power" during his presidential campaign in 1968. Not to be perceived as advocating the black nationalism of the Nation of Islam or the revolutionary politics of the Black Panther Party, Nixon insisted that he meant "black capitalist power." Convincing black people that capitalism could benefit them in a neoliberal society gained traction. In addition to the increased employment opportunities for African Americans, dozens of black people became millionaires in Atlanta. By the close of the 1970s, a group informally known as "Maynard's millionaires" was a visible example of the new development of industrial-level wealth that could be realized with black municipal control. Many local companies became some of the largest black firms in the country. Few were as well-known as H. J. Russell & Co., which would become the largest black construction company in the country, with billions in contracts over the years.[20]

Seeking contracts that expanded black wealth did not always directly address the pressing conditions of poverty and deprivation. The people best positioned to benefit from these contracts were not those living in Bankhead Homes or University Homes public housing. They were the well-heeled heirs (figurative or literal) of the black contractors such as W. E. Evans or Alexander Hamilton and Son. They were the ones with resources and experience forged in the closed markets of a neo-Confederate city. However, some were not so wealthy or high born. Some, such as Russell, had resources and experience but like Evans and Hamilton (both of whom were enslaved at birth) built relatively small businesses that grew when opportunities were made available.[21]

A year after taking office, Jackson created the Atlanta Plan, which would soon become the most visible and significant "minority business enterprise" (MBE) program in the country. Ultimately, it would clearly demonstrate the degree to which local governments can transform economic development in communities previously excluded from public contracts. It would be one of the most consequential efforts of Jackson's terms as mayor. The struggle over the expansion of Atlanta Hartsfield International Airport was a bitter one, with white businesses largely resisting the city's affirmative-action requirements. Jackson appointed Emma Darnell as commissioner of administrator services, which oversaw construction contracts for the airport. Rodney Strong, as compliance officer, reported directly to Darnell. The mayor initially mandated that a minimum of 25 percent of subcontracts would go to women and minority-owned firms, a first for any airport in the country. White business leaders swiftly denounced the new affirmative-action demands. One man, without irony, explained that "like a granite rock," Atlanta's bidding process had withstood years of practice without problem. The efforts to expand economic opportunities was so disruptive to many of the old-guard white elites that economic expansion for black people could only be viewed as inherently antiwhite. Dillard Munford was one of many who expressed opposition to Jackson's effort to widen opportunity for minority business through his Atlanta Plan: "Black leadership must accept their new roles as city leaders and not black city leaders." Munford insisted that "there was no question that he was a full-fledged racist against whites." Jackson's "charge," Munford continued, was to "see this [business contracts with the city] was turned over to blacks."[22]

Munford's sentiments were not rare in white business circles. In fact, the hostility to Jackson's administration was nearly immediate. Central Atlanta Progress, which was an organization of white business leaders that worked closely with the nearly all-white Atlanta Chamber of Commerce, conducted a survey of white business leadership after Jackson's first year in office. It was intended to be an in-house private assessment; however, the study was leaked to the *Atlanta Constitution*, which published it. Known as the Brockey Letter (after its author), the survey revealed that the majority of white business leaders polled viewed the new mayor as "anti-white." They also considered relocating to the suburbs in an effort to escape the mayor's influence "for other than economic or management reasons."[23]

Ivan Allen III, son of the former mayor, served as president of the Atlanta Chamber of Commerce during Jackson's term. In an effort to "mediate," Allen explained to the mayor that white businesses "don't understand why you are pushing so hard." For his part, Jackson wondered why white businesses were protesting so much. The obstinance to opening economic opportunities beyond whites was not only wrong; it was also unhealthy for Atlanta's economy. In 1974 Jackson made an appeal to white-owned Citizens and Southern Bank: "I don't need you guys to get elected, but I need you to govern."[24] In frustration, white business leaders wondered about Allen's chances of becoming mayor. Maybe the white scion of the city's political elite would return city hall to their interests. However, the chamber of commerce president saw a different political landscape when he noted that "we're going to see black mayors for the next fifty years in Atlanta." In 1975, resigned to a fate of whites no longer having exclusive control of city contracts, Allen turned pragmatic. Despite hostility to the Atlanta Plan, white business leadership should "rally around Maynard. If we're going to build this city, we've got to help him."[25] Having access to most development projects was better than no access. Still, many balked at Allen's initiatives.

The resistance and difficulty experienced by black city leadership cannot be separated from the wider social, cultural, and political fabric of the country. Old-guard white leaders were not accustomed to the new gendered and racial circumstances before them. They were met with actual power and authority in the person of Darnell, who was smart, confident, and unapologetically black. With an Afro hairstyle and as one of the only two women appointed to commissioner positions in the history of the city, Darnell (and others) were aware of the symbolism and impact of her role in the Jackson administration. She was a black woman dealing with very powerful white men who had never dealt with black people or women in positions to approve or deny contracts worth millions.

Strong noted that Darnell's commitment to the administration's agenda left no doubt about her importance in an era of substantial changes in both race and gender. Much like black college students who demanded increased access to higher learning for black students, faculty, and staff, black municipal workers often understood their work in a highly politicized context, one that was inextricably bound to the larger political currents of the historical moment. Darnell explained that "we were, for all practical purposes, engaged in a revolution. . . . Those persons during the sixties laid down their lives and died to put us into these positions of power. We did not consider these positions of power to be ends in and of themselves."[26]

Much like Confederates viewed abolition as an abnegation of white freedom to enslave others, many whites in Atlanta viewed challenges to racial discrimination as "reverse discrimination." In fact, many of them sued the city on this very basis. Jackson reasoned with the fuming white business elites: "You can get 75 percent of [hundreds of millions of dollars in] airport contracts, or 100 percent of no contracts." White executives unsuccessfully appealed to Governor Jimmy Carter to place the airport project under state authority rather than Atlanta municipal authority. After nearly two years of wrangling, Jackson's vision won out. The white business leadership relented, agreeing to hire at least 20 percent minority labor in airport construction, and in the process MBEs received record access to contracts worth hundreds of millions of dollars.[27]

On September 21, 1980, Atlanta opened the newly constructed Midfield terminal and landed its first commercial flight. Midfield was the world's largest passenger terminal and a political achievement for Jackson. He successfully courted and kept major airlines in the city while standing firm against recalcitrant businesses. The $700 million airport expansion was completed on schedule and under budget. Moreover, the promotion of black development in Atlanta adhered to the Nixon administration's agenda to open federal contracts to MBEs, an initiative that had bipartisan support. In 1980 President Carter, a Democrat, provided comments at the opening ceremony of the nation's busiest airport. The former Georgia governor (who mentioned in his speech that he had traveled to the event with Herman Russell) celebrated the fact that one-third of the contracts went to minority (almost exclusively black) contractors. The efforts of the Atlanta Plan were significant. Carter explained to the dignitaries and national media that "the minority contractors on this airport comprise 80 percent of all the minority contractors on all the airports in the United States combined." Importantly, the president placed the achievement in context of Atlanta's "progressive" policies on race:

> Mayor Hartsfield many years ago made a famous statement that Atlanta was a city too busy to hate. That was a time when there was indeed a lot of hatred, and it was a remark that swept through the South and made possible many of the achievements that have led to this great day. There's no better way to remember him and

to characterize what he meant and what Ivan Allen meant and what Sam Massell meant and what Maynard Jackson means than to name this airport after him.[28]

As typical in any claim that Atlanta was the South's "most racially progressive city," this declaration ignored widespread and protracted resistance to the celebrated event (in this case, the role of MBEs in the airport renovation). Although Carter was supportive of Jackson, the city's most powerful forces unfurled an intense, expensive struggle against affirmative action. The Herculean efforts of Jackson's administration against inveterate resistance highlight the resilience of Afro-self-determinism rather than any pervasive sense of enlightenment found in the putatively racially progressive "Atlanta." Much like the remarkable success of the city's black colleges and universities or the upscale black suburbs, the successes of the Jackson administration were in spite of local organized neo-Confederate hostility to black advancement. The gaze should rightly shift to the efforts of those who envisioned, implemented, and realized the efforts, not the phantom community of Atlanta's racially progressive whole. Yet the aspirational tenor of the president's speech—as well as that of the slogan itself—is important in shifting popular sentiment and softening hostility to widening opportunities. The fact that both conservative Republicans like Nixon and liberal Democrats like Carter could equally endorse affirmative action proved important to the expansion of the Atlanta Plan across the country.

At the federal level, there were efforts to expand black access to public contracts as well, including a federal law passed in 1977 that created procurement standards for minority businesses. Still holding only a miniscule proportion of the billions in federal contracts, MBEs increased their procurement from $9 million in 1969 to $250 million in 1974. The modest expansion of black economic development through this law prompted some businesses to file lawsuits across the country claiming "reverse racism." In November 1979 the US Supreme Court heard one such case. Several months later, the court issued its decision (*H. Earl Fullilove v. Philip M. Klutznick*) that federal efforts at affirmative action were constitutional. This ruling, coupled with the praise of the overwhelming success of Jackson's efforts, triggered a wave of affirmative-action efforts nationwide. All but fourteen states and nearly two hundred municipalities created MBE programs modeled after the Atlanta Plan by the close of the decade.[29] Federal contracts with MBEs increased from 3.4 percent in 1980 to 8.3 percent by 1994.[30]

The significance of Jackson to the spread of MBE policy expansions across the country cannot be overstated. He was referred to as the "Michael Jordan of black business." Russell argued that Jackson was "like Dr. Martin Luther King Jr. when it came to ensuring African Americans got a chance to participate in the nation's economic marketplace." The Atlanta Plan was so important that its successes "got the attention of black mayors, and some white mayors, in other major cities like Detroit, Los Angeles, Boston, and Chicago. [Jackson] helped put us on another plateau in terms of our dollar volume, the larger jobs, and getting joint ventures with major contractors that would not look at us before. He opened the doors where we otherwise would have been shut out."[31] As seen after other black advancements resulting from public policy, intense challenges to modify or curtail those policies continued. Despite some earlier failures in legal challenges to affirmative action, lawsuits unfolded on various levels throughout the 1980s.

In 1989 the Georgia State Supreme Court ruled that Atlanta's affirmative-action program had failed to provide "convincing evidence" that its program addressed a legacy of discrimination against white women and people of color. Although this was a blow, it did not end the program but created the need for adjustments in the future. An officer in the National Association of Minority Contractors praised the Atlanta Plan and its survival, recognizing how significant it was for the country. It was the "granddaddy of affirmative action programs" because it demonstrated the possibilities of the political economy and it inspired local, state, and federal policies. It continued to do so for decades.[32]

Despite its extraordinary achievements in widening business opportunities to black firms, the Jackson administration still faced significant challenges. In late 1978, more than four years after Jackson took office, the *Los Angeles Times* reported on the troubled landscape of Atlanta in an article written by left-leaning white journalist Robert Scheer. Neither a black nationalist nor a white conservative set against black liberal politics, Scheer unveiled a city full of the sorts of contradictions and mythmaking that had always characterized Atlanta. The "Black Mecca" was a "60 percent black city that floats in a sea of white suburbia whose inhabitants desperately avoid contact with the untouchables."[33] Atlanta was not the shining city on a hill, demonstrating to the world the success of black electoral power and the efficacy of black leadership in the veritable capital of the South. By 1980, Atlanta had a higher poverty rate than any US city except Newark, New Jersey. In 1983, even the city's planning director explained the development as more myth than fact: "If you look at the statistics on a five-county metropolitan basis, Atlanta looks like the booming Sun Belt. . . . But based on the city limits, we look like Newark. It's that simple." Actually, Atlanta's population losses exceeded Newark's.[34]

Despite the propagation of Atlanta exceptionalism among black people (not just elites), the city was burdened by poverty, crime, and inequality as few major cities had ever been. The Scheer article was a shocking revelation to many boosters who continued to spin the narrative of Jackson's success, which in many ways was bound to the hopes of black people across the country who had anticipated witnessing the transformative impact that principled, strong, unequivocally pro-black leadership could realize.

Beyond the challenges with white antipathy, poverty, crime, and white flight, Atlanta received national attention for the horrifying murders of black children. In what became known as the Atlanta murders (or the Atlanta child murders), at least twenty-eight people, most of them children, were victims of what was believed to be a serial killer. Six victims were between twenty and twenty-eight years of age. The youngest victim was seven. Between July 1979 and May 1981, the bodies of mostly poor black children were found in wooded areas, lots, and buildings in the Atlanta area. The murders caused a maelstrom of criticism regarding the city's ability to protect its most politically powerless people. The mayor issued a citywide curfew, and police patrols swept streets. Local people organized vigilance groups.

The mayor offered a reward of $100,000, which was increased to $500,000 when heavyweight boxing great Muhammad Ali added $400,000 to the offer. With hundreds of Atlanta police and FBI agents on the case for more than a year, Wayne Williams, a twenty-three-year-old black man, was arrested in June 1981 and charged with two murders. After his conviction, the cases of the other twenty-six victims were closed. Although debates and conspiracy theories circulated, the murders stopped after his arrest.[35] Through it all, the Black Mecca narrative, though painfully tarnished, endured.

After the tragedy of the murders, the *Los Angeles Times* article's larger critique did not quickly fade from memory. It soon appeared as if the Scheer article was the first in an onslaught of depressing data on Atlanta. Shortly thereafter, the *Atlanta Journal-Constitution* produced its own examination of Atlanta. In the fifteen years after the violent racist protests against integration of restaurants and the recalcitrant white response to the integration of hospitals and schools, as well as the steady white flight from the city, Atlanta had become mostly black, with a black municipal structure and new access to city employment. Yet under these circumstances, whites still controlled 95 percent of the city's wealth. A review of the boards of directors of more than fifty white-owned firms revealed that whites made up 89 percent of directors in the Black Mecca. And although African Americans had access to high-end housing and enjoyed swaths of middle-class, majority-black communities, the city boasted the highest percentage of public housing per capita in the country.[36] In addition to the persistence of black poverty and the concentrated wealth in the white community, the specter of crime loomed across the city. In the same year that the *Los Angeles Times* article pulled back the curtain on the facade of Atlanta's success, the FBI reported that the city had the highest crime rate of any US city with a population of more than 250,000. It was also the murder capital of the country. The *Wall Street Journal* went as far as to call the city's downtown a "war zone."[37]

Despite the disappointing statistics, the list of achievements from Jackson's time in city hall was long and impressive. The municipal structure, its services, and its employees had been transformed. The succeeding mayor, former congressman and US ambassador Andrew Young, held the office from 1982 to 1990. He built on Jackson's successes and similarly reached out to a largely unreceptive white business community when he told the chamber of commerce, "I know none of you voted for me. . . . That's over now. I can't do what I need to do without you. I need your help." A Howard University alumnus and New Orleans native, Young made bureaucratic processes for building permits easier. In his first three years, he approved twenty thousand projects, a record number. As an *Esquire* article in 1985 wrote about Young's leadership as Atlanta's second black mayor, "Andy Young . . . is doing for Atlanta what Reagan has done for America: he is making rich white people feel good again."[38] For the first five years of his tenure, metropolitan Atlanta led the United States in job growth. Delta, Home Depot, United Parcel Service, and Cable News Network are examples of Atlanta's ability to attract top employers and Fortune 500 companies.[39] When Young ran for reelection in 1986, he won by an overwhelming 80 percent of votes cast, capturing the majority of the white vote as well. With his international connections, he successfully helped court over $70 billion in private investment while advancing the

Atlanta mayor Maynard H. Jackson Jr. (right) introduced an aggressive policy to open municipal contracts to black-owned firms known as the "Atlanta Plan." This transformed the political economy and provided a model for cities (and the federal government) across the country, despite intense opposition from local corporate leadership. Andrew Young, his successor (left), proved successful in drawing corporations into the region while extending Jackson's policies, solidifying the Atlanta Plan for subsequent administrations.
CREDIT: MICHAEL PUGH/ATLANTA JOURNAL-CONSTITUTION VIA AP

Atlanta Plan's policies that saw MBEs thrive. In 1990 he, along with white businessman Billy Payne, led the successful bid for Atlanta to host the 1996 Summer Olympic Games. Importantly, Young promoted the city for its "history of racial harmony" and its ability to showcase the best of what the South and the United States could offer the world.

Many people outside the African American community also recognized the successes. In contrast to the scathing coverage of the *Los Angeles Times* in 1978, national media began to send plaudits Atlanta's way. In 1987 the *Christian Science Monitor* noted that Atlanta had become the "mecca of the black middle class." The article highlighted the successes in black business, but it placed the achievements in historical context, with black colleges at the center: "From the orbit of the colleges, Atlanta developed an elite, a wealthy and educated black aristocracy, unmatched in any other American city." These schools graduated "generations of the best and brightest, from Martin Luther King Jr. to four out of five black members of the local Fulton County Commission."[40] The lucrative business contracts with the city were a significant point of celebration, as *Black Enterprise* magazine also stressed in May 1987. Among the scores of large cities in the country, *Ebony* listed Atlanta in its top five for black firms. The accolades put the city at the front of a reverse migration of African Americans leaving northern and western cities for the South. Between 1970 and the 1996 Summer Olympics, African Americans poured into metro Atlanta, increasing their population by 158 percent.[41] However, the expanding sense of promise was not limited to black people. In that same time, white population in the area increased by 78 percent. The highly visible successes in Atlanta—especially in bold business projects—were testimonies to the possibilities of black political power.

There is no question that Maynard Jackson's impact as mayor was consequential not only for Atlanta but also for municipal governments across the country. He had succeeded in opening access to the political economy to African Americans as no mayor had done anywhere else. Mayor Young and the changing dynamics of race then made Jackson's model more attractive than ever.

Perhaps it was the allure of being a political innovator and maverick that drew Jackson back into politics. In 1990 he successfully ran for mayor again, beating his former political lieutenant and Fulton County commissioner Michael Lomax. He governed through the explosive growth of the metropolitan area, its airport, and the city's maturity as the Black Mecca, leading into the preparation for the 1996 Summer Olympic Games, setting Atlanta on the world stage as never before. In 1994 through 2002, Bill Campbell, his successor, though not an alumnus of an HBCU or a native of Atlanta, continued the tradition of

supporting the city's black institutions. He oversaw a dramatic reduction in the violent crime rate and the hosting of the Summer Olympics.
However, his second term was dogged by allegations of corruption. The
city had received a ten-year, $250 million federal program to improve
more than thirty of the city's poorest neighborhoods. Subsequent
reports from the US Department of Housing and Urban Development
and the Georgia Department of Community Affairs found interference from Campbell, waste, and ineptitude.[42]

In many ways, Atlanta, like most US cities, was no paradise. It was
burdened with rates too high in every negative category: crime, poverty, and housing pressures. However, the facts were that the Gate City
of the early twentieth century did not look as violent, racially polarized,
or poor as had its earlier versions. Like any movement—freedom, civil
rights, affirmative action—advancements were met with resistance
from forces hostile to disruptions to the old order. Those would not
relent, even as conditions improved in most sectors of Atlanta and its
metropolitan area. Most notably, as discussed in Chapter 11, there were
serious struggles over who would control city hall and the immense
resources that it regulated.

11 | Atlanta in the New Century
Beyond the Novelty of Black Mayors

> Blacker than a Panther, blacker than Atlanta. . . . Mighty like the builders
> of the pyramids in Africa.
>
> —Blackalicious, 2015

What had once been heralded as a remarkable political feat became a norm: a black mayor of Atlanta had come to be expected—and accepted—by most Atlantans by the start of the twenty-first century. New York, Chicago, Los Angeles, Philadelphia, Houston, Seattle, Baltimore, and Dallas, as well as hundreds of small cities and towns, had elected black mayors since 1973. The election of Shirley Franklin in 2001 was distinguished by her being Atlanta's first woman mayor and the first black woman mayor of any major southern city. A former commissioner of cultural affairs under Maynard Jackson, Franklin saw her successes as mayor lead her to national acclaim. In 2005 *Time* named the Howard University alumna as one of the five best big-city mayors in the country, among other national awards, including recognition for elevating Atlanta to one of the cities with the most LEED buildings for environmentally responsible, energy-efficient design. Under her administration, crime declined while investments grew. She was even in contention for a World Mayor honor. Franklin rode a tidal wave of support to a second term with an astounding 90 percent of the votes cast.[1] In 2007 the city launched a partnership to build a massive museum, the National Center for Civil and Human Rights, to showcase to the world Atlanta's role in the struggle for social justice. Mayor Franklin selected Doug Shipman, who is white, to be the center's first chief executive officer. Crime rates continued to track a national trend downward through her second term. In Franklin's last year of office, 2009, Atlanta saw the lowest number of homicides in the city since 1963.[2] By many measures, the racial tensions, violence, and wave of big-city problems appeared to give way to the sort of progress, stability, and opportunities for which many had longed. No Atlanta mayor in history could boast a record of garnering such electoral popularity across gender, racial, and class lines.

In 2009 Franklin's former campaign manager, State Senator Mohammed Kasim Reed, another Howard alum, decided to run to be her successor. Among other candidates, his major opponent was Mary Norwood, a white city council member and Buckhead resident. A white mayor of Atlanta had seemed out of reach decades earlier, but the racial landscape of the country had shifted considerably since Maynard Jackson's first victory. Many majority-white cities had black mayors, and the mostly white country had a black president. Majority-black cities such as Detroit and Gary had elected white mayors. But in the Black Mecca, what would become of the decades of celebrated black municipal leadership? The black appointments and the aggressive affirmative-action programs with successful minority business enterprise (MBE) records? On Election Day, November 3, 2009, Norwood won more votes than anyone else in the race. At 46 percent of the total votes, she achieved precisely the same percentage of votes that Jackson had won in 1973. Like Jackson, however, she did not secure an initial victory. A runoff with Reed was set for December 1. With 84,000 votes cast, the election was so close that a recount delayed the final result until December 9, when Reed was declared victor by 714 votes.

A native Atlantan, Reed had won a slim victory and inherited a city with a declining crime rate, an expanding metro with growing investments from Fortune 500 companies, and a reversal of decades of population loss. Yet, various challenges still confronted city hall. Under Mayor Andrew Young, the Atlanta Police Department, in its effort to reduce historically high crime rates, created a special unit, Red Dog, to target drug dealers. The aggressive police unit soon became notorious for its brutality and possibly extralegal activities. By the end of the first decade of the twenty-first century, the complaints against the unit for verbal and physical abuse had become a cacophony of alarm from citizens across the areas where the Red Dog squads were most active. Cristina Beamud, executive director of the Atlanta Citizen Review Board, which investigated complaints against police abuse, explained that the board had received "a disproportionate number of complaints about officers who belong to the Red Dog unit as opposed to officers involved in the zones." Chief of Police George Turner explained that "crime—and the drug trade in particular—has gotten more sophisticated, often moving indoors. We, too, have gotten smarter, using technology and intelligence-driven analysis to strategize and shift resources as needed. But let me be clear: That does not mean there still isn't a need for aggressive, street-level crime-fighting—there is."[3] Complaints against the Red Dog squads persisted. In February 2011 Chief Turner, with Mayor Reed's support, announced that the Red Dog Unit would be disbanded. Even a majority-black police force under black administrators could not prevent allegations of abuse against black people.

Simultaneously, the city was reeling from the real estate bubble and the Great Recession. However, it was not among the worst-hit areas.

Among the top-ten largest metros, Atlanta had the sixth-highest fore-closure rate in the country, at 2.04 percent, half the rate of the Washington metro and significantly lower than Miami's 7.08 percent.[4] On the positive side, Reed inherited a thriving and growing television and film industry, which offered copious opportunities to extend the narrative of the city as a cultural center for black America.

Atlanta's cultural landscape has always been extraordinarily rich. Yet that landscape changed dramatically with the rise of African American leadership. In 1974 Mayor Jackson created the city's Bureau of Cultural Affairs. It provided grants and other assistance for artists across platforms, including music, visual arts, drama, and literary arts. It was created in the era of the black power movement, and one cannot disentangle the influence and importance of the bureau from its historical context. A city that had trafficked in hagiographic Confederate traditions for more than a century was under African American leadership for the first time. In the loyal slaves of *Gone with the Wind*, the grinning and dancing magical Negroes in *Song of the South*, the Ku Klux Klan klaverns, and Stone Mountain's massive Confederate monument, the Gate City had a storied tradition of white-nationalist celebrations in popular culture and leisure. Of course, streets, neighborhoods, and parks, from Collier Hills to Ben Hill to Grant Park, have been institutionalized reminders of the city's Confederate heritage. In the same vein as his efforts to open the city's closed access to black firms in city contracts, Jackson charged the new Bureau of Cultural Affairs to widen the cultural representation of the city.

Even as street names were changed to represent the fullness of Atlanta's history of black and white citizens, the popular cultural representations shifted from romantic homages to the Confederacy to a broader expression that included black artistic work. Though not explicitly, the bureau advanced black art in particular, even as white artists always received funding and support as well. Ultimately, the new office, in conjunction with tax incentives from the Georgia Entertainment

Industry's Investment Act, "served as the expressive arm of perceived black political and economic power resulting from Jackson's affirmative action initiatives," as Maurice Hobson explains. Transformative effects of the bureau were felt in various arts. Hundreds of artists, venues, centers, schools, theaters, and organizations received grants to aid the production of programming that elevated the city and enhanced its national reputation as a cultural hub.

In 1988 the Fulton County Arts Council and the Fulton County Commission, under the leadership of Michael Lomax, founded the National Black Arts Festival. Twenty years later, after drawing millions to the city through its annual festivals, the US Congress recognized the NBAF for its importance to the "cultural fabric of greater Atlanta and all of America." Artists across the spectrum of creativity transformed the city into an extravaganza of black expression: Maya Angelou, Wynton Marsalis, Bill T. Jones, Nikki Giovanni, and Gregory Porter. Hosting plays at the 14th Street Playhouse in Midtown and jazz, modern dance, ballet, African dance, blues concerts, and arts and crafts in Piedmont Park, the NBAF has been one of dozens of anchor events that have promoted the city's Black Mecca authenticity.

Music emerged as one of the most visible art forms to emanate from the city. Alternately called the "Motown of the South" or the "Music Capital of the South," the city became a center for music production, especially in R&B and hip-hop, generating over half a billion in revenues per year. *Rap Capital: An Atlanta Story*, published in 2022, is a nearly four-hundred-page tome on Atlanta's music scene. Its author argues that the Gate City continues to have a disproportionate effect on American popular music, shifting the regional importance away from New York and Los Angeles in the process.[5] The city is home to a long list of artists, as well as black-owned studios, production companies, and record labels. The presence of Gladys Knight, OutKast, Toni Braxton, TLC, Usher, Goodie Mob, Ludacris, T. I., Future, 2 Chainz, 21 Savage, and Migos means that Atlanta's impact on music is profound.

Black-owned labels—LaFace, So So Def, the Infamous BMF, Konvict Musik (Akon), RBMG (Usher), Freebanz (Future), and Grand Hustle (T. I.)—continue to shape America's popular culture.[6] Many artists who are not Atlanta natives, such as Mariah Carey, Steve Harvey, and Janelle Monáe, have relocated to the city, drawing in other high-profile entertainers. Along with Miami, New York, and Los Angeles, Atlanta looms large as a site for glamour, leisure, and excess for African American cultural trendsetters and creatives.

Given the prominence of popular music, it is not entirely surprising that TV and film production also took root in the city. In 2006 the breakout *Real Housewives* franchise debuted with an all-white cast of affluent wives in Orange County, California. Two years later, *Real Housewives of Atlanta* debuted with the franchise's first majority-black cast. Through the show, which centered on the lives of the affluent housewives and their families in the Atlanta area, viewers were introduced to a world of conspicuous consumption and excess, on par with the other versions of *Real Housewives*. Of course, the obvious difference was not only the black cast but also the black denizens of the show's supporting cast: real-life family physicians, lawyers, stylists, event planners, restaurateurs, personal assistants, therapists, and personal trainers. The people were not actors cast as extras in a fictional black utopian world. The overwhelming blackness showcased a world that is largely unseen anywhere else. The show was a great success, eventually earning higher ratings than all other shows in the franchise, and it emerged as the highest-rated show on the Bravo network. More than twenty black Atlanta-based reality shows have debuted since the first year that *Real Housewives* aired, highlighting a veritable "Wakanda" of Afro-self-determinism: black physicians (*Married to Medicine* and *Atlanta Plastic*), black real estate titans (*Ladies Who List*, *Married to Real Estate*, and *Selling It: In the ATL*), and black music executives (*Love and Hip-Hop: Atlanta* and *Growing Up Hip-Hop: Atlanta*).[7] It is notable that no other city boasts the draw that the "Hollywood of the South" has for black reality shows, consistently underscoring how visible the city has become as a center for black popular culture.

In 2016 no other US city had as many TV projects and film work outside of Los Angeles and New York. Georgia television and movie production, which has grossed more than $9.5 billion for the state, is centered in metro Atlanta, which has established the Mayor's Office of Film and Entertainment. Like most Atlanta municipal departments, the office is under black executive management. In fact, two black women, Cardellia Hunter and Phillana Williams, serve as comanagers of the office.[8] Atlanta has consistently reflected a level of black executive leadership rarely seen in other cities anywhere.

One of the largest film-production studios in the country is based in Atlanta and is owned by a black billionaire, Tyler Perry.[9] Because of TV shows or films such as *Being Mary Jane*, *Surviving the Pole*, *Black Ink: Atlanta*, and *ATL*, the brand of Atlanta has been conspicuous to such an extent that in 2016 the immensely talented auteur Donald Glover, an area native, launched one of the most critically acclaimed TV shows, aptly named *Atlanta*. The Black Mecca narrative has become so popular that a major tourist industry has developed around attracting the African American business-meeting and tourist market. Black tourists frequently travel to the city for leisure or business, making it the number-one or number-two black tourist destination in the country during the last twenty years. There is no doubt that the centrality of Atlanta in popular culture has continued to promote the Black Mecca narrative.

In clear, quantifiable measures, municipal control of the city became firmly black after Jackson's first election as mayor. The city council has been majority black since 1977. Between 1976 and 2020, all but one of the council presidents were black. Since the 1970s, the Atlanta Public School Board has been majority black. By the late 1980s, most municipal employees were black.[10] A clear effort to expand contracts and employment to African Americans shaped the political economy as whites left the city and the proportion of blacks in Atlanta peaked at 67 percent in 1990. For generations before the era of black mayors, the city refused to allow black Atlantans a wide range of resources, including use of the city's public libraries, even as they supported them with their taxes. W. E. B. Du Bois famously protested this practice when the eminent scholar resided in the city. In 1959 Irene Dodd Jackson, Maynard's mother, was the first African American to secure a library card at the city's previously restricted Central Library. By the twenty-first century, the library system had grown considerably, modernized, expanded its mission, and had successive black executive leaders. The current executive director and 55 percent of the members of the Fulton County Library System Board of Trustees are black.

However, systematic promotion of the city's exceptional, bold, and explicit blackness could be problematic, especially for nonblacks. Because people, across racial lines, generally do not wish to be excluded from the mainstream, the city's emphasis on blackness, though attractive to many African Americans, was less so for others seeking their own affinity with Atlanta. Ultimately, the idea of Atlanta as an open city where all people, of any race, could thrive and be visible in many spheres became critical to city leadership. An unspoken sense of resolve to forge a new narrative was necessary, and the Olympics provided the opportunity to do so on a grand scale. The fact that the two most important players in securing Atlanta for the 1996 Olympic Games were a black man and a white man further confirmed the new narrative that the city was an exemplar of racial cooperation, even if the races remained "separate as the fingers" in most social intimacies across the metro area. Some suggested "Olympic City" as the city's newest nickname.[11]

The Olympic City/Black Mecca continued to draw more black transplants than any other city in America, and the power of the ballot was visible through the city's governance.[12] Along with the expanding percentage of black people in the city, there was a massive influx of black people into suburbs. Notably, most newcomers to the area (of any race) settled in the suburbs, transforming and expanding the abstraction of "Atlanta." By the mid-1990s, the municipality of Atlanta represented only 13 percent of the metropolitan region's three million people, which distinguished it as the smallest core city of any major metropolitan area in the country. By the mid-2000s, an influx of nonblacks lowered the percentage of African Americans in the city. Conversations circulated about how much longer the city would be majority black.

In 2007 Mayor Shirley Franklin, speaking to a political symposium in New York, remarked that some were "concerned" about the declining percentages of black people in the city: "It's not spoken about much, but there are concerns that we will lose, as African Americans, our political base, which has largely been the city of Atlanta for major leadership within the state." Of course, there was immediate outcry from those who found concerns over increasing numbers of nonblacks to be misguided. The fact that Atlanta is a hospitable city for the country's increasing diversity is essential for the business of attracting tourists, investment, and general growth, many insisted.[13]

In accordance with demographic shifts to the suburbs, 57.5 percent of black-owned firms in "Atlanta" were not even in the city limits by the end of the 1990s. About a quarter were in suburbia, near their customer base. Black business owners moved outside of the city and were highly likely to employ black workers, more than a fifth of whom came from low-income, inner-city neighborhoods. Reflecting the demographic shift of black people to the suburbs, black employers on average had a suburban workforce that was 85 percent black, higher than the percentage of black employees in the city.[14]

By the early twenty-first century, literally dozens of articles, videos, and other popular media had focused on Atlanta as the veritable capital of black America. In 1997 *Ebony* revisited Atlanta's status as

Black Mecca, even calling it the "land of milk and honey" for black people. According to a poll of the magazine's one hundred most influential African Americans, Atlanta was rated as the overall best city for blacks, and it "possessed the most employment opportunities for blacks." Although many cities had a higher percentage of black people, or percentages that more closely reflect the national rates of Latinx and Asians (both underrepresented in Atlanta according to the 1990 census), the Gate City was also called America's "most diverse city."[15] Surprisingly, it was lauded for being the city with the best schools and most-affordable housing for blacks. In line with the historical accolades directed at the city, these modern hagiographic claims were rarely accompanied by scientific metrics. Did the city have the best schools for black children? What were the graduation rates? Test scores? Rates of college attendance after graduation? What about poverty rates or homeownership rates? These and other metrics were omitted.

The boosterish stories proliferated. Some of the praise, especially regarding businesses, had merit. These accounts were often tied to the highly successful affirmative-action efforts of city hall. No one else was more visible than Herman J. Russell. From the 1960s to the twenty-first century, Russell had literally shaped the landscape of Atlanta. Because of middle-income apartment complexes, higher-end ones, academic buildings on college campuses, and skyscrapers, the H. J. Russell Company would become the largest black-owned construction company in the United States, largely as a result of the Atlanta Plan. Many black firms scaled up over time to tackle massive projects that had previously been unavailable to them. Other black-owned firms, such as C. D. Moody Construction and Bryson Constructors, emerged later, becoming some of the largest construction companies in the city, regardless of race. These two companies alone have had projects that have netted billions in revenue since the 1980s.

The impact of the construction projects in and around Atlanta has shaped the iconic skyline. The Georgia-Pacific Tower, completed in

1982 and standing at nearly seven hundred feet, was constructed by a joint venture between the H. J. Russell Company and the white-owned J. A. Jones Construction Company. It was the second-tallest skyscraper in the city for several years. The Mercedes-Benz Stadium (home to the Atlanta Falcons NFL team), State Farm Arena (home to the Atlanta Hawks NBA team), Coca-Cola's global headquarters, college and university buildings, and terminals at Hartsfield-Jackson International Airport are some of the notable landmarks built jointly or solely by black developers in the Black Mecca. When the city hosted the world for the 1996 Olympic Summer Games, eighty thousand cheering fans witnessed the former Olympian Muhammad Ali light the flame in the Olympic Stadium (later Turner Field, home of the Atlanta Braves MLB team from 1997 to 2016), which was built, in part, by black contractors. A black firm even emerged as one of the official apparel makers of the Summer Games. Throughout the Olympics, hundreds of thousands of spectators, athletes, government officials, and tourists arrived at the Atlanta airport, which itself showcased Afro-self-determinism to the world. In addition to being the busiest airport in the world, it was under black executive control and had mostly black employees. Its contracts with black firms exceeded all other United States airports *combined*. No other US city comes close to boasting a skyline, three professional sports stadiums, or a major airport fully or partly constructed by black firms.

Russell, who was born poor in segregated Atlanta, became a prominent financial backer of the black freedom movement, was a personal friend of Martin Luther King Jr. and other freedom fighters, and later emerged as one of the city's wealthiest residents and a power broker beyond his hometown. Governors, presidents, congresspeople, and others have sought his support and time. Among many firsts, he became the first black member (and president) of the Atlanta Chamber of Commerce and the Capital City Club. He also served as chairman of the board of Citizens Trust Bank, one of the oldest black banks in the country.

Michael H. Ross, CEO of MHR International, a construction-management company, explains that Russell is a national titan of black business who elevated the visibility of black economic power and potential. Ross, who has worked with cities across the country as a consultant on procurement policies, is a son of professors at Clark Atlanta University. An alumnus of Morehouse, he explains that many municipalities want to achieve the metrics established in Atlanta. The city's reputation of widening economic access has been so significant that he was the only US consultant on a South African procurement task force established by President Nelson Mandela. Ultimately, South African president Thabo Mbeki developed a "black economic empowerment program" that was partially inspired by the Atlanta Plan.[16]

The circulation of black business success stories, such as Russell's, bolstered the narrative of Atlanta exceptionalism, which had, since the black power movement, taken on a significant focus directly tied to financial opportunities for black people. Beyond its black-dominated municipal affairs or even its reputation as a black-majority city, Atlanta had emerged as a city sui generis. It was not a deindustrialized city hollowed out by white flight and the loss of manufacturing jobs, left with a professional class of black people who operated as managers of a crumbling, stressed municipal structure that was overextended, underfunded, and overburdened by poverty, crime, and diminished tax dollars. The city was much more than this cliché. Atlanta was not a tale of two cities but rather a tale of multiple cities—large enough to contain various running narratives of success and failure, of black power and white power, of black political exceptionalism and disproportionate white economic power. Through it all, the political economy and the role of affirmative action proved essential for carving out black access to what had been closed spaces reserved for whites only. Throughout the city's rise in national visibility, mainstream media continued to take notice of the city's conspicuous black success stories.

In 2003 a CBS *60 Minutes* segment, "Going Home to the South," explored the extraordinary appeal of the Gate City. It showed marvelous visuals of the well-manicured lawns of large homes in suburban subdivisions with pools, tennis courts, and basketball courts. From afar, these communities looked similar to affluent, mostly white suburbs outside the majority of American cities. Located in the suburbs to the south, east, and west of the city, these were almost completely black, however. According to the *60 Minutes* report, "Black suburban Atlanta may look like Beverly Hills, but it's Mecca for many new migrants who are buying homes worth from $200,000 to more than $2 million [$320,000 to $3.2 million in today's dollars]. And new subdivisions keep sprouting, marketed especially to blacks." Featuring several black families, the report was clear that many, if not most, were transplants from other cities, especially from the North. "I blazed a trail to get out of New York," explained one transplant. "I just wanted a better way for my kids."[17]

The rise of upscale black subdivisions was not an accident. Like many other features of the city's landscape, an explicit Afro-self-determinist politics played a role in the proliferation of these neighborhoods. Upscale black residential areas or suburbs are not unique to Atlanta. Los Angeles's Baldwin Hills, Ladera Heights, and Windsor Hills enclaves; Chicago's Pill Hill and Chatham; and Harlem's Sugar Hill are high-socioeconomic-status (SES) black neighborhoods that have existed for generations. However, every one of those transitioned from white to black. Atlanta areas such as Guilford Forest, Camp Creek Parkway, Beazer Homes Cascade Place, and Wolf Creek Chase were black since inception. "We were intentional about that," explains Rodney Strong, former director of contract compliance for the city of Atlanta.[18] In the late 1980s, Atlanta's high-SES black areas included sections of Ben Hill, Collier Heights, and Cascade Heights. Ben Hill was particularly prominent. In fact, its namesake, the infamously racist Confederate congressman Benjamin Hill (discussed in earlier chapters), would be astonished to know what happened in an area bearing his name. These neighborhoods became home to old-guard African American leaders in business, education, electoral politics, and even professional sports. Herman J. Russell, Martin L. King Sr., Benjamin Elijah Mays, and MLB great Hank Aaron called these sections home. But the expanding demand for new housing from the growing black middle class required new construction. In the mid-1980s, Greg Baranco, an African American owner of a local car dealership, became one of the lead developers of a sixty-six-home residential subdivision, Sandstone Shores, in Decatur. Around the same time, Guilford Forest was built. These became the largest upscale new black subdivisions in the area since Collier Heights. Their immediate successes demonstrated to banks, realtors, and developers the potential for upscale black subdivisions in the region.

Since the late 1980s, more than twenty middle- to luxury-level black housing developments have been established throughout the metro area. One of the newest, Stonecrest Estates, expanded in 2021, with sprawling mansions on impressive lots in an overwhelmingly black area of DeKalb County. The rise of these stretches of black residential opulence has been heralded as proof of the city's claim to exceptionalism. There are even videos of virtual tours of these communities on YouTube and other social media for people to appreciate. In many ways, the swaths of black suburban affluence feed the narrative of black opportunity, which draws more migration, particularly highly skilled African Americans seeking to optimize their resources. Simultaneously, however, even lower-skilled black people have moved into the metro area, helping to significantly expand the numbers and class diversity of black folks throughout the region. The draw is so great that the black community, purely by its enormous size, affords multiple black communities where a variety of class, culture, politics, sexuality, and religion can thrive.

After the Civil War, black churches became some of the most important institutions forged in the city. In addition to some of the earliest churches (First Congregational Church, Friendship Baptist, Big Bethel AME, and Ebenezer Baptist Church), a series of black megachurches have emerged in metro Atlanta. Megachurches are defined as churches having congregations of more than two thousand members, and Atlanta's metro is home to one of the highest concentrations of black megachurches anywhere.[19] Each week, World Changers Church International draws several thousand people into its 8,500-seat World Dome in College Park and many more virtually. New Birth Missionary Baptist Church has a weekly attendance of 12,000 people in Lithonia, outside of Atlanta. Some of these churches, such as Ebenezer, underscore the importance of a social-justice ministry. Ebenezer draws attention to its history of activist work from the days of former senior pastor Adam Daniel Williams, who was a cofounder of the Atlanta NAACP, through the time of Williams's grandson, Martin Luther King Jr. Black-nationalist churches, such as the Pan-African Orthodox Christian Church, anchor their messages of social justice and "nation building" in sermons and practice, whereas World Changers had, until 2022, put emphasis on the "prosperity gospel," which states that people are rewarded with wealth and material comfort when they demonstrate their faith. Other groups, such as the Nation of Islam and the African Hebrew Israelites, highlight the profound black religious diversity of the city. Though not without critics and controversies, these institutions have remained a constant force of important activity in the black community. Black churches have erected apartment complexes and have promoted health care, scholarships, farms, businesses, and voter-registration drives, remaining deeply engaged with and central to the social, cultural, and political ecology of the city, much as they were a century earlier.

For black LGBQT+ persons, the city has drawn members into a vast community of kindred folk. Multiple publications have regarded Atlanta as a gay-friendly city, whereas others have highlighted its status as a Black Mecca for gays. One blogger writes that "Atlanta became the

Black gay mecca, the most Wakandian of the Black gay metropolises." In 2010 *Advocate* ranked the Gate City as the number one on its "Gayest Cities List," beating out San Francisco, often hailed as a gay mecca. Although Atlanta lost its top spot on subsequent *Advocate* lists, in 2013 the Human Rights Campaign gave Atlanta a perfect score on its Municipal Equality Index. It has received many other awards, reflecting its status as an open, progressive space for LGBTQ+ people. Laypeople often overstate the percentage of gays in the city, but multiple studies, including a Gallup project and a UCLA Law School report, find that the percentages of gays in Atlanta are close to the national average, around 4.5 percent. Because only one metropolitan area in the country (New York) has more black people than Atlanta, it follows that the black gay community would be particularly robust and institutionally supported. Atlanta Black Pride, established in the 1990s, has become one of the largest such events in the country. In its nightclubs and social and intellectual spaces, the city offers a particular "warmth and hospitality" that feeds the community's growth in newcomers.[20]

The sheer size of metro Atlanta's black population makes it significant for almost any subset, subculture, or industry of black America, but no endeavor has as much significance as higher education. As discussed throughout this book, African Americans from across the country have been drawn to the transformative powers of Atlanta's black colleges and universities for generations. In turn, many of these people have contributed to the rich social, political, and cultural ecology of Atlanta. They have enriched the city, thereby making it more attractive to others who might consider the schools for education or employment. Few cities in the country graduate more black college students each year than Atlanta.[21] After desegregation, most of these schools have continued to thrive, some even becoming richer and more successful than the vast majority of white colleges.

By the twenty-first century, Atlanta had expanded its position as a center of black education, even beyond the Atlanta University Center.

Among the thirty-six largest metropolitan areas, only Washington, DC, has a higher percentage of African Americans with college degrees (32 percent, compared to Atlanta's 28 percent).[22] In addition to the storied histories of the highly rated and renowned HBCUs in Atlanta, there are more than a dozen other colleges in the Atlanta metro area. Georgia State University, once a whites-only school for commuter students, now enrolls and graduates more black students than any other brick-and-mortar university in the country, including, of course, any HBCU. Although Georgia State is not an HBCU, its student government, social programs, and general student culture are unlike most traditionally white schools. Student government and homecoming courts are very diverse but also disproportionately black. Brian Blake became its first black president in 2021, overseeing a vast educational enterprise of more than 54,000 students, scores of degree programs, and ten schools and colleges, including law, business, and arts and sciences. Its Andrew Young School of Policy Studies is named after Atlanta's second black mayor. With several high-ranking black administrators, GSU is the largest school in the state and one of the top-ten largest universities in the country. It also ranks fifth nationally in the granting of doctorates to black students.[23]

Another formerly majority-white school, Clayton State University (CSU), was founded in the 1960s and was never for whites only, unlike Emory, Georgia Tech, or many other schools in the area. Like Georgia State University, CSU, several miles south of Atlanta, has attracted a huge volume of black student applications, making the student body nearly two-thirds black. Compared to the private schools of the Atlanta University Center, CSU (like Georgia State) is significantly cheaper, while affording students access to both Atlanta and a heavily black and generally supportive collegiate environment. It also hired its first black president, T. Ramon Stuart, in 2021, who was succeeded by another African American, Georj Lewis, in 2023.

Of course, the HBCUs have expanded and matured in remarkable ways since the election of one of their own alumni as the city's first black mayor. In addition to expanded academic programs within these schools, the Morehouse School of Medicine (an institution fully independent from Morehouse College) was established in 1981, becoming one of four majority-black medical schools in the country. Spelman College has emerged as the wealthiest wholly private HBCU in the country, and it draws some of the most competitive applicants.[24] It simultaneously has the highest ratio of black students of any college or university (around 99 percent) and the highest graduation rate of any HBCU, exceeding the white national average graduation rate by nearly twenty points. It has a per-capita student endowment higher than nearly 90 percent of all colleges and universities, even higher than Georgetown, Tulane, and the University of Southern California.[25] Morehouse College is the fourth-richest HBCU, and it produces more black male graduates who eventually earn doctorates in STEM, humanities, and social sciences than any other school in the country. Both Spelman and Morehouse produce a higher rate of students who eventually earn graduate degrees than do most other colleges. Notably, Spelman outperforms five of the eight Ivy League universities in the rate of black graduates who earn doctorates in STEM.[26] Clark Atlanta University (formed from a merger of Clark College and Atlanta University in 1988) is the largest of the Atlanta University Center (AUC) schools and attracts talented students from across the country in an array of programs, including its celebrated communications major and its business school. Collectively, the nine accredited HBCUs in Georgia generate a total impact of $1.3 billion for the local economy.[27]

Despite the successes of the other schools in the AUC, Morris Brown College lost its accreditation in 2002. It was burdened by mismanagement, scandals, and a paltry endowment before reducing its operations sharply as it tried to reorganize. When it lost its accreditation, it was removed from the Atlanta University Center Consortium, which, among other things, meant that it lost access to the shared resources of the member schools, including the AUC library.

For years, fewer than fifty students were enrolled. The city, as well as Invest Atlanta, the city's economic development agency, provided critical financial assistance in the years following the school's precipitous decline. Morris Brown successfully regained its accreditation in 2022.

In some respects the story of the AUC represents a microcosm of the Black Mecca. When people think of the extraordinary achievements of black people in the city, the successes are celebrated and become the official story, at the expense of the examples that belie the grand narratives of success. The growth, opportunities, and impressive feats of the primarily black women who lead Spelman College are deservedly praised. The extraordinary troubles of Morris Brown's mismanagement, fiscal precarity, and even criminal negligence do not neatly fit into the praises heaped upon the city's black colleges. Similarly, the Atlanta Public Schools scandal shook the city in recent years.

In July 2011 the Georgia Bureau of Investigation (GBI) indicted thirty-five Atlanta public schoolteachers over a massive cheating scandal on standardized tests. According to the GBI, 178 teachers in 44 of 56 schools altered exams to boost school scores. Most teachers took plea deals, and a dozen went to trial.[28] Nearly every defendant was black. This story, like that of Morris Brown, competes with narratives of black excellence. In a society with waves of negative and depressing news, feel-good narratives have a special appeal. Yet fictional narratives of a black utopia can obfuscate problems, evade policy change, and stymie reform and political action.

Despite the occasional negative news, scores of thousands each year migrate to the Atlanta metro area, drawn to the same positive qualities promoted in the popular press: exceptional opportunities for black people. Rodney Strong, who has long played an important role in aiding the political economy under multiple administrations, has become one of the most prominent agents of what was once known as the Atlanta Plan. In 2022 Strong, who entered politics by campaigning for Maynard Jackson's first mayoral bid in 1973, won the Distinguished Service

Award from the Atlanta Business League. A recipient of numerous awards and honors, the former director of contract compliance has become a nationally recognized consultant on disparity studies, public policy, and compliance. He and his firm have advised mayors, city councils, governors, and corporations across the country on the need for and strategies to design and implement public policies to widen economic development for people of color. His shining example for policy makers has long been his adopted hometown, Atlanta. Strong is clear: "No city has achieved what we have done here regarding opening doors and generating black economic development."[29]

The continued attraction of highly skilled African Americans to Atlanta is what Strong calls a "virtuous cycle." This cycle, he details, follows the publicity surrounding a major appointment (or series of appointments) of black CEOs or heads of major segments of the city and county governments, including the areas of public safety, education, and law. The visibility of these figures, Strong explains, underscores Atlanta's reputation as open to black success and opportunity, drawing talented, ambitious, and resource-rich African Americans into the city. The process traverses industries. Recently, tech has enjoyed this virtuous cycle. Local African Americans in tech have gained so much visibility that in 2019 *USA Today* declared Atlanta to be the nation's "black tech capital."[30] According to Strong's comments, the city's reputation as an educational center, tech center, and business center for African Americans would necessarily attract ambitious, highly trained black professionals, perpetuating the virtuous cycle. Whatever the factor, black transplants to metro Atlanta have been significant.

More than a half million African Americans migrated into the area between 2000 and 2010 alone, pushing the total black metropolitan population to 1.7 million. They represented the largest net gain of any racial or ethnic group in the region. And much of the migration has involved highly skilled and educated workers. In Atlanta the rate of African Americans with a bachelor's degree is 40 percent higher than the national average.[31] Atlanta in 2020 was the ninth-largest metropolitan area in the United States, but it ranks second—only to New York City's metropolitan statistical area—in black residents, having more than two million people. Communities that were once known as notorious centers of white-supremacist activity, such as Stone Mountain and Forsyth County, became integrated by the influx of African Americans and other people of color from both the city and other parts of the country. Professionals—white and black—who sought strong school systems, large homes, and affordable luxuries found these communities attractive.

As is typical of the story of Atlanta, these positive statistics are more complicated when seen in relation to the bigger picture. Atlanta is strained by environmental and infrastructure pressures, and, for swaths of the city, concentrated poverty. Although Atlanta has more black businesses and black millionaires per capita than any other US city, it also has the lowest rate of social mobility and greatest wealth disparity among American cities. A child born into poverty in Atlanta has only a 4 percent chance of escaping poverty in her lifetime.[32] By 1990, Atlanta had one of the highest ratios of citizens—10 percent—who lived in public-housing projects. These were often veritable war zones with exponentially high levels of crime. As part of what some have called the "Olympification" of the city, the Atlanta Housing Authority, under chairperson Renee Glover, secured federal funding to destroy much of the public housing and provide residents with vouchers to live in mixed-income areas. In 2011 the first American city to erect public housing became the first to tear down all public-housing projects.[33] Whereas the rate of black affluence increased after 1970, the black poverty rate had risen as high as 35 percent in 1990 before dropping to 28 percent in 2020, only 1 percent lower than in 1970.[34]

Under black administrative control, the city of Atlanta has struggled to make significant progress on reducing black poverty, even as black affluence has increased. For a decade, census data have shown that among cities of more than a hundred thousand people, Atlanta has the largest gap between the poor and wealthy. Poverty has been persistent in the city, although it is much lower in the suburbs. As noted in the data here, it is less a case of poor Atlantans (mostly black) being pushed out of Atlanta as much as more-affluent Atlantans (also mostly black) moving to the suburbs. When the wealth gap is measured among US metropolitan areas (including both a city and its suburbs), Atlanta plummets from the top spot of inequality down to number 227 on the list, far better than dozens of major cities, including Houston (117) and New York City (39). Atlanta's metropolitan area includes, of course, the huge swaths of black upscale subdivisions and integrated neighborhoods stretching across over twenty counties, where African Americans represent approximately one-third of metro residents.[35] Herein lies the increasingly abstract notion of what "Atlanta" is. It is much more than the 136 square miles of its municipality. For most people, "moving to Atlanta" means moving to its metropolitan area because of being drawn by the promises of success and opportunity. Hence the "Black Mecca" is more capacious than the half-million people living in the core of this sprawling urban abstraction. Suburban success stories prevail, but the city, though making notable strides, still struggles in its own way.

Of course, the city alone could not cure all social ills. Scores of grassroots organizations and local branches of national nonprofits have attempted to address the exigencies faced in Atlanta. Some of the wealthiest black Atlantans have been at the forefront of these efforts. Founded by the Herman J. Russell Foundation, the Russell Innovation Center for Entrepreneurs (RICE) seeks to replicate the extraordinary business successes for which Atlanta is known. It provides resources and training, connects investors, and offers grants to create black business development among communities most isolated from traditional methods of investment. Jay Baily, president and CEO of RICE, notes that the disturbing data on black poverty and social immobility demand creative solutions. Baily explains that the city, with its deep wells of talent, has the "greatest potential to get it right."[36]

Challenges notwithstanding, the allure of Atlanta has recently brought into the city the highest percentage of whites since the 1970s. Reflecting national trends which find that today's whites and blacks are not nearly as opposed to integrated neighborhoods as earlier generations were, the racial landscape of the city has continued to evolve. The city peaked in population in 1970 with 496,973, before experiencing a steady decline, driven mostly by whites moving to the suburbs. More than 120,000 whites left Atlanta between 1970 and 1990. Between 1990 and 2000, however, more than 7,300 whites moved into Atlanta, whereas the number of blacks decreased by nearly 26,000. By 2010, continued influx resulted in another 9,504 white people. Simultaneously, the black movement into spacious, middle-class, and upscale suburban areas accelerated as black migration into the metro area continued. Clayton County, south of the city, increased from 24 percent black to 51 percent between 1990 and 2000, and DeKalb County increased its black population from 42 percent to 53 percent. In all, the number of black people who lived in the surrounding suburbs increased by more than one million between 1980 and 2000. Over the next twenty years, the metro Atlanta black population increased by an additional 67 percent. Explosive growth continued into the twenty-first century: Atlanta hit 498,715 in the 2020 census—more people than any other point in its history—and the metro area ballooned to more than six million people.[37] The city of Atlanta was, after fifty years, growing again.

Although some have argued that black people were leaving the city (for various reasons), between 2010 and 2020 there was a net *increase* of black people into the city, even as the black population in the suburbs also increased. Two things were occurring at the same time: an influx of black people into the city and a much larger influx into Atlanta of nonblacks. In fact, there were 21,502 additional African Americans in the city between 2010 and 2020, even as the black percentage of the city decreased from 54 percent to 49.8 percent. The proportion of black Atlantans dropped not because there were fewer black people. It was largely because of the influx of whites, Latinx, and Asian Americans who, collectively, outpaced black in-migration. During this decade, there was also the loss of scores of thousands of black residents to secession.[38] In 2017 a middle-class area in southwest Atlanta, which included parts of black neighborhoods such as Ben Hill and Red Oak, seceded from the city, becoming the state's eighth largest city, South Fulton. Around 90 percent of South Fulton is African American. It became, according to the 2020 census, the blackest city of more than one hundred thousand people in the country. Sixty-seven percent are black homeowners, 59 percent higher than the national average of 42 percent. If the city's population had remained in Atlanta, 2020 would have had recorded more black residents than at any other point in the city's history.[39]

The diversification of the Gate City demographically reflects the increasing diversity of the country as a whole. With larger numbers of Latinx and Asians, it is no longer the archetypal racially bifurcated southern city, although it remains the second-most-segregated city in the country.[40] On the other hand, some of the suburbs reflect unprecedented residential integration. The segregation index of the Atlanta Regional Commission region dropped from 77.4 percent to 46.9 percent. For the Atlanta metropolitan statistical area, residential segregation declined from 68.8 to 48.3 percent. Gwinnett County, once overwhelmingly white, is now one of the most diverse counties in the region; its integration index (the likelihood that two randomly selected households in the same census tract will be of different races) is the highest of any Sun Belt metro area and higher than the richly diverse Kings County, which includes Brooklyn. By 2020, more than seven times as many African Americans lived in the suburbs and exurbs of Atlanta than in the city. Eight of the eleven counties around Atlanta are majority people of color, and most are majority black. Only Cherokee, Forsyth, and Fayette have a white majority.[41] Metro Atlanta has been transformed as an extension of the Black Mecca.

Despite cries of blacks being "pushed out" by white newcomers or by what has nebulously been called "gentrification," the actual data do not reflect any black exodus—of the poor or otherwise. The destruction of public housing, which took place from 1996 to 2011, relocated thousands of people from blighted areas of highly concentrated poverty, drug addiction, and violence. Throughout that period, the overwhelming majority of former public-housing residents remained in the city—between 80 and 85 percent, according to research from Georgia State University.[42] Simultaneously, crime continued to plummet, dropping to historic lows. In fact, at the start of 2011 the homicide rate had dropped around 50 percent from the 1999 level. By 2019, the rate remained roughly comparable to the 2011 level.[43] Black home ownership has also increased as property values have increased. Black home ownership stood at 42 percent in 1980 and has since increased by 16.6 percent to 49 percent, seven points higher than the rate under the first black mayor. It is also 16.6 percent higher than the black national average.[44] Nationally, the city ranked in the top ten among cities with the largest increases of black home ownership. In fact, many of the gentrifiers have been black. In communities across the city, African Americans have been among the higher-income newcomers moving into new apartments, new condominiums, or renovated homes in the West End, Adair Park, Midtown, and other areas. In 2022 Atlanta led the country in new apartment constructions. A few old industrial sections of the city have been transformed, including Atlantic Station and Castleberry Hill. The latter, near the Atlanta University Center, was once home to blighted factories and shops. The area now has a new Paschal's Restaurant, a hotel, and dozens of shops, art galleries, restaurants, and bars. It remains largely African American, although it, like many places in the city, enjoys a diverse clientele of whites, blacks, Latinx, and Asians.

The largest such transformation is the industrial park in Midtown that became the upscale, mixed-use community of Atlantic Station.[45]

Developed on the site of the Atlantic Steel Mill Station, originally built in 1901, Atlantic Station is a standard example of gentrification. A partially abandoned brownfield site in 1974, it was a run-down area with little housing or opportunities for commerce or leisure. The developer, Jim Jacoby, assumed an ambitious task: to create a walkable district with mixed-used development of higher-end apartment rentals, a large movie theater, a bowling alley, restaurants, sports bars, and space for open-air concerts across 138 acres. This community would be anchored by high-rise office buildings and two glistening upscale high-rise condominiums, the Atlantic and the Twelve, the latter being partially a hotel. Opened in October 2005, the area eventually became a significant entertainment space for the city. Most visitors are black, but the clientele continues to be a racially and ethnically diverse one. The occupants of the two new upscale condo developments are largely blacks and other people of color. There is probably no other city in the country that can boast the creation of brand-new, high-end, glistening condominium skyscrapers in prime city locations with mostly black residents.

However, Atlanta continues to be variegated by class and race in incredibly complex ways. Atlanta's racial disparities are gaping. Some people have attempted to focus more on the persistence of black poverty in a city politically dominated by black people rather than on the rise of black affluence. The poor have been overlooked in the grand narrative of black success, they argue. Larry Keating, a professor of city planning and specialist on Atlanta, argues that "even after African Americans gained control of the city government black elected officials largely ignored the problem of black poverty."[46] This attention to stark class differences in the city is not novel. Years earlier, Julian Bond, a veteran of the civil rights movement, explained that "for poor black people without resources, circumstances are no different" in Atlanta than in any other city.[47] Despite the "higher than" rates that black Atlantans have relative to African Americans elsewhere, black Atlantans trail their white counterparts in nearly every positive index and lead them in nearly every negative one: infant mortality, poverty, home ownership, and life expectancy. In fact, most Atlantans—across racial lines—perceive the racial wealth gap as significantly lower than what it actually is in the Atlanta metro. They believe black household wealth to be 40–63 percent of white wealth, but it is actually 10 percent of white household wealth.[48] Racial wealth gaps have not disappeared in the Black Mecca.

Even with these data, Rodney Strong, who has played an important role in shaping the city's aggressive and effective affirmative-action policies, offers a nuanced disagreement with his friend and mentor Julian Bond: "I think that it is not entirely that dismal for African Americans with less training or education. Many of the jobs created [through municipal and country government efforts traced back to Maynard Jackson's model] have benefited working class black people without college degrees." To make his case, Strong points to the airport. In 2002 *Ebony* praised the successes of the airport, noting that around "90 percent of the contracts that go to minority-owned firms that do business with American airports are at Hartsfield."[49] In 2003, four months after Maynard Jackson's death, the city council changed the name of the airport to Hartsfield-Jackson Atlanta International Airport. It has been the busiest airport in the world each year since 1998."[50] With more than 63,000 employees, the airport is the largest employer in the state and generates $83 billion for the Atlanta metro economy. It has been under an unbroken line of executive black leadership since the mid-1980s, and it holds the notable achievement of scores of honors and awards for its management and innovation. In 2021, for the eighteenth consecutive year, the Air Transport Research Society celebrated Hartsfield-Jackson as "the most efficient airport in the world." The Airports Council International awarded the airport the prestigious 2021 Airport Service Quality Award for "Best Airport by Size and Region (over 40 million passengers per year in North America)." In a metro region that is 34 percent black, about 75 percent of the airport's employees are black. Far from regulated to menial jobs, African Americans are pervasive at every level of the airport's administration, even in its contracts with outside firms. The airport, Strong explains, provides access to the middle class for those without college degrees.

Although there is no debate that black poverty has persisted in Atlanta, there is little debate that the black business community has also thrived in the city. Consistently, the city ranks at or near the top for being the best city for black-owned businesses. By 2015, Atlanta led all US cities in its ratio of black-owned businesses. Only New York state had more black-owned businesses than Georgia. Across multiple years, *Forbes* magazine has listed Atlanta as the city where "African Americans are doing the best economically." *Nerd Wallet*, *Smart Assets*, and other financial publications have rated the Gate City at the top of their lists for black economic promise and opportunity. By 2020, black-owned firms in Atlanta employed 62,000 people and produced almost $7 billion in average annual revenue. A study released in 2022 surveying seven criteria in 124 cities found Atlanta to be in the top five "best cities for black-owned businesses."[51] Still, black capitalist enterprise, despite whatever remarkable successes and advancement that have been achieved, has not been a panacea for black people—even in Atlanta. Poverty and stark inequalities persist. But one measure of the fidelity in black leadership and the successes achieved in the black political economy in the region may be found in the unbroken line of black municipal control. Atlanta's seventh consecutive black mayor, Andre Dickens, was elected in 2021. A graduate of Benjamin E. Mays High School, Dickens was born in Atlanta the same year that Maynard Jackson first took office. He is the city's first mayor to have always lived under a black mayor. Today, Atlanta remains one of only three cities of more than 250,000 residents (along with Washington, DC, and Newark, New Jersey) to share the distinction of having only black mayors for nearly fifty years.

By the start of the twenty-first century, Atlanta was firmly ensconced in the popular black imagination as the nation's veritable black capital. With a robust social, political, cultural, and economic landscape, the city itself—not just any segment of the city—was widely perceived as black. Unlike New York, Chicago, or Los Angeles, there were not sections (such as Harlem, Southside, or South Central) relegated to the black experience. There were no provincial signifiers of black space for non-Atlantans. "Atlanta" serves as the signifier of black space. Even a hit rap song from the early 1990s, "Guerillas in the Mist," which celebrated its black-nationalist bona fides, did not use in its lyrics the group's hometown, South Central Los Angeles, or even the nearby Compton. "J. D. is blacker than a city called Atlanta," the line proclaimed. Years later, Bay Area MC Blackalicious similarly rhymed that he was "Blacker than a panther / Blacker than Atlanta." In 2015 the comedic duo of the Comedy Central TV show *Key & Peele* offered a series finale of rich social commentary. A sublime musical skit depicted a black man being magically transported to an Edenic all-black city. His tour guide cheerfully sings that he is in a place "where there ain't no pain and no sorrow. It's the place to be if your skin is brown. . . . I'm talking 'bout Negrotown." Confused about his whereabouts, the man asks his guide, "Negrotown? What, like Atlanta?" The guide smiles, "Almost." Ultimately, the city is a figment of his imagination that is prompted after a racist cop renders him unconscious with a head injury.[52] Although multiple municipalities (Memphis, Baton Rouge, New Orleans, Baltimore, etc.) have higher percentages or higher raw numbers of black people, saying "blacker than Cleveland" does not evoke the same meaning in popular culture.

For well over a decade in the 2000s, when all travelers exited the busiest airport on Earth, they rose on the escalator and were greeted by an expansive, colorful wall depicting a beautiful, smiling black girl with open arms welcoming everyone to Atlanta. Visitors to smaller airports, such as JFK in New York or LAX in Los Angeles, could see a similar warm welcome from a black child, but its meaning in the Gate City strikes a special chord. It invites visitors familiar with the city's history to recognize a particular past meeting the present, wrapped with triumph, defeat, destruction, and resurgence. More than anything else, however, there has always been the optimistic Atlanta spirit, rife with hope, promise, contradiction, tension, and drive. And although the city has always promoted itself as modern, it has never, at any point, ignored the power of history in shaping its present or future.

Even in the putatively Black Mecca, Confederate legacies are everywhere, including the current and several previous iterations of the state flag. As noted earlier, in 1956 the state incorporated the Confederate battle flag to protest desegregation. In 1992 Governor Zell Miller announced plans to change the flag, but without much success. Leading up to the 1996 Summer Olympic Games, activists burned the Confederacy-inspired state flag. In 2003 Governor Sonny Perdue authorized the legislature to draft a new flag. Eventually, the Georgia General Assembly returned to its original flag, which itself was modeled after the Confederacy's national flag. In October 2017, following the violent protests of neo-Nazi, Klan, and neo-Confederate white supremacists in Charlottesville, Virginia, Atlanta mayor Kasim Reed formed a committee to identify and make recommendations about what to do with various Confederate landmarks in the city.[53] The city and its people continue to grapple with its past and its legacies.

Through various struggles in the second decade of the twentieth century, Atlanta has emerged as a massive metropolitan area of six million people—larger than Connecticut and Rhode Island combined—a global hub of commerce, entertainment, education, science, and technological innovation. It is, for many, a shining city on the hill, a testimony to America's ability to transcend the most painful circumstances of racial hatred, violence, and undemocratic traditions. Doug Shipman, the first CEO of the National Center for Civil and Human Rights

(NCCHR), notes that institutions across the city at every level have been transformed over the last half-century. The Junior League, the formerly all-white group that hosted Confederate celebrations in honor of the *Gone with the Wind* premiere, has a local chapter membership that is around one-third women of color. Shipman, who successfully ran for city council president in 2021, explains that his service and engagement on various civic, nonprofit, and corporate boards reveal how different Atlanta is from most cities. The city, despite shortcomings, is not marked by token representation: "Rarely are boards only black or only white." From the Woodruff Arts Center to Piedmont Park and Habitat for Humanity, there is a large proportion of African American membership.[54] In January 2022, Shipman, who led the NCCHR for eight years, became only the second white president of the city council since 1976. A year later, the famed *Atlanta Journal-Constitution*, former journalistic mouthpiece of neo-Confederate nationalism and home of Henry Grady, announced its first black editor-in-chief, Leroy Chapman Jr.

In the suburbs the influx of African Americans has also transformed areas once known for their Confederate legacies. In 1993 Charles Burris, the former student of Martin Luther King Jr., won a seat on the Stone Mountain City Council. The former imperial wizard of the Klan, James Venable, who served as Stone Mountain mayor in 1946–1949, was among the many residents whom Burris convinced to host a campaign sign in their yard. An attorney and former analyst for Mayor Jackson, Burris was elected mayor of the former Klan stronghold in 1997. His election marked the rise of black municipal control in suburbs throughout the metro area. "There's a new Klan in Stone Mountain," Burris told the *New York Times*. "Only it's spelled with a C: c-l-a-n, citizens living as neighbors. And I guess I'm the Black dragon." Venable died before Burris became mayor, but Burris had become close to members of the Venable family, even agreeing to purchase the grand wizard's home. Burris was particularly amused to learn that Venable

and King shared the same birthday. In the shadow of the largest Confederate monument (and the second-largest tourist attraction in the
South, following Disney World), the new mayor made an agreement
with Venable's daughter to halt the annual Labor Day cross burnings at
the base of Stone Mountain.[55]

Although the nearly 80 percent black town of Stone Mountain has
no authority over the Confederate monument, which the state owns, in
2019 the Stone Mountain City Council voted to rename Venable Street
to Eva Mamie Lane, after two black leaders of the city. Two years later,
Stone Mountain elected its second black mayor in its 180-year history:
Beverly Jones, a graduate of Morris Brown College. Its chief of police,
superintendent of schools, and heads of many other municipal departments are African American. A century ago, Venable was a schoolmate
of Nathan Bedford Forrest III at Lithonia High School during the
heyday of the Second Klan. By 2022, the previously whites-only school
was mostly black with a principal, Darrick McCray, who had settled in
the area after graduating from Morehouse College.

Years earlier, Chuck Burris reflected on his election as mayor and
on the vast ways in which Atlanta and its surrounding areas were transformed in his lifetime. Many of these changes were unimaginable
when he first sat in a class to listen to King teach or when he cast his
first vote for Jackson: "This area is rich in history. Some of it is painful
to many people. I want to deal with those facts in a way that people can
[benefit] from. This should be a place where everyone can come to the
table, not just black and white residents but also Hispanic and Asian."
Burris reflected a bit and added, "The place has a tricky history."[56]

EPILOGUE

Dancing with the Past
Looking Ahead in Atlanta

By the time Atlanta had been popularly recognized as a veritable capital of black America in the 1990s, no single site in metro Atlanta attracted more visitors than the Stone Mountain Confederate monument. Located fifteen miles east of Atlanta, it had practical and symbolic significance. It is a massive quartz monzonite dome monadnock with opportunities for expansive sight lines to the engravings. It was also the site of the rebirth of the Second Ku Klux Klan, founded by William J. Simmons on Thanksgiving Day, 1915. Monetary restrictions prevented the engravings of scores of Klansmen, but a massive ode to Jefferson Davis, Robert E. Lee, and Thomas J. "Stonewall" Jackson officially opened on April 14, 1965—exactly a century after the assassination of Abraham Lincoln. It was also only weeks after the infamous Bloody Sunday march for voting rights in Selma, Alabama, drawing global attention to a huge swath of the South's hostility to democracy. Just as the nation debated securing a law to grant all Americans access to the vote, the monument to enslavers and white nationalists opened to great fanfare. This massive structure became the largest Confederacy monument anywhere; it is the largest bas-relief sculpture in the world, even larger than Mount Rushmore. In addition to annual Klan cross burnings and Confederate heritage tours, it emerged as an anchor tourist landmark for Atlanta itself, drawing as many as four million visitors annually. Although it opened in the midst of the civil rights movement, it was not completed until 1971, just as the black power movement was achieving greater reach throughout the country.

The year Stone Mountain was completed, *Ebony* magazine first bestowed a new sobriquet on Atlanta: "the Black Mecca." The Confederate statuary throughout the Black Mecca invited grassroots challenges by activists and politicians alike. In 1992 a group of students from local colleges, Students for Afrikan Amerikan Empowerment (SAAE), gained statewide media attention for demanding a removal of the Stars and Bars and even burning the state flag. Although SAAE was involved with more issues than the state flag, the efforts to change the state flag piqued media attention, with coverage from the *Atlanta Journal-Constitution* in the summer of 1992. The coverage involved death threats directed at three of the most visible members who were pictured in the newspaper: Kevin Donaldson and Lawrence Jeffries, both rising juniors from Morehouse College, and Stacey Abrams, an eighteen-year-old rising sophomore from Spelman College.

In 2018 Abrams, the former eighteen-year-old featured in the 1992 flag-burning controversy, was a member of the Georgia House of Representatives and was then nominated as a Democratic candidate for governor. After hundreds of thousands of voters were purged from the rolls, she lost by fifty thousand votes. However, this loss set in motion her leadership in a massive statewide campaign that registered more than seven hundred thousand new voters, most of them black and Democratic. A year later, Abrams became the first black woman to deliver a response to the State of the Union Address.

In the 2020 presidential elections, the state of Georgia emerged as a critical part of a long, systematic effort to turn a Republican strong-hold into a win for the Democratic candidate. To the surprise of many Americans, the deeply Republican ("red") state was flipped "blue," largely because of the overwhelming turnout of voters in the Atlanta metro area. In fact, the turnout had been unprecedented and heavily African American. More black people cast ballots in the Atlanta met-ropolitan area than in any other area in the United States, smashing the previous records and significantly pushing the state toward the win column in the Democratic presidential campaign.[1] Joseph R. Biden Jr. achieved, with the help of black activists, the highest Democratic per-centage of Georgia votes for a presidential race since Governor Jimmy Carter won in 1976.

The get-out-the-vote efforts of Abrams continued to manifest during a runoff election for two US Senate seats. As in 1864 and 1964, politicians insisted that the nation was looking to Georgia to set the direction. The fate of congressional control rested on Georgia securing two Democratic senators: a long shot. Republican president Donald Trump visited Atlanta and campaigned for the members of his party, calling it "one of the most important runoff elections in the history of our country." Indeed, the nation remained fixed on the outcome, and pundits stressed how consequential the election could be. The Demo-cratic Party mobilized its forces and elevated Abrams as a major polit-ical force throughout the campaign. The same day that Trump spoke, Abrams met across town with Biden and with candidates Jon Ossoff and Raphael Warnock. Biden told crowds that the fate of the country lay in their hands: "One state can chart the course, not just for the next four years, but for the next generation." Another Georgia campaign was underway. On January 6, 2021, both Democratic candidates were declared winners in a massive upset, putting both legislative branches and the executive in Democratic control.[2]

An alumna of Spelman College, a school built on a former Civil War battlefield and designed especially for black women, Abrams offers a fascinating personal story and its relationship to Atlanta. Her activism regarding the Confederate battle flag increased her visibility, leading her to secure a job in the office of Maynard H. Jackson Jr. in the summer of her protests. She eventually ran in—and won—the election for the president of Spelman's student government. Her interest in law led her to Yale Law School and eventually to national attention as a political force. At home in Atlanta, she has embodied the ways in which history and the Confederacy, in particular, continue to shape the present. But, despite whatever enduring imprint the failed rebel experiment has, little is certain about the future.

On the very day that Warnock and Ossoff were declared the winners of the historic Georgia runoff, pro-Trump right-wing insurgents invaded the US Capitol building in an effort to undo the 2020 presidential election results. This was also the day that Joe Biden would be confirmed by the electoral college as the new president. Various white-extremist groups attempted to keep Trump in power on January 6, 2021, despite soon-to-be certified election results. As they attacked Capitol police with pipes, toxic sprays, clubs, and other blunt objects, there was little doubt that they also rejected what both Ossoff and Warnock represented: a Jewish man and a black man as the sole senatorial representatives from the formerly reliably red state of Georgia. One image of a Confederate flag-wielding intruder in the Senate chambers made international news, and various observers viewed it as a through line between generations of white insurgents since the Civil War.

Only days after the Capitol attack, from the pulpit of Ebenezer Baptist Church, Senator Warnock connected the dots. "We saw the crude, the angry, the disrespectful, and the violent break their way into the people's house—some carrying Confederate flags, signs and symbols of an old world order passing away," he said to a captivated and emotional crowd. Amid alternating emotions of exhilaration and frustration, the congregants listened as their pastor implored them to consider the historical context of his victory: "It doesn't matter if you're a Democrat or Republican. If you look with an honest eye at the history of this country and see this moment, you must know that this is a glimpse of God's vision, of a more inclusive humanity that embraces all of God's children." Like Martin Luther King Jr. before him, he shifted the gaze to a resistive and powerful vision that would reject the "signs and symbols of an old order." The past is never really absent, of course. But, he asked, "[On] this day . . . will you stand on the side of . . . justice and truth" to help supplant that old order? [3]

ACKNOWLEDGMENTS

Once, in graduate school, a friend joked that I should be on the payroll of the Atlanta Convention and Visitors Bureau because I praised the city so much: "You need to be fairly compensated for your work!" It was clear that four years of college in that city had a powerful effect on me.

I was born in Chicago but, from age six, raised in Los Angeles. In August 1987 I first arrived in Atlanta for my freshman year at Morehouse College. I remember walking through the airport and seeing a picture of its black chief executive as we exited into the humid night air. Over the course of the next four years, I came to love the city. It was quite different from other cities with which I was familiar. First, it was southern. Finding catfish and grits was never a challenge. The accents, the food, the sense of history made people distinctly aware of its southernness. Civil War markers were scattered across the landscape. Streets were named for Confederates, including Lee Street (for General Robert E. Lee) near Morehouse. The state flag then included the Confederate battle flag, a strong affirmation of the state's identification with the cause of nineteenth-century white southern nationalism.

Simultaneously, the city was already known as the "Black Mecca." Like the other two cities where I had lived, Atlanta had a black mayor. Although Chicago and Los Angeles each had more black people than the entire population of Atlanta, the Gate City was significantly blacker. It was over 65 percent black when I arrived, whereas blacks were minorities in the other two cities. African Americans were migrating into Atlanta and its suburbs in huge numbers. My cousins had recently relocated from Chicago. By the time I was in graduate school, friends from Los Angeles and cousins from both sides of my family had migrated to Atlanta. A friend from New York City said that so many black people from his North Bronx high school had moved to Atlanta that his graduating class holds "Bronx Day" class reunions in the Georgia capital.

Despite whatever homages to the Confederacy dotting the landscape, Atlanta reinvented itself as a major attraction to black people over the next three decades. Its black community is so vast that there is a large home for any segment. A conservative Christian could find a large community of kindred churchgoers in some of the largest black mega-churches anywhere. Simultaneously, exotic dancers have a robust community in what once was the strip-club capital of the country. Atlanta has the highest concentration of black millionaires and black-owned businesses, with expansive, majority-black upscale housing developments. It also has swaths of depressed, impoverished black communities with dilapidated housing. There are robust black communities of vegetarians, skiers, runners, and gun aficionados, and other large black communities of BBQ fans, bourbon lovers, blerds, writers, and artists of every corner of creative expression. You can find gospel and R&B artists in shared studio space with the grimiest rappers. I've always wanted someone to tell this story of black Atlanta—beyond the academic narrative of municipal politics. I set out to write a history of the last half century of Atlanta and its political and wildly diverse cultural contours.

What you have in your hands is not that book. Although I set out to write that book, over the course of nine years my work evolved into a history that explores how the Black Mecca emerged out of the Confederate project of the nineteenth century. Its temporal constraints went from focusing on a fifty-year history to exploring the entire arc of the city's history since the 1840s. I had to learn about the Civil War in ways that exceeded my study in graduate school. Along the twists and turns of this new project, some friends insisted that I seek a publishing agent. Thank you, Baz Dreisinger, for first sharing that insight. Manisha Sinha, Jelani Cobb, and Jacob S. Dorman similarly inspired me to think differently about the audience and scope of this book. Thank you, Charlotte Sheedy and Jessica Salky, for being fantastic agents, believing in and advocating for this project. Thank you, Kyle Gipson, for your enthusiasm for adding this book to the outstanding corpus of works at Basic Books. Your critical eye has made this project a much better one than what you first read.

There are so many people who have helped carry me through this process. My colleagues at the University of Connecticut were immensely helpful in providing me feedback and a space to research and write. No institution was as important as the UConn Humanities Institute and the fellowship that granted me a year to work on this book. I am also quite grateful for the Humanities Book Support Award, from the Humanities Institute as well. Michael Lynch, Richard D. Brown, Peter Baldwin, Micki McElya, Dexter Gabriel, and my many other colleagues are appreciated. A hearty thanks to Andra Gillespe, Carol Anderson, Leroy Davis, and the African American Studies Department at Emory University for the courtesy appointment, as well as the staff at the Emory Robert W. Woodruff Library. The amazing staff at the Atlanta History Center, the Atlanta University Center's Robert W. Woodruff Library's Special Collections, the National Center for Civil and Human Rights, and the Library of Congress were indispensable.

Fruitful writing and research for me cannot happen outside of social engagement peppered with my sharing of research. Many friends have entertained my ramblings about Atlanta history over the fire pit, good drinks, and more. Thanks to Adisa Iwa, Alex Torres, Kirk Bradley, Damon Scott, Anu B. Kemet, Ayize Sabater, Tokunbo Akinbajo,

Michael Mallery, Frank Moore, Wilford Samson, Wilner Samson, Wordy Samson, Ed Lewis, Robert Braswell, Ken Allyene, and so many others for the patience and ears. My cousin Melvin Collier, a leading professional genealogist, helped crack open the case of William Edward Evans, who features prominently in this book. I owe you, cousin! Dave Canton, Scot Brown, Ricky Jones, Monique Bedasse, Derrick White, Treva Lindsey, Fanon Wilkins, Khalil Muhammad, Gerald Horne, Derek Musgrove, and Amrita Chakrabarti Myers provided attention, sounding boards, and insight on urban history, Atlanta, and the South. My friends in Atlanta have, throughout the writing, added depth to how I've conceptualized and intellectually developed this project. Many thanks to Ken Williams, Antan Wilson, Kamau Forman, Jonathan Gayles, Eric Taylor, Akinyele Umoja, and Elyce Strong Mann.

So many scholars have produced incredible work on Atlanta's history. I'm pleased to have benefited from the insight, friendship, and work of Maurice Hobson, who remains faithfully engaged in the city's history in so many ways. I know of no Atlanta historian with a hand in so many institutions critical to the city's legacy than Karcheik Sims-Alvarado, who even helped with the cover art of this book. Many thanks to Kevin Kruse, David Levering Lewis, Tera Hunter, Winston Grady-Willis, Tomiko Nagin-Brown, Jay Winston Driskell Jr., Herman "Skip" Mason, and Marc Wortman for your important work as historians of this amazing city. The influence of the late Alton Hornsby Jr. continues to shape my scholarship in profound ways. Other influential scholars whose work has affected my understanding of race and urban spaces include Robin D. G. Kelly, Clarence Stone, Stefan M. Bradley, Charles Rutheiser, Pero G. Dagbovie, Michael Eric Dyson, Ronald Bayor, Peniel Joseph, Tom Davies, Richard Rothstein, Rhonda Williams, Lance Freeman, Keeanga-Yamahtta Taylor, and Brittney Yancy. Josiah Brown has been an important interlocutor to incredibly helpful people. Thank you, Rodney Strong, for your gracious devotion of time and attention for interviews. Thanks also to the titans, freedom fighters, and servants of the people, Andrew Young, Willie Mukasa Ricks, and Julian Bond, who spent time giving me personal insight into the richness of the Gate City.

For years, my family has endured my days at archives, in the office (Starbucks, campus, or home), at conferences, and more. I promised my son that one day the scattered collection of papers in piles and spewing from my printer would be a book: "Be patient, buddy. By the time you can read, it will be here!" My daughter took some of her early steps balancing and grabbing stacks of books in my office. She later found joy stomping on boxes of notes, channeling Rick James on Eddie Murphy's couch. Even in those moments, she brought me great levity. My mother, aunts, uncles, cousins, and Sandy and Art Miller have been a constant source of support and love. My in-laws—Vera and Asa Grimes and the Andersons—were always exceptionally generous with their time, listening to me eagerly share some new discovery, from General Sherman to Lugenia Burns Hope to Maynard Jackson. However, no one had to deal with more of this ordeal than my wife, Jeanna. From research trips, endless information about Atlanta, and hours in the office, she has been a standard-bearer of support. She has provided perspective and entertained and encouraged me through it all. A "thank you" seems too slight to capture the depth of my gratitude. Our shared humor, curiosity, love, and rare moments of quiet reflection carried this project across the line. I see what you do for me.

NOTES

Introduction

1. *CBS This Morning News*, January 5, 2021; "Trump Throws Grenades into High-Stakes Georgia Senate Runoffs in Final Stretch," *NBC News*, accessed January 8, 2021, www.nbcnews.com/politics/donald-trump/trump-throws-grenades-high-stakes-georgia-senate-runoffs-final-stretch-n1252672; "Trump's Efforts to Overturn Election, Rescue Senate Majority Collide in Georgia," *Politico*, accessed January 8, 2021, www.politico.com/news/2021/01/04/trump-biden-georgia-senate-runoffs-454533.

2. Most of the state's Democratic voters are black, and although Republicans are the majority, the Democrats' turnout surpassed the Republicans' in the runoff. Nate Cohn, "Why Warnock and Ossoff Won in Georgia," *New York Times*, January 7, 2021, www.nytimes.com/2021/01/07/upshot/warnock-ossoff-georgia-victories.html.

3. Wakanda is the name of the fictional country that is the home of Marvel Comics' superherocharacter Black Panther. It is a highly advanced utopian African nation that has successfully resisted Western imperialism. It was popularized in the 2018 blockbuster movie *Black Panther*, parts of which were filmed in Atlanta. Numerous articles in the popular press and comments in social media have referred to Atlanta as an approximation of Wakanda.

4. "Atlanta, Georgia (U.S.)," CRW Flags, www.crwflags.com/fotw/FLAGS/us-ga-at.html#sym.

5. Like advocates of other forms of nationalism (Bosnian, Basque, Irish, or Hutu, for example), advocates of white nationalism may not necessarily insist on the superiority of any race, although the sentiment generally suggests it. See Timothy Baycroft, *Nationalism in Europe, 1789–1945* (New York: Cambridge University Press, 1998); and Jeffrey O. G. Ogbar, "Black Nationalism," in *Routledge Handbook of Pan-Africanism*, ed. Reiland Rabaka (New York: Routledge, 2020), 89–100.

Chapter 1: Capturing the Heart of the Confederacy

1. "Railroad Towns," American History: From Revolution to Reconstruction and Beyond, www.let.rug.nl/usa/essays/1801-1900/the-iron-horse/railroad-towns.php.

2. "Hon. John C. Calhoun's Prediction," *Memphis Daily Appeal*, February 9, 1861. In 1853 Fulton County was formed from the western half of DeKalb County, where 90 percent of Atlanta is currently located.

3. Frederick B. Gates, "The Impact of the Western & Atlantic Railroad on the Development of the Georgia Upcountry, 1840–1860," *Georgia Historical Quarterly* 91, no. 2 (Summer 2007): 169–184; James A. Ward, "Power and Accountability on the Pennsylvania Railroad, 1846–1878," *Business History Review* 49, no. 1 (1975): 37–59.

4. Gates, "Impact of the Western & Atlantic Railroad"; Ward, "Power and Account-ability on the Pennsylvania Railroad." See also Paul DeForest Hicks, *Joseph*

Henry Lumpkin: Georgia's First Chief Justice (Athens: University of Georgia Press, 2002).

5. US Census, 1860, www.civil-war.net/pages/1860_census.html.

6. "Declaration of the Immediate Causes Which Induce and Justify the Secession of South Carolina from the Federal Union (1860)," South Carolina Secession Convention, https://en.wikisource.org/wiki/Declaration_of_the_Immediate_Causes_Which_Induce_and_Justify_the_Secession_of_South_Carolina_from_the_Federal_Union.

7. Stephen Davis, *What the Yankees Did to Us: Sherman's Bombardment and Wrecking of Atlanta* (Macon, GA: Mercer University Press, 2017), 18–21; Wendy Hamand Venet, *Commerce and Conflict in Civil War Atlanta* (New Haven, CT: Yale University Press, 2014), 181.

8. "Gov. Joseph Brown's Open Letter," Civil War Causes, accessed September 21, 2019, www.civilwarcauses.org/jbrown.htm.

9. "1860 United States Census, Slave Schedules," United States Census, 1860, District 85, Jefferson, Georgia, 464–465; "Alexander Stephens," accessed July 26, 2020, www.newworldencyclopedia.org/entry/Alexander_Stephens.

10. T. Conn Bryan, "The Secession of Georgia," *Georgia Historical Quarterly* 31, no. 2 (1947): 98.

11. Quoted in Thomas D. Morris, *Southern Slavery and the Law, 1619–1860* (Chapel Hill: University of North Carolina Press, 1996), 18.

12. Bryan, "Secession of Georgia," 93.

13. Quoted in Bryan, 103.

14. State of Georgia, "Georgia Declaration of Causes of Secession," *Journal of the Public and Secret Proceedings of the Convention of the People of Georgia*, January 29, 1861, https://web.archive.org/web/20150213033216/http:/civilwarcauses.org/reasons.htm.

15. *Atlanta Intelligencer*, March 21, 1866, 2.

16. *Atlanta Intelligencer*, 2.

17. David T. Dixon, "Augustus R. Wright and the Loyalty of the Heart," *Georgia Historical Quarterly* 94, no. 3 (Fall 2010): 365–368; Brian Melton, "'The Town That Sherman Wouldn't Burn': Sherman's March and Madison, Georgia, in History, Memory, and Legend," *Georgia Historical Quarterly* 86, no. 2 (2002): 201; Bryan, "Secession of Georgia," 98–100.

18. Quoted in Bryan, 103–104.

19. Quoted in Miles Parks, "Confederate Statues Were Built to Further a 'White Supremacist Future,'" NPR, August 20, 2017, www.npr.org/2017/08/20/544266880/confederate-statues-were-built-to-further-a-white-supremacist-future.

20. Jon Guttman, "Which States Referred to Slavery in Their Cause of Secession?," accessed January 17, 2018, www.historynet.com/which-states-referred-to-slavery-in-their-cause-of-secession.htm.

21. John M. Coski, "The Birth of the 'Stainless Banner,'" *New York Times*, May 13, 2013, https://archive.nytimes.com/opinionator.blogs.nytimes.com/2013/05/13/the-birth-of-the-stainless-banner.

22. Quoted in George Henry Preble, *Our Flag: Origin and Progress of the Flag of the United States of America, with an Introductory Account of the Symbols, Standards, Banners and Flags of Ancient and Modern Nations* (Albany: Joel Munsell, 1872), 535.

23. Quoted in J. William Harris, *Plain Folk and Gentry in a Slave Society: White Liberty and Black Slavery in Augusta's Hinterlands* (Baton Rouge: Louisiana State University Press, 1998), 65–66.

24. For a detailed discussion of the forms of codified segregation in the North in the antebellum era, see Leon F. Litwack, *North of Slavery: The Negro in the Free States* (Chicago: University of Chicago Press, 1965). See also C. Vann Woodward's classic *The Strange Career of Jim Crow* (New York: Oxford University Press, 2001 [1955]); and Stacey Close, "Connecting with the Ancestors," Hartford African American Heritage Trail, https://hartfordheritagetrail.org/historical-figures.

25. For years, scholars and laypeople alike have argued that various European ethnic groups were not legally understood as white in the US. Arguments that they were racially liminal, marginally white, or "near black" have circulated. Being poor, being called ethnic epithets, and being viewed as a threat to the native white social order have been used as justifications for the "almost white" thesis. All of these arguments avoid clear, unequivocal legal definitions of race that define people from any part of Europe as "white." No Irish, Italians, Poles, or Greeks have ever been legally banned from voting anywhere. No whites-only public university banned them. As noted in the text, all Europeans—Irish, Poles, Italians, and others, across religions—fought in all-white regiments in all of America's wars. Their whiteness was legally unequivocal, despite any cultural, social, or ethnic rivalries and tensions between various groups of whites. Despite ahistorical assumptions to the contrary, whiteness has never been dependent on all white people forging loving bonds of friendship, camaraderie, class equality, and cultural acceptance. Ethnic and class tensions have never nullified whiteness as a legal designation with substantive benefits exclusive to white people, including citizenship, access to land, housing, suffrage, education, testifying in court, marrying other whites when interracial marriage was illegal, and health care. For discussion of these debates, see Noel Ignatiev, *How the Irish Became White* (New York: Routledge, 1995); Thomas A. Guglielmo, *White on Arrival: Italians, Race, Color, and Power in Chicago, 1890–1945* (New York: Oxford University Press, 2004); Jennifer Guglielmo and Salvatore Salerno, eds., *Are Italians White? How Race Is Made in America* (New York: Routledge, 2003); Matthew Frye Jacobson, *Whiteness of a Different Color: European Immigrants and the Alchemy of Race* (Cambridge, MA: Harvard University Press, 1999); David R. Roediger, *Working Toward Whiteness: How America's Immigrants Became White: The Strange Journey from Ellis Island to the Suburbs* (New York: Basic Books, 2018); and Richard Rothstein, *The Color of Law: A Forgotten History of How Our Government Segregated America* (New York: Liveright, 2017).

26. William F. K. Marmion, "Generals of Irish Birth in the U.S. Civil War: The Complete List," *Irish Sword* 23, no. 91 (Summer 2002), http://irishamericancivilwar.com/generals.

27. Quoted in Leon F. Litwack, *Been in the Storm So Long: The Aftermath of Slavery* (New York: Vintage, 1980), 100–101.

28. Pamela Herr and Mary Lee Spence, eds., *The Letters of Jessie Benton Frémont* (Urbana: University of Illinois Press, 1992), 266.

29. Quoted in Ta-Nehisi Coates, "What This Cruel War Was Over," *Atlantic*, June 22, 2015, www.theatlantic.com/politics/archive/2015/06/what-this-cruel-war-was-over/396482.

30. Quoted in Edward H. Bonekemper III, *The Myth of the Lost Cause: Why the South Fought the Civil War and Why the North Won* (Washington, DC: Regnery History, 2005), 68.

31. John C. Calhoun, "Speech to Senate, August 12, 1849," https://web.archive.org

/web/20070123074414/http://www.claremont.org/publications/pubid.667/pub
_detail.asp.

32. For a wider exploration of slave patrols in the context of whiteness, citizenship, power, and class, see Sally E. Hadden, *Slave Patrols: Law and Violence in Virginia and the Carolinas* (Cambridge, MA: Harvard University Press, 2003); Jeff Farret, *Race Relations at the Margins: Slaves and Poor Whites in the Antebellum Southern Countryside* (Baton Rouge: Louisiana State University Press, 2010); and Harris, *Plain Folk and Gentry in a Slave Society*.

33. Henry Lewis Benning, "Speech of Henry Benning to the Virginia Convention, February 18, 1861," *Proceedings of the Virginia State Convention of 1861*, 62–75, http://civilwarcauses.org/benningva.htm.

34. Although most poor white southerners were loyal to the Confederacy, they were measurably less loyal to the rebel cause than was the planter class. Poor whites were more likely to desert and had lower casualty rates than those from slaveholding families. Unionist support was higher among whites from the hill country (where slavery was not common) and among poor whites. For discussions on class and the Civil War South, see Bonekemper, *Myth of the Lost Cause*, 28, 38.

35. Inter-university Consortium for Political and Social Research, "Historic, Demographic, Economic and Social Data: The United States, 1790–1970," 1977, www.icpsr.umich .edu/web/pages.

36. Ted Tunnell, "Confederate Newspapers in Virginia During the Civil War," *Encyclopedia Virginia*, accessed May 5, 2018, https://encyclopediavirginia.org/entries/newspapers -in-virginia-during-the-civil-war-confederate; Thomas Copper De Leon, *Four Years in Rebel Capitals: An Inside View of Life in the Southern Confederacy from Birth to Death* (New York: Time Life Books, 1984); J. Cutler Andrews, *The South Reports the Civil War* (Princeton, NJ: Princeton University Press, 1970).

37. "Federal Retaliation," *Carolina Spartan* (Spartanburg, SC), December 6, 1860.

38. John C. Inscoe, "Georgia in 1860," *New Georgia Encyclopedia*, www.georgiaencyclopedia .org/articles/history-archaeology/georgia-1860.

39. Among the five largest cities in the state, Atlanta had the smallest percentage of slaves. In the other cities (Macon included), about a third of the population was enslaved. The highest concentration of enslaved people, at 35 percent, was in the largest city, Savannah. Virtually all black people in the state, 99.3 percent, were enslaved in 1860. Most free blacks were in Savannah and Augusta. Inscoe, "Georgia in 1860."

40. "Southern Confederacy. (Atlanta, Ga.) 1861–1865," Georgia Historic Newspapers, Digital Library of Georgia, https://gahistoricnewspapers.galileo.usg.edu.

41. "Judicially Blind," *Southern Confederacy*, March 4, 1861, 2, https://gahistoricnewspapers .galileo.usg.edu/lccn/sn82014677/1861-03-04/ed-1/seq-2. If passed, the Corwin amendment would have been the thirteenth amendment to the US Constitution. The actual Thirteenth Amendment, passed in December 1865, outlawed slavery in the United States.

42. "Southern Confederacy. (Atlanta, Ga.) 1861–1865."

43. Timothy Hughes Rare & Early Newspapers, "A Memphis Confederate Newspaper Printed in Atlanta . . . ," accessed May 5, 2018, www.rarenewspapers.com/view /586631.

44. "Slavery and the Bible," *DeBow's Review*, September 1850, http://fair-use.org/debows -review/1850/09/slavery-and-the-bible.

45. Quoted in Gordon Rhea, "Why Non-slaveholding Southerners Fought," address to

the Charleston Library Society, January 25, 2011, www.civilwar.org/learn/articles /why-non-slaveholding-southerners-fought.

46. Quoted in Rhea, "Why Non-slaveholding Southerners Fought."

47. Merton E. Coulter, *The Confederate States of America, 1861–1865* (Baton Rouge: Louisiana State University Press, 1950), 100.

48. Both sides eventually employed regiments of Indians in separate, segregated units. Otherwise, all whites, regardless of national origin or religion, fought in all-white regiments. Some groups were organized by nationality for the efficacy of battle (including all-German and all-Irish groups), but Americans of German and Irish descent were never barred from white units. See also "Black Regiments," accessed April 8, 2018, http://spartacus-educational.com/USACWcolored.htm; David T. Gleeson, *The Green and the Gray: The Irish in the Confederate States of America* (Chapel Hill: University of North Carolina Press, 2016); Kevin M. Levin, *Searching for Black Confederates: The Civil War's Most Persistent Myth* (Chapel Hill: University of North Carolina Press, 2019); James M. McPherson, *The Negro's Civil War: How American Blacks Felt and Acted During the War for the Union* (New York: Vintage, 2003); and Robert N. Rosen, *The Jewish Confederates* (Columbia: University of South Carolina Press, 2000).

49. Ronald Franklin, "How Abraham Lincoln Fired General John C. Fremont," Owlclation, December 8, 2017, https://owlcation.com/humanities/How-Abraham-Lincoln -Fired-General-John-C-Fremont.

50. "Maj. Gen. David Hunter, Department of the South, General Order No. 11, May 9, 1862,"*Freedman & Southern Society Project*, www.freedmen.umd.edu/hunter .htm#HUNTER.

51. Quoted in Ira Berlin, Barbara J. Fields, Steven F. Miller, Joseph P. Reidy, and Leslie S. Rowland, eds., *Free at Last: A Documentary History of Slavery, Freedom, and the Civil War* (Edison, NJ: Blue and Grey Press, 1997), 56–59.

52. Doris Kearns Goodwin, *Team of Rivals: The Political Genius of Abraham Lincoln* (New York: Simon & Schuster, 2005), 352, 549; J. G. Randall and David Donald, *The Civil War and Reconstruction*, 2nd ed. (Boston: Heath, 1961), 391.

53. Randall and Donald, *Civil War and Reconstruction*, 392.

54. Coulter, *Confederate States of America*, 264.

55. Coulter, 255.

56. David Donald, ed., *Inside Lincoln's Cabinet: The Civil War Diaries of Salmon P. Chase* (New York: Longmans, Green, 1954), 149–152.

57. "Confederate President Jefferson Davis, Address to the Confederate Congress, January 12, 1863," *Journal of Confederate Congress* 3:13–14, http://memory.loc.gov/ammem /amlaw/lwcc.html.

58. Coulter, *Confederate States of America*, 265.

59. "War Department General Order 143: Creation of the U.S. Colored Troops (1863)," www.ourdocuments.gov/doc.php?flash=false&doc=35.

60. Quoted in David W. Blight, *Frederick Douglass, Prophet of Freedom* (New York: Simon & Schuster, 2018), 409.

61. Deborah Gray White, Mia Bay, and Waldo E. Martin Jr., *Freedom on My Mind* (Boston: Bedford/St. Martin's, 2013), 1:335; Russell Duncan, *Freedom's Shore: Tunis Campbell and the Georgia Freedmen* (Athens: University of Georgia Press, 1986), 42–67.

62. Quoted in Blight, *Frederick Douglass*, 395.

63. Quoted in Berlin, Fields, Miller, Reidy, and Rowland, eds., *Free at Last*, 448–449.

64. "On This Day: The President's Order No. 252," *New York Times*, https://archive .nytimes.com/www.nytimes.com/learning/general/onthisday/harp/0815.html.

65. Noah Andre Trudeau, *Southern Storm: Sherman's March to the Sea* (New York: Harper Perennial, 2009); Davis, *What the Yankees Did to Us*; Marc Wortman, *The Bonfire: The Siege and Burning of Atlanta* (New York: PublicAffairs, 2010).

66. Richard Fuchs, *An Unerring Fire: The Massacre at Fort Pillow* (Mechanicsburg, PA: Stackpole, 2002), 14; "The Fort Pillow Massacre. Report of the Committee on the Conduct of the War. All Previous Reports Fully Confirmed. The Horrors and Cruelties of the Scene Intensified. Report of the Sub-committee," *New York Times*, May 6, 1864, www.nytimes.com/1864/05/06/archives/the-fort-pillow-massacre-report-of-the -committee-on-the-conduct-of.html; William W. Freehling, *The South vs. the South: How Anti-Confederate Southerners Shaped the Course of the Civil War* (New York: Oxford University Press, 2002); David Downing, *A South Divided: Portraits of Dissent in the Confederacy* (Nashville, Cumberland House, 2007).

67. Steve Balestrieri, "Fort Pillow: A Massacre of Black Troops During the Civil War," April 15, 2020, *SOFREP*, https://sofrep.com/news/fort-pillow-a-massacre-of-black -troops-during-the-civil-war. See also Paul Horton, "A Model for Teaching Secondary History: The Case of Fort Pillow," *History Teacher* 33, no. 2 (2000): 175–183.

68. Stephan Benzkofer, "The Civil War: The Fort Pillow Massacre," *Chicago Tribune*, April 6, 2014, www.chicagotribune.com/news/ct-fort-pillow-massacre-flashback-06 -20140406-story.html.

69. William T. Sherman, *Memoirs of General W. T. Sherman* (New York: Library of America, 1990), 470.

70. Abraham Lincoln, "Abraham Lincoln to Cabinet, Tuesday, May 3, 1864 (Fort Pillow Massacre)," Abraham Lincoln Papers at the Library of Congress, May 3, 1864, http:// memory.loc.gov/ammem/alhtml/malhome.html; William H. Seward, "William H. Seward to Abraham Lincoln, Wednesday, May 4, 1864 (Opinion on Fort Pillow)," Abraham Lincoln Papers at the Library of Congress, May 4, 1864, http://memory.loc .gov/ammem/alhtml/malhome.html; Abraham Lincoln, "Abraham Lincoln to William H. Seward, Tuesday, May 3, 1864 (Fort Pillow Massacre)," Abraham Lincoln Papers at the Library of Congress, May 3, 1864, http://memory.loc.gov/ammem /alhtml/malhome.html.

71. Litwack, *Been in the Storm So Long*, 70.

72. "Non-southern" includes white men from all other regions—the North and the West. About 100,000 of the Union's forces were white southerners. Though smaller in proportion and number than the black men who fought for the United States, these loyalist white men were drawn from every state in the Confederacy. In fact, all but South Carolina provided at least one battalion of soldiers for the federal forces, in contrast to promises from southern lawmakers that no men from their states would serve in the Union. American patriotic duty did, in fact, transcend state lines, even deep into Confederate territory. Richard Nelson Current, *Lincoln's Loyalists: Union Soldiers from the Confederacy* (Boston: Northeastern University Press, 1992), 5; "War Department General Order 143," www.ourdocuments .gov/doc.php?flash=true&doc=35; Inter-university Consortium for Political and Social Research, "Historical, Demographic, Economic, and Social Data"; "The Civil War Facts," National Park Service, accessed April 8, 2018, www.nps.gov/civilwar/facts.htm.

73. Martha S. Jones, *Birthright Citizens: A History of Race and Rights in Antebellum America* (New York: Cambridge University Press, 2018), 11.

Chapter 2: "No Capes for Negroes"

1. Stephen Davis, *What the Yankees Did to Us: Sherman's Bombardment and Wrecking of Atlanta* (Macon, GA: Mercer University Press, 2017), 8–9, 188; "The Death of Solomon Luckie," *Civil War Picket*, June 9, 2017, http://civil-war-picket.blogspot.com/2017/06/the-death-of-solomon-luckie-lamppost-to.html; Thomas Schott, *Alexander H. Stephens of Georgia: A Biography* (Baton Rouge: Louisiana State University Press, 1996), 87–90.

2. Davis, *What the Yankees Did to Us*, 3, 8–9, 188; Samuel Carter III, *The Siege of Atlanta, 1864* (New York: St. Martin's, 1973), 283–284; "Antebellum Lamppost Move Revealing Black Barber's Story," WABE, June 6, 2017, www.wabe.org/antebellum-lamppost-move-revealing-black-barbers-story; Chattahooch 33, "Tidbits of Wartime Atlanta," *Civil War Talk*, April 23, 2014, https://civilwartalk.com/threads/tidbits-of-wartime-atlanta.98491; "Death of Solomon Luckie"; Wendy Hamand Venet, *A Changing Wind: Commerce and Conflict in Civil War Atlanta* (New Haven, CT: Yale University Press, 2014), 169.

3. Benjamin Joseph Klebaner, "American Manumission Laws and the Responsibility for Supporting Slaves," *Virginia Magazine of History and Biography* 63, no. 4 (1955): 443–453; "Slave Laws of Georgia, 1755–1860," www.georgiaarchives.org/assets/documents/Slave_Laws_of_Georgia_1755-1860.pdf; Ralph B. Flanders, "The Free Negro in Antebellum Georgia," *North Carolina Historical Review* 9, no. 3 (1932): 268.

4. Amrita Chakrabarti Myers, *Forging Freedom: Black Women and the Pursuit of Liberty in Antebellum Charleston* (Chapel Hill: University of North Carolina Press, 2014); Mary Gehman, *Free People of Color of New Orleans: An Introduction* (Marrero, LA: Margaret Media, 1996); Carl Lane and Rhoda Freeman, "John Dipper and the Experience of the Free Black Elite, 1816–1836," *Virginia Magazine of History and Biography* 100, no. 4 (1992): 485–514.

5. Davis, *What the Yankees Did to Us*, 8–9; "Atlanta," accessed January 29, 2021, www.georgiaencyclopedia.org/articles/counties-cities-neighborhoods/atlanta; "Death of Solomon Luckie."

6. Anthony Gene Carey, *Parties, Slavery, and the Union in Antebellum Georgia* (Athens: University of Georgia Press, 1997), 250–254.

7. Mark Wortman, *The Bonfire: The Siege and Burning of Atlanta* (New York: PublicAffairs, 2009), 83; "The Two Atlantas," *Atlanta Constitution*, May 12, 1968, 20.

8. Venet, *Changing Wind*, 97–98.

9. Although various sources have reported that the first black landowner was "Mary Combs," an extraordinary effort of research has found her actual name to be Laura. For greater detail on the complexity of Laura Combs's life and times, see Paul K. Graham, "The Life and Family of Laura (Lavinia) Kelley Combs," *National Genealogical Society Quarterly*, December 2013, 245–266.

10. Quoted in Flanders, "Free Negro in Antebellum Georgia," 267.

11. Carter, *Siege of Atlanta*, 58–59; "Inauguration of President Lincoln," *Atlanta Intelligencer*, March 6, 1861, 2; Davis, *What the Yankees Did to Us*, 18–22.

12. Carter, *Siege of Atlanta*, 58–59.

13. Quoted in Gary M. Pomerantz, *Where Peachtree Meets Sweet Auburn* (New York: Scribner, 1996), 49.

14. "Mayor's Proclamation," *Southern Confederacy*, June 9, 1864, 1.

15. Pomerantz, *Where Peachtree Meets Sweet Auburn*, 47.

16. Quoted in Charles H. Wesley, *The Collapse of the Confederacy* (Columbia: University of South Carolina Press, 2001), 63.

17. Pomerantz, *Where Peachtree Meets Sweet Auburn*, 47–48.

18. William T. Sherman, *The Capture of Atlanta and the March to the Sea* (Mineola, NY: Dover, 2007) 185; Hill, quoted in Wesley, *Collapse of the Confederacy*, 85.

19. Quoted in Sherman, *Capture of Atlanta*, 185.

20. Quoted in Wesley, *Collapse of the Confederacy*, 86.

21. Quoted in Wortman, *Bonfire*, 158. See page 189 on newspaper reports on Yankees and race.

22. Robert L. O'Connell, *Fierce Patriot* (New York: Random House, 2015), 144.

23. Wallace Putnam Reed, *History of Atlanta, Georgia: With Illustrations and Biographical Sketches of Some of Its Prominent Men and Pioneers* (Syracuse, NY: D. Mason, 1889), 123, 171.

24. Quoted in Gilbert H. Muller, *Abraham Lincoln and William Cullen Bryant: Their Civil War* (New York: Palgrave, 2007), 192.

25. Quoted in O'Connell, *Fierce Patriot*, 145.

26. For an elaborate discussion of the Battle of Atlanta, see Lee Kennett, *Marching Through Georgia: The Story of Soldiers and Civilians During Sherman's Campaign* (New York: HarperCollins, 1995). See also Carter, *Siege of Atlanta*; and Jacqueline Glass Campbell, *When Sherman Marched North from the Sea: Resistance on the Confederate Home Front* (Chapel Hill: University of North Carolina Press, 2003).

27. Deborah Redin Van Tuyll, "Nineteenth-Century Georgia Newspapers," *New Georgia Encyclopedia*, accessed May 6, 2018, www.georgiaencyclopedia.org/articles /history-archaeology/nineteenth-century-georgia-newspapers.

28. "The Front," *Southern Confederacy*, July 9, 1864, 1.

29. Wortman, *Bonfire*, 184–185.

30. Venet, *Changing Wind*, 145–146.

31. Thomas Reade Rootes Cobb was a brother of Howell Cobb, a fire-eater. They were cousins of Thomas W. Cobb, former US representative and senator, for whom Cobb County, adjoining Atlanta, is named. For Charles D'Alvigny's military service, see Clement A. Evans, ed., *Confederate Military History* (Atlanta: Confederate Publishing, 1899), 6:593.

32. Quoted in Carter, *Siege of Atlanta*, 275.

33. Wayne Bengston, "James Birdseye McPherson: Sherman Loses His 'Right Bower,'" *About North Georgia*, accessed September 22, 2019, www.aboutnorthgeorgia.com /ang/James_Birdseye_McPherson.

34. Quoted in Carter, *Siege of Atlanta*, 239.

35. William T. Sherman, "Headquarters, Military Division of the Mississippi, in the Field, Near Atlanta, August 10, 1864," in *The War of the Rebellion: Official Records of the Union and Confederate Armies* (Washington, DC: Government Printing Office, 1891), 452.

36. Quoted in Davis, *What the Yankees Did to Us*, 127.

37. Quoted in Carter, *Siege of Atlanta*, 275.

38. Davis, *What the Yankees Did to Us*, 278.

39. Sherman, "Headquarters," 409.

40. Quoted in Carter, *Siege of Atlanta*, 284–285.

41. Davis, *What the Yankees Did to Us*, 188–189; Carter, *Siege of Atlanta*, 284; Venet, *Changing Wind*, 169; Franklin Garrett, *Atlanta and Environs: A Chronicle of Its People and Events* (Athens: University of Georgia Press, 1969), 1:628.

42. There is some uncertainty about the exact date of the "red day" that resulted in Luckie's death. Most reports suggest that it was August 9, but some suggest that it was August 15. There is also some imprecision in the number of people who attended to him when he was struck. Some reports indicate one person, some indicate two, and others indicate three. I have chosen to cite the names of the three men found in multiple sources. See Carter, *Siege of Atlanta*, 284; Davis, *What the Yankees Did to Us*, 188–189; Luckie Family Photographs, Kenan Research Center, Atlanta History Center, Collection Number: vis20, accessed January 28, 2021, https://aspace-atlantahistorycenter.galileo.usg.edu /repositories/2/resources/2444; and "Death of Solomon Luckie."

43. Kerry Walters, *Outbreak in Washington, D.C.: The 1857 Mystery of the National Hotel Disease* (Charleston, SC: History Press, 2014), 1–9; "The National Hotel Epidemic," *Unresolved*, accessed January 8, 2021, https://unresolved.me /the-national-hotel-epidemic; Rebecca Boggs Roberts and Sandra K. Schmidt, *Historic Congressional Cemetery* (Charleston, SC: Arcadia, 2012), 72; US Federal Census for Washington City, 1830, 123.

44. Quoted in Marc Wortman, "Why Was Robert Webster, a Slave, Wearing What Looks Like a Confederate Uniform?," *Smithsonian Magazine*, October 2014, www.smithsonianmag.com/history/why-was-robert-webster-slave-wearing-what -looks-confederate-uniform-180952781.

45. Styles was a member of Company A, 15th US Colored Troops. See "Styles Linton Hutchins," accessed June 16, 2021, https://sharetngov.tnsosfiles.com/tsla/exhibits /aale/hutchins.htm.

46. "Spies in Atlanta," *Atlanta Intelligencer*, April 3, 1862, 1; Thomas G. Dyer, "Half Slave, Half Free: Unionist Robert Webster in Confederate Atlanta," in *Inside the Confederate Nation: Essays in Honor of Emory M. Thomas*, ed. Lesley J. Gordon and John C. Inscoe (Baton Rouge: Louisiana State University Press, 2005), 295–300; Venet, *Changing Wind*, 53, 69, 165, 178; Davis, *What the Yankees Did to Us*, 50; Wortman, *Bonfire*, 314.

47. Wortman, "Why Was Robert Webster?" One dollar in 1860 was worth $35.22 in 2022, making Webster's wartime savings an estimated $563,520 today.

48. Wortman, "Why Was Robert Webster?"; Thomas Walter Reed, *History of the University of Georgia* (Athens: University of Georgia Press, 1949), 388–390; Dyer, "Half Slave, Half Free," 295–300; Venet, *Changing Wind*, 165.

49. Davis, *What the Yankees Did to Us*, 201–203.

50. Carter, *Siege of Atlanta*, 238.

51. Sherman, *Capture of Atlanta*, 95.

52. Carter, *Siege of Atlanta*, 311–316.

53. Garrett, *Atlanta and Environs*, 1:633–638; Calhoun and Coburn, quoted in Davis, *What the Yankees Did to Us*, 261–262; Wortman, "Why Was Robert Webster?"; Carter, *Siege of Atlanta*, 323–324.

54. "The Fall of Atlanta; the Official Report of Maj. Gen. Sherman," *New York Times*, September 5, 1864, www.nytimes.com/1864/09/05/archives/the-fall-of-atlanta-the -official-report-of-majgen-sherman-his.html.

55. O'Connell, *Fierce Patriot*, 148–149.

56. Quoted in Muller, *Abraham Lincoln and William Cullen Bryant*, 192.

57. White southerners fought in the Union Army and raised battalions from every state in the Confederacy except South Carolina. For a detailed examination of white southern loyalists during the Civil War, see Richard Nelson Current, *Lincoln's Loyalists: Union Soldiers from the Confederacy* (Boston: Northeastern University Press, 1992), 5–7.

58. Davis, *What the Yankees Did to Us*, 262.

59. Quoted in Wortman, *Bonfire*, 279–281.

60. Quoted in Davis, *What the Yankees Did to Us*, 273.

61. Mary's enslaver died and bequeathed his estate to his white daughter, Eliza, who married Milton. "A Worthy Colored Man," *Atlanta Constitution*, December 29, 1890, 2; "Cities of Georgia," *New York Times*, December 3, 1865, 2; Venet, *Changing Wind*, 200.

62. Quoted in Davis, *What the Yankees Did to Us*, 188; Garrett, *Atlanta and Environs*, 1:639.

63. May A. H. Gay, *Life in Dixie During the War* (Project Gutenberg, 2012), 125, www.gutenberg.org/files/41548/41548-h/41548-h.htm.

64. Gay, *Life in Dixie*, 126.

65. Quoted in Carter, *Siege of Atlanta*, 336.

66. Quoted in Garrett, *Atlanta and Environs*, 1:637–639.

67. Quoted in Carter, *Siege of Atlanta*, 335.

68. Davis, *What the Yankees Did to Us*, 325.

69. Quoted in Carter, *Siege of Atlanta*, 339.

70. Davis notes that 86 servants were tallied in addition to 705 adults and 860 children, making 1,651 in total. See *What the Yankees Did to Us*, 308.

71. Quoted in Carter, *Siege of Atlanta*, 336.

72. "Fighting Words Between Sherman and Hood," *HistoryNet*, accessed July 17, 2018, www.historynet.com/fighting-words-sherman-hood.htm.

73. "Fighting Words." In fact, President Lincoln had directly communicated to Sherman in July 1864 that he should break the whites-only policy among his regiments. The use of black troops was law, Lincoln reminded him. "I have the highest veneration for the law, and will respect it always," Sherman explained. But beyond support as "teamsters, cooks and servants," he thought to start them with "duties of local garrisons." O'Connell, *Fierce Patriot*, 154.

74. "Fighting Words."

75. Quoted in Davis, *What the Yankees Did to Us*, 325.

76. "The Civil War and Emancipation," *PBS Resource Bank*, www.pbs.org/wgbh/aia/part4/4p2967.html. See also William M. Brewer, "Poor Whites and Negroes in the South Since the Civil War," *Journal of Negro History* 15, no. 1 (January 1930): 26–37; and Stephen V. Ash, "Poor Whites in the Occupied South, 1861–1865," *Journal of Southern History* 57, no. 1 (February 1991): 39–62.

77. Garrett, *Atlanta and Environs*, 1:633–638.

78. Garrett, 1:633–638. "The Bonnie Blue Flag" was a Confederate marching song written by Harry McCarthy in the spring of 1861. The song's title is taken from the name of the first unofficial flag of the Confederate States of America. See Steven Schoenherr, "Bonnie Blue Flag," accessed May 9, 2018, http://history.sandiego.edu/gen/snd/bonnieblueflag.html.

79. Quoted in Wesley, *Collapse of the Confederacy*, 86.

80. *Richmond Examiner*, September 5, 1864, quoted in James M. McPherson, "No Peace Without Victory, 1861–1865," presidential address, 118th annual meeting of the American Historical Association, Washington, DC, January 3, 2004, www.historians.org/about-aha-and-membership/aha-history-and-archives /presidential-addresses/james-m-mcpherson#REF52, accessed January 11, 2023.

81. Quoted in Wesley, *Collapse of the Confederacy*, 86.

82. "Fall of Atlanta," 1.

83. Glyndon G. Van Deusen, *Horace Greeley: Nineteenth-Century Reformer* (Philadelphia: University of Pennsylvania Press, 1953), 310–311.

84. Doris Kearns Goodwin, *Team of Rivals: The Political Genius of Abraham Lincoln* (New York: Simon & Schuster, 2005), 656.

85. Quoted in Sherman, *Capture of Atlanta*, 106.

86. Quoted in Goodwin, *Team of Rivals*, 658.

87. James M. McPherson, *Tried by War: Abraham Lincoln as Commander in Chief* (New York: Penguin, 2008), 231–250.

88. Quoted in Goodwin, *Team of Rivals*, 655.

89. Goodwin, 655.

90. Andrew Rolle, *John Charles Frémont: Character as Destiny* (Norman: University of Oklahoma Press, 1991); "John C. Fremont," Civil War Home, accessed April 8, 2018, www.civilwarhome.com/fremontbio.htm.

91. Quoted in David W. Blight, *Frederick Douglass, Prophet of Freedom* (New York: Simon & Schuster, 2018), 439.

92. J. G. Randall and David Donald, *The Civil War and Reconstruction*, 2nd ed. (Boston: Heath, 1961), 424–425; William C. Davis, *Lincoln's Men: How President Lincoln Became Father to an Army and a Nation* (New York: Simon and Schuster, 1999), 211; "Atlanta Campaign (1864)," Heritage Preservation Services, accessed February 16, 2018, https://web.archive.org/web/20131019062057/http://www.nps.gov/history/hps /abpp/battles/ga017.htm; Stephen W. Sears, *George B. McClellan: The Young Napoleon* (Boston: Houghton Mifflin Harcourt, 2014), 385–386.

93. Ella Lonn, *Desertion During the Civil War* (Big Byte Books, 2016), 6–8, 18.

94. S. Kittrell Rushing, "Garnett Andrews (1798–1873)," *New Georgia Encyclopedia*, last modified September 9, 2014, www.georgiaencyclopedia.org/articles/history -archaeology/garnett-andrews-1798-1873.

95. Sherman, *Capture of Atlanta*, 107–108.

96. Quoted in Kevin M. Levin, *Searching for Black Confederates: The Civil War's Most Persistent Myth* (Chapel Hill: University of North Carolina Press, 2019), 58.

97. "F. Kendall to President Jefferson Davis, September 16, 1864," in *Free at Last: A Documentary History of Slavery, Freedom, and the Civil War*, ed. Ira Berlin et al. (New York: New Press, 1992), 151.

98. Quoted in Levin, *Searching for Black Confederates*, 61.

99. "The Freedman's Savings Bank: Good Intentions Were Not Enough," Office of the Comptroller of the Treasury, www.occ.treas.gov/about/who-we-are/history /1863-1865/1863-1865-freedmans-savings-bank.html; Carl R. Osthaus, *Freedmen, Philanthropy, and Fraud: A History of the Freedman's Savings Bank* (Urbana: University of Illinois Press, 1976).

100. Levin, *Searching for Black Confederates*, 64–65.

101. Although some small groups of black men were brought to Confederate camps for training, the Confederate Army, though in shambles and short on uniforms, shoes, food, and munitions, did not use armed, uniformed black soldiers in any battle. For an outstanding scholarly book-length exploration of the myth of black Confederates, see Levin, *Searching for Black Confederates*. See also Randall and Donald, *Civil War and Reconstruction*, 522.

102. Wendy Hamand Venet, *A Changing Wind: Commerce and Conflict in Civil War Atlanta* (New Haven, CT: Yale University Press, 2014), 188.

103. Graham, "Life and Family of Laura (Lavinia) Kelly Combs," 250–265. The current location of the Combs property is currently valued at more than $3 million. See also "A Love Story Proved: The Life and Family of Laura (Lavinia) Kelly Combs," Ancestry .com, March 31, 2014, www.ancestry.com/corporate/blog/a-love-story-proved -the-life-and-family-of-laura-lavinia-kelly-combs.

104. The bank was white administered, yet black schools, churches, and others poured money into it. The national economic panic in 1873 and internal mismanagement critically destabilized the bank. Its board recruited Frederick Douglass to become the bank president in 1874 to reassure African Americans of its solvency. The venerated leader even deposited $10,000 of his own money (over $250,000 in value today) to convince depositors that the bank could be trusted. Tragically, the bank was too far gone. It closed that same year. Only about half of the depositors received some of their money. "The Story of the Freedman's Bank," US Department of the Treasury, accessed July 9, 2022, www.youtube.com/watch?v=zkxcSuIWC1I; "Freedman's Savings Bank." See also Osthaus, *Freedmen, Philanthropy, and Fraud*.

105. Graham, "Life and Family of Laura (Lavinia) Kelley Combs," 245–264.

106. Linda O. McMurry, *To Keep the Waters Troubled: The Life of Ida B. Wells* (New York: Oxford University Press, 2000), 13.

107. Pomerantz, *Where Peachtree Meets Sweet Auburn*, 7. Pomerantz refers to Combs by the name that was ascribed to her in earlier histories, Mary Combs.

108. "Increasing Wealth," *Atlanta Constitution*, August 21, 1880, 1; "A Worthy Colored Man," *Atlanta Constitution*, December 29, 1890, 2; Catherine M. Lewis and J. Richard Lewis, eds., *Jim Crow America: A Documentary History* (Fayetteville: University of Arkansas Press, 2009), 15–16.

109. "Luckie Family Photographs."

Chapter 3: Sherman's Shadow

1. "The Two Atlantas," *Atlanta Journal-Constitution*, May 12, 1968, 20.

2. Quoted in Robert L. O'Connell, *Fierce Patriot* (New York: Random House, 2015), 163; Jim Miles, *To the Sea: A History and Tour Guide of the War in the West, Sherman's March Across Georgia and Through the Carolinas, 1864–1865* (Nashville: Cumberland House, 2002), 138–139.

3. O'Connell, *Fierce Patriot*, 168–169.

4. Ira Berlin, Thavolia Glymph, Steven F. Miller, Joseph P. Reidy, Leslie S. Rowland, and Julie Saville, eds. *Freedom: A Documentary History of Emancipation 1861–1867: Selected from the Holdings of the National Archives of the United States*, series 1 (Chapel Hill: University of North Carolina Press, 1991), 3:331–338.

5. "Negroes of Savannah," *New-York Daily Tribune*, February 13, 1865, Consolidated Correspondence File, series 225, Central Records, Quartermaster General, Record Group 92, National Archives, www.freedmen.umd.edu/savmtg.htm.

6. As noted earlier, many of the philosophical architects of white supremacy and slavery

argued that they did not hate black people but in fact had great affection for what they considered an inferior group. Slavery, they insisted, was a benign, divinely sanctioned institution that provided a reciprocal and symbiotic relationship between the enslavers and those whom they enslaved.

7. Many histories of black leadership in the late nineteenth and early twentieth centuries have explored the impulse of black nationalism, integration, or accommodation. See Michele Mitchell, *Righteous Propagation: African Americans and the Politics of Racial Destiny After Reconstruction* (Chapel Hill: University of North Carolina Press, 2004); Kevin Gaines, *Uplifting the Race: Black Leadership, Politics, and Culture in the Twentieth Century* (Chapel Hill: University of North Carolina Press, 2012); Deborah Gray White, *Too Heavy a Load: Black Women in Defense of Themselves, 1894–1994* (New York: W. W. Norton, 1999); Hazel Carby, *Race Men* (Cambridge, MA: Harvard University Press, 2000); V. P. Franklin, *Black Self-Determination: A Cultural History of African-American Resistance* (Chicago: Lawrence Hill, 1993); and Evelyn Brooks Higginbothom, *Righteous Discontent: The Women's Movement in the Black Baptist Church, 1880–1920* (Cambridge, MA: Harvard University Press, 1994).

8. For a richer exploration of the concepts of black nationalism and integration, along with their twentieth-century outgrowth, black power, see E. U. Essien-Udom's classic study of the Nation of Islam, *Black Nationalism: A Search for Identity in America* (Chicago: University of Chicago Press, 1962); Wilson J. Moses, *On the Wings of Ethiopia* (Ames: Iowa State University Press, 1991); William Van De Burg, ed., *Modern Black Nationalism: From Marcus Garvey to Louis Farrakhan* (New York: New York University Press, 1996); Wilson J. Moses, *The Golden Age of Black Nationalism, 1850–1925* (New York: New York University Press, 1988); Wilson J. Moses, *Classical Black Nationalism: From the American Revolution to Marcus Garvey* (New York: New York University Press 1996); Manning Marable, *Black Leadership* (New York: Columbia University Press, 1998); Jeffrey O. G. Ogbar, *Black Power: Radical Politics and African American Identity* (Baltimore: Johns Hopkins University Press, 2019); Keisha N. Blain, *Set the World on Fire: Black Nationalist Women and the Global Struggle for Freedom* (Philadelphia: University of Pennsylvania Press, 2019); and Robyn C. Spencer, *The Revolution Has Come: Black Power, Gender, and the Black Panther Party in Oakland* (Durham, NC: Duke University Press, 2016).

9. Quoted in David Lindsey, *Americans in Conflict: The Civil War and Reconstruction* (Boston: Houghton Mifflin, 1974), 139.

10. Russell Duncan, *Freedom's Shore: Tunis Campbell and the Georgia Freedmen* (Athens: University of Georgia Press, 1986), 15–23; Edmund L. Drago, *Black Politicians and Reconstruction in Georgia: A Splendid Failure*, revised ed. (Athens: University of Georgia Press, 1992).

11. Leon F. Litwack, *North of Slavery: The Negro in the Free States* (Chicago: University of Chicago Press, 1965), 34–37; Duncan, *Freedom's Shore*, 67–74.

12. Herbert Aptheker, "Negro Casualties in the Civil War," *Journal of Negro History* 32, no. 1 (January 1947): 11–19.

13. (1857) Frederick Douglass, 'If There Is No Struggle, There Is No Progress,'" BlackPast.org, January 25, 2007, www.blackpast.org/african-american-history/1857-frederick-douglass-if-there-no-struggle-there-no-progress.

14. E. Merton Coulter, "Tunis G. Campbell, Negro Reconstructionist in Georgia," *Georgia Historical Quarterly* 51, no. 4 (December 1967): 402–445.

15. Quoted in "Sherman Meets the Colored Ministers in Savannah," Civilwarhome.com, accessed June 6, 2018, https://civilwarhome.com/shermanandministers.htm.

16. "Sherman Meets the Colored Ministers"; O'Connell, *Fierce Patriot*, 169.

17. Eric Foner, *Reconstruction: America's Unfinished Revolution* (New York: Harper and Row, 1988), 70; John Buescher, "Forty Acres and a Mule," Teachinghistory.org, accessed June 1, 2018, https://wikisummaries.org/special-field-order-no-15-forty-acres -and-a-mule.

18. Quoted in David W. Blight, *Frederick Douglass: Prophet of Freedom* (New York: Simon & Shuster, 2018), 442.

19. William T. Sherman, "Order by the Commander of the Military Division of the Mississippi: In the Field, Savannah, GA., January 16th, 1865," *Freedom & Southern Society Project*, accessed May 6, 2018, www.freedmen.umd.edu/sfo15.htm.

20. Foner, *Reconstruction*, 70; Buescher, "Forty Acres and a Mule."

21. Quoted in Stephen Davis, *What the Yankees Did to Us: Sherman's Bombardment and Wrecking of Atlanta* (Macon, GA: Mercer University Press, 2017), 301, 312.

22. Doris Kearns Goodwin, *Team of Rivals: The Political Genius of Abraham Lincoln* (New York: Simon & Schuster, 2005), 697.

23. Quoted in Goodwin, *Team of Rivals*, 697, 699.

24. Initially, security at the White House stopped Douglass, insisting that a whites-only policy would prevent his entrance. The president himself intervened and welcomed the famed abolitionist. Goodwin, *Team of Rivals*, 699–700.

25. Frederick Douglass, "Eulogy for Abraham Lincoln," Library of America, http:// storyoftheweek.loa.org/2020/02/eulogy-for-abraham-lincoln.html.

26. "Mary Chesnut: News of Lincoln's Assassination," in *Mary Boykin Chesnut from A Diary from Dixie, Reading Vine*, accessed December 11, 2020, www.readingvine .com/passages/mary-chesnut-news-of-lincolns-assassination; Wendy Hamand Venet, *A Changing Wind: Commerce and Conflict in Civil War Atlanta* (New Haven, CT: Yale University Press, 2014), 183.

27. John Hope Franklin, *Reconstruction After the Civil War*, 2nd ed. (Chicago: University of Chicago Press, 1994), 33–34.

28. "Freedpeople Protest Loss of Their Land," accessed September 17, 2019, www .facinghistory.org/reconstruction-era/freedpeople-protest-loss-their-land.

29. Duncan, *Freedom's Shore*, 34–36; Drago, *Black Politicians and Reconstruction in Georgia*.

30. Foner, *Reconstruction*, 358.

31. Quoted in Jacqueline Glass Campbell, *When Sherman Marched North from the Sea: Resistance on the Confederate Front* (Chapel Hill: University of North Carolina Press, 2003), 17.

32. Donna Lee Dickerson, *The Reconstruction Era: Primary Documents on Events from 1865 to 1877* (Westport, CT: Greenwood, 2003), 43–46.

33. Elizabeth Studley Nathans, *Losing the Peace: Georgia Republicans and Reconstruction, 1865–1871* (Baton Rouge: Louisiana State University Press, 1968); Drago, *Black Politicians and Reconstruction in Georgia*.

34. E. Merton Coulter, *The South During Reconstruction, 1865–1877* (Baton Rouge: Louisiana State University Press, 1947), 380–381.

35. Barry Godfrey and Steven Soper, "Prison Records from 1800s Georgia Show Mass Incarceration's Racially Charged Beginnings," *Conversation*, May 22, 2018, https:// theconversation.com/prison-records-from-1800s-georgia-show-mass-incarcerations -racially-charged-beginnings-96612.

36. Equal Justice Initiative, *Lynching in America: Confronting the Legacy of Racial Terror*, 3rd ed. (Birmingham: Equal Justice Initiative, 2017); W. Fitzhugh Brundage, ed.,

Under Sentence of Death: Lynching in the South (Chapel Hill: University of North Carolina Press, 1997); W. Fitzhugh Brundage, *Lynching in the New South: Georgia and Virginia, 1880–1930* (Urbana: University of Illinois Press, 1993); National Association for the Advancement of Colored People, *Thirty Years of Lynching in the United States, 1889–1918* (New York: Arno, 1969); Stewart E. Tolnay and E. M. Beck, *A Festival of Violence: An Analysis of Southern Lynchings, 1882–1930* (Urbana: University of Illinois Press, 1995).

37. Edwin L. Jackson, "Georgia's Historic Capitals," *New Georgia Encyclopedia*, June 6, 2017, www.georgiaencyclopedia.org/articles/counties-cities-neighborhoods/georgias-historic -capitals; Barry L. Brown and Gordon R. Elwell, *Crossroads of Conflict: A Guide to Civil War Sites in Georgia* (Athens: University of Georgia Press, 2010).

38. Coulter, "Tunis G. Campbell," 407–408.

39. Quoted in Foner, *Reconstruction*, 325.

40. Quoted in Jackson, "Georgia's Historic Capitals."

41. Lee W. Formwalt, "The Camilla Massacre of 1868: Racial Violence as Political Propaganda," *Georgia Historical Quarterly* 71 (Fall 1987): 399–426; Lee W. Formwalt, "Petitioning Congress for Protection: A Black View of Reconstruction at the Local Level," *Georgia Historical Quarterly* 73 (Summer 1989): 305–322.

42. Quoted in Blight, *Frederick Douglass*, 477.

43. Coulter, *South During Reconstruction*, 57, 60.

44. Quoted in Coulter, 59.

45. Quoted in Coulter, 56.

46. Quoted in Lisa Cardyn, "Sexualized Racism/Gendered Violence: Outraging the Body Politic in the Reconstruction South," *Michigan Law Review* 100, no. 4 (2002): 692.

47. Quoted in Litwack, *Been in the Storm So Long*, 277–278.

48. Litwack, *Been in the Storm So Long*, 280.

49. Cardyn, "Sexualized Racism/Gendered Violence."

50. Quoted in Cardyn, 696.

51. Quoted in Coulter, *South During Reconstruction*, 143.

52. Coulter, "Tunis G. Campbell," 405–410; Duncan, *Freedom's Shore*, 62–72.

53. Quoted in Coulter, *South During Reconstruction*, 83.

54. Quoted in Foner, *Reconstruction*, 428.

55. Quoted in Jacqueline Jones, *Soldiers of Light and Love, Northern Teachers and Georgia Blacks, 1865–1873* (Athens: University of Georgia Press, 2004), 78–79.

56. Jones, 78–80.

57. Foner, *Reconstruction*, 38–39; Coulter, *South During Reconstruction*, 85–86; Drago, *Black Politicians and Reconstruction in Georgia*; Duncan, *Freedom's Shore*.

58. Quoted in Coulter, *South During Reconstruction*, 82–85; Jones, *Soldiers of Light and Love*, 78–79.

59. Jones, 80.

60. Duncan, *Freedom's Shore*, 25, 63, 92; Tunis G. Campbell, *Suffering of Rev. T. G. Campbell and His Family* (Ithaca, NY: Cornell University Library, 1877), 12–15.

61. Other counties in the district included McIntosh and Tattnall.

62. Robin Kadison Berson, *Marching to a Different Drummer: Unrecognized Heroes of American History* (Westport, CT: Greenwood, 1994); Coulter, "Tunis G. Campbell."

63. For the most detailed and sweeping history of Reconstruction, see Foner, *Reconstruction*.

64. Foner, 423.

65. Quoted in Coulter, *South During Reconstruction*, 117, 169. See also Cardyn, "Sexualized Racism/Gendered Violence," 686–687.

66. Quoted in Litwack, *Been in the Storm So Long*, 265.

67. Quoted in Litwack, 267.

68. Quoted in Litwack, 264–265.

69. Michael Newton, *White Robes and Burning Crosses: A History of the Ku Klux Klan from 1866* (Jefferson, NC: McFarland, 2014), 12.

70. "Black-American Members by Congress, 1870–Present," US House of Representatives: History, Art, and Archives, Office of the Historian, http://history.house.gov/Exhibitions-and-Publications/BAIC/Historical-Data/Black-American-Representatives-and-Senators-by-Congress.

71. "Long, Jefferson Franklin," History, Art, and Archives, United States House of Representatives, http://history.house.gov/People/Detail/17115.

72. Samuel Denny Smith, *The Negro in Congress* (Port Washington, NY: Kennikat, 1940), 73–74.

73. Quoted in Blight, *Frederick Douglass*, 523.

74. Quoted in Blight, 471.

75. Quoted in Blight, 472.

76. Quoted in Blight, 477.

77. George C. Rable, *But There Was No Peace: The Role of Violence in the Politics of Reconstruction* (Athens: University of Georgia Press, 1984), 130–134; C. Vann Woodward, *Reunion and Reaction: The Compromise of 1877 and the End of Reconstruction:* (New York: Oxford University Press, 1951), 3–15; Eric Foner, *A Short History of Reconstruction* (New York: Harper Collins, 1990), 253–255.

78. Curt Holman, "How Well Do You Know Atlanta's Historically Black Neighborhoods?," *Atlanta Journal-Constitution*, March 4, 2016, www.ajc.com/lifestyles/how-well-you-know-atlanta-historically-black-neighborhoods/XI5oFU29CIqhw24Sw7w9QJ.

79. Holman, "How Well Do You Know?"

80. Holman.

81. Quoted in Litwack, *Been in the Storm So Long*, 314.

82. Campbell Gibson, *Population of the 100 Largest Cities and Other Urban Places in the United States: 1790 to 1990*, Population Division, US Bureau of the Census. (Washington, DC: United States Government Publishing Office, 1998).

83. Quoted in Venet, *Changing Wind*, 211.

84. Venet, 212.

85. Quoted in Coulter, *South During Reconstruction*, 129.

86. Frederick Douglass, "Lesson of the Hour, January 9, 1894 (Excerpt)," *Teaching American History*, accessed November 10, 2019, https://teachingamericanhistory.org/library/document/lessons-of-the-hour-excerpt.

87. Quoted in Henry Louis Gates, "The 'Lost Cause' That Built Jim Crow," *New York Times*, November 8, 2019, www.nytimes.com/2019/11/08/opinion/sunday/jim-crow-laws.html?smid=nytcore-ios-share&fbclid=IwAR0GwT8s9x-4cJKy_1Va1xJdpnrQz_7nYcLEQW9wOjsB9nWj7pP2v8rD1bI.

88. Drago, *Black Politicians and Reconstruction in Georgia*, 56–57.

89. See Franklin's classic *Reconstruction After the Civil War*, especially Chapter 3, from which this term is borrowed.

Chapter 4: Redeeming Atlanta

1. "Cyclorama Document Based Questions," Atlanta History Center, 8, accessed January 10, 2023, www.atlantahistorycenter.com/app/uploads/2020/12/EDU_School Tours_Cyclo_TeacherGuide_DBQ.pdf.

2. Daniel Judt, "Atlanta's Civil War Monument, Minus the Pro-Confederate Bunkum," *Atlantic*, March 17, 2019, www.theatlantic.com/ideas/archive/2019/03/how-atlanta -cyclorama-lost-its-confederate-overtone/584938.

3. J. Morgan Kousser, *The Shaping of Southern Politics: Suffrage Restriction and the Establishment of the One-Party South, 1880–1910* (New Haven, CT: Yale University Press, 1974), 71, 76, 107.

4. Ella Myers, "Beyond the Wages of Whiteness: Du Bois on the Irrationality of Antiblack Racism," *Items: Insights from the Social Sciences*, March 21, 2017, https://items .ssrc.org/reading-racial-conflict/beyond-the-wages-of-whiteness-du-bois-on-the -irrationality-of-antiblack-racism.

5. Campbell Gibson, "Population of the 100 Largest Cities and Other Urban Places in the United States: 1790 to 1990," US Census Bureau, 1998, www.census.gov/library /working-papers/1998/demo/POP-twps0027.html.

6. Joel Chandler Harris, "Life of Henry W. Grady" (1890), in *Major Problems in the History of the American South*, ed. Paul D. Escott and David R. Goldfield (Lexington, MA: Heath, 1990), 2:71–73.

7. Henry Grady, "New South" speech, December 22, 1886, http://georgiainfo.galileo .usg.edu/topics/history/article/late-nineteenth-century-1878-1900/henry-gradys -new-south-speech-dec.-22-1886.

8. Grady, "New South."

9. Wendy Hamand Venet, *A Changing Wind: Commerce and Conflict in Civil War Atlanta* (New Haven, CT: Yale University Press, 2014), 188.

10. *Proceedings of the National Association of Life Underwriters* (Boston: Standard, 1893), 61–62.

11. Jo Ann Rayfield, "Tragedy in the Chicago Fire and Triumph in the Architectural Response," *Illinois History Teacher*, 1997, www.lib.niu.edu/1997/iht419734.html.

12. Joseph E. Brown, "Education of the Negroes," *New York Times*, March 5, 1879, 2.

13. Karen L. Cox, *Dixie's Daughters: The United Daughters of the Confederacy and the Preservation of Confederate Culture* (Gainesville: University Press of Florida, 2003), 10–12; David S. Williams, "Lost Cause Religion," *New Georgia Encyclopedia*, October 2, 2017, www.georgiaencyclopedia.org/articles/arts-culture/lost-cause-religion.

14. Edward A. Pollard, *The Lost Cause: A New Southern History of the War of the Confederates* (Louisville: E. B. Treat, 1867), 216, 323.

15. Gary W. Gallagher and Alan T. Nolan, eds., *The Myth of the Lost Cause and Civil War History* (Bloomington: Indiana University Press, 2000), 13–14; Gaines M. Foster, *Ghosts of the Confederacy: Defeat, the Lost Cause, and the Emergence of the New South* (New York: Oxford University Press, 1987).

16. Cox, *Dixie's Daughters*, 12.

17. "Is Your Atlanta Street Named for a Confederate Leader? Here's the List," *Atlanta*

Journal-Constitution, November 21, 2017, www.ajc.com/news/local/your-atlanta
-street-named-for-confederate-leader-here-the-list/2L3cc7ceKs5BTMRcqcgC8L.

18. The war crime attributed to Forrest is the 1864 Fort Pillow Massacre, discussed in Chapter 1. See Albert Castel and John Allan Wyeth, *That Devil Forrest: Life of General Nathan Bedford Forrest* (Baton Rouge: Louisiana State University Press, 1989); Jack Hurst, *Nathan Bedford Forrest: A Biography* (New York: Knopf Doubleday, 2011), 247; and "Forrest, One of Klan Organizers, Dies," *Brooklyn Daily Eagle*, March 12, 1931, 1.

19. Kenneth K. Krakow, *Georgia Place-Names: Their History and Origins* (Macon, GA: Winship, 1975), 119.

20. Quoted in Judt, "Atlanta's Civil War Monument."

21. C. Vann Woodward, *Origins of the New South: 1877–1913* (Baton Rouge: Louisiana State University Press, 1981), 154–155.

22. *Sacramento Daily Union*, December 4, 1868, 1. Center for Bibliographic Studies and Research, California Digital Newspaper Collection.

23. Cox, *Dixie's Daughters*, 1–2.

24. That flag, or some variation of it, remained in place until 1956, when state lawmakers, in protest of the *Brown v. Board of Education* Supreme Court decision, added the more well-known Confederate battle flag to the state flag. Alexander J. Azarian and Eden Fesshazion, "The State Flag of Georgia: The 1956 Change in Its Historical Context," Senate Research Office, State of Georgia, August 2000, www.senate.ga.gov/sro /documents/studycommrpts/00stateflag.pdf; Edwin L. Jackson, "State Flags of Georgia," www.georgiaencyclopedia.org/articles/government-politics/state-flags-georgia. See also Isabell S. Buzzett, *Confederate Monuments of Georgia* (Atlanta: United Daughters of the Confederacy, 1984), for a general conversation about the honorific nods to the Confederacy in the state.

25. Many monuments, streets, and counties, too many to list here, were named to honor Confederates in Atlanta and throughout Georgia. Evans County and Turner County, among others, are named for Confederate veterans. Kenneth Coleman, gen. ed., *A History of Georgia*, 2nd ed. (Athens: University of Georgia Press, 1991).

26. W. E. B. Du Bois, "Postscript," *Crisis*, August 1931, 279.

27. "Homes at the Park: Beautiful Residences That Make Inman Park an Ideal Home Place," *Atlanta Constitution*, March 26, 1896, 9.

28. Edward L. Ayers, *The Promise of the New South: Life After Reconstruction* (New York: Oxford University Press, 1992), 67–68. For more information on the long history of institutionalized housing discrimination and its sanction on the federal, state, and local levels, see the outstanding study by Richard Rothstein, *The Color of Law: A Forgotten History of How Our Government Segregated America* (New York: Liveright, 2016).

29. *Weekly Atlanta Intelligencer*, April 26, 1871, 1.

30. Leon F. Litwack, *Been in the Storm So Long: The Aftermath of Slavery* (New York: Vintage, 1980), 276–277.

31. Quoted in Litwack, *Been in the Storm So Long*, 274.

32. Franklin Garrett, *Atlanta and Environs: A Chronicle of Its People and Events* (Athens: University of Georgia Press, 1969), 876–878; Venet, *Changing Wind*, 205.

33. G. Wright and Kenneth H. Wheeler, "New Men in the Old South: Joseph E. Brown and His Associates in Georgia's Etowah Valley," *Georgia Historical Quarterly* 93, no. 4 (2009): 363–387.

34. Barton C. Shaw, "Populist Party," *New Georgia Encyclopedia*, September 29, 2020, www

.georgiaencyclopedia.org/articles/history-archaeology/populist-party; Barton C. Shaw, *The Wool-Hat Boys: Georgia's Populist Party* (Baton Rouge: Louisiana State University Press, 1984); Alex Mathews Arnett, *The Populist Movement in Georgia: A View of the "Agrarian Crusade" in the Light of Solid-South Politics* (1922; reprint, Ithaca: Cornell University Library, 2009).

35. Quoted in James M. Beeby, ed., *Populism in the South Revisited: New Interpretations and New Departures* (Oxford: University Press of Mississippi, 2016), 158–159.

36. Beeby, *Populism in the South Revisited*, 159.

37. C. Vann Woodward, *Tom Watson: Agrarian Rebel* (New York: Macmillan, 1938), 8–19.

38. Benjamin Houston Turner Purvis, "Sectionalism, Nationalism, and the Agrarian Revolt, 1877–1892" (PhD diss., University of Mississippi, 2014).

39. Mab Segrest, *Memoir of a Race Traitor: A History of Racism in the United States* (Boston: South End, 1994), 209.

40. Segrest, *Memoir of a Race Traitor*, 209.

41. Quoted in Richard Wormser, *The Rise and Fall of Jim Crow* (New York: St. Martin's, 2004), 73.

42. Beeby, *Populism in the South Revisited*, 159–160.

43. Purvis, "Sectionalism, Nationalism, and the Agrarian Revolt," 254–255.

44. Kenneth Coleman, ed., *A History of Georgia* (Athens: University of Georgia Press, 1991), 299.

45. Joseph Gerteis, *Class and the Color Line: Interracial Class Coalition in the Knights of Labor and the Populist Movement* (Durham, NC: Duke University Press, 2007), 164.

46. Wormser, *Rise and Fall of Jim Crow*, 74; "Black, James Conquest Cross," *Biographical Directory of the United States Congress, 1774 to the Present*, https://bioguideretro .congress.gov/Home/MemberDetails?memIndex=B000502.

47. Shaw, "Populist Party"; Shaw, *Wool-Hat Boys*.

48. R. B. Rosenburg, "The House That Grady Built: The Fight for the Confederate Soldiers' Home of Georgia," *Georgia Historical Quarterly* 74, no. 3 (1990): 404.

49. Arnett, *Populist Movement in Georgia*, 178–183.

50. Rosenburg, "House That Grady Built," 405.

51. Barton Shaw, "Populist Party," *New Georgia Encyclopedia*, last modified September 29, 2020, www.georgiaencyclopedia.org/articles/history-archaeology/populist-party/.

52. Rosenburg, "House That Grady Built," 400–401.

53. Rosenburg, 400, 402; Wallace Putnam Reed, ed., *History of Atlanta, Georgia, with Illustrations and Biographical Sketches of Some of Its Prominent Men and Pioneers* (Syracuse, NY: D. Mason, 1889), 89–92; "Shadrach Walker Inman," *Geni*, www.geni .com/people/Shadrach-Inman/6000000011148796328.

54. See John B. Gordon, *Reminiscences of the Civil War* (New York: Charles Scribner's Sons, 1904); Beeby, *Populism in the South Revisited*; and Woodward, *Tom Watson*.

55. Rosenburg, "House That Grady Built," 405.

56. Karen Cook Bell, "Black Politics in Lowcountry Georgia After the Civil War," https:// startingpointsjournal.com/black-politics-in-lowcountry-georgia-after-the-civil -war; Sarah A. Soule, "Populism and Black Lynching in Georgia, 1890–1900," *Social Forces* 71, no. 2 (1992): 431–449; Francis M. Wilhoit, "An Interpretation of Populism's Impact on the Georgia Negro," *Journal of Negro History* 52, no. 2 (1967): 116–127.

57. Quoted in Rosenburg, "House That Grady Built," 407.

58. Rosenburg, 411.

59. Note that the legislator's surname is spelled "Humphries" in the article, yet when listed among those who voted against the home, it is spelled "Humphreys." See "Defeated," *Atlanta Constitution*, August 27, 1891, 1.

60. Quoted in Rosenburg, "House That Grady Built," 415–416.

61. "Refused to Accept," *Americus Times-Recorder*, August 28, 1891, 1; Lucian Lamar Knight, *A Standard History of Georgia and Georgians* (New York: Lewis, 1917), 6:3218.

62. Bell, "Black Politics in Lowcountry Georgia"; Soule, "Populism and Black Lynching," 431–449; Rosenburg, "House That Grady Built," 415–416.

63. Rosenburg, 419.

64. "A Soldiers' Home," *Atlanta Constitution*, November 24, 1891, 8.

65. Quoted in "Favorably," *Atlanta Constitution*, December 3, 1891, 5.

66. Quoted in Rosenburg, "House That Grady Built," 420–421.

67. Rosenburg, 430–431.

Chapter 5: The New South Mecca

1. Although the recorded testimony is clear about his mother, Ellen, it is unclear if William Edward's father, George, was enslaved by Hill.

2. The left wing of Sherman's troops that marched through Georgia was led by General Henry Slocum. It would have been Slocum, not Sherman, who led forces through Madison that day. Evans, in reporting the events of his childhood from more than sixty years earlier, also misnamed his enslaver's first name as "John," not Joshua. However, he did properly name Joshua's wife, Emily. Many other details, including Hill's former membership in the Whig Party, being a congressman, and the specific town corroborate that the informant from 1939, "E. W. Evans," was enslaved on the plantation of Joshua Hill. Geneva Tonsill, "Interview with E. W. Evans, Bricklayer and Plasterer," *American Life Histories: Manuscripts from the Federal Writers' Project, 1936–1940*, Library of Congress, www.loc.gov/item/wpalh000565. Tonsill, the interviewer, misspelled her informant's name as "E. W. Evans," transposing the first two initials. Census records confirm the address of Evans as the same as that found in the WPA interview: 610 Parsons Street, Atlanta. Census documents also confirm the same birth year for both men, 1855. His full name is recorded as William Edward Evans Sr. in federal records. *Fourteenth Census of the United States: 1920*, Place: Atlanta Ward 1, Fulton, Georgia; Roll: T625_250; Page: 10B; Enumeration District: 49 (Washington, DC: United States Government Printing Office, 1921).

3. Kim Tolley, "Slavery," in *Miseducation: A History of Ignorance-Making in America and Abroad*, ed. A. J. Angulo (Baltimore: Johns Hopkins University Press, 2016), 13–33.

4. Tonsill, "Interview with E. W. Evans." In this manuscript Evans refers to his enslaver as a "Whig Senator." Hill was once a member of the Whig Party until it collapsed in Georgia. In 1857 he was elected to the House of Representatives as a member of the American Party, also called the Know Nothing Party. After the war, Hill became the first Republican elected to the Senate from Georgia. Despite these slight inaccuracies, the testimony from Hill, more than sixty years later, proves quite impressive. See "Senator Joshua Hill," accessed January 17, 2021, http://rancho.pancho.pagesperso-orange.fr/Joshua.htm; and "Emily (Reid) Hill (1820–1889)," WikiTree, accessed January 17, 2021, www.wikitree.com/wiki/Reid-13978.

5. Stephen Davis, *What the Yankees Did to Us: Sherman's Bombardment and Wrecking of Atlanta* (Macon, GA: Mercer University Press, 2017), 298–314.

6. Thomas Walter Reed, *History of the University of Georgia* (Athens: University of Georgia Press, 1949).

7. Maurice J. Hobson, *The Legend of the Black Mecca: Politics and Class in the Making of Modern Atlanta* (Chapel Hill: University of North Carolina Press, 2017), 15.

8. The university traces its founding to October 1885; however, the school did not actually enroll students until three years later. "History and Traditions," Georgia Tech, www.gatech.edu/about/history-traditions, accessed October 25, 2021.

9. Kenneth Robert Janken, *White: The Biography of Walter White, Mr. NAACP* (New York: New Press, 2003), 4–5.

10. Walter White, *A Man Called White: The Autobiography of Walter White* (Bloomington: Indiana University Press, 1948), 14.

11. Janken, *White*, 3–4. See also Elizabeth Fox-Genovese's classic *Within the Plantation Household: Black and White Women of the Old South* (Chapel Hill: University of North Carolina Press, 1988).

12. Augustus Ware died in 1872, and his estate went to his white family. Little is known about how much wealth and support was ever provided to Marie and her four children with Ware.

13. For an outstanding study of the collusion of public and private forces to ensure racial segregation in housing, see Richard Rothstein, *The Color of Law: A Forgotten History of How Our Government Segregated America* (New York: Liveright, 2017).

14. Edward L. Ayers, *The Promise of the New South* (Oxford: Oxford University Press, 2007), 64.

15. Homer C. McEwen, "First Congregational Church, Atlanta," *Atlanta Historical Society Bulletin* (Spring 1977): 129–142; Clara Merritt DeBoer, *His Truth Is Marching On—African Americans Who Taught the Freedom for the American Missionary Association, 1861–1877* (Abingdon, UK: Routledge, 2016); Richard S. Selcer, *Civil War America, 1850 to 1875* (New York: Facts on File, 2006), 308; Euell A. Nielsen, "First Congregational Church, Atlanta, Georgia (1867–)," December 9, 2015, BlackPast.org, www.blackpast.org/african-american-history/first-congregational -church-atlanta-georgia-1867.

16. Clarence A. Bacote, *The Story of Atlanta University: A Century of Service, 1865–1965* (Atlanta: Atlanta University Press, 1969), quoted in "National Registry of Historic Places—Inventory Nomination Form," National Park Service, https://npgallery.nps .gov/NRHP/GetAsset/NHLS/74000680_text.

17. In 1929, when Atlanta University moved a few blocks south, it leased the building to Morris Brown College, which had relocated to the Atlanta University Center neighborhood, near Morehouse, Spelman, and Atlanta University. Renamed Fountain Hall, after Bishop William A. Fountain, the building became a central part of Morris Brown College. It was named a National Historic Landmark in 1974.

18. Ernie Suggs, "Grant Could Be Key Step in Restoring Morris Brown's Historic Building," *Atlanta Journal-Constitution*, December 27, 2019, www.ajc.com /news/grant-could-key-step-restoring-morris-brown-historic-building/evMmHr 1jIQ2lJdhsAl0RzJ; Tonsill, "Interview with E. W. Evans, Bricklayer and Plasterer."

19. Quoted in Dorothy Cowser Yancy, "William Edward Burghardt Du Bois' Atlanta Years: The Human Side—A Study Based upon Oral Sources," *Journal of Negro History* 63, no. 1 (1978): 60.

20. Tonsill, "Interview with E. W. Evans."

21. The term *Creole* is very nebulous and indistinct between countries and time periods. Even in Louisiana, it can refer to self-defined white people or self-defined people

of African descent. Its roots in the colonial era in Latin America applied its meaning to people of nearly pure Portuguese or Spanish descent born in the Americas. The French adopted a similar meaning. People of mixed African, European, and Native ancestry in Louisiana adopted the term for themselves in the nineteenth century. Many whites, as well, understood them to be a separate and distinct group from both whites or blacks. For more discussion of these terms, see Shirley Elizabeth Thompson, *Exiles at Home: The Struggle to Become American in Creole New Orleans* (Cambridge, MA: Harvard University Press, 2009); Munro Martin and Celia Britton, *American Creoles: The Francophone Caribbean and the American South* (Liverpool: University Press, 2012); Sybil Kein, *Creole: The History and Legacy of Louisiana's Free People of Color* (Baton Rouge: Louisiana State University Press, 2009); Andrew Jolivette, *Louisiana Creoles: Cultural Recovery and Mixed-Race Native American Identity* (Lanham, MD: Lexington, 2007); Mary Gehman, *The Free People of Color of New Orleans: An Introduction* (Donaldsonville, LA: Margaret Media, 2012); Emily Clark, *The Strange History of the American Quadroon: Free Women of Color in the Revolutionary Atlantic World* (Chapel Hill: University of North Carolina Press, 2012); and Virginia Dominguez, *White by Definition: Social Classification in Creole Louisiana* (New Brunswick, NJ: Rutgers University Press, 2012).

22. *Berea College v. Kentucky*, 211 U.S. 45 (1908).

23. "Savannah State University," *New Georgia Encyclopedia Online*, last modified July 29, 2014, www.georgiaencyclopedia.org/articles/education/savannah-state-university; "Morrill Land-Grant Act Sesquicentennial," Digital Library of Georgia, https://blog .dlg.galileo.usg.edu/?p=3589. See also Bobby L. Lovett, *America's Historically Black Colleges and Universities: A Narrative History, 1837–2009* (Macon, GA: Mercer University Press, 2015).

24. For a fascinating study of the ways in which rigidly codified forms of racial oppression in the United States compared to the class-based systems of access in Brazil's "racial democracy," see Carl N. Degler, *Neither Black nor White: Slavery and Race Relations in Brazil and the United States* (Madison: University of Wisconsin Press, 1986). See also Edward E. Telles, *Race in Another America: The Significance of Skin Color in Brazil* (Princeton: Princeton University Press, 2006); Francine Winddance Twine, *Racism in a Racial Democracy: The Maintenance of White Supremacy in Brazil* (New Brunswick, NJ: Rutgers University Press, 1997); and Anthony W. Marx, *Making Race and Nation* (New York: Cambridge University Press, 1999).

25. *Fourteenth Census of the United States: 1920*, Place: Atlanta Ward 1, Fulton, Georgia; Roll: T625_250; Page: 10B; Enumeration District: 49; 1930; Place: Atlanta, Fulton, Georgia; Page: 17B; Enumeration District: 0008; Year: 1940; Place: Atlanta, Fulton, Georgia; Roll: m-t0627-00729; Page: 7B; Enumeration District: 160–135 (Washington, DC: United States Government Printing Office, 1921).

26. Jay Winston Driskell Jr., *Schooling Jim Crow: The Fight for Atlanta's Booker T. Washington High School and the Roots of Black Protest Politics* (Charlottesville: University of Virginia Press, 2014), 4.

27. Johnetta Cross Brazzell, "Bricks Without Straw: Missionary-Sponsored Black Higher Education in the Post-Emancipation Era," *Journal of Higher Education* 63 (January/February 1992): 26–49; Beverly Guy-Sheftall and Jo Moore Stewart, *Spelman: A Centennial Celebration, 1881–1981* (Atlanta: Spelman College, 1981).

28. Guy-Sheftall and Stewart, *Spelman*.

29. White, *Man Called White*, 27.

30. Quoted in Driskell, *Schooling Jim Crow*, 9.

31. Driskell, 116–117.

32. William and Sarah Evans had four boys and three girls living with them: Arther (18), Alpheus (17), Thomas (15), Ethel (13), Delilah (10), George (8), and Adell (6). *United States Census*, 1900; Census Place: Atlanta Ward 1, Fulton, Georgia; Page: 9; Enumeration District: 0045.

33. Driskell, *Schooling Jim Crow*, 201, 203.

34. Alton Hornsby Jr., *A Short History of Black Atlanta, 1847–1990* (Atlanta: APEX Museum, 2003), 8.

35. Homer C. McEwen, "First Congregational Church, Atlanta," *Atlanta Historical Society Bulletin* (Spring 1977): 129–142.

36. Quoted in Marc Wortman, *The Bonfire: The Siege and Burning of Atlanta* (New York: PublicAffairs, 2009), 84.

37. For a thorough examination of the strike, see Tera Hunter's *To 'Joy My Freedom: Southern Black Women's Lives and Labors After the Civil War* (Cambridge, MA: Harvard University Press, 1997).

38. Friendship Baptist Church, "Our History," accessed August 6, 2018, https://fbcatlanta.org/who-we-are/about; Leroy Davis, *A Clashing of the Soul: John Hope and the Dilemma of African American Leadership and Black Higher Education in the Early Twentieth Century* (Athens: University of Georgia Press, 1998).

39. Edward A. Jones, *A Candle in the Dark: A History of Morehouse College* (Valley Forge, PA: Judson, 1967); Cross-Brazzell, "Brick Without Straw"; Addie Louise Joyner Butler, *The Distinctive Black College: Talladega, Tuskegee, and Morehouse* (Metuchen, NJ: Scarecrow, 1977); Guy-Sheftall and Stewart, *Spelman*; Lawrence Otis Graham, *Our Kind of People: Inside America's Black Upper Class* (New York: Harper Perennial, 1999); Tonsill, "Interview with E. W. Evans, Bricklayer and Plasterer."

40. For clarity and continuity, I will generally refer to Atlanta Baptist College as Morehouse College when referring to the school before its official name change in 1913.

41. Louie D. Newton, "Good Morning," *Atlanta Constitution*, April 15, 1942, 9; "Historic Friendship Baptist Church Celebrates 151 Years of Service," *Atlanta Daily World*, April 19, 2013, https://atlantadailyworld.com/2013/04/19/historic-friendship-baptist-church-celebrates-151-years-of-service; "Rev Edward Randolph Carter," Find a Grave, www.findagrave.com/memorial/10391031/edward-randolph-carter; "Photographs: Rev. E. R. Carter," Auburn Avenue Research Library on African American Culture and History, https://aafa.galileo.usg.edu/repositories/2/archival_objects/42099.

42. Quoted in Jacqueline M. Moore, "Booker T. Washington's 1895 Atlanta Exhibition Speech," National Registry, Library of Congress, 2002.

43. Quoted in Ridgely Torrence, *The Story of John Hope* (New York: Macmillan, 1948), 114–115.

44. After the 1906 Atlanta Racial Massacre, the *Voice of the Negro* relocated to Chicago but ceased operations the following year.

45. Stephanie R. Wright, "Self-Determination, Politics, and Gender on Georgia's Black College Campuses, 1875–1900," *Georgia Historical Quarterly* 92, no. 1 (2008): 96–97.

46. B. P. Lovasik, P. R. Rajdev, S. C., Kim, J. K. Srinivasan, W. L. Ingram, and B. A. Sayed, "'The Living Monument': The Desegregation of Grady Memorial Hospital and the Changing South," *American Surgery* 86, no. 3 (March 2020): 213–219.

47. David Levering Lewis, *W. E. B. Du Bois: Biography of a Race, 1868–1919* (New York: Henry Holt, 1993), 227–228; Lovasik et al., "'Living Monument,'" 213–219.

48. Lewis, *W. E. B. Du Bois*, 227–228.

49. See Alexa Benson Henderson, *Atlanta Life Insurance Company: Guardian of Black Economic Dignity* (Tuscaloosa: University of Alabama Press, 1990); E. R. Carter, *The Black Side: A Partial History of the Business, Religious, and Educational Side of the Negro in Atlanta, Georgia* (Atlanta: n.p., 1894).

50. Carole Merritt, *The Herndons: An Atlanta Family* (Athens: University of Georgia Press, 2002), 91–119.

51. Henry L. Morehouse, "Talented Tenth," *American Missionary* 50, no. 12 (December 1896): 182–183.

52. Alexa Benson Henderson, "Alonzo Herndon and Black Insurance in Atlanta, 1904–1915," *Atlanta Historical Bulletin* 21 (Spring 1977): 34–47; Henderson, *Atlanta Life Insurance Company.*

53. Henderson, *Atlanta Life Insurance Company*, 78–92. See also Merah Stevens Stuart, *An Economic Detour: A History of Insurance in the Life of American Negroes* (New York: Wendell Malliett, 1940); and Merritt, *Herndons.*

54. Lewis, *W. E. B. Du Bois*, 220–221.

55. Lewis, 220.

56. Allen D. Candler, "'Fools and Fanatics' Roasted by Gov. Candler," *Warren (NC) Record*, August 11, 1899, 2.

57. Lewis, *W. E. B. Du Bois*, 220–221; "National Negro Business League," Library of Congress, http://memory.loc.gov:8081/ammem/amrlhtml/dtnegbus.html.

58. Quoted in "National Negro Business League."

59. Eugene J. Watts, "Black Political Progress in Atlanta: 1868–1895," *Journal of Negro History* 59, no. 3 (July 1974): 268.

60. For a detailed history of Populism and late nineteenth-century Georgia politics, see Alex Mathews Arnett, *The Populist Movement in Georgia: A View of the "Agrarian Crusade" in the Light of Solid-South Politics* (1922; reprint, Ithaca: Cornell University Library, 2009); Steven Hahn, *The Roots of Southern Populism: Yeoman Farmers and the Transformation of the Georgia Upcountry, 1850–1890* (New York: Oxford University Press, 2009); Barton C. Shaw, *The Wool-Hat Boys: Georgia's Populist Party* (Baton Rouge: Louisiana State University Press, 1984). and C. Vann Woodward, *Tom Watson, Agrarian Rebel* (Eastford, CT: Martino, 2014).

61. Watts, "Black Political Progress in Atlanta," 271.

62. Quoted in Facing History and Ourselves, *The Reconstruction Era and the Fragility of Democracy* (Brookline, MA: Facing History Facing Ourselves, 2015), 43.

63. Henry Epps, *A Concise Chronicle History of the African-American People Experience in America: From Slavery to the White House* (Scotts Valley, CA: CreateSpace, 2012), 199.

64. Georgia Humanities Council, *The New Georgia Guide* (Athens: University of Georgia Press, 1996), 32.

65. It is estimated that around 5,000 men from Georgia served in the Union Army; most (3,500 of them) were black. John D. Fowler, "Civil War in Georgia," *New Georgia Encyclopedia*, last modified August 24, 2020, www.georgiaencyclopedia.org/articles /history-archaeology/civil-war-in-georgia-overview. See also F. N. Boney, *Rebel Georgia* (Macon, GA: Mercer University Press, 1997); and Clarence L. Mohr, *On the Threshold of Freedom: Masters and Slaves in Civil War Georgia* (Athens: University of Georgia Press, 1986).

66. Melvin B. Hill Jr., *The Georgia State Constitution: A Reference Guide* (Westport, CT: Greenwood, 1994), 14–15; Ethel K. Ware, *A Constitutional History of Georgia* (New York: Columbia University Press, 1947).

67. Quoted in Driskell, *Schooling Jim Crow*, 37.

68. Lewis, *W. E. B. Du Bois*, 335; Watson, quoted in Driskell, *Schooling Jim Crow*, 37.

69. Kwame Anthony Appiah and Henry Louis Gates Jr., *Africana: Civil Rights: An A-to-Z Reference of the Movement That Changed America* (Philadelphia: Running Press, 2005).

70. Henderson, "Alonzo Herndon and Black Insurance in Atlanta"; Henderson, *Atlanta Life Insurance Company*; Merritt, *Herndons*.

71. For further scholarly investigation of the history of the African American elite, with roots in the nineteenth century, see Willard B. Gatewood, *Aristocrats of Color: The Black Elite, 1880–1920* (Fayetteville: University of Arkansas Press, 2000); Elizabeth Downing Taylor, *The Original Black Elite: Daniel Murray and the Story of a Forgotten Era* (New York: Amistad, 2018); and August Meier and David Lewis, "History of the Negro Upper Class in Atlanta, Georgia, 1890–1958," *Journal of Negro History* 28, no. 2 (Spring 1959): 128–139. Several journalists have produced popular histories of this class as well. See Graham, *Our Kind of People*; Lawrence Otis Graham, *The Senator and the Socialite: The True Story of America's First Black Dynasty* (New York: Harper Perennial, 2007); Carol Jenkins and Elizabeth Garner Hines, *Black Titan: A. G. Gaston and the Making of a Black American Millionaire* (New York: One World, 2005); and Shomari Wills, *Black Fortunes: The Story of the First Six African Americans Who Survived Slavery and Became Millionaires* (New York: Amistad, 2019).

72. Meier and Lewis, "History of the Negro Upper Class in Atlanta, Georgia," 128.

73. Meier and Lewis, 130.

74. Meier and Lewis, 128–129; Driskell, *Schooling Jim Crow*, 9–11.

75. Meier and Lewis, "History of the Negro Upper Class in Atlanta, Georgia," 130–133; Tomiko Brown-Nagin, *Courage to Dissent: Atlanta and the Long History of the Civil Rights Movement* (New York: Oxford University Press, 2011), 27–28.

76. Driskell, *Schooling Jim Crow*, 45.

77. Quoted in Driskell, 9.

78. Quoted in E. Merton Coulter, *The South During Reconstruction, 1865–1877* (Baton Rouge: Louisiana State University Press, 1947), 164.

79. Lewis, *W. E. B. Du Bois*, 334.

80. Leo Alilunas, "Legal Restrictions on the Negro in Politics: A Review of Negro Suffrage Policies Prior to 1915," *Journal of Negro History* 25, no. 2 (April 1940): 153–160; "Black-American Members by Congress, 1870–Present," http://history .house.gov/Exhibitions-and-Publications/BAIC/Historical-Data/Black-American -Representatives-and-Senators-by-Congress.

Chapter 6: To Ashes, Again

1. Dewey W. Grantham Jr., *Hoke Smith and the Politics of a New South* (Baton Rouge Louisiana State University Press, 1967), 143; Eric Tabor Millin, "Defending t] Sacred Hearth: Religion, Politics, and Racial Violence in Georgia, 1904–19((master's thesis, University of Georgia, 2002).

2. Grantham, *Hoke Smith*, 143; Millin, "Defending the Sacred Hearth."

3. At age thirteen, Samuel W. Small volunteered for the Confederate reserves i home state of Tennessee in the waning months of the war. He eventually ser the US military during the Spanish-Cuban-American War in 1898. See Dr. S W. Small scrapbook, MSS 316, Kenan Research Center at the Atlanta] Center; and "Rev Samuel White 'Georgia Cyclone' Small," Find a Grave, January 25, 2022, www.findagrave.com/memorial/39031718/samuel-white·

4. A representative style of Old Si can be found in the column "A Mear

Atlanta Constitution, November 18, 1875, 3. "Old Si" stories from the *Constitution* were reprinted in papers across the United States, often in virtually all-white locales outside of the South. See especially "Old Si on Sunday Niggers," in the *Altoona (PA) Tribune*, October 16, 1902. See also the *Benton (WI) Advocate*, October 31, 1901, 7; the *Virginia (MN) Enterprise*, November 1, 1901, 3; and the *Beatrice (NE) Evening Times*, November 5, 1901, 2. Small left the newspaper in 1876, prompting the editor to hire Joel Chandler Harris to take over Small's Old Si column. Harris first published his Uncle Remus tales in the newspaper in 1876 and went on to publish entire volumes on Uncle Remus and achieve great fame. The appeal of an Old Si–type of plantation literary figure was national in scope.

5. For more information on minstrelsy and its development, see Yuval Taylor, *Darkest America: Black Minstrelsy from Slavery to Hip-Hop* (New York: W. W. Norton, 2012); Jeffrey O. G. Ogbar, *Hip-Hop Revolution: The Culture and Politics of Rap* (Lawrence: University Press of Kansas, 2007); Tim Brooks, *The Blackface Minstrel Show in Mass Media: 20th Century Performances on Radio, Records, Film and Television* (Jefferson, NC: McFarland, 2019); and Eric Lott, *Love and Theft: Blackface Minstrelsy and the American Working Class* (New York: Oxford University Press, 2013).

6. "Sam Small and Tom Hardwick Debate on 'Disenfranchisement,'" *Atlanta Constitution*, January 27, 1906, 1.

7. The civil unrest has been generally called the "Atlanta Race Riot." I do not avoid "riot" altogether. In recent years, "Atlanta Racial Massacre" has come into use. The evolving nomenclature more effectively captures the scale, scope, and nature of the event. Whereas "riot" may be used to describe a wide range of civil unrest, including the rowdy celebrations after a college football team wins a championship, "racial massacre" is clear. It does not provide room for imprecise allusions to overturned cars, smashed windows, and perhaps physical assaults. It was an elevated scale of racial mob violence that resulted in more than two dozen murdered. In addition to vast property damages, the actual lethal and savage nature of the mobs evinced an event more dramatic than "riot" alone captures.

8. Walter F. Willcox, "Negroes in the United States: The Negro Population," Bureau of the Census (Washington, DC: Government Printing Office), 12.

9. W. E. Burghardt Du Bois, "Some Notes on Negro Crime," in *Atlanta University Publications* 2, publication 9 (New York: Octagon, 1968), 19. Originally published 1904.

10. Quoted in "80,000 White Men Are Disenfranchised Under Virginia Law," *Atlanta Constitution*, August 15, 1906, 1.

11. Quoted in Dewey W. Grantham, "Georgia Politics and the Disfranchisement of the Negro," *Georgia Historical Quarterly* 32, no. 1 (1948): 3.

12. Numan V. Bartley, *The Creation of Modern Georgia* (Athens: University of Georgia Press, 1990), 149.

13. Quoted in "Foolish and Perilous So Brantley Declares of Disenfranchisement," *Atlanta Constitution*, August 15, 1906, 1.

14. "Sam Small and Tom Hardwick Debate," 1.

15. Jane Dailey, "Baltimore's Confederate Monument Was Never About 'History and Culture,'" *Huffington Post*, August 17, 2017, www.huffingtonpost.com/entry /confederate-monuments-history-trump-baltimore_us_5995a3a6e4b0d0d2cc 84c952.

16. Quoted in Karen L. Cox, *Dixie's Daughters: The United Daughters of the Confederacy and the Preservation of Confederate Culture* (Gainesville: University Press of Florida, 2003), 87.

17. Quoted in Jay Winston Driskell Jr., *Schooling Jim Crow: The Fight for Atlanta's Booker T. Washington High School and the Roots of Black Protest Politics* (Charlottesville: University of Virginia Press, 2014), 38.

18. Driskell, *Schooling Jim Crow*, 45.

19. "Georgia Equal Rights Convention ca. 1906," W. E. B. Du Bois Papers, Series 1A, General Correspondence, University of Massachusetts, Amherst, https://credo.library .umass.edu/view/pageturn/mums312-b002-i289/#page/1/mode/1up.

20. "Georgia Equal Rights Convention."

21. "Georgia Equal Rights Convention."

22. Duncan Maysilles, "Hoke Smith," *New Georgia Encyclopedia*, last modified November 10, 2021, www.georgiaencyclopedia.org/articles/government-politics/hoke-smith-1855 -1931.

23. Quoted in Gary M. Pomerantz, *Where Peachtree Meets Sweet Auburn* (New York: Scribner, 1996), 73.

24. "Adamson Asserts," *Atlanta Constitution*, June 10, 1906, 1.

25. Reverdy C. Ransom, "The Spirit of John Brown," *Voice of the Negro* 3, no. 10 (1906): 412–417.

26. David Levering Lewis, *W. E. B. Du Bois: Biography of a Race, 1868–1919* (New York: Henry Holt, 1993), 352.

27. "Negroes Ask Suffrage," *Bristol (IN) Banner*, August 24, 1906, 3.

28. "The Convocation of Negroes at Harper's Ferry," *Sentinel* (Grenada, MS), August 25, 1906, 4; "Niagara Movement Asks Government for Measures in Behalf of the Negro," *Rutland (VT) Daily Herald*, August 20, 1906, 1.

29. Dominic J. Capeci and Jack C. Knight, "Reckoning with Violence: W. E. B. Du Bois and the 1906 Atlanta Race Riot," *Journal of Southern History* 62, no. 4 (1996): 739.

30. "Hoke's Speech Lost Him Votes," *Atlanta Constitution*, August 10, 1906, 2.

31. Dewey W. Grantham Jr., "Hoke Smith: Progressive Governor of Georgia, 1907– 1909," *Journal of Southern History* 15, no. 4 (1949): 427.

32. Although the bitter contest between Smith and Howell occupied much of the press, Richard B. Russell, John H. Estill, and James M. Smith were also on the ballot. Smith received 104,796 popular votes and 312 county-unit votes, four times as many votes as Howell or any other candidate. In fact, Smith won over 20,000 more votes than all opposing candidates combined. Grantham, "Hoke Smith," 426.

33. Gregory Mixon, "'Good Negro—Bad Negro': The Dynamics of Race and Class in Atlanta During the Era of the 1906 Riot," *Georgia Historical Quarterly* 81, no. 3 (1997): 604, 605.

34. Quoted in Mixon, "'Good Negro—Bad Negro,'" 602, 605.

35. Quoted in Mixon, 605.

36. Mixon, 609.

37. Quoted in Mixon, 606.

38. "Drive out the Dives," *Atlanta Constitution*, August 29, 1906, 6.

39. Clifford Kuhn and Gregory Mixon, "Atlanta Race Riot of 1906," *New Georgia Encyclopedia*, last modified August 27, 2020, www.georgiaencyclopedia.org/articles /history-archaeology/atlanta-race-riot-of-1906.

40. "Race Riots Black People Need to Know About," *Coli*, www.thecoli.com/threads /race-riots-black-people-need-to-know-about.251677. See also Ian Hernon, *The*

Wild East Gunfights, Massacres and Race Riots Far from America's Frontier (Stroud, UK: Amberley, 2019); and Clifford Kuhn and Gregory Mixon, "Atlanta Race Massacre of 1906," *New Georgia Encyclopedia*, last modified November 14, 2022, www.georgiaencyclopedia.org/articles/history-archaeology/atlanta-race-massacre -of-1906.

41. Pomerantz, *Where Peachtree Meets Sweet Auburn*, 72–73.

42. Pomerantz, 72–73.

43. Kuhn and Mixon, "Atlanta Race Riot of 1906."

44. "Chased Negroes All the Night," *Atlanta Constitution*, August 23, 1906, 1.

45. "Atlanta Is Swept by Raging Mob," *Atlanta Constitution*, August 23, 1906, 1.

46. Capeci and Knight, "Reckoning with Violence," 740.

47. Lewis, *W. E. B. Du Bois*, 333.

48. Capeci and Knight, "Reckoning with Violence," 740.

49. "Governor Calls All Troops Out," *Atlanta Constitution*, August 23, 1906, 1.

50. Capeci and Knight, "Reckoning with Violence," 727; Rebecca Burns, *Rage in the Gate City: The Story of the 1906 Atlanta Race Riot* (Athens: University of Georgia Press, 2009).

51. "Miss Ethel Evans Smith," *Atlanta University Bulletin*, December 1951, 34.

52. Geneva Tonsill, "Interview with E. W. Evans, Bricklayer and Plasterer," *American Life Histories: Manuscripts from the Federal Writers' Project, 1936–1940*, Library of Congress, www.loc.gov/item/wpalh000565.

53. Pomerantz, *Where Peachtree Meets Sweet Auburn*, 76.

54. Walter White, *A Man Called White: The Autobiography of Walter White* (Bloomington: Indiana University Press, 1948), 9.

55. There is some speculation that the story is remembered differently by some family members. See Kenneth Robert Janken, *White: The Biography of Walter White, Mr. NAACP* (New York: New Press, 2003), 14–17; and White, *Man Called White*, 11–12.

56. "115 Years Ago, a Deadly Race Riot Reshaped Atlanta," *Atlanta Journal-Constitution*, September 21, 2021, www.ajc.com/news/115-years-ago-a-deadly-race-riot-reshaped -atlanta/437DMCYOKNG5RNOUZIIMM5BHQA.

57. Morris Brown relocated to Atlanta University's old campus in 1932; Clark University (renamed Clark College) relocated to the cluster in 1941.

58. Mixon, "'Good Negro—Bad Negro,'" 608–609.

59. Hasan Kwame Jeffries, *Bloody Lowndes: Civil Rights and Black Power in Alabama's Black Belt* (New York: New York University Press, 2009), 9.

60. Nicholas Johnson, *Negroes and the Gun: The Black Tradition of Arms* (Amherst, NY: Prometheus, 2014), 151–157.

61. White, *Man Called White*, 8–11.

62. Capeci and Knight, "Reckoning with Violence," 740–741; "Two Blacks Riddled by Posse," *Atlanta Constitution*, August 25, 1906, 1.

63. "Riot's End All Depends on Negroes," *Atlanta Constitution*, August 25, 1906, 1.

64. Quoted in Pomerantz, *Where Peachtree Meets Sweet Auburn*, 75.

65. "Atlanta Mob Kills 10 Negroes," *Hartford Courant*, September 24, 1906, 1; "Savagery of the Night's Work," *Chicago Tribune*, September 24, 1–2; Richard Maxwell Brown, *Strain of Violence* (New York: Oxford University Press, 1975), 210–213; Kuhn and Mixon, "Atlanta Race Riot of 1906"; "Atlanta Riot of 1906," Encyclopedia

.com, March 29, 2022, www.encyclopedia.com/history/encyclopedias-almanacs -transcripts-and-maps/atlanta-riot-1906; Walter C. Rucker and James N. Upton, *Encyclopedia of American Race Riots* (Westport, CT: Greenwood, 2007), 14–20; "3,000 Georgia Troops Keep Peace in Atlanta," *New York Times*, September 26, 1906.

66. "3,000 Georgia Troops Keep Peace in Atlanta."

67. Quoted in "Whites and Negroes Killed in Atlanta," *New York Times*, September 25, 1906; Mixon, "'Good Negro—Bad Negro,'" 609.

68. Quoted in "Thousand Atlantans Meet to Pledge Law and Order," *Atlanta Constitution*, September 26, 1906.

69. Quoted in Mixon, "'Good Negro—Bad Negro,'" 609.

70. Brown, *Strain of Violence*, 210–213; "3,000 Georgia Troops Keep Peace in Atlanta."

71. LeRae Umfleet, *A Day of Blood: The 1898 Wilmington Race Riots* (Raleigh: North Carolina Office of Archives and History, 2009); Timothy B. Tyson, "The Ghosts of 1898: Wilmington's Race Riot and the Rise of White Supremacy," *News and Observer* (Wilmington, NC), November 17, 2006, https://media2.newsobserver.com/content /media/2010/5/3/ghostsof1898.pdf; Andrea Meryl Kirshenbaum, "'The Vampire That Hovers Over North Carolina': Gender, White Supremacy, and the Wilmington Race Riot of 1898," *Southern Cultures* 4, no. 3 (1998): 6–30; David Zucchino, *Wilmington's Lie: The Murderous Coup of 1898 and the Rise of White Supremacy* (New York: Atlantic Monthly Press, 2020).

72. Eric Foner, *Reconstruction: America's Unfinished Revolution* (New York: Harper and Row, 1988), 119–123; W. Fitzhugh Brundage, *Lynching in the New South: Georgia and Virginia, 1880–1930* (Urbana: University of Illinois Press, 1993).

73. Thomas Dixon Jr., *The Clansman: An Historical Romance of the Ku Klux Klan* (New York: A. Wessels, 2007), iv.

74. Joel Williamson, *The Crucible of Race: Black/White Relations in the American South Since Emancipation* (New York: Oxford University Press, 1984), 209–233. See also "The 'Clansman' Barred by Macon," *Atlanta Constitution*, September 25, 1906, 3.

75. Quoted in W. E. B. Du Bois, "From the Point of View of the Negroes," *The Tragedy at Atlanta*, 1173. See W. E. B. (William Edward Burghardt) Du Bois, John Temple Graves, The Tragedy of Atlanta, W. E. B. Du Bois Papers (MS 312), Special Collections and University Archives, University of Massachusetts Amherst Libraries.

76. The editorials were reprinted in the *Atlanta Constitution*, September 27, 1906, 4.

77. Capeci and Knight, "Reckoning with Violence," 741.

78. Paula Bevington, "Henry Hugh Proctor," *New Georgia Encyclopedia*, last modified October 31, 2017, www.georgiaencyclopedia.org/articles/arts-culture/henry-hugh -proctor-1868-1933.

79. Capeci and Knight, "Reckoning with Violence," 741.

80. Capeci and Knight, 727–741.

81. White, *Man Called White*, 12.

82. Allison Dorsey, *To Build Our Lives Together: Community Formation in Black Atlanta, 1875–1906* (Athens: University of Georgia Press, 2004); "How Well Do You Know Atlanta's Historically Black Neighborhoods?," *Atlanta Journal-Constitution*, March 4, 2016, www.ajc.com/lifestyles/how-well-you-know-atlanta-historically -black-neighborhoods/XI5oFU29CIqhw24Sw7w9QJ.

83. Grantham, "Hoke Smith," 427.

Chapter 7: The Second Resurgence

1. Gary M. Pomerantz, *Where Peachtree Meets Sweet Auburn: The Saga of Two Families and the Making of Atlanta* (New York: Scribner, 1996), 90–91.

2. Quoted in Pomerantz, *Where Peachtree Meets Sweet Auburn*, 88–92; Darren Grem, "Henry W. Grady," *New Georgia Encyclopedia*, last modified February 1, 2022, www .georgiaencyclopedia.org/articles/arts-culture/henry-w-grady-1850-1889; Harold E. Davis, *Henry Grady's New South: Atlanta, a Brave and Beautiful City* (Tuscaloosa: University of Alabama Press, 1990).

3. Quoted in James Weldon Johnson, ed., *The Book of American Negro Poetry* (Project Gutenberg), www.gutenberg.org/ebooks/11986.

4. Dominic J. Capeci and Jack C. Knight, "Reckoning with Violence: W. E. B. Du Bois and the 1906 Atlanta Race Riot," *Journal of Southern History* 62, no. 4 (1996): 728.

5. Ida B. Wells became Ida B. Wells-Barnett after marrying Ferdinand Barnett in 1895.

6. Dewey W. Grantham Jr., "Hoke Smith: Progressive Governor of Georgia, 1907–1909," *Journal of Southern History* 15, no. 4 (1949): 434.

7. "Prison Records from 1800s Georgia," *Conversation*, accessed March 1, 2022, https:// theconversation.com/prison-records-from-1800s-georgia-show-mass-incarcerations -racially-charged-beginnings-966121.

8. Richard H. Steckel, "Slave Mortality: Analysis of Evidence from Plantation Records," *Social Science History* 3 (October 1979): 86–114; William Todd, "Convict Lease System," *New Georgia Encyclopedia*, last modified July 17, 2020, www .georgiaencyclopedia.org/articles/history-archaeology/convict-lease-system; "Prison Records from 1800s Georgia."

9. Grantham, "Hoke Smith," 424; Todd, "Convict Lease System."

10. W. E. B. Du Bois, "The Niagara Movement Declaration of Principles," *Sphinx* 55, no. 5 (Spring 1969): 23, 30.

11. Todd, "Convict Lease System."

12. Grantham, "Hoke Smith," 427.

13. For greater details on class, race, and education, see Thomas V. O'Brien, *The Politics of Race and Schooling: Public Education in Georgia, 1900–1961* (New York: Lexington, 1999); and Grantham, "Hoke Smith," 425.

14. Grantham, 432.

15. Walter White, *A Man Called White: The Autobiography of Walter White* (Bloomington: Indiana University Press, 1948), 30–31.

16. White, *Man Called White*, 31.

17. White, 33.

18. Jay W. Driskell Jr., *Schooling Jim Crow: The Fight for Atlanta's Booker T. Washington High School and the Roots of Black Protest Politics* (Charlottesville: University of Virginia Press, 2014); Alton Hornsby, "Black Public Education in Atlanta, Georgia, 1954–1973: From Segregation to Segregation," *Journal of Negro History* 76, no. 1 (1991): 21–47.

19. Robert A. Margo, "Race and Schooling in the South: A Review of the Evidence," in *Race and Schooling in the South, 1880–1950: An Economic History*, ed. Robert A. Margo (Chicago: University of Chicago Press, 1990), 17.

20. "Campaigning for the African American Vote in Georgia, 1894," Gilder Lehrman Institute of American History, accessed March 1, 2022, www.gilderlehrman.org

/history-resources/spotlight-primary-source/campaigning-african-american-vote
-georgia-1894.

21. "GSU Researcher Takes Deep Dive into Summerhill's Fascinating, Turbulent History," *Atlanta Curbed*, June 27, 2019, https://atlanta.curbed.com/2019/6/27/18761209 /gsu-historian-deep-dive-georgia-avenue-summerhill.

22. Jacqueline Rouse, *Lugenia Burns Hope, Black Southern Reformer* (Athens: University of Georgia Press, 1989), 1–2.

23. Rosalyn Terborg-Penn, "Afro-Americans in the Struggle for Woman Suffrage" (PhD diss., Howard University, 1977), 318–319.

24. Rouse, *Lugenia Burns Hope*, 1–5.

25. The United States was not yet at war when the Great Migration began in 1915. It unfolded in two parts, 1915–1930 and 1940–1970.

26. The black population had increased in Memphis to 37 percent but was slightly smaller than Atlanta's black population in raw numbers. Theodore Kornweibel, "An Economic Profile of Black Life in the Twenties," *Journal of Black Studies* 6, no. 4 (1976): 307–308; *1920 Census, United States Census Bureau* (Washington, DC: Government Printing Office, 1920); Marcus E. Jones, *Black Migration in the United States with Emphasis on Selected Central Cities* (Saratoga, CA: Century Twenty One, 1980), 137; Reynolds Farley, "The Urbanization of Negroes in the United States," *Journal of Social History* 1 (Spring 1968): 250; Fredric Miller, "The Black Migration to Philadelphia: A 1924 Profile," *Pennsylvania Magazine of History and Biography* 108, no. 3 (1984): 315–316.

27. Over the last decade historians have begun to move away from the term "Harlem Renaissance" and prefer "New Negro Movement" or "New Negro Renaissance." This revised nomenclature decenters Harlem, giving attention to the intellectual, political, and artistic work that black people were producing across the country and beyond. As demonstrated here, Atlanta was a critical locus of much of what was known in the 1920s as the New Negro Renaissance. It has been a heretofore underrated site for so much of what has given this era historical importance.

28. Geneva Tonsill, "Interview with E. W. Evans, Bricklayer and Plasterer," *American Life Histories: Manuscripts from the Federal Writers' Project, 1936–1940*, Library of Congress, www.loc.gov/item/wpalh000565; Robert Craig, "Alexander Hamilton and Son," *New Georgia Encyclopedia*, last modified August 7, 2013, www.georgiaencyclopedia.org /articles/arts-culture/alexander-hamilton-and-son. Martin Luther King Jr., future civil rightsleader, lived in Robert Hall (now called Robert House) as a student at Morehouse in the 1940s. See "Robert House," www.morehouse.edu/life/housing/robert-house.

29. Tragically, Adrienne Herndon became ill with Addison's disease as the home was being completed. She died on April 6, 1910, only a week before her family's home was finished. "Herndon Home," National Historic Landmark Nomination form, National Park Service, 4–5.

30. "Negro Business League Sessions Start Wednesday," *Atlanta Constitution*, August 16, 1921, 3; "Weekly Bulletin, Urban League," *Atlanta Constitution*, August 21, 1921, 5. Ethiopia was the other independent country.

31. Quoted in Kevin M. Kruse, *White Flight: Atlanta and the Making of Modern Conservatism* (Princeton, NJ: Princeton University Press, 2005), 30–31.

32. Alexa Benson Henderson, "Heman E. Perry and Black Enterprise in Atlanta, 1908–1925," *Business History Review* 61, no. 2 (1987): 216–242.

33. Henderson, "Heman E. Perry," 216–217.

34. Jesse B. Blayton Sr., an ambitious man of many trades, including being a bank president and Atlanta University professor, purchased the radio station WERD in 1949. He introduced a black format for the station and put it under black management. "Jesse B. Blayton, Sr," www.blackpast.org/african-american-history /blayton-sr-jesse-b-1897-1977; "Newspapers: The Atlanta Daily World," www.pbs .org/blackpress/news_bios/newbios/nwsppr/atlnta/atlnta.html.

35. See Tim Darnell, *The Crackers: Early Days of Atlanta Baseball* (Athens, GA: Hill Street, 2003); Darnell, "Atlanta Black Crackers," *New Georgia Encyclopedia*, last modified March 20, 2021, www.georgiaencyclopedia.org/articles/sports-outdoor -recreation/atlanta-black-crackers; and "An Atlanta Crackers–Atlanta Black Crackers Happy Short Story," Ebbets Field Flannels, www.ebbets.com/blogs /news-and-history/atlanta-crackers-atlanta-black-crackers-whats-the-deal.

36. Remarkably, there is little documentation on Joyland Park. Photographs, details about the amenities, and when it exactly closed are rare, conflicting, or unavailable. Later the same month of Joyland's opening, Suburban Gardens opened in Washington, DC. It was black owned and operated, and it lasted for two decades. Another park with the same name as Atlanta's famed park was founded in Chicago in 1923. Some have come to call the Chicago version the "first black amusement park," but Atlanta's preceded it by two years. "Urban League Weekly Bulletin," *Atlanta Constitution*, May 22, 1921, 8; "Fed Indians Win," *Atlanta Constitution*, May 30, 1921, 6; "Leopard Freed as Wind Wrecks Joyland Park," *Atlanta Constitution*, June 24, 1921, 7; "Macon Is Given Fine Struggle," *Atlanta Constitution*, August 23, 1921, 8; "Remembering Suburban Gardens, D.C.'s Only Amusement Park," *Washington Post*, October 26, 2013, www.washingtonpost .com/local/remembering-suburban-gardens-dcs-only-amusement-park/2013/10/26/62b b1c9a-3d72-11e3-a94f-b58017bfee6c_story.html. See also "Joyland Park," https:// blackthen.com/joyland-park-first-owned-operated-amusement-park-established -chicago-1923.

37. For an extensive exploration of black Atlanta in the 1920s, see Herman "Skip" Mason Jr., *Black Atlanta in the Roaring Twenties* (Charleston, SC: Arcadia, 1997); and Eloise McKinney Johnson, "Langston Hughes and Mary McLeod Bethune," *Langston Hughes Review* 2, no. 1 (1983): 5.

38. Richard Rothstein, *The Color of Law: A Forgotten History of How Our Government Segregated America* (New York: Liveright, 2017), 46; Ronald H. Bayor, "The Civil Rights Movement as Urban Reform: Atlanta's Black Neighborhoods and a New 'Progressivism,'" *Georgia Historical Quarterly* 77, no. 2 (1993): 286–309.

39. Pomerantz, *Where Peachtree Meets Sweet Auburn*, 64.

40. Tonsill, "Interview with E. W. Evans," 4.

41. "Evans, Mr. William E. Sr.," *Atlanta Constitution*, February 27, 1944, 14.

42. "Our History," South-View Cemetery, accessed April 7, 2022, https://southviewcemetery .com/our-history.

Chapter 8: Black Nationalism in the Klan's Sacred Kapital City

1. Note that the usage of "race" in this context refers to our contemporary notion of "ethnicity." Watson uses the term in a colloquial sense, not "race" in any legal sense. The US government has never offered any recognition of any Jewish "race," nor has it for a "Slavic race," "Celtic race," or "Germanic race," yet these were all in circulation in late nineteenth-century and early twentieth-century nomenclature. See Richard McMahon, "The Races of Europe: Anthropological Race Classification of Europeans 1839–1939" (PhD thesis, Florence: European University Institute, 2007); Beverly M. Pratt, Lindsay Hixson, and Nicholas A. Jones, "Measuring Race

and Ethnicity Across the Decades: 1790–2010," United States Census Bureau, www .census.gov/data-tools/demo/race/MREAD_1790_2010.html.

2. R. Barri Flowers, "Murder at the Pencil Factory: The Killing of Mary Phagan 100 Years Later," *True Crime*, October 6, 2013, 8.

3. "Jews Fight to Save Leo Frank," *New York Sun*, October 12, 1913, 1.

4. Brent M. S. Champney, "State Studies and the Whiteness of White-on-White Lynching," *Journal of the Gilded Age and Progressive Era* 20, no. 1 (2021): 104–113; David Barton, *Setting the Record Straight: American History in Black and White* (Aledo, TX: Wallbuilder, 2004).

5. "The Various Shady Lives of the Ku Klux Klan," *Time*, April 9, 1965, https:/content .time.com/time/subscriber/article/0,33009,898581,00.html.

6. Kenneth T. Jackson, *The Ku Klux Klan in the City, 1915–1930* (New York: Oxford University Press, 1967), 29–31.

7. David Blight, *Race and Reunion: The Civil War in American Memory* (Cambridge, MA: Belknap, 2001), 272–273; W. Fitzhugh Brundage, "White Women and the Politics of Historical Memory in the New South, 1880–1920," in *Jumpin' Jim Crow: Southern Politics from Civil War to Civil Rights*, ed. Jane Dailey, Glenda Elizabeth Gilmore, and Bryant Simon (Princeton, NJ: Princeton University Press, 2000), 115–139, esp. 119, 123, 131.

8. David M. Chalmers, *Hooded Americanism: The History of the Ku Klux Klan* (Chicago: Quadrangle, 1965), 282.

9. Quoted in Charles Rutheiser, *Imagineering Atlanta: The Politics of Place in the City of Dreams* (New York: Verso, 1996), 38.

10. Rutheiser, *Imagineering Atlanta*, 38; Howard Shaff and Audrey Karl Shaff, *Six Wars at a Time: The Life and Times of Gutzon Borglum, Sculptor of Mount Rushmore* (Sioux Falls, SD: Center for Western Studies, St. Augustana College, 1985), 197.

11. As the civil rights movement was reaching its crest of activity and legal success in 1964 (the same year that the landmark Civil Rights Act was passed), and after decades of financial and other challenges, the Georgia Assembly stepped in to provide financial resources and authorization for the completion of the dedication to the Confederacy. Rutheiser, *Imagineering Atlanta*, 38.

12. Catholic, Jewish, and protestant whites fought unfettered in the Confederacy and served as officers of ethnically diverse all-white regiments. Given their service, the United Daughters of the Confederacy recognized these various groups as veterans and granted membership in the UDC to their widows, wives, and progeny. See Michael Pasquier, "Catholic Southerners, Catholic Soldiers: White Creoles, the Civil War and Lost Cause in New Orleans" (master's thesis, Florida State University, 2003); and Thomas C. Mandes, "More Than 10,000 Jews Fought for the Confederacy," *Washington Times*, June 18, 2002, www.rense.com/general26/morethan10000.htm.

13. Chalmers, *Hooded Americanism*, 71; Jim Bishop, *FDR's Last Year: April 1944– April 1945* (New York: William Morrow, 1974), 420–421.

14. Isadore Barmash, "Rich's Plans to Close Its Main Store," *New York Times*, April 18, 1991, www.nytimes.com/1991/04/18/business/rich-s-plans-to-close-its-main-store .html; Jeff Clemmons, *Rich's: A Southern Institution* (Charleston, SC: History Press, 2012), 26, 30–31.

15. Jackson, *Ku Klux Klan in the City*, 38.

16. Ronald H. Baylor, *Race and the Shaping of Twentieth-Century Atlanta* (Chapel Hill: University of North Carolina Press, 1996), 17.

17. James Cobb, quoted in Stephannie Stokes, "Stone Mountain and the Rebirth of the KKK, One Century Ago," November 25, 2015, WABE, www.wabe.org/stone -mountain-and-rebirth-kkk-one-century-ago.

18. Jackson, *Ku Klux Klan in the City*, 37–39.

19. Chalmers, *Hooded Americanism*, 70–71.

20. Gary M. Pomerantz, *Where Peachtree Meets Sweet Auburn* (New York: Scribner, 1996), 162.

21. Kevin M. Kruse, *White Flight: Atlanta and the Making of Modern Conservatism* (Princeton, NJ: Princeton University Press, 2005), 34.

22. Kruse, *White Flight*, 52.

23. Kruse, 14.

24. Jackson, *Ku Klux Klan in the City*, 37–39.

25. Felix Harcourt, "White Supremacists Within: The Ku Klux Klan in 1920s Atlanta," *Atlanta Studies*, December 12, 2017, https://atlantastudies.org/2017/12/12/felix -harcourt-white-supremacists-within-the-ku-klux-klan-in-1920s-atlanta.

26. Jackson, *Ku Klux Klan in the City*, 39.

27. Jackson, 74–75; M. William Lutholtz, *Grand Dragon: DC Stephenson and the Ku Klux Klan in Indiana* (West Lafayette, IN: Purdue University Press, 1991).

28. Quoted in Rutheiser, *Imagineering Atlanta*, 34–35.

29. Mary G. Rolinson, "Universal Negro Improvement Association," www.georgia encyclopedia.org/articles/history-archaeology/universal-negro-improvement -association.

30. Marcus Garvey, *The Philosophy and Opinions of Marcus Garvey, Or Africa for the Africans*, 2nd ed. (Hoboken, NJ: Taylor and Francis, 2013), 71.

31. Danielle L. McGuire, *At the Dark End of the Street: Black Women, Rape, and Resistance—A New History of the Civil Rights Movement from Rosa Parks to the Rise of Black Power* (New York: Vintage, 2011).

32. Mary G. Rolinson, "The Universal Negro Improvement Association in Georgia: Southern Strongholds of Garveyism," in *Georgia in Black and White: Explorations in the Race Relations of a Southern State, 1865–1950*, ed. John C. Inscoe (Athens: University of Georgia Press, 1994), 202–224.

33. "African Prince Speaks to Negroes on 'Heathen Life,'" *Atlanta Constitution*, April 30, 1925, 2.

34. "Many Lots Sold in Sub-division for Colored Folk," *Atlanta Constitution*, October 3, 1926, 32.

35. See www.loc.gov/resource/cph.3b39508 for a photograph of the group.

36. Erin D. Chapman, "New Negro Renaissance," in *Keywords in African Americans Studies*, ed. Erica R. Edwards, Roderick A. Ferguson, and Jeffrey O. G. Ogbar (New York: New York University Press, 2018), 125. There is a growing body of scholarship on the shifting nomenclature for and narratives on African Americans (and other black people) in the 1920s. See also Jeffrey O. G. Ogbar, ed., *The Harlem Renaissance Revisited: Politics, Arts, and Letters* (Baltimore: Johns Hopkins University Press, 2010).

37. Felix Harcourt, "White Supremacists Within"; Shawn Lay, "Ku Klux Klan in the Twentieth Century," *New Georgia Encyclopedia*, last modified August 12, 2020, www.georgiaencyclopedia.org/articles/history-archaeology/ku-klux-klan-in-the -twentieth-century.

38. Oliver H. Prince, *A Digest of the Laws of the State of Georgia*, 2nd ed. (Athens, GA: 1837), 662.

39. Harold Henderson, "Ellis Arnall," *New Georgia Encyclopedia*, last modified August 19, 2020, www.georgiaencyclopedia.org/articles/arts-culture/ellis-arnall -1907-1992/.

40. Tomiko Brown-Nagin, *Courage to Dissent: Atlanta and the Long History of the Civil Rights Movement* (New York: Oxford University Press, 2011), 49–50.

Chapter 9: The Dixie Reprise

1. Ernie Suggs, "Once the 'Richest Negro Street,' Sweet Auburn Tries to Hold On," *Atlanta Journal-Constitution*, January 3, 2022, www.ajc.com/news/once-the-richest-negro -street-sweet-auburn-tries-to-hold-on/LK6NKKVEPVBUNJZDBVS32XH3VQ; Louis Chu, "Atlanta's Sweet Auburn Is Being Revived," *Washington Post*, August 1, 2004, www.washingtonpost.com/archive/politics/2004/08/01/atlantas-sweet-auburn -is-being-revived/5192a9fc-4d1f-49ab-a2ec-3196cdb1492c.

2. Nigel Richardson, "Civil War and Civil Rights," *Telegraph*, March 27, 2008, www .telegraph.co.uk/travel/destinations/northamerica/usa/943274/Martin-Luther -King-and-Gone-With-the-Wind-Civil-war-and-civil-rights.html.

3. Hamilton Cravens, ed., *Great Depression: People and Perspectives*. Perspectives in American Social History (Santa Barbara, CA: ABC-CLIO, 2009), 221.

4. The literature on the ubiquity of racism in federal, state, and local law is considerable. See George M. Fredrickson, *The Black Image in the White Mind* (Middletown, CT: Wesleyan University Press, 1987), 172; Gerhard Peters and John T. Woolley, "Franklin D. Roosevelt: "Statement on Signing the Bill to Repeal the Chinese Exclusion Laws," December 17, 1943, American Presidency Project, www.presidency .ucsb.edu/documents/statement-signing-the-bill-repeal-the-chinese-exclusion -laws. See also Kyle G. Volk, *Moral Minorities and the Making of American Democracy* (New York: Oxford University Press, 2014), 104–116; George Lipsitz, *The Possessive Investment in Whiteness: How White People Profit from Identity Politics* (Philadelphia: Temple University Press, 2006); David R. Roediger, *The Wages of Whiteness: Race and the Making of the American Working Class* (New York: Verso, 2007); Ira Katznelson, *When Affirmative Action Was White: An Untold History of Racial Inequality in Twentieth-Century America* (New York: W. W. Norton, 2007); and Richard Rothstein, *The Color of Law: A Forgotten History of How Our Government Segregated America* (New York: Liveright, 2017).

5. "AH History," Atlanta Housing Authority, www.atlantahousing.org/about-us/ah -history.

6. William Anderson, *The Wild Man from Sugar Creek: The Political Career of Eugene Talmadge* (Baton Rouge: Louisiana State University Press, 1975), 190–194; Louis Mazzari, "New Deal," *New Georgia Encyclopedia*, last modified August 12, 2020, www.georgiaencyclopedia.org/articles/history-archaeology/new-deal.

7. Kevin M. Kruse, *White Flight: Atlanta and the Making of Modern Conservatism* (Princeton, NJ: Princeton University Press, 2005), 48–50.

8. "Platform of the States Rights Democratic Party, August 14, 1948," American Presidency Project, University of California, Santa Barbara. www.presidency.ucsb .edu/documents/platform-the-states-rights-democratic-party.

9. "Platform of the States Rights Democratic Party, August 14, 1948."

10. Kari Fredrickson, *The Dixiecrat Revolt and the End of the Solid South, 1932–1968* (Chapel Hill, University of North Carolina Press, 2001).

11. Kruse, *White Flight*, 131–132.
12. Stetson Kennedy, *The Klan Unmasked* (Tuscaloosa: University of Alabama Press, 1990), 67–69.
13. Kruse, *White Flight*, 52.
14. Kruse, 54–55; Kennedy, *Klan Unmasked*, 68.
15. Allison L. Murphy, "Fifty Years of Challenges to the Colorline, Montgomery, Alabama" (master's thesis, Georgia State University, 2009). See also Rothstein, *Color of Law*.
16. Maria Krysan and Kyle Crowder, *Cycle of Segregation: Social Processes and Residential Stratification*, Chapter 1, wwwrussellsage.org/sites/default/files/Krysan-Crowder chapter1.pdf.
17. Kruse, *White Flight*, 61.
18. Oral History Interview with Grace Towns Hamilton, July 19, 1974, Interview G-0026, Southern Oral History Program Collection (#4007) in the Southern Oral History Program Collection, Southern Historical Collection, Wilson Library, University of North Carolina at Chapel Hill.
19. Tomiko Brown-Nagin, *Courage to Dissent: Atlanta and the Long History of the Civil Rights Movement* (New York: Oxford University Press, 2011), 81–83; Kruse, *White Flight*, 59–61.
20. "Isaac Cuthbert Collier, son of Robert Marshall and Amanda F. Greene Collier," Collier Heritage Foundation, www.collierheritage.org/page/15; David Reiss, "The Federal Housing Administration and African-American Homeownership," *Journal of Affordable Housing and Community Development Law* 26, no. 1 (2017): 123–150; "George Washington Carver House," https://tomitronics.com/old_buildings/collier/index .html; "History Abounds the Streets of Buckhead," www.mdjonline.com/neighbor _newspapers/northside_sandy_springs/history-abounds-on-the-streets-of-buck head/article_83e479ae-b3fb-11eb-918c-9397d21ecc9c.html; "Why Buying a House Today Is Much Harder Than in 1950," *Curbed*, https://archive.curbed.com/2018 /4/10/17219786/buying-a-house-mortgage-government-gi-bill; "Houses, Sale, E. Atlanta 122," *Atlanta Constitution*, July 4, 1948, 30.
21. Ruth Glass, *London: Aspects of Change* (London: MacGibbon & Kee, 1964); Maureen Kennedy and Paul Leonard, "Dealing with Neighborhood Change: A Primer on Gentrification and Policy Choices," Brookings Institution, April 1, 2001, www .brookings.edu/research/dealing-with-neighborhood-change-a-primer-on-gentri fication-and-policy-choices.
22. Kruse, *White Flight*, 97–101; Ronald H. Bayor, *Race and the Shaping of Twentieth Century Atlanta* (Chapel Hill: University of North Carolina Press, 1996), 64–65; "The Epic of Collier Heights," *99 Percent Invisible*, https://99percentinvisible.org /episode/the-epic-of-collier-heights.
23. Quoted in Kruse, *White Flight*, 97–101; "Epic of Collier Heights."
24. Kruse, *White Flight*, 4.
25. Quoted in Kruse, 3–4.
26. Ralph McGill, "Negro March Was Typical American Showmanship," *Daily Journal* (Franklin, IN), September 23, 1963, 4.
27. Theo Lippman, "McGill and Patterson: Journalists for Justice," *VQR*, Autumn 2003, www.vqronline.org/essay/mcgill-and-patterson-journalists-justice.
28. Quoted in Kruse, *White Flight*, 4.

29. Heather Gray, "Part Two: Atlanta and the Klan 1982—Interview with James Venable," Justice Initiative International, October 5, 2017, https://justiceinitiative international.wordpress.com/2017/10/04/part-two-atlanta-and-the-klan-1982-inter view-with-james-venable.

30. Charles Rutheiser, *Imagineering Atlanta: The Politics of Place in the City of Dreams* (New York: Verso, 1996), 47.

31. Quoted in Alexander J. Azarian and Eden Fesshazion, "The State Flag of Georgia: The 1956 Change in Its Historical Context," Senate Research Office, State of Georgia, August 2000, www.senate.ga.gov/sro/documents/studycommrpts/00stateflag.pdf.

32. Quoted in Azarian and Fesshazion, "State Flag of Georgia."

33. E. Merton Coulter, *The South During Reconstruction, 1865–1877* (Baton Rouge: Louisiana State University Press, 1947), 141–144; Eric Foner, *Freedom's Lawmakers: A Directory of Black Officeholders During Reconstruction* (Baton Rouge: Louisiana State University Press, 1996), xii.

34. Foner, *Freedom's Lawmakers*, xii.

35. William Alexander Percy, "Georgia History Textbooks," *Georgia Encyclopedia*, www.georgiaencyclopedia.org/articles/education/georgia-history-textbooks; "How Southern Socialites Rewrote Civil War History," *Vox*, www.youtube.com /watch?v=dOkFXPblLpU, accessed April 2, 2018.

36. SAC, Atlanta, Director, FBI, "Citizens Council Movement," December 13, 1956, https://archive.org/stream/CItizensCouncilMovement/CitCouncils-Atlanta _djvu.txt.

37. Charles M. Payne, *I've Got the Light of Freedom: The Organizing Tradition and the Mississippi Freedom Struggle* (Berkeley: University of California Press, 2007), 34–35.

38. Executive Order 10450 "charged the heads of federal agencies and the Office of Personnel Management, supported by the Federal Bureau of Investigation (FBI), with investigating federal employees to determine whether they posed security risks."

39. SAC, Atlanta, Director, FBI, "Citizens Council Movement."

40. SAC, Atlanta, Director, FBI, "Citizens Council Movement."

41. Les Payne and Tamara Payne, *The Dead Are Arising: The Life of Malcolm X* (New York: Liveright, 2020), 358–361.

42. Bayor, *Race and the Shaping of Twentieth Century Atlanta*, 190.

43. Bayor, 229; Stephen Meyer, *As Long As They Don't Move Next Door: Segregation and Racial Conflict in American Neighborhoods* (Lanham, MD: Rowman & Littlefield, 1999), 104.

44. Payne and Payne, *Dead Are Arising*, 364.

45. Bayor, *Race and the Shaping of Twentieth Century Atlanta*, 150–151.

46. Bayor, 226.

47. Bayor, 229.

48. Quoted in Susan M. McGrath, "From Tokenism to Community Control: Political Symbolism in the Desegregation of Atlanta's Public Schools, 1961–1973," *Georgia Historical Quarterly* 79, no. 4 (1995): 851.

49. Kruse, *White Flight*, 156–157.

50. Kruse, 238.

51. "Atlanta Blazes with KKK Crosses with Martin L. King Main Target," *Philadelphia Independent*, May 7, 1960, 2.

52. Winston A. Grady-Willis, *Challenging U.S. Apartheid: Atlanta and Black Struggles for Human Rights, 1960–1977* (Durham, NC: Duke University Press, 2006), 23.

53. "Josephine Baker Miffed," *New York Times*, June 18, 1951, www.nytimes.com /1951/06/18/archives/josephine-baker-miffed-cancels-appearance-in-atlanta -after-hotels.html.

54. Kruse, *White Flight*, 208.

55. Quoted in "Revamp of Atlanta's First Integrated Hotel Pays Homage to Its History," *Atlanta Journal-Constitution*, December 2, 2017, www.ajc.com/travel/revamp-atlanta -first-integrated-hotel-pays-homage-its-history/3wr2ccJv03Lkdc70ZzgAcP.

56. Quoted in Brown-Nagin, *Courage to Dissent*, 230.

57. *Atlanta Motel v. United States*, 379 U.S. 241 (1964), accessed March 2, 2018, http://law2.umkc.edu/faculty/projects/FTrials/conlaw/heartofatlanta.html; Grady-Willis, *Challenging U.S. Apartheid*, 39; "WSB-TV Newsfilm Clip of Attorney Moreton Rolleston Speaking to a Reporter Following the United States Supreme Court Ruling Upholding the Public Accommodations Section of the 1964 Civil Rights Act and the Integration of the Heart of Atlanta Motel in Atlanta, Georgia, 1964 December 14," Civil Rights Digital Library, http://crdl.usg.edu/cgi/crdl?format =_video&query=id%3Augabma_wsbn_31715&_cc=1.

58. Billy Hathorn, "The Frustration of Opportunity: Georgia Republicans and the Election of 1966," *Atlanta History: A Journal of Georgia and the South* 31 (Winter 1987–1988): 38.

59. Hathorn, "Frustration of Opportunity," 38.

60. "Civil Rights: And the Walls Down Came Tumbling," *Time*, July 17, 1964, https:// content.time.com/time/subscriber/article/0,33009,875944,00.html.

61. Quoted in Frederick N. Rasmussen, "Back Story: Maddox Openly Defied Civil Rights Act in Georgia," *Baltimore Sun*, September 5, 2013, www.baltimoresun.com/maryland /bs-md-lester-maddox-backstory-20130905-story.html.

62. Quoted in James H. Cone, *Martin and Malcolm and America: A Dream or a Nightmare* (Ossining, NY: Orbis, 1991), 226.

63. Quoted in Jeffrey O. G. Ogbar, *Black Power: Radical Politics and African American Identity* (Baltimore: Johns Hopkins University Press, 2019), 64.

64. Quoted in Ogbar, *Black Power*, 62.

65. Martin Luther King Jr., *The Radical King*, ed. Cornel West (Boston: Beacon, 2015), 165.

66. King, *Radical King*, 166–167, emphasis added.

Chapter 10: "Atlanta Is Ours and Fairly Won"

1. Phyl Garland, "Atlanta: Black Mecca of the South," *Ebony*, August 1971, 152–157.

2. Alton Hornsby Jr., *A Short History of Black Atlanta, 1847–1990* (Atlanta: APEX Museum, 2003), 70.

3. Martin Luther King Jr., *The Radical King*, ed. Cornel West (Boston: Beacon, 2015), 171–180.

4. Susan M. McGrath, "From Tokenism to Community Control: Political Symbolism in the Desegregation of Atlanta's Public Schools, 1961–1973," *Georgia Historical Quarterly* 79, no. 4 (1995): 864–870.

5. Frederick Allen, *Atlanta Rising: The Invention of an International City 1946–1996* (Atlanta: Longstreet, 1996), 176.

6. Paul West et al., "School Desegregation in Metro Atlanta, 1954–1973," Research Atlanta, February 1973, https://files.eric.ed.gov/fulltext/ED074204.pdf; McGrath, "From Tokenism to Community Control," 865.

7. McGrath, 864–865.

8. Quoted in McGrath, 870.

9. Elizabeth Fussell, "Constructing New Orleans, Constructing Race: A Population History of New Orleans," *Journal of American History* 94, no. 3 (December 2007): 846–855; Richard Campanella, "An Ethnic Geography of New Orleans," *Journal of American History* 94, no. 3 (December 2007): 704–715; "Louisiana—Race and Hispanic Origin for Selected Cities and Other Places: Earliest Census to 1990," US Census Bureau, www.census.gov/population/www/documentation/twps0076/twps0076.pdf.

10. Rodney K. Strong, interview with author, October 28, 2016.

11. Gary M. Pomerantz, *Where Peachtree Meets Sweet Auburn* (New York: Scribner, 1996), 417–419.

12. Strong, interview with author, October 28, 2016.

13. Rodney Strong, interviews with author, October 28, 2016, and February 17, 2017.

14. Interview with Maynard Jackson ("Eyes on the Prize II," October 24, 1988), Washington University at Saint Louis University Library, http://repository.wustl.edu/downloads/qz20sx258.

15. Pomerantz, *Where Peachtree Meets Sweet Auburn*, 453; J. Douglas Allen-Taylor, "Black Political Power: Mayors, Municipalities, and Money," *Race, Poverty and the Environment* 17, no. 1 (Spring 2010): 72.

16. Tom Adam Davies, *Mainstreaming Black Power* (Berkeley: University of California Press, 2017), 209.

17. Quoted in Pomerantz, *Where Peachtree Meets Sweet Auburn*, 447, 474, 449.

18. Pomerantz, 446–449; Strong, interview with author, October 28, 2016.

19. Thomas Boston, *Affirmative Action and Black Entrepreneurship* (New York: Routledge, 1999), 4, 14.

20. Herman J. Russell with Bob Andelman, *Building Atlanta: How I Broke Through Segregation to Launch a Business Empire* (Chicago: Chicago Review Press, 2014), 148–151; Tom Davies, *Mainstreaming Black Power* (Berkeley: University of California Press, 2017), 213–214; Derek T. Dingle, "Maynard Jackson: The Ultimate Champion for Black Business," *Black Enterprise*, February 10, 2009, www.blackenterprise.com/maynard-jackson-the-ultimate-champion-for-black-business.

21. Russell with Andelman, *Building Atlanta*, 139–140.

22. Quoted in "Is Race at Play in Atlanta Airport Takeover Bid?," *Atlanta Journal-Constitution*, March 30, 2019, www.ajc.com/news/race-play-atlanta-airport-takeover-bid/54IPY7AvoHczN7FYDvRa8K. See also "ATL Fact Sheet," Hartsfield-Jackson Atlanta International Airport, www.atl.com/about-atl/atl-factsheet.

23. Charles Rutheiser, *Imagineering Atlanta: The Politics of Place in the City of Dreams* (New York: Verso, 1996), 172.

24. Kruse, *White Flight*, 240.

25. Quoted in Pomerantz, *Where Peachtree Meets Sweet Auburn*, 447, 448, 50.

26. Henry Hampton and Steve Fayer, *Voices of Freedom: An Oral History of the Civil Rights Movement from the 1950s Through the 1980s* (New York: Random House, 2011), 637.

27. Strong, interview with author, October 28, 2016.

28. Jimmy Carter, "Remarks at Dedication Ceremonies for Hartsfield-Atlanta International Airport," September 16, 1980, www.presidency.ucsb.edu/documents/atlanta-georgia-remarks-dedication-ceremonies-for-the-harts-field-atlanta-international.

29. Terry H. Anderson, *The Pursuit of Fairness: A History of Affirmative Action* (New York: Oxford University Press, 2005), 156–157; Marcus K. Garner, "Disparity Studies Provide Evidence to Confirm Contracting Inequalities: Remembering the Impact of Atlanta's First Disparity Study on Policies to Support Minority Business," *American DBE* (Summer 2020): 28–30; Boston, *Affirmative Action and Black Entrepreneurship*, 34, 17, 40.

30. Boston, 12; Robert E. Weems Jr., *Business in Black and White: American Presidents and Black Entrepreneurs in the Twentieth Century* (New York: New York University Press, 2009), 219–220; "The Benefits of Increased Equity in Federal Contracting," December 1, 2021, www.whitehouse.gov/cea/written-materials/2021/12/01/the-benefits-of-increased-equity-in-federal-contracting.

31. Quoted in Dingle, "Maynard Jackson."

32. Ronald Smothers, "Atlanta Affirmative Action Plan Is Upset," *New York Times*, March 3, 1989, www.nytimes.com/1989/03/03/us/atlanta-affirmative-action-plan-is-upset.html.

33. Quoted in Allen, *Atlanta Rising*, 205.

34. Kevin M. Kruse, *White Flight: Atlanta and the Making of Modern Conservatism* (Princeton, NJ: Princeton University Press, 2005), 243.

35. For a longer discussion, see Maurice J. Hobson, *The Legend of the Black Mecca: Politics and Class in the Making of Modern Atlanta* (Chapel Hill: University of North Carolina Press, 2017). See also Audra D. S. Burch, "Who Killed Atlanta's Children?," *New York Times*, April 30, 2019, www.nytimes.com/2019/04/30/us/atlanta-child-murders.html; and Joshua Sharpe, "Wayne Williams: 'Ready and Willing to Cooperate' in New Atlanta Child Murders Probe," *Atlanta Journal-Constitution*, April 1, 2019, www.ajc.com/news/local/wayne-williams-ready-ad-willing-cooperate-new-atlanta-child-murders-probe/TQocGPTkK6SftY9kQI95qJ.

36. Allen, *Atlanta Rising*, 205; Jamiles Lartey, "Nowhere for People to Go: Who Will Survive the Gentrification of Atlanta?," *Guardian*, October 23, 2018, www.theguardian.com/cities/2018/oct/23/nowhere-for-people-to-go-who-will-survive-the-gentrification-of-atlanta.

37. Allen, *Atlanta Rising*, 206.

38. Quoted in Kruse, *White Flight*, 241.

39. Kruse, 242.

40. Marshall Ingwerson, "Atlanta Becomes Mecca for Black Middle Class in America," *Christian Science Monitor*, May 29, 1987, www.csmonitor.com/1987/0529/amecca.html.

41. David L. Sjoquist, "The Atlanta Paradox: Introduction," 1, www.russellsage.org/sites/default/files/sjoquist_chapter1_pdf.pdf.

42. Scott Henry, "Federal Grants Go to Groups with Shaky Past," *Creative Loafing*, September 26, 2007, https://creativeloafing.com/content-170454-federal-grants-go-to-groups-with-shaky.

Chapter 11: Atlanta in the New Century

1. "US Elections 2005," City Mayors, accessed July 18, 2022, www.citymayors.com/politics/usa_elections05.html.

2. "Atlanta Homicides Second Lowest in 50 Years," *Atlanta Journal-Constitution*, January 10, 2013, www.ajc.com/newscrime--law/atlanta-homicides-2nd-lowest -years/5KZDukpRGDMGUwXb5maL4K; "Murders in Atlanta," *Atlanta Journal-Constitution*, January 31, 2017, www.ajc.com/news/crime--law/murders-atlanta-are -way-but-overall-crime-way-down/dBSfTIdF7afBJ38yGmqVrM/.

3. Quoted in Steve Visser, "Police Red Dog Unit Disbanded in Atlanta," *Atlanta Journal-Constitution*, February 9, 2011, www.wsbtv.com/news/atlanta-police-chief -disbands-red-dog-unit_nd9w2/241792890.

4. "Foreclosure Pain Index: 10 Cities," *CNN Money*, last modified January 27, 2011, https://money.cnn.com/galleries/2011/real_estate/1101/gallery.foreclosures_in _major_cities/7.html.

5. Joe Coscarelli, *Rap Capital: An Atlanta Story* (New York: Simon & Schuster, 2022).

6. Stereo Williams, "How Atlanta Became the New Cultural Capital of America," *Daily Beast*, last modified April 11, 2017, www.thedailybeast.com/how-atlanta-became -the-new-cultural-capital-of-america.

7. "Wakanda," from the blockbuster movie *Black Panther*, mostly filmed in Atlanta, has come to signify an unrivaled space of black excellence, freedom, and self-determination.

8. City of Atlanta Office of Film and Entertainment, www.atlantaga.gov/government /mayor-s-office/executive-offices/office-of-film-entertainment.

9. Perry's studio is on a 330-acre lot that is part of the former Fort McPherson Army Base, which the Union Army established after the Civil War and named for General James McPherson, who died in the Battle of Atlanta.

10. Ronald H. Bayor, "Race and City Services: The Shaping of Atlanta's Police and Fire Departments," *Atlanta History: A Journal of Georgia and the South* (Fall 1992): 19–27.

11. Steve Hummer, "On 25th Anniversary of Atlanta Olympics, Two Icons Steadfast in How Far City Has Come," *Atlanta Journal-Constitution*, July 15, 2021, www.ajc.com /sports/state-sports/on-25th-anniversay-of-atlanta-olympics-two-icons-steadfast -in-how-far-city-has-come/N5PXIYHT7VDERF4FYK5U5.

12. Maurice J. Hobson, *The Legend of the Black Mecca: Politics and Class in the Making of Modern Atlanta* (Chapel Hill: University of North Carolina Press, 2017), 205.

13. Tom Crawford, "Outlines of a New Georgia," *Georgia Trend*, January 1, 2008, www .georgiatrend.com/2008/01/01/outlines-of-a-new-georgia.

14. Thomas D. Boston, "Trends in Minority-Owned Businesses," in *America Becoming: Racial Trends and Their Consequences*, ed. Neil J. Smelser, William Julius Wilson, and Faith Mitchell (Washington, DC: National Academies Press, 2001), 2:195.

15. "Atlanta Is New Mecca for Blacks," *Ebony*, September 1997.

16. Michael H. Ross, "How Cities Create Systems to Support the Growth of Black-Owned Businesses," *Empowerment Zone* (podcast), hosted by Dr. Ramona Houston, https://ramonahouston.com/podcast/how-cities-create-systems-to-support-the -growth-of-black-owned-businesses/?utm_term=jeffreyogbar@yahoo.com&utm _campaign=podcast%20update%20220628&utm_medium=email&utm_source =mail_from_10/29/2022.

17. "Going Home to the South," *60 Minutes*, June 12, 2003, www.cbsnews.com/news /going-home-to-the-south.

18. A similar pattern has emerged in the nation's wealthiest black-majority counties: Maryland's Prince Charles County and Prince George's County. The latter has more black people than all but three cities: New York, Chicago, and Philadelphia.

19. Tamelyn Tucker-Worgs, *The Black Megachurch: Theology, Gender, and the Politics of Public Engagement* (Waco, TX: Baylor University Press, 2012).

20. Charles Stephens, "Got Something to Say: How ATL Became the Black Gay Mecca," *Cassius*, https://cassiuslife.com/66017/atlanta-black-gay-mecca; "Atlanta, Georgia Population 2022," World Population Review, https://worldpopulationreview .com/us-cities/atlanta-ga-population; "U.S. Estimate of LGBT Population Raises to 4.5%," Gallup, March 22, 2018, https://news.gallup.com/poll/234863/estimate -lgbt-population-rises.aspx; "LGBT Adults in Large US Metropolitan Areas," UCLA School of Law, Williams Institute, https://williamsinstitute.law.ucla.edu/wp-content /uploads/MSA-LGBT-Ranking-Mar-2021.pdf.

21. New York City has dozens of schools, as does Boston and Chicago. However, none of these cities have a school that graduates more black students than Georgia State University does. Only a handful of schools graduate more black males than Morehouse College.

22. Jamie Boschma and National Journal, "Best and Worst Cities for Educating Blacks," *Atlantic*, www.theatlantic.com/politics/archive/2015/06/best-and-worst-cities-for -educating-blacks/432099.

23. "Survey of Earned Doctorates," National Center for Science and Engineering Statistics (NCSES), Directorate for Social, Behavioral and Economic Sciences, National Science Foundation, December 2020, https://ncses.nsf.gov/pubs/nsf21308 /data-tables#group1.

24. Howard University, more than five times the size of Spelman College, has a larger endowment but is a semipublic school, receiving more than $200 million in annual special appropriations from the federal government. When comparing Spelman's endowment against Howard's on a per-capita basis, however, the former's is more than 80 percent larger. "Howard University Fiscal Year 2021 Budget Request," US Department of Education, www2.ed.gov/about/overview/budget/budget21 /justifications/t-howard.pdf.

25. CollegeRaptor, accessed July 24, 2022, www.collegeraptor.com/colleges/rankings /Spelman-College-GA--141060.

26. "Baccalaureate Origins of Underrepresented Minority Research Doctorate Recipients," National Science Foundation, NSF 22-335, August 9, 2022, https:// ncses.nsf.gov/pubs/nsf22335.

27. "HBCUs Make America Strong," United Negro College Fund (UNCF), 2018, https://cdn.uncf.org/wp-content/uploads/PDFs/fy_2018_budget_fact_sheets /HBCU_FactSht_Georgia_5-17D.pdf?_ga=2.163650175.1357827528.1658710657 -499068884.1658710657.

28. Shani Robinson and Anna Simonton, *None of the Above: The Untold Story of the Atlanta Public Schools Cheating Scandal, Corporate Greed, and the Criminalization of Educators* (Boston: Beacon, 2019); Mark Niesse, "Jury Finds Cotman Not Guilty in First Atlanta Cheating Trial," *Atlanta Journal-Constitution*, September 6, 2013, www.ajc.com/news/local/jury-finds-cotman-not-guilty-first-atlanta-cheating-trial /dIPiWt0aXRIgoV1U9UHPbM.

29. Rodney Strong, interview with author, May 31, 2022.

30. "Goodbye, Silicon Valley, Hello Atlanta: Black Entrepreneurs Part of New Migration to South," *USA Today*, March 10, 2019, www.usatoday.com/story/news/2019/03/10 /bye-silicon-valley-black-entrepreneurs-part-new-migration-atlanta/2982120002.

31. "Cities: Atlanta," Black Demographics, accessed July 3, 2015, http://blackdemo graphics.com/cities-2/atlanta.

32. Charles Jaret, "Black Migration and Socioeconomic Inequality in Atlanta and the Urban South," *Humboldt Journal of Social Relations* 14, no. 1/2 (1987): 62–105; Byron E. Small, "Economic Disparities in the 'Black Mecca,'" *Atlanta Business Chronicle*, June 26, 2020, www.bizjournals.com/atlanta/news/2020/06/26/a-walk-together-economic-disparities-black-mecca.html; David Sjoquist, "Racial Differences in Atlanta's Median Household Income Widespread, Deeply Rooted," *Saporta Report*, July 19, 2020, https://saportareport.com. See also "Racial Wealth Gap," Atlanta Wealth Building Initiative, www.atlantawealthbuilding.org/racial-wealth-gap; Sarah Foster and Wei Lu, "Atlanta Ranks Worst in Income Inequality in the U.S.," October 10, 2018, *Bloomberg*, www.bloomberg.com/news/articles/2018-10-10/atlanta-takes-top-income-inequality-spot-among-american-cities?leadSource=uverify%20wall; and Josh Green, "Study: Atlanta Ranks Dead Last in Upward Mobility," *Curbed Atlanta*, July 23, 2013, https://atlanta.curbed.com/2013/7/23/10217118/study-atlanta-ranks-dead-last-in-upward-mobility.

33. "Comprehensive Annual Financial Report and Independent Auditor's Report," Annual Board Plan Fiscal Year 2019, Atlanta Housing Authority, www.atlantahousing.org/wp-content/uploads/2019/12/Fiscal-Year-2019.pdf.

34. The black poverty rate in Atlanta in 2020 was 28 percent, but the white rate was only 7.68 percent. "Poverty Status in Past 12 Months," American Community Survey, https://data.census.gov/cedsci/table?tid=ACSST5Y2020.S1701&g=1600000US1304000; David L. Sjoquist, "The Atlanta Paradox: Introduction," www.russellsage.org/sites/default/files/sjoquist_chapter1_pdf.pdf.

35. Dylan Jackson, "Atlanta Has the Highest Income Inequality in the Nation, Census Data Shows," *Atlanta Journal-Constitution*, November 28, 2022, www.ajc.com/news/investigations/atlanta-has-the-highest-income-inequality-in-the-nation-census-data-shows/YJRZ6A4UGBFWTMYICTG2BCOUPU.

36. Neima Abdulahi, "Is Atlanta Really Wakanda?," *11Alive* (WXIA television, Atlanta), August 26, 2020; Russell Innovation Center for Entrepreneurs, "About Us," https://russellcenter.org/about-us.

37. Moshe Haspel, "Changing Demographics: Race and Ethnicity, 1990 to 2020," *Finding Meaning at 33.7°n*, November 15, 2021, https://33n.atlantaregional.com/monday-mapday/changing-demographics-race-and-ethnicity-1990-to-2020; "Doubling of Nonwhite Population Leads Demographic Changes over Past 45 Years in Atlanta Region," *Georgia State News Hub*, April 24, 2017, https://news.gsu.edu/2017/04/24/nonwhite-population-demographic-changes; "Atlanta's Nonwhite Population Doubles Since 1970," *Atlanta Agent*, April 24, 2017, https://atlanta agentmagazine.com/2017/04/24/atlantas-nonwhite-population-doubles-since-1970.

38. "Atlanta in Focus: A Profile from Census 2000," Brookings Institution, 2013, https://web.archive.org/web/20111221063813/http://www.brookings.edu/~/media/Files/rc/reports/2003/11_livingcities_Atlanta/atlanta; "City of Atlanta Quick Facts, US Census Bureau," accessed October 17, 2017, www.census.gov/quickfactsat lantacitygeorgia; "Profile of General Population and Housing Characteristics: 2010" (Select Atlanta (city), Georgia), US Census Bureau, www.census.gov/newsroom/releases/archives/2010_census/cb11-cn137.html.

39. "Quick Facts: Atlanta City, Georgia," United States Census Bureau, www.census.gov/quickfacts/fact/table/atlantacitygeorgia#; "Black High School Attainment Nearly on Par with National Average," United States Census Bureau, www.census.gov/library/stories/2020/06/black-high-school-attainment-nearly-on-par-with-national-average.html; "About Us," South Fulton, www.cityofsouthfultonga.gov

/3009/About-Us; "City of South Fulton Council Districts," http://share.myfulton countyga.us/datashare/fultoncounty/maps/CityofSouthFulton_ProposedCouncil Districts_el_v2.pdf.

40. Nate Silver, "The Most Diverse Cities Are Often the Most Segregated," *FiveThirtyEight*, May 1, 2015, https://fivethirtyeight.com/features/the-most-diverse -cities-are-often-the-most-segregated.

41. Jim Skinner, "A Decade of Change: Population and Demographics in Metro Atlanta," *Finding Meaning at 33.7°n*, August 13, 2021, https://33n.atlantaregional .com/friday-factday/a-decade-of-change-population-and-demographics-in-metro -atlanta; "Doubling of Nonwhite Population"; "Atlanta's Nonwhite Population Doubles Since 1970"; Jarrod Apperson, "An Afterward to White Flight: Atlanta's Return to Community & Long Road Toward Integration," *Patch*, January 28, 2013, https://patch.com/georgia/eastatlanta/bp—an-afterward-to-white-flight-atlantas -return-to-cd126722ab4.

42. Deirdre Oakley, quoted in Paul Kersey, *Black Mecca Down: The Collapse of the City Too Busy to Hate* (CreateSpace, 2012), 76.

43. "Atlanta GA Crime Rate 1999–2018," macrotrends, www.macrotrends.net/cities /us/ga/atlanta/crime-rate-statistics. Nationally, crime rates increased during and following the COVID-19 pandemic, which started in early 2020. Atlanta's rates also increased yet remained significantly lower than the rates of the 1990s. See www .atlantapd.org/i-want-to/crime-data-downloads.

44. "The Black Homeownership Gap in Atlanta," Stacker, March 22, 2022, https:// stacker.com/georgia/atlanta/black-homeownership-gap-atlanta; Jim Skinner, "Black Homeownership: A Look at the 11-County Area, 1980–2019," *Finding Meaning at 33.7°n*, February 18, 2022, https://33n.atlantaregional.com/friday-factday/black -homeownership-a-look-at-the-11-county-area-1980-2019.

45. Sherah Faulkner, "It Makes Atlanta Feel Like a Real City: Biopolitical Urbanism and Public Art on the Atlanta BeltLine" (master's thesis, Georgia State University, 2014), 32, https://scholarworks.gsu.edu/cgi/viewcontent.cgi?article=1041&context=wsi _theses; "Atlanta Leads U.S. in Intown Apartment Development," *Atlanta Agent*, September 14, 2009, https://atlantaagentmagazine.com/2022/09/14/atlanta-leads-u- s-in-intown-apartment-development; "Atlantic Station Shopping a Retail Rush for City," *Atlanta Business Chronicle*, March 3, 2006, www.bizjournals.com/atlanta/stories /2006/03/06/focus7.html.

46. Larry Keating, *Atlanta: Race, Class, and Urban Expansion* (Philadelphia: Temple University Press, 2001), 76. See similar concerns expressed more recently in Michael Kruse, Brittany Gibson, and Delece Smith-Barrow's article on the secession of South Fulton from Atlanta: "What Will Become of 'America's Blackest City?,'" *Politico*, September 16, 2022, www.politico.com/news/magazine/2022/09/16 /americas-blackest-city-political-power-00054676.

47. Julian Bond, interview with author, spring 2007.

48. Note that African Americans are more likely to live in nonmarried households than any other ethnic group. The wealth gap between married black households and married white households, though still wide, is narrower than without controlling for marriage. Similarly, per-capita income finds even narrower gaps between whites and blacks. Jim Skinner, "Income Inequality and Black Wealth: Opinions from Metro Atlanta Speaks," *Finding Meaning at 33.7°n*, February 25, 2022, https://33n .atlantaregional.com/friday-factday/income-inequality-and-black-wealth-opinions -from-metro-atlanta-speaks.

49. "Hartsfield-Jackson Wins 2021 Airport Service Quality Award," AviationPros.com,

March 10, 2022, www.aviationpros.com/airports/press-release/21259906/hartsfield jackson-atlanta-international-airport-atl-hartsfieldjackson-wins-2021-airport -service-quality-award; "Atlanta's Hartsfield-Jackson Named Most Efficient Airport in the World," WSBTV.com, September 6, 2021, www.wsbtv.com/news/local /atlantas-hartsfield-jackson-named-most-efficient-airport-world/K3XLEYAOZ 5FSLGJPRTMK6EG7VU; Charles Whitaker, "Is Atlanta the New Black Mecca?," *Ebony*, March 2002, 148–158, 162.

50. Hartsfield briefly lost its title as busiest airport in 2020 during the global COVID pandemic, but it regained the rank in 2021. Marnie Hunter, "This US Airport Has Reclaimed Its Title as the World's Busiest," *CNN Travel*, April 11, 2022, www.cnn .com/travel/article/worlds-busiest-airports-2021/index.html.

51. Eric Moore, "The Best Cities for Black-Owned Businesses in 2022," June 12, 2022, *Overheard*, https://overheardonconferencecalls.com/business/best-cities-for-black -owned-businesses; U.S. Census Bureau, Annual Business Survey, 2018 (TableID: AB1700CSA01); "5 Reasons Why Atlanta Is the Best City for Black-Owned Businesses," *Black Business*, August 24, 2015, www.blackbusiness.com/2015/08why -atlanta-is-best-city-for-black-owned-businesses.html; "Best Places for Black-Owned -Businesses," *Nerd Wallet*, February 9, 2015, www.nerdwallet.com/article/small -business/best-places-for-black-owned-businesses; Stephanie Horan, "Best Places for Black Entrepreneurs—2022 Study," *SmartAsset*, February 17, 2022, https:// smartasset.com/data-studies/best-places-for-black-entrepreneurs-2022; Jovonne Ledet, "Here Are Some of the Best Places to Start a Black-Owned Business," *Black Information Network*, August 29, 2022, www.binnews.com/content/2022-08 -29-here-are-some-of-the-best-places-to-start-a-black-owned-business; Joel Kotkin, "The Cities Where African-Americans Are Doing the Best Economically 2018," *Forbes*, January 15, 2018, www.forbes.com/sites/joelkotkin/2018/01/15/the-cities-where -african-americans-are-doing-the-best-economically-2018/?sh=2ca486da1abe.

52. See Joanna Robinson, "How the *Key & Peele* Series Finale Paid Off 4 Seasons of Cutting Social Commentary," *Vanity Fair*, September 10, 2015, www.vanityfair .com/hollywood/2015/09/key-and-peel-finale-2015-negrotown.

53. Becca J. G. Godwin, "Atlanta Forms Committee to Review Confederate Monuments and Streets," *Atlanta Journal-Constitution*, October 13, 2017, https://www.ajc .com/news/local/atlanta-forms-committee-review-confederate-monuments-and -streets/TfWbmD8g9VWbdonTwERXGI/.

54. Doug Shipman, interview with author, October 28, 2016.

55. D. L. Chandler, "Chuck Burris Becomes 1st Black Mayor of Stone Mountain on This Day in 1997," *News One*, https://newsone.com/2755472/charles-chuck-burris -stone-mountain.

56. Quoted in Minna Morse, "The Changing Face of Stone Mountain," *Smithsonian*, January 1999, 56–67; Kevin Sack, "Birthplace of Klan Chooses Black Mayor," *New York Times*, November 22, 1997, A1; Kelly Starling, "Chuck Burris: Stone Mountain Mayor," *Ebony*, October 1998, 128–131; Duane Stanford, "Councilman Practices Open Door Policy," *Atlanta Constitution*, March 25, 1993, XA3; November 5, 1997, C5. Chuck Burris died in 2009.

Epilogue

1. "Georgia Election Results 2020," *NBC News*, accessed January 1, 2021, www.nbc news.com/politics/2020-elections/georgia-results.

2. Richard Fausset, Rick Rojas, and Maggie Astor, "As Georgians Prepare to Vote,

Trump Interference Draws Rebuke," *New York Times*, January 4, 2021, www.nytimes
.com/2021/01/04/us/politics/georgia-voters-trump.html; Lauren Gambino, "One
State Can Chart the Course': Biden Rallies in Georgia on Eve of Senate Runoffs,"
Guardian, January 4, 2021, https://amp.theguardian.com/us-news/2021/jan/04
/georgia-senate-runoffs-trump-biden-rallies.

3. Aaron Morrison, "Warnock Condemns Capitol Rioters in Post-election Sermon,"
Associated Press, January 10, 2021, https://apnews.com/article/senate-elections
-georgia-elections-riots-jon-ossoff-8a603c46c220d2e3cd143d57a57a37ad.

INDEX

Jeffrey O. G. Ogbar is professor of history and founding director of the Center for the Study of Popular Music at the University of Connecticut. He earned his PhD in US history from Indiana University Bloomington and his BA in history from Morehouse College, in Atlanta. He lives in Hartford, Connecticut.